Books by Eugenia Price

NONFICTION

The Eugenia Price Treasury of Faith
   Beloved World
   No Pat Answers
   Share My Pleasant Stones
   The Burden Is Light

FICTION

St. Simons Trilogy
   Lighthouse
   New Moon Rising
   Beloved Invader

Florida Trilogy
   Don Juan McQueen
   Maria
   Margaret's Story

Savannah Quartet
   Savannah
   To See Your Face Again
   Before the Darkness Falls
   Stranger in Savannah

Georgia Trilogy
   Bright Captivity

Beloved World

EUGENIA PRICE

Beloved World

The Story of
God and People
as Told
from the Bible

DOUBLEDAY

NEW YORK   LONDON   TORONTO   SYDNEY   AUCKLAND

PUBLISHED BY DOUBLEDAY
a division of Bantam Doubleday Dell Publishing Group, Inc.
666 Fifth Avenue, New York, New York 10103

DOUBLEDAY and the portrayal of an anchor with a dolphin
are trademarks of Doubleday, a division of Bantam Doubleday Dell
Publishing Group, Inc.

Beloved World was originally published in paperback by
Zondervan Publishing House in 1961. The Doubleday edition
is published by arrangement with Eugenia Price.

Library of Congress Cataloging-in-Publication Data
Price, Eugenia.
  Beloved world: the story of God and people
  as told from the Bible / Eugenia Price.
      p.   cm.
  —(The Eugenia Price treasury of faith)
  Reprint. Originally published: Grand Rapids,
  Mich.: Zondervan, c 1961.
  Includes bibliographical references.
  1. Bible stories, English.   I. Title.
II. Series: Price, Eugenia.
Eugenia Price treasury of faith.
BS550.2.P7   1991   90-21326
220.9′505—dc20   CIP
ISBN 0-385-41716-0

Preface

Most authors write their Prefaces after the entire book is finished. Few have the chance to update a Preface more than three decades later. I have that chance now with *Beloved World*, thanks to Doubleday, currently publishers of my long historical novels laid on the southeastern coast of the United States.

Here is a portion of the first Preface, written sometime in 1959: "Whatever the ultimate destiny of this book, the months spent in research, arranging and blending the altogether magnificent array of material between the covers of the Holy Bible have been an adventure to mark every remaining year of my life. The attempt to communicate the amazing 'story of God and people' to those living now in His 'beloved world' stimulated me as no other writing has ever done. I have lived with this greatest of all stories for more than two years. It will live with me forever. *Beloved World* is the true story of God's consistent behavior toward *us*—in spite of our behavior toward Him. It has been written with *everyone* in mind—as we are always in the mind of God."

That is true. Long ago, when I was working on the story, I had only been a believer for twelve years or so. I had studied the Bible as literature in college, but for most of those twelve exciting years, I lived in the ever-opening adventure of learning for the first time that the world and all of us in it are indeed *beloved* by God Himself. Those early days were too short—always too short for all I needed to learn. For twelve years, the big complex book we know as the Bible had almost overwhelmed me and yet I could not slow my urge to discover. Still in my thirties, I was too impatient to tackle long intricate commentaries—I was confused anyway by theological language. To me, it lacked life and I had discovered *life*. Books of Bible stories for young people—to which I turned in some desperation—were too simplistic, written as though they were tales of ancient history. I needed a *story* of God's ways with us now—a book that simply made plain His intentions toward us—His heart.

From the age of fifteen, I had wanted above all else to learn to write novels, to tell stories. All my books until then had been nonfiction works. I terrified my scholarly friends by trying the hardest possible kind of storytelling—straight from the Bible. Had I been older, I might have had sense enough to be afraid. I wasn't. The actual writing, I now know, planted deep the seed of future novels for me. It also made plain my own path of discovery.

Doubleday is bringing back into print many of my older books. All have special meaning for me. None more—perhaps none as much as *Beloved World*. The title, of course, came from John 3:16, in which we are told that God loved all of us enough to become one of us in Jesus Christ.

He did love us that much.

He still does.

And this is my telling of the story He gave us to prove it.

EUGENIA PRICE
St. Simons Island, Georgia

Contents

Beloved World

Chapter 1

In the Beginning

One day we may be able to stand on another planet and look through a powerful telescope at the Earth. If and when this day comes, it will be hard to believe that there was once a time when there was no such thing as the planet Earth. Just as it is hard to imagine as we look at the other planets now, that once there was nothing but space, not only in our universe, but in all the others.

Once there was no place to stand at all. Once there was nothing to look at. More than this, there was no one to look.

Then one day in deepest heaven a great light broke. Brighter than the great light already there. Every shining mountain and every bright angel leaned expectantly toward the light and listened.

God was about to speak.

A deep rhythm swelled and subsided, and God said: "Let us make man in our own image."

He did not speak to the angels or to the shining mountains. He spoke to Someone else. Someone who was a part of Himself.

"Let Us make man in Our image—after Our likeness. . . ."

In God's heart was so much love that He needed to create other beings for His own sake. Beings who would be completely dependent upon His love. And so that these new creatures would have a place to live, God began to create the heavens and the earth, and all that is in both.

Into space He flung the stars and the suns and the moons.

Over the dark waters that hung in one particular part of that trackless space, His Spirit brooded, and there was dry land. The mountains, valleys, little hills and meadows of the planet Earth.

Between the stretches of dry land, God limited the rivers to their banks and the big oceans to their shores. And when rivers began to run their courses and when oceans met shores, a new rhythm was born on the earth. A rhythm that met and mingled with the rhythm of the wind that blew the clouds, and the rain that fell when the thunder came across the sky.

Then under the sound of this rhythm which we can hear,

9

another sound we cannot hear was born. The sound of seeds cracking in the dark ground, and the sound of little green sprouts pushing their way toward the sun. Little sprouts which became great trees and bright fragrant flowers and grass.

In the seas, God put fish.

In the skies, He put birds.

On the dry land, big and little horned and furry animals began to roam and scamper and chatter and roar.

God was busy creating the heavens and the earth for love of the man He would create and watch over forever. Then when everything on Earth was ready, God created man, and called him Adam, which means red earth, because God created Adam out of the dust of the earth.

Adam and God

There was no other human being there that first day to be glad that Adam had come. But even though he was the first man on earth, he did not feel at all unwelcome.

When he opened his eyes, he was not surprised to find the bright, heavy-petaled flowers all around him. He was not surprised to find the blue sky carrying white plumed clouds high over his head. He was not surprised to find the tall, dark, pointed cedar trees, nor the thick green palms, nor the fruit trees, gray-green and green and hanging with fruit.

Adam wasn't at all surprised when a big, lumbering animal plodded toward him. He knew no surprise and no fear. When the big beast nudged his bare foot, he quietly nudged back, as though he had always been doing just that.

He didn't examine his long muscular legs and arms, or run his strong fingers through his thick hair, wondering what it was. He just stretched and stood up and picked a big, round fruit from the nearest tree—ate its sweet, juicy meat and threw the empty rind on the green grass, as though he had always done it. Adam wasn't surprised. He didn't yet understand about being surprised. This was his first day of life. He was prepared for everything and so expected everything. And it was all familiar to him, in spite of the fact that he had never been there before.

Adam walked quite calmly upon the newly created earth and took whatever he needed as though it all belonged to him. And it did.

God, for love of Adam, had created out of space the blue sky which Adam saw hanging above him, and the solid ground on which he walked and sometimes ran. Out of the dense darkness, God had created the light by which he could see the green and red and yellow and purple of the trees and flowers and fruit in the garden which God called Eden. All of which He had created just because He loved Adam.

This first man upon the earth was not afraid because nothing had yet harmed him. He was not lonely because he had never known the companionship of another human being. He did not feel unwelcome that first day because no one had ever welcomed him before.

He was a man, with God's own breath in him, with the whole world at his disposal, and God came every day to walk with him in the cool of the evening.

If Adam had known unhappiness before, he would have realized that now he was in Paradise. But he had never known anything but this peace and joy and so he must have realized very little of what he had.

For a long time, Adam lived alone in the beautiful Garden of Eden, eating when he felt like eating, sleeping when he was tired. Every day, all day long, while the great sun filled even the deep valleys of the garden with light, he went from one flowering bush to another fruitladen tree, smelling the pungent blossoms and tasting the sweet pink meat of the fruit. He walked along the banks of the four rivers that flowed through the garden, watching the sun dance on the swift shallow places. He picked up pebbles and rocks. Brilliant, iridescent stones, some of them like jewels. And all of them his.

One day Adam had seen the whole of the beauty of the garden and since there was nothing else to do, he sat down to wait for God to come for His walk with him in the cool of the evening. That evening, and God must have known that even though Adam hadn't realized it, the first man was lonely. He was friends with all the animals and the birds in the garden, because one day God had paraded all the animals and birds before Adam and had let Adam give them each a name. But somehow he felt shut out of their world. The birds hatched young birds, each according to their kind. The animals gave birth to young animals, each according to their kind.

But Adam was alone. There was no one like him anywhere on the Earth.

God walked every day in the cool of the evening with Adam, but this was not the only time God saw him. Every minute, He was aware of everything Adam did and thought. And God saw that it was not good for Adam to be alone.

So while Adam slept, God created woman.

Adam and Eve and Paradise

When the Lord brought the first woman to Adam, he looked at her a long time and then went to her as though he had always known her.

She was like Adam, and yet unlike him in all the ways that made him know she needed him to complete her. And that he needed her to complete him.

They both loved to run beside the rivers and they both loved the beautiful stones along the river banks. But she was more pleased when Adam brought her a handful of glistening rocks as a gift than when she found them for herself. And she could see that Adam much preferred to hunt the most unusual stones and bring them to her.

They thought alike on many things. But in the way they looked and the way they thought there was enough difference so that both of them felt complete in each other.

Now there was someone else to wait happily with Adam for the Lord's visit in the cool of each evening. Now there was someone else to be glad with him in the Lord's presence.

Neither Adam nor his woman wore any clothing, but because they had, from the beginning of their lives, been one with God, they were not at all embarrassed or ashamed. Up to now they had nothing to hide, and so neither of them even understood or thought of shame.

They were in Paradise. But the peace and love and purity that filled their Paradise were not there only because of the beautiful surroundings in the Garden of Eden. Adam and his woman were in Paradise because their hearts were open in love to the Lord their God and because they were in one accord with Him in every thought and in every action.

Adam and Eve and Paradise Lost

Of all the animals in the Garden of Eden, there was one which Adam had called a "serpent," more beautiful and tantalizing than all the rest. The serpent moved about in a rhythmic, upright, undulating fashion, and both Adam and his woman loved to watch him. Apparently the serpent enjoyed watching them, too. And on the day God gave the first man and woman their simple instructions for the full, happy life He had planned for them in their beautiful Garden, the serpent was nearby, listening.

The Lord God told His beloved man and woman that they were welcome to eat and enjoy all the fruit from every tree in the garden except one. In the center of the garden stood the tree of the knowledge of good and evil. God pointed to this one magnificent tree and said, "You shall not eat of it lest you die."

Above all, God wanted this man and woman He had created to live in harmony with Him forever.

But one unusually lovely afternoon, the wily, attractive field animal, which Adam had named a serpent, came quite close to the woman as she sat looking at the forbidden tree in the center of the garden. Sensing the serpent's presence she turned to look at him and showed no surprise at all when he spoke to her.

"So God has told you not to eat from any tree in the garden?"

The woman got up and walked closer to the beautiful animal. "Oh, we may eat the fruit of the garden's trees; but about the fruit of the one tree in the center of the garden God has said, 'You shall not eat of it, or even touch it, lest you die.' "

The serpent seemed to mock her as he moved his graceful body and laughed. "No, you would not die at all! But God knows that whenever you eat of it your eyes will be opened and you will be like gods! You will know good and evil."

The woman turned away from the serpent and studied the tree in the center of the garden, unaware that he watched her closely. "So, I'll know all that God knows if I eat that fruit! I hadn't thought about it that way. It is the most beautiful tree in all the garden. Surely its fruit would be more delicious than any of the others. And think of it! Adam and I would become like gods!"

She looked back at the serpent who seemed to be smiling his approval and encouragement. Walking rapidly toward the tree, the woman stopped a moment beneath its fruit-laden branches.

"Why, this tree is so filled with fruit, its branches almost touch the ground! The fruit is easier to reach than all the others. And it must be much more delicious to eat."

For a long moment there was a deathlike silence in the garden. Then after a quick look around, the woman lunged toward the lowest-hanging branch, and with one ugly jerking motion she grabbed a luscious fruit and stood clutching it in her hands. Her lovely body trembled, and as she stood hunched awkwardly over the fruit, she said, "I'll eat it! It's mine now—I have a right to eat it!"

As the once graceful woman gulped the succulent meat of the fruit, suddenly she became aware of her awkward, naked body. The other fruit from the trees in the garden had brought only joy and hunger fulfilled, but this was different. The fruit was good to her taste, but she ate like an animal and the trembling in her body was so great she could no longer bear it alone.

"Adam! Adam!"

Her voice frightened and charmed him.

Her face and the new awkwardness of her body stopped him a few feet from her. She stood holding out the half eaten fruit, its juices running down her chin and onto her white, smooth throat.

For a quick moment, Adam wanted to run. But there she was with the luscious fruit, moving toward him. There was a frightening new authority in her eyes. Adam could not look away from her.

And in another instant, he, too, grabbed the fruit from her hand and ate.

For the first time his strong, muscular body began to shake. And as though to take their minds off this strange, new trembling, for the next few moments they both grabbed one after another of the forbidden fruit.

They gulped noisily and rapidly as though they were afraid to stop. Neither looked at the other. The joy and gratitude they had known as they shared the fruit of the other trees in the garden was gone.

Finally they could eat no more. Even though the fruit was delicious to the taste, it made them ill. Both of them still felt hungry, but with their hands over their faces, they turned and ran away from the tree in the center of the garden.

After awhile, Adam dared to look at the woman again.

And when he did, she looked back at him.

But only for an instant. Because for the first time they knew they were naked and both of them were ashamed. Still wanting to do things for her, Adam gathered some fig leaves and together they began to try to make skirts to cover themselves.

But they worked in silence. The joy and the laughter and the peace had gone out of the garden forever.

"In the cool of the day they heard the sound of the Lord God taking a walk in the garden and the man and his wife hid themselves among the trees of the garden from the presence of the Lord God. Then the Lord God called out to the man, 'Where are you?' "

Adam stood, still trembling, trying to hide himself behind a wide, green bush. "I heard Thy sound in the garden and I was afraid because I am naked; so I hid myself."

In a moment the Lord God asked, "Who made you know you are naked, Adam? Have you eaten from the tree of which I forbade you to eat?"

Adam was ashamed, but he was not really repentant. He quickly put the blame on his wife and even left some of it resting on the Lord God Himself! "The woman Thou gavest me for a companion, she gave me from the tree and I ate."

The Lord God turned to the woman. "Just what have you done?"

As unrepentant as Adam, she snapped back, "The serpent tricked me and I ate."

There in the cool of the evening in the garden He had given them, God saw that self-will and sin had entered the hearts of His loved ones. They had dared to put themselves in God's place! When they ate from the tree of the knowledge of good and evil, they had opened their hearts to know what only God was able to know and remain good.

One thing only had He asked of them, and He had asked it for their own well-being. He had asked it because, loving them as He did, He longed to keep them from the knowledge of evil. But the first woman and the first man disobeyed God in the one thing He had asked.

God could no longer trust them with the Paradise He had created for love of them. And sadly, the Lord God began to tell them what their life would be on earth from that time on.

Adam would have to earn his bread by the sweat of his brow. He would have to work hard in the earth to make it yield food. And the woman would bring children into the world in great agony and suffering. But she would bear children, and so Adam named her Eve, which means "life."

God sent them out of the garden. He could not leave them there, because now that sin had entered their lives, now that they knew evil, how could He be sure they would not eat of the tree of life as they used to do, and live forever in their unhappy state? They had disobeyed Him once. If He now asked them not to eat of the fruit of the tree of life, how could He be sure they would obey?

Because He had great future plans to redeem them and bring them back to Himself, He had to send them from the garden. But He did not send them in anger. He sent them not only in sorrow, but also in love. He showed His love by Himself making for them robes of skins, and with His own hands He clothed them before they left.

As the first man and woman wandered out into the unknown world, beyond the old safety of their Paradise, there began the long and glorious story of God's efforts to bring man back once more into the peaceful, happy relationship with Himself which He intended in the first place.

God loved them no less for their sin. He saw them exactly as they were and He loved them still with all His heart. What lay ahead for Adam and Eve, only God knew. But in it all, He knew Himself, and He was beginning His work of winning men back to Himself by attempting to show His sinful loved ones what He is really like.

He alone has always known that if man could only see God as He is, he would want to obey Him forever.

Adam and Eve had seen God during their first peaceful days in the garden, but having never known evil then, they took His goodness for granted.

Chapter 2

The First Family

Holding her first-born son, Cain, in her arms in the shelter of their crude home outside Paradise, Eve tried to tell the child about the Lord God. Cain was the first baby born in the world and it puzzled his mother that he couldn't understand.

But a new pain disturbed the first woman's heart. The wrinkled, ruddy-faced boy in her arms screamed and kicked and cried seemingly without reason; and Eve may have sensed that Cain was born, not of God's nature, but of her disobedient, rebellious nature and of Adam's.

The drudgery of their life outside the garden was made still harder to bear because she was seeing that the suffering begun at the tree in the center of the garden that rebellious day would go on in worry and anxiety over their children.

Now and then she and Adam knew happiness together and now and then they laughed over something their son, Cain, did as a little boy. But most of the time Adam was tired from working in the fields all day. The sun beat hotter outside the garden. And Eve was pale and worn from bearing her child and from all the other endless work of woman, feeding and clothing her family. The means to exist was in the earth God had made. But only hard, backbreaking work could wrench food and shelter from it.

Adam tried, too, to explain about the Lord God. Especially when their second child, Abel, was born and their sense of being responsible for the very lives of their sons made them feel more anxious and afraid.

One night in particular, when the boys were growing taller, and the first family was gathered around a stick fire outside their tent house, Adam began to talk. He tried to tell Cain, his hot-tempered, thick-shouldered older son, and Abel, the younger and gentler boy, about the garden west of Eden. For quite some time he spoke of the joy he and their mother had known when God came in the cool of the evening to walk in the garden with them.

"Why doesn't God come to visit us now, Father?" Abel asked.

"He is watching over us, son, but——" Adam frowned and

17

rubbed his head with his knuckles and Eve shared his shame.

"Go on, Father," the boy persisted. "I want to know about the Lord God. You and Mother know Him, but I've never heard Him talk to me, and I want you to tell me about Him."

Adam looked at Abel's eager face, and then he looked at his first-born son, Cain. "Do you want to know about the Lord God, too, Cain?"

Cain shrugged. "If you want to tell me."

Eve stroked Cain's hand. A helpless little woman-gesture. "Oh, Cain, your father and I want you both to know about the Lord God. Neither of you boys must make the same terrible mistake we made!"

"What did you and Father do?" Abel's eyes were wide with interest.

Adam thought a moment and then he said, "We disobeyed the Lord God. He asked us not to eat the fruit of one certain tree and we ate it anyway!"

"That sounds like what I do sometimes." Abel was thoughtful, as a young boy can be thoughtful. "And you too, Cain. We both disobey Mother and Father often."

Cain shoved his brother off the rock where he was sitting. "You talk too much!"

Abel climbed back on his rock. "But I want to know how I can keep from disobeying. Do you and Mother still disobey God, Father?"

Adam looked at Eve with love and sorrow in his eyes.

Eve answered for them both. "Yes, son, I'm afraid we do."

"But God said something just before He sent us out of the Garden of Eden which gives your mother and me great hope." Adam patted his wife's arm and left his hand there. "The serpent that tempted your mother in the first place was punished for his deed. You see, boys, back in those days serpents didn't crawl on their bellies as they do now."

"What did they do, Father?" Abel asked.

"They moved about in an upright position, with beautiful motions of their body, Abel. But your mother and I heard the Lord God tell the serpent before we left, that from that time on, he would crawl on his belly."

Abel jumped up excitedly. "That's right. He does, too! I killed a serpent this afternoon with a rock."

Cain shoved his brother off his perch again. "You killed a serpent? Why, you're too soft to kill anything!"

Adam helped Abel up from the ground and went on with his story. "And when the Lord God promised the serpent that he would crawl on his belly forever, He also said something which gave your mother and me great hope. The Lord God said that someday an offspring of woman would bruise the head of the serpent."

"I killed one today, Father!" Abel was jumping around now with excitement. "Is that what the Lord God meant?"

Adam smiled and stroked his youngest son's bare foot. "It might be something like that, Abel. But it will be much more. The Lord God said the serpent would crush the heel of the woman's offspring, but He also promised that this great offspring who will be born of a woman would crush the head of the serpent. Your mother and I take great hope in this somehow."

Eve tried to help Adam explain. "Crushing the head is much more final than crushing the heel, you know."

Cain got up and strode away from the family group, his face bored and sullen. "None of it makes any sense to me."

Eve reached toward her first-born son. "Cain, wait—the Lord God promised us help and we must believe Him."

But Cain, the rebel, was out of sight in the darkness which lay all around the world beyond the circle of yellow light from their stick fire.

Abel sat quietly for a few moments and then he said, "I believe the Lord God, and I certainly hope He does find a way to make me obedient. To my mother and father, and to Him."

Adam slipped his arm around his wife's waist, and although their hearts ached over their first-born son, Cain, they thanked God for what they saw in Abel.

The First Murder

When Cain was a man, he chose to be a farmer. And when Abel was a man, he made his living by caring for a herd of cattle.

The time came for both sons to make offerings to the Lord God. Abel picked out the firstlings from his flock. Cain brought an offering of the grain and vegetables he had grown on the land he worked as a farmer.

Both men brought their offerings, but only one brought himself with his offering. Abel gave himself to the Lord God as he gave his choice young cattle. Cain gave some of his produce, but that was all.

Outwardly, it would seem that both men were obeying God in their offerings. We are told, however, that the Lord approved of Abel and his offering, but He did not approve of Cain and his offering.

God approved of Abel.

God did not approve of Cain, because He saw into his heart. Instead of having peace in his heart like that Abel felt after his offerings were made, Cain flew into a violent rage toward Abel, his brother.

And in the midst of his anger, the Lord God spoke, "Why are you angry, Cain, and why is your face downcast? If you do right, will there not be a lifting up? But if you misbehave, sin is crouching at the door; its intention is toward you, and you must master it."

To have his brother Abel overhear the Lord God talking to him this way only blackened Cain's anger.

"Get out of my sight, Abel!"

"Why should I get out of your sight, Cain? We're brothers!"

Cain's tall, thick body shook with rage gone out of control.

"I'm warning you, get out of my sight because I want you out of my sight. I hate the very look of your smug, sweet face. Why should this Lord God approve of your bloody offering and not mine? Anyone can walk around after a few cattle on a green countryside! I worked for the crops I grew!"

"You've no right to talk to me like that, Cain!" Abel was a gentle man, but in him, too, was the rebel blood of his mother and father, and his temper flared hot against his brother, Cain. "There's room for both of us to make a living here. Why drive me to be like you! This is what we are not supposed to do if we obey God."

"I'll decide what I'm to do," Cain roared.

"I say you're jealous, Cain!"

Cain made a beast noise, all growl and fury. "I'll decide what I'm to do and I don't need a soft-faced brother to tell me what makes my own belly ache! I'll obey myself!"

"But we're all to obey God, Cain! You know what happened to our mother and father."

20

The older man reached for a stone, sharp and heavy, the size of his hand.

"Cain, no! I don't want to fight with my own brother."

But Cain moved toward him, growling now, belonging to his fury. The sin that had crouched at his door was inside, rushing him to violence. A wild leap toward Abel! Then one, two, three, four hard blows against his head.

Abel crumpled to the ground at his brother's feet. And in the first family on earth, there was the first murder.

Fluid fire seemed to be pounding through Cain's body instead of blood. But there was blood spreading around Abel's body on the ground. He was glad to be rid of his brother, but a sudden fear rushed through his brain, pushing out the rage. And as Cain stood shaking now from a new thing, he heard the voice of the Lord God again.

"Where is your brother, Cain?"

Almost brightly, and flip, as one is when shocked at being caught in the act, Cain snapped, "I do not know. Am I my brother's keeper?"

"Listen!" the Lord God commanded. "Your brother's blood is crying to Me from the ground, and now you, Cain, are cursed from this very ground that has opened its mouth to receive your brother's blood from your hand. When you till the soil from now on, it shall no longer yield its full produce for you. What's more, you will be a vagrant and a wanderer on the earth."

Cain forgot his arrogance and trembled and began to cry out to the Lord God, "My punishment is worse than I can stand. Someone will surely kill me."

Over Cain's cries, the voice of the Lord spoke again, and promised that even though Cain would be a wanderer on the earth, God would put a mark on him, so that no one who found him could kill him.

In no way did God approve of Cain, but all that Cain did could in no way change God's love for him.

Cain went out from the presence of God. The Lord God did not leave Cain. Cain left the Lord God and began to wander on his own, over the strange, dangerous face of the earth.

The First Civilization

Another son was born to Adam and Eve, after their beloved

Abel was killed. They named him Seth, which meant "a substitute." And he was well named, because Seth did grow up to be like Abel. He was gentle and he believed the Lord God.

No one knows exactly how many children were born to Adam and Eve before they died at an old, old age, but there were many and some of them were daughters.

Cain and Seth evidently married among them, since the population of the earth increased rapidly.

Of Cain, it is said that he built the first city. And in this and other cities which sprang up, men began to follow the trades and arts. Civilization on the earth advanced rapidly, both among the descendants of Cain and of Seth. People fell in love and married and some of them were happy and peaceful people. Especially among those descended from Seth. Those descended from Cain were often brilliant and inventive. Tubal-Cain became the first man to make all kinds of sharp tools of bronze and of iron. But in Cain's family, for generation after generation, there was violence and rebellion. When the descendants of Cain began to marry among the descendants of Seth, the balance shifted heavily toward the side of evil and debauchery and trouble.

A few remained true to the Lord God, but none of them was perfect. Sin had been born into the human race in the long-forgotten garden west of Eden. Human conscience was awake to the knowledge of right and wrong, but it found, as men still find, that the less we think about God, the less we think about our own sin. And so, although God still yearned over the people of the earth, there is no indication that many thought much about God. In all the long years that followed, there is only one mention of one man who walked with God. His name was Enoch.

As the earth's population grew and grew, God saw that with the growth in the numbers of people, "human wickedness was growing out of bounds on the earth." Men had taken things into their own hands. Nothing was working out as the God of love had planned it. Men murdered each other, stole from each other, and spent their time in pleasing themselves.

When it seemed that sin had laid hold of all that He had planned, the Lord said, "I will wipe what I have created from the face of the earth, man and beast, and reptile and birds of the air; for it is grief to Me that I have made them."

But God's grief over the earth did not spring from hatred. It sprang from love and sorrow over the sins of the people. Although He had promised to send help to mankind, as yet not many people had heard of this promise. Only those who had known Adam and Eve or some of the other descendants of Seth. At this point the promise could not have been understood. But a few had believed it, and God knew it was true. He was going to send this mysterious Redeemer to the people of the earth, so of course He would not bring an end to the earth and its people forever.

God longed, rather, to give the world a fresh start. And so He looked among the descendants of Seth for one man and his family who had loved and obeyed Him. The man He found was Noah.

Chapter 3

Civilization Destroyed

Noah was an upright man who walked with God. And with Noah, God began to talk about His plan to give the earth a new start.

Realizing that the people who knew Noah would think he was crazy, God was careful to give him exact instructions so the jeers and criticisms of his friends wouldn't throw him off the course God had set for him. After all, God did ask Noah to build a boat on a vast stretch of dry land with no water in sight! People were bound to laugh. They laughed, too, at Noah's earnest warnings about the events to come. God did not act without warning, but the people turned deaf ears to His message.

Explaining to Noah that the whole earth would be washed clean by a mighty flood, He gave the one man who obeyed Him detailed dimensions and plans for the building of a great boat or ark into which Noah would take his wife, his three sons and their families, and two of every living thing on the earth—one male and one female. God told Noah how much food to take into the ark, so that he and all those with him could stay alive and well during the flood that would come.

Noah carried out God's orders to the letter, and with his wife, his sons and his sons' wives, a male and female of each of the living things on earth, he boarded the ark just ahead of the flood-waters.

That very day all the fountains of the great deep broke through and all the sluices of the heaven were opened up; the rains gushed down upon the earth for forty days and forty nights. But Noah and those he took with him were safe. God Himself had sealed the door behind them from the outside.

For forty days the flooding continued on the earth. The waters mounted and lifted the ark so that it rose from the ground, and still the waters kept rising on the earth with overwhelming volume, while the ark floated on top of the waters. Higher and higher the waters rose until all the high mountains under heaven were covered, and every living creature that moved on earth. Only Noah and those with him in the ark remained alive. For one hundred and fifty days the waters dominated the earth.

But God kept Noah and his family in mind, as well as all the animals and all the livestock with him in the ark.

Then a great wind began to blow over the water-covered mountains and valleys of the earth, and the rain stopped. Steadily the waters moved back from the mountains first and then moved back still more from the low hills and the edges of the valleys, and the ark was grounded at last on a mountain range called Ararat, in Armenia.

Realizing that the rains must have stopped, Noah decided to try an experiment. But to be sure, he waited another forty days and then opened one small window in the ark. Picking up one of the two ravens with him, Noah held the ugly black bird at the open window and watched it stretch its cramped wings and soar first in circles near the ark and then farther and farther out until the dark speck it made in the sky was gone.

Ravens thrive on dead and rotting things and so the raven did not come back at all. The water-logged land and trees and the dead bodies floating in the remaining flood-waters made the raven feel right at home.

Next Noah released a dove from the little window in the ark. Knowing that the dove would not put her dainty foot down on any unclean thing, Noah could tell when the dove came back that the waters were not yet drained from the earth. He put out his hand and caught the dove and brought her back into the safety of the ark.

After seven more days, he again sent the dove out over the silent earth outside, and about twilight Noah had his answer. Back came the dove with a freshly plucked olive leaf in her beak!

All the people in the ark were restless to get outside again, as were the animals and birds, but Noah thought it wise to wait another seven days, and when once more he released the dove she did not return at all.

Noah removed the covering from the ark, looked out, and saw that the empty earth was dry at last.

After they had all left the big boat, safe and healthy, Noah built an altar to the Lord and gave thanks. And they all breathed deeply of the fresh, sweet, rain-washed air.

A Rainbow in the Sky

God blessed Noah and his sons and told them, "Be fruitful, multiply and populate the earth. . . . Every living, moving thing shall be yours for food; I have given it all to you like the vegetables."

God was talking once again with one family about a fresh start on the earth.

"Take note! I Myself am establishing My covenant with you, with your descendants and with every living creature—of all that left the ark. I covenant with you that never shall all flesh again be eliminated by the waters of a flood, nor shall there be another deluge to destroy the earth."

Here God was making a binding covenant with man. Noah and his family were not one with God as Adam and Eve had been. They were the descendants of Adam and Eve, and the downpull of sin was still strong upon them. God had not yet sent His promised offspring of woman to redeem them. But Noah had done his best to obey God, and so God had made another great gesture of love toward all human nature.

"This is the sign of the covenant I am making between Me and you. . . . I will set My bow in the clouds; it shall be for a token of a covenant between Me and the earth. When I collect my clouds above the earth, then the bow shall appear in the clouds and I will remember My covenant that exists between Me and you and every living creature. . . ."

As a token of His love and to remind us of His faithfulness to us, God put a rainbow in the sky that day.

And when He collects His clouds still, there stretches across the sky the sign of the love of God, arched and glowing above those who love Him and above those who do not.

Chapter 4

God Called Abram

About the year 2000 B.C., from the greatest of all the flourishing cities in the fertile valley of the Tigris and Euphrates rivers, God called another man, named Abram.

This time there was apparently no choice on God's part where obedience to Himself was concerned. Although Abram was a cultured gentleman, from a good Semitic family, there is no record that he nor any member of his family worshiped the Lord God. Almost certainly, they were moon-worshipers.

Abram was, however, a descendant of Noah, and at the time God called him, lived with his wife, Sarai, his two brothers, and his father, Terah, in a city known as Ur of the Chaldees, in the south of Mesopotamia, near the Persian Gulf.

Today there is little left of the great city of Ur except a desolate pile of rubble and some ruined walls. For in three thousand years, Ur, which in Abram's time had been a center of highly developed arts, writing, carving, and well-established legal systems, was eventually buried out of sight by the hot, wind-driven sands of the desert. Once the city was crisscrossed by canals. Once it had two thriving harbors, milling throngs of prosperous people who wore daggers and helmets of gold, and who drank from golden cups and ate from golden plates. Ur was a city of streets, squares, good houses, temples, palaces and city towers, with their thick stone battlements, some of which still stand in ruins.

But the Euphrates River changed its course in time and the sea retreated almost sixty miles from Ur. Nothing remained to be seen of the city until modern archeologists laid bare its ruins to the scorching desert sun in the 1920's and 1930's. But the life of the one man, Abram, whom God called, has kept the name of his home town of Ur alive.

The direct call of God to Abram, a man whose life was rooted in pagan culture and tradition, throws a still brighter light on the loving perseverance of the Lord God. He could find no descendant of Noah who still believed Him, but this did not stop God from keeping His promise to redeem His people. Most likely Abram had heard one of the several stories of the flood. Perhaps through the caravans that passed through, or from sailors on the ships that docked in the great harbors, he had even heard about his ancestor, Noah. His father, Terah, knew the story of Adam and Eve. But realizing that He could not depend upon any inherited knowledge of Himself, God spoke to Abram directly, telling him to leave this pagan land and return to the land of his ancestors north in Haran.

So Abram and his wife, Sarai, his father, Terah, his two brothers and their wives and children, prepared to leave the noisy bustle and jolt of the seacoast city of Ur. It is never easy to leave one's home, but their departure was made even more difficult because one of Abram's brothers died in the arms of their old father, Terah, just before they left. Their heavy hearts at having to leave the brother's body behind made the miles seem longer during the days and nights as they moved slowly, with all their possessions, north along the Euphrates River to Haran.

They settled in Haran and life went on for them peacefully year after year. Then Abram's beloved father, Terah, died, and Abram's thoughts turned once more to the One who had spoken to him at Ur so long ago.

In his need for comfort, his heart again caught words spoken directly to him: "Abram, as for you, leave this land, your relatives and your father's household for a land which I will show you, and I will make you into a great nation. I will bless you and make your name famous and you shall be a blessing."

A great and deep wondering began in Abram's heart.

God had moved him from the confusion and ambition of the thriving city of Ur to a quieter Haran. But once more He seemed to be wanting Abram still farther away from cultural temptation and family ties. God had need of Abram to carry on the active fulfillment of His promise made so long ago.

And having no idea where he was going, but knowing in his heart that he had heard the voice of the Lord God, Abram took his wife, Sarai, now also well along in years, and his nephew, Lot, packed up all his belongings, and with his servants once more began to move across the semi-desert land toward a land called Canaan (now Palestine).

At Shechem, in Canaan, where the travelers found the tall mountains, Gerazim and Ebal, standing in front of each other like two giants, and the little valley between, God once more spoke to

Abram: "I know, Abram, there are Canaanites in the land now, but to your offspring I will give this land."

As God spoke, Abram stood beside a terebinth (oak) tree and listened. And to show God that he believed Him, Abram, the man who had grown up worshiping the moon-god, built his first altar to the Lord.

A new life surged through Abram's heart and body after that. And this time when he and his family and servants moved on to the hills east of Bethel, it was not so hard to go.

His faith in the Lord God grew, and when they pitched their tents between Bethel and Ai, the first thing Abram thought of doing was to worship the Lord his God who had guided him safely this far.

Here he also built an altar to the Lord and spent much time with Him. We are told that Abram called on the Name of the Lord. God's Name stood for His personality, His character. So we know that Abram was intent upon learning more about the real character of God. In his deep desire to learn what God was like, Abram spent much time communing with Him person to Person.

The Lord God had found a friend on the earth.

A Mere Man in Egypt

Abram believed God. But he was a mere man for all that!

As he and his wife Sarai and his nephew Lot moved on over the hot, arid land of Canaan, a famine caused them to make a detour down into the rich, fertile land of Egypt. Egypt had reached one of the high peaks of her ancient and amazing history. Great pyramids, containing hundreds of thousands of blocks of granite, each one weighing several tons, had been so skillfully cut and worked into shape by Egyptian artisans that no mortar was needed to hold them together. These still fantastic examples of art and engineering were already seven hundred years old when Abram and his family detoured into Egypt because of the famine in Canaan.

There is no particular indication that the Lord God told Abram to go to Egypt, but the Lord did make use of this side-excursion of His chosen man to show still more definitely that He did not intend to allow even Abram's lack of mature faith to hinder His long-range, over-all plan to bring a Redeemer to mankind through Abram's line.

Here is the story. Just as they were crossing into Egypt, Abram pulled his camel alongside Sarai's and a pointedly human and faithless conversation took place.

"Sarai, I know and anyone knows you're a good-looking woman!" Abram began.

"Well, what's the occasion for talk like this?" Sarai was a little suspicious.

"You *are* a good-looking woman, Sarai. And when those Egyptians catch sight of you, I'll be in trouble! They're bound to say, 'So this beautiful fair-skinned woman is his wife! We'll kill the man and then keep his wife alive.'"

Sarai frowned. "Now, Abram, don't you think you're just imagining things? And at my age, too?"

Abram was emphatic now. "No, Sarai, I'm not imagining things! I have eyes. I can see how beautiful you are and I want you to say you're my sister. That way I'll be favored because of your beauty. Don't you see what I mean?"

"I see that you're a clever man, my husband. But then I always knew that."

Abram, rolling along unevenly on his tall camel, pressed his point. "Sarai, you are to say you're my sister! And by doing that, my dear, you'll save your own husband's life."

"All right, Abram. You knew all along I'd do it." Sarai said nothing else, but her eyes were troubled as Abram swung his camel around and resumed his place in the long procession of animals and people.

Entering Egypt at the head of his caravan, atop his tall camel and his brand new lie, Abram looked and acted more like a reasonably prosperous pagan living by his wits than a man who believed God.

In the course of their journey into Egypt, Sarai came to the attention of two of the Pharaoh's nobles, and was immediately introduced as Abram's sister!

The Egyptian nobles from the court of Pharaoh led Abram and Sarai and their caravan straight to the palace of the ruler of Egypt, where Sarai was recommended highly. And with much misgiving the poor woman was taken into the palace to the Pharaoh himself. Because of her, just as he had hoped, Abram was treated most generously. So beautiful did the Pharaoh find Sarai that he gave Abram choice flocks, herds, donkeys, male and female servants, she-donkeys and camels.

As her brother, Abram's life was in no way endangered. However, suppose the Pharaoh had kept Sarai as his wife, believing her to be Abram's sister? Had not God promised that He would make of Abram's offspring a great nation?

Abram took a tremendous chance. But God was aware of all that went on at Pharaoh's court and some people have been surprised that God made use of a pagan ruler to get Abram out of his difficulty, but that's exactly what He did.

Almost everyone in Pharaoh's household became ill suddenly and perhaps Sarai realized that the time had come for honesty! At any rate, Abram was summoned to appear before the ailing Pharaoh, who roared angrily (and who can blame him?), "Look here, Semite! What is this you have done to me? Why did you not let me know she is your wife? Why did you say, 'She is my sister'? so that I took her for a wife?"

Abram hung his head and began to stammer some sort of weak explanation, but the Pharaoh had had enough of Abram. More than enough.

"Stop muttering! Here is your wife. Take her and get out!"

Abram got out, and with no delay. His shame and humiliation were only increased by the fact that this pagan ruler ordered an escort for him to conduct him on his way, and heaped on more shame by allowing Abram to take with him not only his beloved wife, Sarai, but all the gifts the Pharaoh had given him—including a beautiful young Egyptian girl, Hagar, whom Sarai particularly wanted as her personal slave.

Abram rode out of Egypt rocking atop a new and finer camel, at the head of a larger and richer caravan of beasts and slaves. But somehow he rocked along without much dignity now.

God had found a friend in Abram, but as yet this man's faith was new and weak and, although it grew stronger as time went by, this was not the only time it wobbled and then collapsed awkwardly at God's feet.

None of this surprised the Lord God. He knew He had chosen to carry out His plan through a mere man, born of Adam.

Abram Went Back to Canaan and God

Abram and his wife and nephew returned to Canaan with their new wealth. Their caravan was much larger, there were more animals to herd together, more tents to pack, because of the slaves given them in Egypt during the days in which Abram hid behind Sarai's beautiful skirts. The way back was long and Abram had plenty of time to think about the Lord God, and his own behavior in Egypt. He rode alone, apart from the others, much of the way back across the sandy hills and plains toward the place where his heart drew him. From the Negeb, he trekked by stages toward Bethel. Abram stopped a day or two along the way for rest for his people and animals, but mostly he pressed back toward the spot between Bethel and Ai where his tent had been pitched before the trip to Egypt.

"What progress is there in coming back here?" Lot demanded of his Aunt Sarai as the servants made camp at the old spot.

"You've no right to question, Lot, but if you must, it's best to bother me. And not your uncle."

"Do you know why he brought us back here again, Aunt Sarai?"

Sarai watched Abram's long strides as he walked away from their encampment alone, over a dry swell in the hilly ground and out of her sight.

"Yes, Lot," the woman didn't look at her nephew as she spoke. Her eyes were still turned toward the rise in the ground over which Abram had disappeared. "Yes, I know why we've come back here."

"Then tell me."

"Your uncle built an altar to the Lord here, Lot."

"What difference does that make? He built one in Shechem, too."

"I don't know *what* difference, boy. But your uncle communes with the living God. A communion goes two ways, remember. God speaks to Abram and Abram speaks to God. It's not for us to butt into their conversations!" Then Sarai smiled, but there was compassion and understanding in her smile. "I just have a woman's feeling that your uncle feels his need to come back here. Especially after our trip to Egypt."

"You mean after the trick he pulled there."

"I said," Sarai snapped, "after our trip to Egypt!"

Canaan was a quiet, silent land. It was the land to which God had sent Abram and perhaps this was part of the reason He sent him there. The people who lived in Canaan were separated from the rest of the hurried civilized world, on the west by the sea, on the east and south by the desert, and on the north by high mountains. Canaan was crossed by the trade routes connecting the rest of the world around it, but it was an isolated land, cut off by desert, sea and mountains from the more civilized countries.

A man could think in Canaan.

A man could hear the voice of God here.

On the other side of the little sandy rise in the ground, as Sarai and Lot talked, Abram called once more on the Name of the Lord. He called from his heart to all that he knew then of the nature of the Lord God. And he called for forgiveness for his faithless behavior on the trip to Egypt.

Chapter 5

The Household of Abram

It took faith for Abram to obey God's call to leave his native lands and his relatives and begin his wandering over the earth. And although this faith faltered at times, it also seemed to grow stronger even as a result of its faltering. To Abram's faith were added love and wisdom as the months passed by over the hilly countryside around his encampment in Canaan, between Bethel and Ai.

Lot Made a Choice

And then one day a singular chance to prove his maturing faith came when the conflict, which had been brewing between Abram's herdsmen and Lot's herdsmen, exploded. Lot also owned many cattle and tents, and both their possessions increased until the land where they lived became too small for them. When the herdsmen on both sides began to fight and throw stones at each other, Lot, as usual, went to Sarai to air his views.

"It won't do a bit of good for you to remind me that he's my uncle, Aunt Sarai. I know he's my uncle. I know he's been good to me. But I have my own interests to protect. And there's not pasture enough for us both here!"

"Oh, Lot," she shrilled. "You need a good beating!"

Sarai tried to relieve her annoyance with her nephew by shaking him good and hard by the shoulders. That her annoyance was justified there is no doubt. But the aging little woman's fury only made Lot angrier. She moved him not an inch no matter how hard she shook!

Abram strode into the tent just as Sarai broke into uncontrollable womanly weeping.

"Sarai, stop crying!"

"Oh, my husband," she wailed, "do something!"

"Exactly what I intend, but let there be an end to that sniffling and snorting so I can be heard. Now, Lot," Abram's voice was suddenly kind and tender. "Please, nephew, let there be no disputing between you and me or between my herdsmen and yours, for we are kinsmen. Is not the whole country open to you? I wish, boy, that you might separate yourself from me now. If you turn to the left, then I will turn to the right. Or if you turn to the right, then I will turn to the left."

Lot's hands hung limp at his sides. "Do you mean, Uncle, that you are giving me my choice of which land to take?"

"Abram, have you thought this over carefully?" Sarai knew what Lot would do.

"Silence, woman. I would not have made the offer otherwise, would I?" Abram returned to Lot. "Go take a good look, nephew, and let me know which land you decide you want."

Lot took a good look and saw how well-watered the whole Jordan district was as far away as Zoar. It seemed to him to be as lush and fruitful as the legendary Garden of Eden.

So, without a moment's hesitation, Lot chose the whole Jordan basin for himself. And as he packed his possessions and lined up his camels and donkey and herds and tents to leave with his wife and slaves, Abram and Sarai stood and watched. It would be hard to know what Abram thought, except that this time his conscience was clear. He had tried no tricks. He had given Lot first choice and he had been able to do it willingly.

Other than these things, it would be difficult to read Abram's thoughts as his brother's son separated from him, having brazenly chosen the choicest land for himself.

Abram watched Lot's caravan raising the dust far, far in the distance and was so silent it was hard to know what he thought.

But not so with Sarai.

Not as she stood fuming beside Abram, and not as she hurried, still fuming and fussing, back to their tent home.

When Sarai was out of sight and when Lot was gone from him toward the district of Jordan to make his new home, Abram stood alone looking around at the empty camp grounds where Lot's tents had stood.

It was then that the Lord spoke once more to him: "Now, Abram, raise your eyes and look from where you stand northward, southward, eastward and westward, for all the land you are viewing I will give you and your offspring forever."

Abram raised his eyes. "My offspring, Lord God?"

"Yes, Abram, I will make your descendants as countless as the dust of the earth, so that, if anyone is able to count the dust particles by number, so may your offspring be numbered. Now, rise! Travel over the land in its length and breadth, for to you will I give it."

That very night Abram gave orders to pack the tents and move on. And he settled next in a grove of oak trees near Hebron.

As soon as they arrived there, Abram built an altar to the Lord.

Sarai's Heartache

Sarai, Abram's wife, stood alone just outside the entrance to their large black goat's-hair tent at Hebron on a warm windy evening.

Her beloved husband was gone on a dangerous mission. The basin cities of Sodom and Gomorrah had been attacked. This would have been no affair of Abram's except that his nephew, Lot, attracted by the glitter and prosperity of Sodom, had moved his possessions and his family inside the city gates. Both Sodom and Gomorrah were captured by the attacking armies, and an escaped messenger ran to Abram to tell him that Lot and his family were taken captive, too.

Abram, with the aid of his friendly neighbors, the Amorites, gathered a force of three hundred and eighteen of his own trained men and hurried away in the direction of Lot's captors.

Sarai hated the thought of Abram in battle. What would become of her in this silent, lonely land if Abram should be killed?

"I would have no life without him! No life at all." Sarai spoke to herself, as the sun swelled to a heavy ball on the horizon and lit the cloudless desert sky with orange and then red and then darker red-orange.

"He should be back by now. Even by yesterday!" Sarai wrung her hands.

"Is my mistress ill?"

"Hagar! You startled me. No, I'm not ill. But stay to talk with me a little. I'm so worried about the master."

"It is hard to wait, Mistress." The slim, lovely dark-skinned Egyptian servant girl stood a respectful distance from Sarai. There seemed to be a real bond between them.

"If he is killed, Hagar—it is the end of everything! I've borne him no child." Sarai tried to laugh, but the sound was not a laugh. It creaked out from the bitterness in her heart. She had failed her husband in not giving him an heir.

"Come inside and rest, Mistress. I'll bring you a cool drink and then I'll watch the plain for my master's return."

"How can I rest!" Sarai shuddered and clasped her arms tight over her aging breast. Then she faced her maid-servant almost in anger. "Hagar, why would God create into a woman such a strong desire to hold a child to her bosom and then deprive her of one?"

"My heart aches for you, Mistress, but didn't you tell me that the God you worship promised your husband that he would have many offspring?"

"Yes, Hagar. I know what God promised. I think my husband believes it, too. Most of the time."

"Do you not believe it, Mistress? You have talked to me so much about the Lord God, I—I think even I believe Him now."

"Sometimes I don't understand about believing, Hagar. Oh, I do believe the Lord God, but, girl, I am too old to have a child! How will God bring it about?"

"Perhaps that is not for us to know, Mistress." The beautiful slave girl's eyes grew soft and she moved closer to Sarai. "Oh, when your child comes, I shall be so glad to nurse him. I'll take such good care of him. He will be your child and you are—you are dear to me, Mistress. Like a second mother."

Sarai looked at the girl. "Hm—tears in your eyes, Hagar. Was it cruel of me to take you from your mother and family in Egypt? I hope not. You are also dear to me."

Then Sarai stiffened. "Hagar. What did they think in the Pharaoh's court?"

"What did they think, Mistress? About what?"

"Oh, about my husband's passing me off as his sister. Did they—think he loved me less than his own life?"

Hagar touched her arm tenderly. "Forget about them, Mistress. Forget about all of Egypt. The whole thing. Your husband loves you. We are here now. If I can put it all behind me, can't you, Mistress?"

Sarai smiled at Hagar. "I must be getting old. My bondservant not only clothes and bathes me, she now has to give me advice. Good advice, Hagar. I'm grateful."

Far out over the beige-pink rocky plain, as though they rode up from the red sun itself, a large group of men came toward them.

"Hagar, look! Do my old eyes serve me well? Or is my heart calling him back by a deceit? Are they coming? Are they coming, girl?"

"Yes, Mistress, it must be the master coming home!"

Sarai paced the hard earth in front of her tent back and forth, back and forth as the riders came closer.

"Don't worry, Mistress. I'm sure the master's come back alive and well."

"If only God had created me with patience instead of beauty, I'd be the better for it." The old woman laughed then. "Go on, you may laugh, too, Hagar. I forget sometimes how old I've grown."

"My mistress is still a beautiful woman."

"I am neither beautiful nor patient—nor fruitful. I am a waste, Hagar, except for the love in my heart for Abram."

"Few women would follow him as you have done on such a wild chase across a strange land, Mistress."

"Then there are few wise women in the world, Hagar! When a woman has a man like Abram, she follows him. But—my old heart sighs within me when I remember my grumblings. Especially the day we first packed to leave Ur of the Chaldees."

The women spoke together and kept their watch outside the big dark tent until a bigger and blacker tent settled down over the hot earth. When night came completely, Abram and his men reached the encampment among the grove of oak trees.

Alone in their tent, Abram and Sarai embraced each other.

"Look here, Sarai, I've come home! Is this any time to weep?"

"A woman sometimes weeps when she's happy! Let me look at you well. Are you sure you're not hurt, my husband?"

"Not at all. The hand of the Lord God protected me all the way. And thanks to His goodness, Sarai, Lot and his wife are both safe now."

"That Lot! All of this fighting is because of him."

"Sarai, Lot is blood of my blood and bone of my bone. Whatever he has done, I love the boy. And he is not a bad fellow."

"Then his wife's a bad influence on him! Choosing to live in that wicked city of Sodom. What happened, Abram? Was there much fighting?"

"There was more chasing than fighting, Sarai."

"And hard on you at your age, too!"

"We overtook them near Dan, chased them almost to Damascus, jumped them by night, recovered Lot and his family, *plus* all the spoil the marauders had stolen from Sodom, too!" Abram smiled and squared his shoulders like a bragging boy.

"I hope you brought all that spoil back here with you!"

Abram laughed at his fiery wife. "No, I took it all back where it came from. I didn't want one thread or sandal-strap from the King of Sodom. This way he can never say he made Abram rich."

Sarai sighed deeply. "Abram, you have the best heart and the kindest ways of any man on earth. You're a good man. You're a real servant of the Lord God. And you're my husband! Was any woman ever so blest as I?"

Abram cradled his wife in one big arm. "I am the man most blest on the earth to have such a wife."

Then a familiar, helpless feeling gripped Abram. He felt all thumbs and big feet. Sarai had begun to weep again on his shoulder. It was not happy weeping this time.

"You are not the most blest man, Abram. I have failed you. All these years we've been man and wife and although I have loved you with all the love of my woman heart, I have not been able to give you a child! Don't call yourself blest, Abram! You are poor—poor!"

Abram still held Sarai close to him, but when he spoke she heard that strange authority which came sometimes to his voice.

"Sarai, the Lord God has said He would make me a great nation. That my offspring would be greater in number than the particles of dust on the earth. Can we not believe Him?"

"But, Abram, I am old. You are old. How can we have children? It frightens and confuses me even more when you mention the Lord God."

Tenderly Abram picked his wife up in his arms and held her wet face close in the silken warmth of his long, thick beard. For a moment, he stood there with her in his arms, looking helplessly toward heaven, aware of the strange fear in his beloved wife's heart. A woman fear he could sense, but not understand fully. Then he carried her back to her part of the big tent, to the thick pile of carpets where she slept, and laid her down gently.

"You treat me like the child you never had, my husband."

"I treat you like the beloved and loyal wife you have always been to me, Sarai."

The woman slept at last, and Abram sat beside her alone. Hating it, he remembered Egypt and his trickery with the Pharaoh. Did Sarai doubt his love sometimes since then? Manlike, Abram hadn't considered this at all in Egypt. Did it appear to her that he placed the safety of his own life above his life with her? What if the Lord God had not broken up the Pharaoh's plans to take Sarai as his wife? Was this new fear in her heart an Egyptian worm eating at the childlike trust she always had in him? Or was Sarai's despair only that she was barren and old?

A man who loves a woman hates himself hotly when he thinks he might be the cause of her sorrow. Tears glistened on his bearded cheeks in the dim light of the olive oil lamp. Abram put out the lamp and sat hoping with all his heart that Sarai's misery did not go back to Egypt. He reminded himself that the Lord God knew how much they both longed for a child. This was sorrow enough. Abram stood up. Not one word had Sarai said about his behavior in Egypt. It must be the child they didn't have that haunted her heart. It haunted his heart, too.

God's Covenant with Abram

There was no one to see Abram's tears as he sat alone beside his sleeping wife. No one, that is, but God. And in a vision, as he sat there, the Lord God spoke to Abram as to a troubled child.

"Have no fear, Abram; I am your shield; your reward is marvelously rich."

"O Lord God, what canst Thou give me, since I am ending life childless? What could be my rich reward? My only heir according to the law is my servant, Eliezer. He is a good servant, Lord, but he is not my son. Thou hast given me no offspring, and please consider the facts, Lord. Just a member of my household, a servant, will be heir to me!"

"Abram, Eliezer shall not be your heir; your heir will be born from your own body."

As though to be nearer the Lord, away from any distraction, Abram felt a desire to go outside under the giant white stars.

"Now look toward the heavens and count the stars, Abram, if you can number them."

"I can't count them, Lord. They are too many."

"So shall your offspring be."

"*My* offspring, Lord?" the old man cried.

"So shall *your* offspring be, Abram."

For a long moment, Abram was silent. Then in a voice younger and stronger than his had been for years, he said, "I believe You, Lord God. I do believe You."

Abram felt a strange new sense of peace. At that moment he was closer to God and less troubled by anything on the earth than ever before in his life.

"Abram, I am the Lord who brought you from Chaldean Ur to give you this land to possess."

"But, Lord, this land belongs to the Canaanites. In what way can I be assured it will be mine?" There was still the new oneness with God of a moment ago, but strong faith built slowly in Abram, as it does in most men.

"You may be sure, Abram. Listen to Me. Get Me a three-year-old heifer, a three-year-old she goat, a three-year-old ram, a turtle dove and a young pigeon."

With these instructions in his mind, Abram went back to his tent and waited for dawn when he could begin to carry out the sacrifice the Lord had asked of him.

All day long, Abram worked, selecting the heifer, the goat, the ram, the turtle dove and the pigeon. With his own hands he butchered the animals, cut them into halves, then laid the halves opposite each other on the altar. The dove and the pigeon he did not halve.

When the sacrifice was laid out and ready, Abram himself drove away the vultures and ravens which swept down to devour the carcasses. Waiting for further instructions from the Lord, Abram kept his watch at the altar alone.

Then about sunset a deep sleep overcame him and a horror of dense darkness got hold of him. If one could have seen into the unconscious mind of the sleeping Abram, there would have been a foretaste of sorrow and suffering and frustration and death. Into the depths of this man's being rushed a prophetic stream of all the sorrows and trials of the generations to come. His darkness was so dense and filled with horror that no one man's life could have held so much trouble. *Abram was the father of a great nation yet to be.* A suffering nation. A rebellious nation. A chosen nation. Chosen by God Himself and about to be brought into being through the man from the pagan city of Ur—Abram, the chosen servant of God.

41

When the dark agony of his vision had complete hold of him so that it was too much to bear, the clear voice of the Lord came again. "You will know with certainty that your descendants shall be aliens in a land not theirs for 400 years, working for those who shall oppress them. In turn I will punish the nation they shall be serving and afterward they will come away with ample wealth. As for yourself, Abram, you will join your fathers in peace; you will be buried in ripe old age. But they (your offspring) will come back here at the end of 400 years."

The story of the yet unborn nation of Israel was carefully foretold to Abram as he was allowed to share in the wonder and the suffering that lay ahead for the people who would be born of his body. The body of an old man.

When the sun had set and night blotted the altar and the sacrifice from Abram's waking eyes, he saw a smoking oven with no man near it. And a burning torch passing between the pieces of the offering he had laid out to the Lord.

God Himself was lighting the offering for him, and as it burned God made a covenant with Abram, saying, "To your descendants I will give this country from the river of Egypt to the Great River, the River Euphrates."

As God's own fire burned on the altar, Abram had his sign in detail from the hand and from the mouth of the Lord God Himself.

Doubt is always possible for anyone. But Abram now had no reason to doubt that God would give him an heir.

Chapter 6

Trouble in the Tent House

Both Sarai and Abram were old. It was ridiculous to think of Sarai bearing children. No doubt she had signed a marriage contract promising children to Abram. And so it is not surprising that one day she urged her husband to bring this promised heir to life through her well-favored Egyptian handmaid, Hagar.

Abram knew what this suggestion cost his beautiful, proud wife. Undoubtedly he was running ahead of God when he agreed to follow Sarai's plan, but he loved her and in his own heart was a deep desire for a son. So Abram went in to Hagar and she conceived.

As soon as it became known that Hagar, the slave girl, would bear Abram's child, the whole atmosphere of the tent home of Sarai and Abram changed. Like the coming of a sudden summer storm, thick heavy clouds of resentment and envy rolled across Sarai's disposition!

Hagar's devotion to her once-beloved mistress vanished like the sun gone out. Where once she had consoled and comforted her mistress, now her pride and disdain for the woman who could not bear a child snapped and slashed like lightning before the thunder of Sarai's jealousy.

Frantic in her new hatred of Hagar, Sarai flew at Abram.

"May the injury I suffer at the hands of this upstart slave girl from a pagan land come home to you!"

"To me, Sarai? Why to me?"

"I entrusted my maid to your bosom and as soon as she found herself with child, I became *her* slave! Or so she would have it."

"Sarai, be reasonable," Abram pleaded with her. "Hagar's young. We couldn't expect her to behave like a mature woman."

Sarai stomped her foot. "So, now you remind me of my age! And of her youth! I expect her to act as I would have her act. This is enough! She is my slave. I will decide what happens to her. Let the Lord do justice between you and me over this thing, Abram, but about that Egyptian slave, I will decide!"

Abram turned away, hurt and disgusted. "Then why bring me into it? Your maid is in your power. Do with her as you please."

Sarai turned her fury and jealousy upon Hagar in every harsh way her woman's cunning could devise. She gave her such hard work that no woman could have endured it. She saw to it that the girl had little sleep, improper food, and the life of the Egyptian slave girl so far away from her homeland became a nightmare of fear and wounded pride and exhaustion.

The child Hagar carried was her life, and one day she felt she would never be able to bear the child if she stayed with Sarai. The strength was gone out of her heart and her body.

Hagar ran away.

Someone Cared About Hagar

Weary when she left the encampment to begin her flight across the hot, hard desert, Hagar fell heavily to the ground beside the first spring of water she found.

With all her young heart she wanted to live for the child's sake. But there remained in her heart little else to go on. Lying face down on the rough earth, the Egyptian girl desperately needed inner strength for the long, long journey back to her homeland.

Her body was young and strong. A night's rest, even on the hard ground, would revive her physically. But fear and shock from the treatment she had received at the hands of the mistress she once loved had drained her of courage. And almost of reason.

Her unborn child stirred within her. Somehow Hagar had to get hold of herself.

"If only I could think about something else. If only I could concentrate on something—anything." Lifting herself until her bare elbows dug into the rough ground, she began arranging pebbles in little circles. One inside the other. It forced her to concentrate. At least she wasn't thinking of Sarai's anger and the bewildering circumstances of her life since the day she knew about her child.

Suddenly she sat up. "Hagar." There was someone there with her!

"Hagar."

His voice was like no voice she had ever heard. She half rose and there He stood. The sun was almost out of sight, streaming dark thick shadows across the world. But where He stood it was as light as day, without the pain and heat of the desert sun. Hagar felt somehow rested, just looking at Him. He was a stranger to her.

She had never seen a Man like this anywhere in Egypt or in Canaan. And yet she didn't feel at all strange with Him.

He smiled at her. "Hagar, Sarai's maid, where have you come from and where are you going?"

The girl stood up, forgetting her tiredness. How did He know her name? How did He know that she was Sarai's maid? None of these questions formed into words, though. She felt only quiet and something in her wanted to answer His questions. And to answer them truthfully.

"I am running away from my mistress, Sarai."

There was no need to tell Him more of what had happened. Hagar felt sure He knew all about it. When He spoke again not one pang of resistance did she feel, even though He was telling her to do exactly what she did not want to do!

"Go back to your mistress and humble yourself under her authority."

Hagar didn't fight. She just stood there hoping He would speak again. In a moment, as though He had heard the details of the turmoil in her heart, He said, "I will greatly increase your descendants beyond all counting, they will be so numerous." And as though to further reassure her that He knew everything there was to know, He said, "You are with child and you will give birth to a son, whom you will name Ishmael, which means *God has heard*. Name him Ishmael, Hagar, because the Lord Himself has noticed your harsh treatment."

Hagar stood looking at Him, no longer weary, no longer afraid. When she spoke at last, her voice was clear and strong and filled with bold awe. The simple Egyptian girl sensed who He was.

"Thou seeing God." Hagar had forgotten herself. "Thou seeing God."

In another moment, He was gone.

But Hagar thought of only one thing all through the dark night as she walked unafraid back toward Sarai's tent.

"Have I really seen God and remained alive after seeing Him?"

Would God Himself become a Man so that one frightened, proud, confused Egyptian girl could be sure that He watched over her?

Hagar named the spring by which He saw her troubled heart Beer-Lahai-Roi, which means, "Well of the living One who sees me."

Hagar went back to Sarai, and a little later on, bore Abram a son, and Abram, believing what Hagar had seen and heard beside the desert spring, named his son Ishmael.

Visitors at the Tent House

When Abram was 99 years old and his son Ishmael 13, Abram heard again from the Lord God. And what he heard brought a surprising reaction from the old man.

God once more renewed His promise to make many great nations of Abram's offspring, and in view of this God instructed him that his name would no longer be Abram, but Abraham, which means "father of a multitude."

With his new name, the heart of Abraham leaped with new hope and a deeper belief in the Lord God. But the next thing God said brought the unexpected reaction.

God said to Abraham: "As for Sarai, your wife, do not call her Sarai, for her name shall be Sarah; I will bless her, yes, and give you a son by her. I will bless her so that she shall become a mother of nations and from her, kings of peoples shall spring."

By now, Abraham must have believed that Ishmael, his child by the Egyptian maid, Hagar, was God's promised heir. And when God brought Sarah, then ninety, into the picture as having a child of her own, it was too much for Abraham. He fell on his face and laughed—in shock, in amazement. Over and over to himself he said, "Shall a child be born to a hundred-year-old man, or can Sarah bear at ninety?"

Abraham loved his son, Ishmael, and his next words to God may have been a plea for Ishmael's safety, but surely he also presumed to reason with God. At any rate, this is what he said: "O that Ishmael might live before Thee!"

God's answer was firm. "No, Sarah, your wife, is about to bear you a son and you will name him Isaac. With him, too, I will establish My covenant as an everlasting covenant for his children after him." But the Lord God knew how Abraham loved Ishmael, and so did not exclude the boy. "I have also heard you regarding Ishmael and will indeed bless him and render him fruitful. I will multiply him immensely; he will be ancestor to twelve princes and

I will set him up for a great nation. But My covenant I will establish with Isaac, whom Sarah will bear you this season next year."

Sometime later, Abraham sat in his tent door in the hottest part of the day, the early afternoon. He was pondering the strange things which God had told him about the son who would be born of his ninety-year-old wife, whose name was now Sarah.

Abraham had heard no one approach, but suddenly standing a little way from the tent door were three magnificent-looking men. Extreme hospitality was a "must" in the eastern culture of those days and so Abraham bowed to the ground and begged to be allowed to wash the dust from the travelers' feet and to feed them and give them rest.

"I beg of you, recline under the tree while I get refreshment for you." When they agreed, Abraham hurried inside the tent to instruct Sarah to prepare fresh cakes made of fine meal. Then he ran to the herd to select a fine calf which he gave to a servant to prepare for his three visitors. When the food was ready, Abraham placed it ceremoniously before his guests, standing by to care for their every need as they ate.

Sarah and Hagar (their relationship somewhat mended) eavesdropped from within the women's part of the tent. Hagar particularly kept trying to see one of the visitors without being seen. In those days, women had to remain out of sight. But the Voice of one visitor caused Hagar's heart to pound with excitement. She felt so sure she had heard that Voice before beside the spring in the desert!

Both women were listening intently as the most arresting of the three visitors spoke. He spoke with the Voice Hagar remembered!

"Abraham, where is your wife, Sarah?"

"There in the tent, honored visitor."

Then the same Voice spoke again. "Without fail I shall come back to you at the reviving season and Sarah, your wife, will have a son."

Hagar, who had been peeping around the side of the goat's hair tent, jumped back inside. Sarah had begun to laugh aloud. Surely they would hear her! Her laughter was like a cackle. And well it should be. Sarah was old.

"Such a thing for me worn out as I am? And my husband a hundred years old!" Sarah laughed and laughed and laughed.

47

The Visitor with the Voice Hagar remembered was silent during Sarah's laughter. Then He spoke again.

"Abraham, why did Sarah laugh just then, saying, 'How could I possibly bear a child, old as I am?' Is anything beyond the Lord's reach? At the appointed time I will return to you, at the reviving season, and Sarah will have a son."

Inside the tent, Sarah's laughter had stopped at the sound of the Lord's Voice.

"He heard you, Mistress. The Lord God heard you laugh!"

"Hush, girl. I did not laugh." Sarah was pale now.

From outside the tent the same Voice answered her denial to Hagar. "But you did laugh, Sarah. You did laugh."

A dreadful and uncomfortable silence hung around the tent, inside and outside. Even Sarah dared not utter a word.

Finally the three visitors rose as if to depart, looking toward the city of Sodom where Lot and his family now lived. Abraham walked with the men to show them the way. The Visitor who had heard Sarah's whisper of denial inside the tent began to speak again, almost to Himself, and Abraham realized it *was* the Lord who walked beside him as a Man!

"Am I hiding from Abraham what I am about to do? I have known him. So that he may charge his children and his household after him to keep the way of the Lord, doing what is right and fair, so that the Lord may bestow upon Abraham what He has told him." Then, confiding in his friend, Abraham, the Lord said as He walked beside him that day, "Abraham, the Sodom and Gomorrah outcry is loud and their sin is very grievous." Turning to the two visitors with Him, the Lord sent them in the direction of Sodom to investigate.

Abraham sensed the doom of the two wicked cities and remembered Lot and his family in Sodom. Standing alone facing the Lord, his Visitor, he dared to move closer to Him. "Lord, wilt Thou wipe out the good, too, with the bad? There are perhaps 50 good persons in the city; wilt Thou indeed wipe out and not pardon the community because of the 50 good people among them? Far be it from Thee to do such a thing, to slay the good with the bad, to treat righteous and wicked alike. Far be it from Thee. Shall not the Judge of all the earth deal justly?"

The Lord looked at Abraham a long moment. His friend, the husband of Sarah, was learning about Him at last. "Abraham, if

I find within the city of Sodom 50 righteous, then I will grant pardon to the whole place for their sake."

Something in His manner gave Abraham added courage and faith. "Lord God, I am aware that I have undertaken to speak to the Lord although I am but dust and ashes. But if there should be only 45 righteous, wilt Thou destroy the city?"

"If I find there 45, Abraham, I will not destroy it."

"What if only 40 are found, Lord?" Abraham's heart yearned over the city.

"For the sake of 40 I will take no action," the Lord showed His own yearning heart in His reply.

"O let not the Lord be angry, but perhaps there will be 30 found there."

Abraham was engaged in real prayer. The kind God answers.

"I will not act, Abraham, if I find 30."

Old Abraham trembled now with longing over the wicked city of Sodom, but also from this face-to-face conversation with his Lord. "Thou seest I am undertaking to speak to the Lord, but perchance 20 only shall be found there." The Lord once more agreed.

"Let not the Lord be angry, so that I may speak just once more. But perchance only 10 shall be found in Sodom, what then, Lord?"

"I will not destroy it, Abraham, for the sake of the 10."

As Abraham walked back toward his tent, after the Lord went away, his blood raced through his body like a young man's, so deep was his desire over Lot's family and so deep was his joy at the fact of this rare converse with God Himself. Surely Lot's family would make up almost all of the 10 good persons. Would the Lord find even two or three others, so that Sodom could be saved?

The messengers of the Lord had gone ahead to the wicked city. The decision would soon be made. Abraham slept little that night, and early in the morning he hurried to the spot where he had spoken directly to the Lord.

As he looked down upon Sodom and Gomorrah and upon that whole valley, he saw the smoke of the country rising like the smoke from a furnace. The wicked cities had been wiped out. Ten good people had not been found. But when God wiped out the basin cities, He remembered Abraham, and His messengers led Lot out of the catastrophe.

His whole family could have been saved. God's messengers gave careful instructions. One of the instructions was that no one was to look back toward the evil cities as they fled.

Lot's wife looked back. Her heart was still there in the sin and wealth and ease of Sodom. She has gone down in history as the woman who turned into a pillar of salt.

But God kept His promise. As always, He did all He could do in the face of human disobedience.

Chapter 7

God's Kind of Laughter

Old Abraham paced the hard rocky ground outside their big, black skin tent the night Sarah was due to give birth to their own child. Surely he had no reason to fear. The birth itself was a miracle of God! Wasn't God in charge now? Couldn't Abraham trust Him with Sarah's life and the life of their long-awaited son?

But the old man was a human old man. "Lord God, I'm trying to trust. I do trust you with the life of my son. It's Sarah's life that frightens me. She is so old, Lord. So old and frail. Watch over her. Keep her. Keep her with me. Let her see our child grow to be a strong, fine man."

Abraham's footsteps crunched on the dry pebbly ground back and forth. Back and forth. Praying, as he awaited some sound from inside the tent. Some sound, other than the low voices of Sarah's attending slaves. Overhead the stars, great and clear and endless, reminded him that God had said He would give him as many offspring as the stars in the sky.

Crunch, crunch, crunch - - and then the sandaled footsteps stopped! The quiet night tingled suddenly with what could only be the first lusty cry of Abraham's son and heir. Over it, the murmur of the women's voices inside the tent rose sharply to the usual woman exclamations as though a time like that had never happened before.

Later, inside the tent, Abraham knelt beside old Sarah's bed of soft rugs. She looked radiant. Both Sarah and the baby were fine. Abraham thanked God in his heart as he kept saying over and over again, "Sarah, beloved, beloved Sarah."

Her voice was weak, but there was strength in her old arm as she circled Abraham's neck and chuckled, "Who would have thought it, Abraham? Who would have told Abraham, 'Old Sarah will nurse a child'?"

Her happy weeping overwhelmed her. His joy and concern overwhelmed him. For a long moment the two old people could say nothing. They could only cling to each other and mix their tears of thanksgiving and relief.

After awhile, Sarah lifted her husband's head and wiped his

eyes with her hand. "I laughed at God's promise, my husband. Now, God has prepared laughter for me. How can a woman be ashamed of laughter and glad about laughter at one and the same time? How, Abraham?"

"Because of what our God is like, Sarah. He has prepared His kind of laughter for us now. And we will call our son Isaac. Our beautiful, strong son will be called Isaac."

Because Isaac meant "laughter."

Laughter and Tears and God's Heart

Laughter surrounded the young life of Isaac. Laughter of many kinds. In those days children were not weaned until they were five years of age and then there was a special weaning day with much celebration and a big feast for everyone. On Isaac's weaning day, the little boy whose name meant "laughter" was the brunt of some laughter which threw his hot-tempered, possessive mother, Sarah, into a fit of rage.

Abraham's son, Ishmael, behaved on Isaac's weaning day as any teen-ager might behave toward a mere five-year-old who was being made the center of attention. He laughed at Isaac.

"Is that *all?* What a lot of fuss over one brother teasing his younger brother!" Abraham obviously said the wrong thing to his wife.

"Is that all? Is that all? Where is your pride in our son Isaac, Abraham?" Sarah was screeching.

"I'm as proud of Isaac as a father could be, Sarah. But I think you're making a big thing out of—"

"—out of nothing, I suppose you're about to say! Well, you listen to me. No son of a heathen slave woman is going to make fun of my son and get away with it!" Sarah's voice rocketed with fury. "And don't remind me that he's your son, too. I well remember! But I've had him thrown in my face long enough. *Isaac* is God's promised heir. I want that slave and her big, ugly, rough child out of here! Do you hear me, Abraham? I want them sent away. Both of them!"

"But, Sarah, have pity on me. Ishmael is my boy, too. I love him."

The old woman's voice dropped, the way it always did when she was going to have her way. "I want them both sent away at once! The son of a slave is not going to inherit with *my* son. He is not, Abraham. He is not!"

Early the next morning, Hagar and her teen-aged son, Ishmael, carrying food and water tearfully given to them by Abraham, began their long walk across the Beersheba desert. Hagar tried to be cheerful for the boy's sake. Ishmael did his best for his beloved mother's sake. But their heavy hearts overtook them both like the sickening heat of the sun, as a few weary miles moved behind them and an endless number stretched ahead.

On the third day, Ishmael dropped first. The water was gone. So was the food. They would both surely die. They were together, mother and son, but by now neither of them spoke anymore. They were just there together and that was all. Ishmael was a husky boy. It took all the strength Hagar had left in her aching body to drag him to the scant shade of a dry, dusty desert shrub to die.

His feverish, questioning eyes watched his mother walk away from him. Their hearts cried to each other, but still there were no words. Hagar staggered backward a few steps. It is not easy for a mother to turn her back on her dying child. She was walking away, but backwards, so he was still in her sight. Suddenly she turned and stumbled as fast as she could away from the boy about the distance a bow could send an arrow.

"I cannot see him die! I cannot see him die!" Her cry seemed to strike the hot, empty sky and crash back on her.

Maybe Ishmael heard. Maybe not.

As she lay flat on the rocky ground sobbing violently into the tear-streaked, dusty sleeve of her garment, she hoped Ishmael hadn't heard. "I —cannot —I cannot see him—die!"

There was nothing in Hagar that did not weep. She would die, too, but that didn't seem to matter now. Neither did it matter that she relieved the desperation by beating her fists brutally against the sharp, rocky ground. Beating them until the blood ran into the round, dark rosettes her tears had scattered in the dry dust.

And then, over her weeping there was a Voice.

"Hagar!"

She *could* be losing control of her mind! Still her heart was the same heart that broke in a young girl's breast years before when the same Voice spoke to her alone in the same desert. Her mind was tormented now. Her body older and more tired. But hearts don't grow old. And in themselves, they never lose their ability to respond.

"Hagar, what is troubling you?"

If she looked up from her weeping, would He be there again as He was before?

"Hagar, what is troubling you?" Gentle, insistent, the Voice went on now. "Have no fear, God has heard the lad's voice over there where he is."

Not in words, but up from her heart suddenly alive, rang a question. "Did my dying son Ishmael pray to the Lord God? Did his father teach him so well?"

Hagar raised her head now to look for the Visitor who had come to her before. She saw no one, but His Voice was all around her. Above her, cooling the sun; beneath her, softening the dry earth; within her, helping her to think.

"Have no fear, Hagar. God has heard the lad's voice there where he is. Rise up! Go lift the boy up and hold him by the hand, for I will make him into a great nation."

Hagar raised herself upright, feeling no pain from the open gashes in her hands. She must find Him again. Swaying on her feet now, she looked wildly around for some glimpse of the Person who had spoken these strange, comforting words. He was not visible this time, but He was there. And to the left, not more than ten steps away, was a cool, clear spring of water!

Water for Hagar to take to her son who had been dying of thirst but a few minutes before. Water for her to drink. Water and new strength, just as before from the person-to-Person encounter with the Lord God who had once more shown Himself to care greatly about a once pagan slave girl and her sick child.

For all of their lives, God was with the child, Ishmael, and with his mother. Ishmael grew up and lived in the Paran desert, becoming an expert hunter, and his mother got him a wife from her native land of Egypt.

Today, Arabians who follow the Moslem faith believe they are descended from Ishmael, the cast-out son of Abraham, who, as a teen-ager, called on the Lord God for help as he and his frightened mother, Hagar, lay dying in the desert.

Abraham—a Fool for God!

After she had forced Abraham to get rid of Hagar and his son,

Ishmael, the days were as difficult for old Sarah as for Abraham. Abraham was kind to her as always. But when he came to her for a talk or asked her to walk with him in the cool of the evening when the giant stars flashed one after another into the still blue sky, Sarah always felt a little twinge of nervousness. Would he ever be able to speak of Ishmael again?

She hoped so and she hoped not.

"Sarah," Abraham's voice was deep and serious. They were walking together and their teen-aged son, Isaac, walked with them —striding a little ahead. "Sarah, God has spoken to me again."

Without meaning to, Sarah shuddered.

"Last night, when I was outside our tent alone, God called 'Abraham,' and I answered 'Here I am, Lord.' "

Isaac was interested at once. "What did God say to you, Father?"

"You and I are taking a trip tomorrow, Isaac, to the region of Moriah."

Sarah stopped walking.

"Abraham, no! The boy's perfectly happy here. Time enough for more of that hard traveling later on."

"Oh, Mother, I want to go!" Isaac linked his arm with Abraham's, laughing. "Don't pay any attention to Mother. She thinks I'm still a baby. Do we really go tomorrow, Father?"

Sarah stood a little apart from them now, tight with a strange sudden fear.

"Yes, my son. We go tomorrow. Early tomorrow morning."

The dawn came slowly that morning. Softly, carefully, the mountains in the distance piled themselves toward the sky that hung, changing gently, above them. Pale rose. Pale blue. Gold. Isaac and the two young men Abraham took with them on their journey only reveled in the bright vast confusion of craggy peaks and tender clouds, and had trouble matching their young energies to the slow, almost heart-heavy steps of the old man.

"Ride your donkey, Father," Isaac urged. "We can carry the wood and supplies."

Abraham let his wrinkled hand remain longer than was necessary on the boy's strong, broad shoulder, gripping it, as Isaac helped him mount the donkey.

"You are all the joy of this old man's heart, Isaac." His voice trembled under the weight of the heavy, dark-bright secret he carried in his heart.

Isaac laughed. "Look here, Father, a morning like this one is no time to look sad! You're tired already. You see? You should have been riding all the time."

Abraham smiled. "It is a most glorious sunrise, my son. God is in it all."

"God is in everything, Father. And everything is good out here." Isaac took a deep breath of the air growing sweet with the coming day and stretched his muscular young arms ahead of him, relishing the uncomplicated joy of being alive and young.

"Yes, God is in everything. And He will handle it all in a good way. He is a good God." Abraham's voice was still trembling. He still held the heavy secret burden in his heart. The burden of what he knew he had to do. But it *was* somehow a bright-dark burden he held. One he more and more felt able to trust to God to handle—in a good way.

The mountains piled themselves higher into the clearing sky. Their rising pale blue and rose and gold veils revealing more and more of the tumble of giant rock slabs stacked on a slant to their summits. Soon the fierce desert sun would take over. But God would be in that, too.

Little rocks skittered gaily under the clopping hoofs of Abraham's donkey. The first day of their journey came on and then went back again into sunset and night. Abraham and Isaac and the two faithful servants slept.

On the third day, Abraham cupped his hands around his old eyes and looked up toward the sun-bare summit of one mountain. Isaac and the two young men waited for him, slowing their pace, as he reined in his donkey.

After a long moment, Abraham spoke to the servants. "Stay here by yourselves with the donkey. The lad and I will go yonder, so we may worship—and return."

One of the servants, who loved the old man as a father, said, "We will gladly walk along to help you, Sir."

"No, my boy. Only Isaac and I can go to the place God will show me—to make an offering and worship."

"Then put the wood for the fire on my back, Father. I don't have these muscles for nothing, you know!" As always, Isaac was laughing, proud of his broadening shoulders the way a boy who is almost a man is proud because he is no longer scrawny.

Abraham took the wood for the burnt-offering and laid it on Isaac and they began to climb together. In one hand, Abraham carried the torch to light the sacrificial fire, and in the other a long, sharp knife to slay the living thing to be sacrificed.

Isaac sang a carefree song as they walked along together up the steep side of the rocky mountain. Then, as though he had just remembered: "Father, we have the fire and the wood and the knife, but where is the lamb for the burnt-offering?"

There was now no trembling at all in Abraham's voice. In fact, Isaac had never heard his father's voice sound so young and strong. "My son, God will provide Himself the lamb for the offering."

The climb was something of a struggle after that, for a way, and neither of them spoke. Above them rose the great silent boulders, and the flat, piled plates of shingle and slate sloped away downward. Then they reached a thickety shelf and father and son stood silent in the midst of a silence neither of them had felt before. There were the huge knobs of stone against the sky, the soundless sunlit slopes sliding away to the quiet valley below where the servants and the donkey waited. And there was a new fresh aloneness around them, seeming to close them into the silence.

After a few moments of merely joining the great silence, Abraham stooped and began to gather rocks for an altar. Isaac dumped the firewood on the ground and started to help, gathering five or six suitable stones to his father's one.

As he had done so often in the past, Abraham once more built an altar to the Lord God. Then he arranged the wood on the altar.

Isaac had stood by during this, watching his father from deep-set, dark eyes that revealed interest, fear, dismay, confusion, curiosity or all of these. One thing anyone who had been there would have noticed was the boy's accelerated breathing. He had been climbing, yes. But the pulse in his smooth temple throbbed like a blue, wavy rope tugging there. The pulse in his strong throat thumped rapidly. But Isaac said nothing at all to his beloved father, when the old man led *him* to the altar and bound him there securely on top of the wood the boy had carried up the mountain for the sacrifice!

The tall, deep canyon of silence around them seemed suddenly to open out, when before, it had closed them in so that they were aware only of each other. Still no word passed between them.

Isaac only continued to look up at his father who stood above him with one hand behind his back. He looked straight into the sunken eyes of the old man whom he knew loved him with all his heart. And even Abraham could not distinguish exactly what Isaac's look said. Whatever, it was clear now and quiet. God was in the boy's look.

God was in the silence that continued to open around them. Abraham's heart quavered for one instant as he thought of Sarah and her consuming love for their son, but it quieted itself again and he raised his hand into the air, clutching the long, sharp knife, ready to make the death thrust quick and sure.

Suddenly the silence squeezed about them, closed them in once more, and a Voice from heaven rolled commandingly around the mountainside: "Abraham! Abraham!"

The old man still held the knife above his son. "Here I am, Lord! Here I am!"

"Do not lay hands on the lad. Do nothing to him! For now I know that you revere God. You have not held back from Me your only son, your beloved one."

Instantly there was a crashing and bleating in a thicket nearby. Abraham looked, and there, caught by its horns in a thicket, he saw a ram. God had supplied His own sacrifice!

For a moment Abraham could not move, except to loose his fingers from the handle of the knife. As it dropped to the ground, the old man fell on his son, kissing him and praising God.

After Abraham and Isaac had sacrificed the ram on the altar, the Lord called to the old man a second time. "Because you have not held back your son, your only one, I will bless you beyond words; I will greatly multiply your descendants so as to compare with the stars of heaven and the sand on the seashore for numbers. Your offspring shall possess the gate of his enemies and through your offspring all peoples of the earth shall be blessed."

The Lord God was going to continue to fulfill that promise through Isaac long after Abraham's death. But in order to do it, He had to act (as He always does) through some quite unlikely people. Among them Jacob, one of Isaac's twin sons.

Chapter 8

Isaac's Household—a Family Divided

Isaac was a good man who loved his wife dearly. He prospered materially all the days of his life. But as the saying goes, "he was not the man his father was." A quiet, gentle man, so far as is known. A man who revered God. Things happened around Isaac, but unlike his father, Abraham, he seldom took part in them.

No doubt this was the reason his big, danger-loving, red-haired son, Esau, was his favorite of the twin sons born to him and his wife, Rebekah. Esau was a hunter—restless in the quiet calm of their tent-life, discontented unless he was moving, roaming the hills, bringing down wild bucks not fleet enough to escape his arrows. Esau laughed a lot, sang loudly, joked with his father. Through him, Isaac took part in life second-hand, from the sidelines. Old Sarah had over-protected Isaac as a child. Now he had one son, at least, through whom he could be a man of action.

"You'd never know our sons were twins, Rebekah," Isaac mused one day as his wife smoothed his bed and straightened the pile of cushions against which the old man spent most of his hours.

"Of course you wouldn't think they were twins!" Rebekah snapped, tossing a clean robe over the top of his bed. But they did not mean the same thing by their remarks about their sons. Rebekah's very life centered around Jacob, the quiet, more thoughtful son. The clever one of the two.

Isaac was losing his eyesight and growing feeble from inactivity. He hated quarrels of any kind, especially with Rebekah.

"I suppose the fact that Esau brought back three bucks last night has stirred all that fatherly pride in you today." She took Isaac's hand firmly and helped him back to his bed. "The thought of all that venison to eat has you excited again. All Esau has to do is keep you stuffed with venison and you're a happy, proud father."

Isaac settled back on his cushions with a sigh. "I didn't mean to start an argument, Rebekah. They're both our boys. We should love them both."

"You don't care about Jacob, and you know it!" She pulled the buckskin robe up over him. "It's always Esau, Esau, Esau."

"And with you it's always Jacob, Jacob, Jacob."

"Jacob and I have more in common, that's all. How do you expect a woman to get excited about Esau's one-track mind and gamy-smelling clothes? He's a roughneck and you encourage him in it! You don't try to influence him to mend his ways. You worship that boy, Isaac!"

"And you worship Jacob."

"Jacob responds to me, that's why. He's intelligent. He can converse with me."

"When you give him a chance." Isaac wasn't irritated. He loved Rebekah. But he seemed unable to remember that she could never take his teasing. "Rebekah! Come here and take my hand."

"What now, Isaac? I have work to do." But she gave him her hand.

"Thank you, Rebekah. I love your hand. We have been happy together, haven't we?"

"I've never been sorry I left my father's house to marry you, Isaac. You're a good man. It's been good to be with you."

"Our own sons must not come between us, Rebekah. Tell me they won't."

"If that wild buck Esau would learn to act like a civilized human being, there'd be no need to worry about—"

Isaac interrupted her gently. "Esau is Esau and Jacob is Jacob. We can't change them. I'm proud of Esau's ability as a hunter, that's all. He's a man. A real man."

"He's a boor and he'll break your heart by marrying a heathen woman one of these days, too. His kind always does!"

"Esau is so good to me, Rebekah, he couldn't break my heart. Esau loves his old father."

"I suppose that means Jacob does not?"

"Jacob is different. He's a—a thinker. Like you. I can't understand Jacob all the time. I'll leave him to you, Rebekah, and you leave Esau to me. But they mustn't come between us."

Isaac didn't understand Jacob. He didn't try to. He left him to Rebekah and the arrangement worked out toward a strange and embittering end.

But as in all things involving human beings, God was in even this.

No one could really say that Jacob was totally dominated by his mother. He had a mind of his own. A strong mind. A curious, perceptive mind. One that worked overtime and was fully aware of his mother's favoritism toward him. They had much in common, Rebekah and Jacob. Both of them made big Esau the brunt of their caustic jokes. Both of them resented the fact that Esau had been born a few minutes before Jacob, making him the first-born and entitled to inherit all of Isaac's wealth, plus his blessing. According to the social laws of their society, these privileges fell always to the first-born son, regardless of his worth.

When Isaac died, Jacob, from that time on, would be forced to serve Esau. This ground deeply into Rebekah's sense of justice. And into Jacob's.

At every opportunity he and his mother discussed the unbearable situation. Alone, of course, well away from the tent where old Isaac lolled on his bed hour after endless hour.

"Mother, tell me again what the Lord God told you before my 'mighty' brother and I were born. I keep turning it over in my mind. Just what did He say?"

"Jacob, I've told you so many times, you must know it by heart!" Rebekah patted his knee as he lay sprawled on a pile of rugs beside where she sat in her tent.

"I know, I know. But tell me again. Maybe one of these times we'll find a way out of this sickening mess."

"All right, my son, after your father prayed to the Lord God that I would conceive and bear him a child—you remember, I've told you that for years and years I remained childless—"

"Yes," Jacob grinned. "That seems to run in the family. Look how old my grandparents, Abraham and Sarah, were before my father was born."

"But God heard your father's prayer and soon you and your brother were jostling and struggling violently within me!"

"We haven't changed a bit, have we?" Jacob sat up, laughing. "Excuse me, Mother, go on."

"I appealed to the Lord God myself then, asking Him what was happening to me."

"And His reply? That's what I want, Mother—tell me again exactly what you think the Lord said to you!"

Rebekah straightened her back. "What I *think*, Jacob! I *know* what He said."

"All right, all right—what?"

"He said this strange thing: 'Two nations exist in your womb, and two peoples shall separate from your body, one stronger than the other, and the older shall serve the younger.' "

"That's it!" Jacob jumped up and paced the tent. "That's the part I keep turning over and over in my mind, Mother. 'The older, Esau, shall serve the younger'—me! But how? How? Oh, I know you and Father insist that I was born hanging onto Esau's foot—"

"You were, Jacob!" Rebekah's eyes snapped with pride as she watched her lean son pace back and forth. "You were hanging onto Esau's heel for dear life. Just as though you were determined, even then, not to let that oaf get ahead of you! He just blundered into life first, the way he blunders into everything. You were *thinking*, even then, Jacob. The fact that Esau was born first is just a trick of fate. And it's wrong, dead wrong. You are the son to inherit your father's wealth and blessing. Esau would make a mess of everything if he became head of our house."

Jacob stopped pacing and patted his mother's cheek. "You're my favorite woman because you're so smart, Mother. But just because you and I are so smart doesn't alter the fact that the big ox was born first! Still I keep thinking—what did God mean when He said to you that 'the older shall serve the younger'? What did He mean?"

Rebekah stood up and threw her arms around her favorite son. "I don't know what He meant, Jacob, but I know we have to do something to keep Esau from taking what should be yours! I waited so many long years for a son I could love as I love you, and now that I have you, I will not allow anyone else to take from you what is rightfully yours. You were conceived in my womb, Jacob. You are *mine*. You are the reason I like to open my eyes to each new day. Your father is old and blind and almost unaware of everything. Esau is not like my son at all. I open my eyes each morning for you, Jacob. Only for you! And together we will do something to get for you what I demand that you have out of life. Whatever God meant, that is my interpretation of what He said!" She clutched his sensitive face in her wrinkled old hands. "We will get for you what my whole heart demands that you have, Jacob. The older *shall* serve the younger!"

"But how, Mother? How?"

"I don't know how, but we will think of something in time." She drew his head down to her shoulder and embraced him until her knuckles showed white. "I am *your* mother. And a mother always finds a way to get what her own must have!"

Over Jacob's bowed head, Rebekah's eyes were fierce, not tender.

Jacob loosed his mother's arms and laughed at her affectionately. "We'll think of something, I guess. But one thing is sure—we have to keep our wits about us—every minute!"

A Birthright and a Pot of Stew

Jacob had his wits about him the very next day, as he stood stirring a large pot of red lentil stew.

Jacob's wits worked quickly and Esau, who usually moved according to the lumbering ease of his big, hairy body, literally plunged into Jacob's plan. The whole thing took only a few minutes.

"Ho, there!" Esau shouted as he came within smelling distance of the pot of steaming stew. "Who's cooking what? It smells so good! That you, Mother?"

Jacob scarcely looked at his brother as he hove into the shelter where the pot boiled, drawn like a magnet to the spicy aroma. "No, mighty brother, it is only I."

"Oh, so you're becoming a woman for fare, are you, Jacob? And the way that stew smells, you'd make a good woman, too!"

Esau grabbed the big ladle roughly, or tried to.

"Oh, no, dear brother! Not with those blood-smeared hunter's hands."

"Don't tell me what I can do in my own father's house, you slim-waisted mother's boy! Give me some of that stew before I starve to death!"

Jacob jumped in front of the steaming pot. "All right—but sell me your birthright!"

"What good's a birthright when a man is famished?" Esau shoved him out of the way. But Jacob meant the bargain to stick. He leaped back to the pot, covering it with his body. "Is it a bargain, Esau? Your birthright for this pot of stew? Will you swear to it?"

"Look here! I'm starving—that stew is what I want. I swear to you, take the birthright and get out of my way."

Jacob picked himself up from the ground where Esau had sent him sprawling. He smiled as he dusted himself off. "Dear, dear brother of mine. Allow me to serve you this delicious stew! After all, you've just paid dearly for it."

Esau didn't even notice as Jacob left the tent. He was literally guzzling the spicy stew and cramming large hunks of bread into his mouth. Esau was happy. And so was Jacob. At least, he was almost happy. Through the years he would be keeping his wits about him, because after all, he had only Esau's word that the birthright had been sold. Esau went his earthy, carefree way, hunting and eating and living each moment to satisfy just what he wanted for that moment. He had sworn that the transaction was final. But he acted as though nothing at all unusual had happened. As though he had never really thought about the birthright one way or the other.

Rebekah kept her wits about her, too, through the years. They were very much about her on the day old blind Isaac called his beloved son Esau to his tent. As soon as she saw Esau's big hulk stoop to enter his father's tent, she flattened her thin body against the side of the tent just behind the entrance and listened, tense and desperate as the two men who loved each other talked affectionately.

From habit, when he spoke with his favorite son about his mother, the old man whispered, as though he knew she might hear. "Come closer, son," Isaac chuckled brokenly. "You know, your mother thinks I ought to be angry because you up and married not one heathen woman—but two!"

Esau's voice was big and it boomed when he laughed or when he didn't. He laughed now. "Well, Father, haven't I always done everything in a big way? Why one, when I can have two—heathen or not?" Both men roared with laughter. Isaac cackling, Esau booming.

"Sh! We'd better mind how we talk, son." The old man sighed against his pillows. "I wish with all my heart you had married among our own people, but nothing you could do would change my love for you. You're a good son to me, Esau. I've always been proud to be your father."

Esau roughed Isaac's thinning hair with his big calloused hand. Words often stuck in Esau's throat when he spoke to his father. His heart got in the way. And so he just kept on roughing the old man's head, grinning broadly.

Then, because he could wait no longer to tell Esau what burdened his mind, Isaac clutched his son's big, coarse hand and stroked the thick red hair on it nervously.

"Esau, I'm blind now and getting old and tired. Who knows how long I'll live? I may die any day. So, listen to me. Take your hunting outfit, your arrow-case and your big, strong bow, and go out in the open country and hunt game just for me. Prepare me a tasty dish, the kind I'm fond of, and bring it to me to eat, son, so that I may give you my blessing before I die."

Rebekah heard every word. And even before Esau had time to leave for the all-important hunt, she and Jacob were together in her tent making plans.

Rebekah held Jacob's arm tightly as she told him what Isaac had in mind. "Now, son, listen to what I order you to do. Go to the flock right now and fetch me two well-fed kids of the goats. I will prepare them as a tasty dish for your father just the way he likes it. Then, you will take it in to him, so he can eat and give you the blessing before he dies!"

"But, Mother, my brother is a hairy man and I'm smooth. I could bring a curse upon myself instead of a blessing if he touches me to stroke me as he always strokes my 'mighty' brother!"

Rebekah's hand flew to his forehead, caressing it anxiously. She took his dark, sleek head in both her hands and pressed it for a quick moment. "Jacob, my beloved, I'll take your curse upon me, if such comes to you!"

Then, stepping back like a brisk little general—all business now—the old woman snapped, "Just go and fetch the kids for me. Go, Jacob. Do as I tell you!"

Their time had come. And every deliberate move by mother and son for the next few hours was a "now or never" action. Jacob, selecting the well-fed kids from the flock of goats, Rebekah carefully preparing the tasty dish—just the way Isaac liked it— Rebekah hurrying to Esau's tent for his choicest clothes to dress Jacob in her tent. And then, the last minute act of fitting the skins of the goats carefully around Jacob's wrists and over the backs of his smooth, slender hands.

Jacob was nervous, but he relished the excitement. "What about my neck and chest, Mother? Father delights in stroking my 'mighty' brother's hairy chest and neck!"

"I've another goat skin ready. Here, lean toward me."

The last cord was tied, binding the rough, hairy goat-skin over the smooth of Jacob's throat and chest. Rebekah stepped back for one quick look. They both smiled, and ceremoniously his mother handed him the tasty meat and fresh baked bread.

On his way to his father's tent, Jacob realized that he must somehow imitate his older brother's big husky voice. But he had his wits about him, completely.

Inside old Isaac's tent, Jacob stopped, holding the steaming meal steadily in his camouflaged hands. He laughed loudly. Then, in a voice like Esau's he bellowed: "My Father?"

Isaac raised himself on his cushions, sniffing the food. "Here! Here I am. Who are you, my son?"

The big voice boomed again, "I am Esau, your first-born; I have done as you told me, my Father. Please, sit up and eat of my game, so that you yourself may heartily bless me."

"Yes, yes, Esau, my boy." The old man raised himself in his bed. "It smells good! But, how is this, that you found it so quickly, my son?"

At this crucial moment, Jacob had no fear, even of the Lord God. In Esau's voice, he replied glibly, "Why, because the Lord your God brought it direct to me, my Father! Now, enough of this talk. Smell this delicious meat I have prepared just for you."

The old man smiled at the thought of the food, but then a slight frown hung over his sightless eyes. "Please come close to me, so I may stroke you, my son. So that I may know whether you are really my son Esau or not."

Jacob was prepared for this, thanks to his scheming mother. He moved closer to Isaac and after he placed the tempting meat near his father, he held out both his hands to be stroked. The goat skins held as the old man stroked them, at first cautiously, then affectionately.

"The voice sounds like Jacob playing a joke! But the hands are Esau's hands. The strong hairy wrists of my beloved older son.

66

Are you truly my son, Esau?" The old man's smile of recognition made his question seem almost forced.

"I am, my Father," Jacob replied in a softer voice, but still imitating Esau. And to make it stick, he roughed the old man's head as he had seen Esau do so often.

"Ah, then bring the food near me that I may eat of my son's game and then I will personally bless you."

Jacob brought him wine, too, and his blind father ate heartily and drank deeply.

"Now, Esau, my son, come close and kiss me." Jacob's own beard sufficed here. He kissed his father, and the old man clutched at Esau's cloak he wore, smiling broadly. "Oh, I bless you, my son. Truly, the smell of my son is like the smell of a field which the Lord has blessed. God grant you from heaven's dew and from earth's fatness, abundance of grain and wine. May nations serve you and peoples bow down to you. Be master over your kinsman and may your mother's sons prostrate themselves to you. A curse on those who curse you and a blessing on those who bless you."

Jacob and his mother danced for joy in her tent when the great deception was over. And as they were rejoicing, Esau was entering his father's tent, bearing the tasty dish of venison which he had prepared.

After the first few moments of dreadful confusion, while Esau and old Isaac both talked at once—each experiencing the first shock at what had happened—a dreadful silence fell between the two who loved so deeply.

Then a sob broke from the old man, as he muttered over and over, "I ate of all of it. I ate of all of it, before you came in, Esau. I also blessed him. I also blessed him! Yes, and he shall be blessed."

Another hard silence and big, powerful Esau wailed suddenly like a wounded animal. Loudly and bitterly, he wailed and then pleaded, "Bless me, too, my Father. Bless me, too!"

Isaac's voice was wooden, still unbelieving. "Your brother came in with pretense and stole your blessing. He stole it. He stole it, my beloved son!" Anger shook Esau's big body, as he paced the tent, bellowing. "Twice now, he has over-reached me! He robbed me of my birthright for a mess of stew and now he has stolen my blessing, too." The big man stopped pacing and fell to his knees like a child before his father's bed. "But, Father, my beloved Father, have you not reserved a blessing for me? I am Esau, your son. We are close. Like one man. Have you not reserved a blessing for me, too?" Tears streamed down over Esau's thick, red beard. He was weeping openly now.

Isaac's thin old hands trembled as he groped for his son's hand. Tears fell from his sightless eyes, too. "But, my son, my beloved son, I have made him your master and I have given him all his kinfolk for servants; I have provided him with grain and wine. As much as my heart breaks, what can I do for you now, my son? What can I do?"

Esau's sobs split his big voice as he cried for some kind of blessing from his father. Like a desperate child surrendered utterly to his pain, the big man cried aloud for some kind of blessing.

Isaac's shattered heart responded as best it could at that dark moment. Brokenly, slowly, the old man began to speak: "You will live, Esau, my beloved son, on the fatness of the earth and from the dews of heaven above. You will sustain yourself by your sword and you will serve your—brother." Isaac forced the words through his thin, old lips. And then, with all the strength he could muster, he finished his would-be blessing: "But—but, when you strenuously exert your power, you will break his yoke from your neck."

Esau rose to his feet unsteadily. Perhaps for the first time the value of the blessing he had lost swept over him. His father had done his best, but there was actually no blessing left for Esau. Isaac had merely made a statement of a bad situation and a suggestion for making the best of it. He roughed the old man's head once more, so he would know that the hatred in his heart was not toward his father. And as he trudged heavily out of Isaac's tent, toward his own, the hot grudge burst into words. Unaware that his mother lurked nearby, he relieved himself by bellowing at the night sky: "Mourning time for my father is not far off. He will die soon. Then—then I will kill my brother Jacob! Then will I surely kill him!"

Rebekah waited until Esau's big frame vanished inside his own tent. Then she ran to Jacob, frantic and determined.

"He's going to kill you, my son. He knows! I heard him with my own ears. As soon as your father dies, Esau will murder you. He's consoling himself with this black thought and he'll do it."

For once, Jacob had no quick answer. His mother clung to his arm for a moment, as though waiting for him to say something to lessen her fear. But the boy said nothing. He just stood there, staring past her toward the darkness outside where his brother was. Rebekah took hold of the situation then, her panic pushed aside by the plan that fit itself together in her busy mind.

"Jacob, don't look out there. Look at me. And listen to me. Get ready quickly and hurry to my brother Laban at Haran. Stay with him for a few days, my son, until your brother's fury has blown over. You know how stupid he is! One good long hunt and Esau will forget all about the blessing. He won't remember what you did to him for long. He hasn't brain enough!" Rebekah embraced Jacob suddenly. "Then I'll send for you and get you back from there, my beloved. Back here with me. If your father is dying, why should I be deprived of you both at once?"

"But what about my father? Will he agree to my going?"

"I'll make sure that he will. Go now, and gather your belongings. Just as few as possible. You must leave at once, Jacob!"

Jacob felt nauseated and tired. Rebekah was pushing him toward his own tent now, and as usual he did as she ordered him to do.

Inside blind old Isaac's tent, Rebekah watched her husband for a moment before she let him know she was there. He lay back on his bed, his pale eyes open, seeing nothing. One old hand lay tenderly on the thick rim of the clay vessel in which his beloved Esau had brought the venison to him. He seemed almost not to be alive, except for the slight movement of that one hand, as he literally fondled the bowl of untouched, cold venison. All of Isaac's heartbreak was in that hand, caressing the coarse clay bowl of cold meat.

Rebekah began speaking rapidly and nervously. "Isaac, I can't stand it a moment longer. The presence of those Hittite women Esau married wears me down, and if Jacob marries one of them my life won't be worth living!"

Isaac's head turned slowly toward the sound of her voice, but he said nothing.

"Call Jacob to your tent, Isaac, and command him to leave at once for my brother Laban's household! I won't rest until the boy is gone." Rebekah hadn't talked with her husband since Jacob's trickery, but with no pause except for a long, deep breath, she plunged right into the matter.

"Now that you have given your blessing to Jacob, my husband, it is up to you to see to it that he does not marry any but our own kind! Isaac, do you hear me? Command Jacob to leave at once for Haran to get him a wife."

For a long moment old Isaac continued to lie there still fondling the bowl of stiff, cold venison. Rebekah's cheek twitched as she waited through the long moment until he spoke at last.

"Send Jacob to me, Rebekah." His voice was thin and hollow, like an old reed. Even his wife couldn't tell what he intended to do, but she ran at once for Jacob, pushed him inside his father's tent, and flattened herself against the outside to listen. She didn't need to hide from Isaac, but suddenly some of the closeness she had always known with Jacob was gone. She hid from her own beloved son so she could find out for herself just how much of his determination had gone with their old closeness. She had to know that she could still trust the boy to carry out their scheme. Even though she stood eavesdropping outside the tent, her possessiveness squeezed around the slender, dark young man as he stood uneasily beside his father's pallet.

At last the old man spoke. His voice was steadier now, but there was no heart in it.

"Jacob, my son? Is that you there?"

"Yes, my Father. It is I."

"So it is. And this time, I know you. Too well." A tear dropped off Isaac's thin, graying beard and onto the cushion which held his head. But in a moment he went on speaking to Jacob.

"Once more I bless you, Jacob, my son, and I also charge you that you are to marry no Canaanite girl. Get ready at once and go to Padan Aram to the family of Bethuel, your mother's father, and get you a wife there from your Uncle Laban's daughters."

Jacob seemed almost too overjoyed. "Yes, Father, I'll go at once!"

"God Almighty bless you, and make you prolific and multiply you so that you may become an association of peoples. May He grant you and your descendants after you the blessing He bestowed on Abraham, so as to possess the land in which you are now a stranger, which God gave to Abraham."

"Thank you, my Father. I will go at once." Rebekah's heart

leaped. Jacob's voice was strong again and determined. His old, self-confident smile was back when he strode outside the tent and across the corner of the compound to collect his belongings.

Sometime later, dressed for his journey, Jacob stood impatiently, almost patronizingly, before his mother in her tent. He had come to say good-by. His determination was back, but she had been mistaken to think that with it would come their old closeness.

"Your mother will send for you in just a few days, Jacob, my son. Don't worry. Don't be afraid. God watch over you."

Jacob laughed and patted her head carelessly. "Me afraid? Now? Let's let God watch over you and Father and poor, stupid Esau. I don't need your prayers, Mother. Everything's going my way now!"

The old woman grabbed his arm. "But you want to come back, don't you, Jacob? You want to come back here to me, don't you?"

He smiled impudently. "All right, Mother. Let's do it your way. Let's leave it all in God's hands."

Her panic almost choked her. Jacob was pulling away from her right before her eyes! "How dare you speak lightly of the Lord God, Jacob? We are only doing His will! Didn't He tell me before you and Esau were born that the older shall serve the younger?"

The boy laughed again. "Have it your way, Mother. And smile as you say good-by to me, woman! This is what we've wanted, isn't it?"

He was pulling away literally now, as her fingers clutched his cloak. "Even though we tricked your father, my son, we were only doing God's will, weren't we?" Jacob was striding away now, waving cheerfully at her, seemingly unmindful of the woman's shrieks of anguish stabbing pathetically at him and falling off his slender shoulders like hailstones.

"Jacob! Jacob, my son! I'll send for you. Trust God. What we did was God's will! Be careful, my son. You are all I have now. I'll send for you, Jacob. I'll send for you."

Jacob was swinging out of sight now, with no more waving. No look back. Gone, into the thick night as though she were not his mother at all.

Rebekah sank to the ground and sobbed until her throat ached, knowing suddenly in her empty heart that she would never see her strange, beloved, devious son again.

71

Chapter 9

Jacob's House Divided by Joseph

Looking back on one's own life, if one has a perceptive mind, is usually a disturbing experience. Whatever Jacob lacked in honesty and integrity, he did not lack in perception. His mind was tricky, but it was not dull. As he grew older Jacob saw himself in relation to the strange events through which he schemed and maneuvered his way during the long years since the night he walked away from his mother, Rebekah, and the encampment of old Isaac, to find a wife among his own people.

As an old man, Jacob looked back and *saw*. The years had not dulled his quick mind. They had added a strange helplessness, bit by bit, as they passed, but it was a helplessness of the emotions, not the mind.

"You promised, Father, that you would tell me about all that happened to you after you left my grandfather Isaac's house. On my twelfth birthday, you said. My brothers are all out in the fields and Benjamin is asleep, so tell me now, Father! I'll be twelve years old tomorrow." Young Joseph spoke with the certainty and ease of a favored son. He was a mature twelve years and his handsome, sensitive face showed him to be at a delicate place in his emotional development. A boy so loved and spoiled by his father could easily turn out to be arrogant and conceited. His brothers hated him already and would have agreed that he was heading in this direction fast. But Joseph was still innocent. As yet he hadn't acted on the security of his position with old Jacob.

He was barely twelve and seemed still waiting to discover his own exciting nature. Whichever way the balance tipped, Joseph would have an exciting nature. This anyone could see. So far, he was merely young and when he wounded other people, as he sometimes did, it was due mainly to the quick energy of his mind whipped along by an admirable, if not always considerate, imagination.

"You told me just enough, Father, to give me the idea that you pulled a neat trick on Uncle Esau and my grandfather! Did you think up getting the blessing yourself, or did Grandmother Rebekah help you?"

Jacob winced and then smiled at the boy. Joseph's candor flicked even his adoring father on occasion.

The two sat at the open door of Jacob's tent, close together in the small shade of the propped-up canopy.

"It was a two-way thing, Joseph." Old Jacob stretched his legs and sighed, his hand on the boy's head. "Your grandmother and I were a lot alike, I guess. What I did was wrong. I love you too much to lie to you, son. But God has dealt mercifully with me, and if you can benefit from your father's mistakes, then bear with me and I will tell you the whole story."

Joseph sat erect, looking intently at his father as he spoke. Jacob's eyes rested on the low, rocky hill to the south, not seeing it. Not really seeing anything around him. Rather seeing back through the years to the third night of his journey from his own home to his Uncle Laban's place.

"It was a strange night, that third night of my journey, Joseph. I grew tired and stretched upon the ground to sleep, grateful for the chance. But I couldn't sleep for a long time. The stone I had selected for a pillow seemed the most uneven one in the field!"

"Were you afraid out there alone in the dark, Father?" The boy was flushed with interest.

"No, not afraid of the dark, Joseph. Strange thing, it wasn't dark enough! The sky didn't seem to grow black as usual that night. It was almost as though the sun had forgotten to go all the way down. There was a strange light everywhere. And then I thought I had fallen asleep. I suppose I did, but suddenly I saw a bright, strong ladder standing on the ground not far from me. Its top reached all the way into heaven and, Joseph, there were angels of God going up and down the ladder between heaven and earth! And the Lord Himself stood above the ladder and said so clearly that I understood every word: 'I am the Lord, the God of Abraham and the God of Isaac. The land on which you are lying I will give you and your descendants; your offspring shall be as the dust of the earth; you will enlarge westward and eastward, northward and southward, and in you and in your offspring all the families of the earth shall be blessed. See now, I am with you and I will watch over you wherever you go, and I will bring you back to this country; for I shall not forsake you.' "

The old man's voice shook with emotion and in the silence after

73

he had stopped speaking, young Joseph whispered, "Can you imagine God saying something wonderful like that to you right after you had played such a trick on your own brother?"

The boy's penetrating words stabbed Jacob back to the present. Then he smiled approvingly at his son. "You amaze me, Joseph. You are seeing God's nature more clearly than I saw it and you are only a boy of twelve years! Oh, I can look back now and see that I woke from that dream with perhaps my first real awareness of God. I knew my father and mother believed in Him, but I personally spoke to Him for the first time after the dream. I told Him I knew He was in that place. It was God's house, son! It was the very gate of heaven. I sensed the living God, but I've always been a bargain hunter, Joseph, and so I made a deal with the Lord God the next morning. I told Him that if He would take good care of me and get me back home safely, that He would be *my* God! Shame covers me to remember it. But your father was no saint, son. I've had to learn the hard way. Profit by my mistakes. Obey God. Don't use your good mind to get things to go your way."

"Get on with the story, Father. You can give me a lecture later on."

Even the boy's impudence delighted Jacob. And he got on with his story.

"Well, the next thing that happened was the glorious moment in the middle of one hot afternoon, when I met your mother, Joseph. At the well on the property of her father, Laban. Rachel was the loveliest girl I had ever seen. Slim, rounded shoulders. A delicate throat; strong, slender hands and a way of walking that made my heart turn over in my breast as I watched her. Flower-blue eyes she had, and long, thick black lashes around them. I loved her from the first moment I saw her. I love her still, Joseph, although she has been dead for all the years your brother, Benjamin, has been alive. Only you and Benjamin were her sons, only you and Benjamin have first place in my heart. You first, perhaps, because even though I love Benjie dearly, his coming meant her death."

"Mother told me once that you worked fourteen years for her, Father. Isn't that a queer thing to have to do?"

The old man smiled a crooked, humorless smile. "Your Great-Uncle Laban was a queer man, Joseph. I told him the only wages I wanted for the good work I did for him—(and if I do say so, he prospered enormously from the moment I began to supervise his flocks)— but the only reward I wanted was to be given Rachel, his lovely daughter, for my wife. He agreed and then double-crossed me on my wedding night. Instead of your mother, he sent in to me his older daughter, Leah. A good soul in her way, but dull-eyed and homely."

Joseph spoke with no conscious conceit. He was just stating a profound discovery as a serious twelve-year-old states a discovery: "No doubt that's why Benjamin and I are so much better looking than our other brothers."

Jacob smiled broadly. His beloved son should watch his candor, he supposed, but heaven knew it was the truth!

Joseph was weighing the story. "After fourteen years of work! Whew! You surely must have loved my mother very much."

The afternoon moved on, young Joseph and his father shifted once or twice, following the shade, and the boy heard his father tell of his decision to leave his wily Uncle Laban's house, with his wives, children and possessions. Great herds of fine sheep Jacob owned by then, because Laban could not outsmart his clever nephew. In spite of Jacob's trickery, God had kept His promise. Had literally invaded the dream of this self-centered young man to make Himself known to Jacob and then had kept His promise to watch over him and his offspring. Now and then the boy Joseph interrupted his father with a pertinent question, like this one: "What about Uncle Esau, Father? Didn't you worry about meeting him again someday? After all, he threatened to kill you!"

Then old Jacob told his son the most amazing part of the whole story. He confessed his nervousness through the years every time Esau came to mind. He confessed his guilt at what he had done. "I felt somehow worse than ever, Joseph, because now I was a rich man myself, in my own right. I didn't need the blessing I had stolen from my brother. It all seemed wasted by then. I hated every thought of my mother's lonely life with me gone. You see, I never saw her again. She died long before my father. I was rich and I had the woman I loved, I had children, and yet my own behavior didn't seem to back up the blessings God had given me. Much of the time I was confused. Oh, so confused, Joseph."

The boy astounded his father once more. "But I'm not confused, Father. It just goes to show that God is good and does what He says He will do, even if we are bad!"

Jacob embraced the boy warmly before he went on with his story. "How well you see God for one so young, boy. But you are right. And more than that, God's very goodness causes us to want to mend our ways. But, your father was slow to learn, and God knew this. He knew He had to do some startling things to bring me to my senses. Like the night just before I saw your Uncle Esau again for the first time."

"Did you just happen to see him, Father?"

"No, God did two amazing things to prepare me for seeing my brother again, son. First of all, He had to bring me to the place of realizing that something must be done about the breach between us, between my brother Esau and me. So, right after your mother and I and the others parted (amicably at last) with Uncle Laban, I saw the angels of God again."

"On another ladder, Father?" The boy was all attention.

"No, I just saw them this time. It was as though God was drawing my attention back to Himself again. And when our attention is on God, we begin to think always of the wrong we have done. So, I began to think of Esau. Of my poor old blind father. Of my mother's loneliness at never seeing me again. I made up my mind, Joseph, that I'd make it right. But, even though God was doing so much to bring me to the place of trusting Him, I still worked up a scheme of my own! I sent messengers to Esau in the Seir range of the Edom country where he lived by then, with instructions to tell him that I no longer needed the benefits of the blessing I had stolen from him. I suppose I hoped to impress him, too, with word of my vast possessions after my years with your Uncle Laban."

"Weren't you scared to see Uncle Esau, Father?"

"Yes, son, I was. I admit it. But I was trying to gain his favor, hoping to soften the blow somewhat. And when my messengers came back saying that Esau was on his way to me with four hundred men, I panicked! I divided my possessions and people into two camps, reasoning that if Esau's terrible temper brought him upon one camp with destruction in his heart, I wouldn't lose all I had. And I prayed, too, son. Oh, how I prayed! I told God I knew I didn't deserve the kindness He had promised me, but I called on Him that night for protection. I reminded Him that Esau could slay me, along with women and children. But, being me, I didn't stop with the prayer. I separated a generous bribe for my brother, too! Goats, ewes, rams, camels, cows, bulls and donkeys. I sent my servants ahead with the stock, telling them to leave plenty of room between the herds. I would bring up the rear, well protected, at least for a time."

"But you're not a coward, Father. I know you're not."

"God is my judge on that, son, but I was using every trick I could think of to appease my violent brother, Esau. I figured that after he kept meeting herd on herd of fine stock which I sent along as gifts for him, by the time he got to the end of the line, he just might accept me."

"Did you really think those presents would change my Uncle Esau's mind about murdering you?"

"I don't know what I really thought, son. But I know now that God was in charge. He was in charge even of me! Because that night, after I saw to it that your mother and the others were safe, I went off alone and that night I had an experience with God Himself that no man could forget!"

"What happened? Did you see some more angels?"

"I wrestled, son, all night long with a magnificent Man!"

"You actually wrestled with Him, Father?"

"I did, Joseph, and when this strange Man saw that I was not going to give up, He struck my hip socket so that my thigh was dislocated! Then He asked me to let Him go because it was almost daybreak."

"Were you holding onto the Man still, Father, after all that?"

"Yes, son. It is probably the only worthwhile thing I ever did. But I heard myself gasp out, 'I will not let You go unless You bless me!' He blessed me, Joseph, and said from that time my name would be Israel. I knew I had wrestled with God Himself!"

"You're a great man, Father. I love you very much. I'm proud that you're my father!" The boy's eyes were wide with open admiration.

"Thank you, Joseph. Only God knows what that means to me. But you haven't heard the strangest part of the story yet. The part that made me begin to see something of what a great God the God of Abraham really is! The sun was up full when I limped away from that place, and as I looked ahead, over a rise in the land, I saw coming straight toward me my brother Esau and his four hundred men! I hurried to your mother and to you and the others, and separated you quickly into small groups—you and your mother, Rachel, I put far in the rear for safety."

"I wish I remembered some of this, Father! Then what did you do? Were you still limping from wrestling all night?"

"Yes, but the sudden shock of seeing Esau coming toward me almost caused me to forget my leg. I went straight toward him and when I got near, I bowed to the ground seven times and kept on bowing until Esau had time to get nearer. Suddenly, I heard heavy footsteps, running!"

"Uncle Esau?"

"Yes, son—and here is the part I still find hard to believe. Your uncle, who had every right to avenge himself upon me, did no such thing. Suddenly, I felt his big strong arms lifting me to my feet. And instead of murdering me as he had sworn to do, the big clumsy oaf threw his arms around me and kissed me over and over again! He even wanted us to travel together, but I thought better of that. He offered me some of his men to help me with my livestock, but I quickly settled for the unbelievable gift of God I had already received."

"You mean God kept my uncle from killing you?"

"Indeed He did, Joseph! God has given me much in my years on earth, but nothing greater than the gift of my brother's favor. Completely undeserved, it was. But God gave it to me for reasons of His own, I guess."

"Maybe God doesn't give to us because we deserve something or keep things from us because we don't deserve them. Could that be right, Father? Can anyone figure out God?" The boy's smooth forehead was wrinkled with the interesting perplexity of the thought he had just had. Joseph was unusually interested in God, especially for a boy of twelve years.

"Can anyone understand God, son? I don't know. But I believe God understands us. And whether we can know much about Him or not, we can obey Him."

"And we can trust Him, too, can't we?" Joseph was still wrinkling his brow over the matter.

"Yes, son, we can. But who does trust God enough?"

"Perhaps I can learn to trust God, Father." The boy's serious face twisted the old man's heart with love. Love for his handsome son, Joseph. Love for Joseph's mother, Rachel. Love for the soul of her which he saw in the boy. Even love for the better part of himself which he knew in the son of his very own heart and soul. A little later, as Joseph walked away to join his brother Benjamin in the courtyard, Jacob (Israel) thought, "I would have no life at all without Joseph. Even with my other eleven sons, I would surely go to my grave without Joseph."

Another Deception

Old Jacob (Israel) lay exhausted upon the hard ground in the land of Canaan where he lived with his sons.

His knuckles were bruised from beating his sunken chest, heaving and red with the welts from his own fists. Even as he lay spent on the ground, his grief still drove him to try to tear the free edge of his garment. He could only try, though. His hands were too sore and his strength was gone.

Jacob would not be comforted.

One by one, and then in groups of two and three, his sons were trying to calm the anguish in his breast. But Joseph was dead! And Jacob could only go on trying to beat his breast to rid himself of some of the pain that tore at his heart.

Judah tried being clever with him. "Look here, Father, you have not lost your best son! Joseph was a braggart. What about the dreams he had? Even you rebuked him for it."

Levi joined Judah sarcastically. "And why not, Father? How dare that young blow-hard tell us he dreamed that our sheaves bowed down to his? That in another dream even the sun, the moon and eleven stars bowed to him?"

Judah pressed the point where he knew it hurt his father most. "To grieve like this for an impudent upstart who dared to tell that he dreamed you and his mother and all his brothers would bend their knees to him? Father, consider the facts!"

Israel's answer was another attempt to ease his own pain. The old man raised himself to his elbow weakly and wailed piteously against the hot, flat, relentless afternoon sky.

Joseph's long, beautiful coat, which Israel had given him, lay blood-soaked on the ground beside the old man. He seemed not to notice as his sons came and went. He tore at his sackcloth girdle as best he could, and wailed at the sky. Joseph was dead! Left to him was only the once beautiful, princely coat soaked with the blood of his beloved son.

Over and over in his grieving mind, Jacob stabbed himself with wild, futile questions: "Why did I send Joseph to see after his brothers as they pastured the flock? How could I send the prize of my old age, the son of my heart?" Then he would try to talk to Rachel, the boy's dead mother. "Rachel? Rachel, hear me! Why did I do it? Our boy! Our Jóseph! Our first-born! What flock is worth the apple of my eye? What flock?"

Reuben, the gentler of the sons, aside from Benjamin, stood near the writhing old man for a long while. Reuben had wanted not to kill Joseph. In fact, although he didn't have any special love for him, he did talk the others into removing Joseph's coat and abandoning him in a pit without water. "No bloodshed," Reuben had begged. And in his heart, he planned to return later alone to rescue Joseph. Reuben loved his father. As he stood in silence beside him, some of his love reached Israel. But Reuben couldn't bring himself to tell him the truth. Joseph was not really dead! By now he could be anywhere. In Reuben's absence, the others had sold Joseph to a band of passing Midianite slave-dealers for twenty dollars. It was truly Joseph's beautiful coat which Jacob kept beside him. But the brothers had dipped it in the blood of a kid they killed for that purpose.

Reuben half wanted to tell his father the truth. But he didn't love the old man quite that much. He wanted Joseph out of his hair, too! Believing him to be dead, the old man would not send them to find him.

He would just continue to grieve.

"But in the name of heaven, how long, Father?" Judah strode angrily back to where the old man sat tearing at his sackloth girdle.

Israel's long life of trickery floated grotesquely before him. With Joseph gone, there was now nothing to live for.

"How long can a man grieve like this?" Judah snapped.

"I will *not* be comforted," Israel clenched and unclenched his fists. "I will go down to the grave mourning for my son!"

When the others had gone once more, young Benjamin came at last to his father. Benjamin, Rachel's other son, who loved Joseph and whose soft, brown eyes pooled with tears as he stooped to pat his father's trembling shoulder. Benjie didn't offer any words of comfort. But he was there to offer himself as best he could, to take Joseph's place in the old man's heart.

But Joseph was not dead. The Midianite slave-dealers sold him in Egypt to a man named Potiphar, captain of the guard to Pharaoh.

The handsome, sensitive seventeen-year-old boy was suddenly alone in a lavish, pagan land among cultivated, sometimes cruel men and women who worked and schemed and danced and loved aimlessly in a society which was unlike anything Joseph had ever known.

Young Joseph was alone now except for the Lord God, who had had the boy's attention for all of his short life up to that strange time.

More Than a Beautiful Woman

"The Lord blessed the Egyptian's household for Joseph's sake; the Lord's blessing rested on all Potiphar's belongings in house and field. So he committed everything to Joseph's care. Potiphar did not bother about anything; he simply ate his meals."

Joseph, grown tall and unusually handsome, stood erect and solemn before the warm, brown beauty of Potiphar's wife. The woman was smiling at him and in a moment she moved toward him and slipped one fragrant, slim arm around his neck.

"Embrace me, Joseph!"

Not one muscle in his young body moved. And his face remained remote and solemn.

"I command you!" The woman's blood was stirred by this strange, serious young genius to whom her husband had turned over everything except the eating of his own meals. She was bored and lonely. *Potiphar did not bother about anything; he simply ate his meals!*

The gold bangles on her ankle bracelets clanged when she stamped her foot at him. "I command you, Joseph. Embrace me! We are alone. Who will know? Who will care, for that matter?"

She embraced him again. Joseph was aware of his own blood racing, faster than when he ran after his father's flocks on a sunny day in his youth. Faster and different. Her perfume was costly and Joseph felt it cover his senses like great plunging waves without a shore to break on.

"Embrace me, Joseph . . . Joseph . . . Joseph."

He had not moved. He had not looked at her except for one quick moment. His eyes looked beyond her now, and the solemnity which had broken from his face for that brief instant was back. He looked beyond her and spoke firmly, rapidly.

"Look here! My master does not bother about anything in the house. He has put me in charge of everything. No one in the house is superior to me. He has kept nothing from me except you, because you are his wife. How could I commit so great a crime and sin against God!"

The woman's eyes narrowed and she backed away, then slowly she walked away, still looking at him. But day followed day and sometime during the passing of each one, as Joseph went about his responsible position as head of Potiphar's household and fields, she managed to find him alone. And each time she found him, she talked long and persuasively. Commanding, cajoling, pleading, weeping, tantalizing him in every woman's way she knew. Any one way would have broken the defenses of most men. True, Joseph did stop trying to reason with her. But always he stood serious and silent and relentless in his refusal of her generous offer of herself.

One day she found him alone in the house, with all the servants gone. This time she did not talk or plead. With one sudden movement, she leaped toward him like a glorious cat and grabbed his coat, demanding that he obey her!

Joseph's sinewy body responded to his quicker brain and he moved, too! Not toward her. Away, with long, swift steps, he ran from the house and from the woman who had tormented him day after day after day.

But in order to escape, he had to slip from his coat and the coat hung suggestively from the bejeweled, scented hand of Potiphar's wife. She herself took the suggestion quickly! In no time her screams brought men servants running and soon not only the household, but Potiphar himself, knew her story.

"That Hebrew slave you brought in to us came to my room to molest me! But when I raised my voice and screamed, he left his coat with me and ran outdoors!"

Perhaps old Potiphar believed the story, perhaps he did not. At any rate, he threw Joseph into prison, when he might have had him executed instead.

In prison, Joseph continued his success story. The warden liked the young man at once, and in no time Joseph was in complete charge of all the convicts. Not once did the warden check on anything for which Joseph was responsible. He, too, saw that the Lord was with him and apparently gave the boy success in every thing he touched. And the afternoon when the Pharaoh's own butler and baker were thrown into prison, they, too, were under Joseph's surveillance.

The Lord God was with him, and this made Joseph keener than ever to discern trouble among the prisoners, either outwardly or in their hearts. He was interested in each man, and God chose this very concern of Joseph's as His way of moving along His own plan through the life of the young shepherd boy who made good in a rich pagan land.

Instead of dreaming his own dreams, Joseph was about to make a new name for himself as an interpreter of dreams. The dreams of some important people.

A Butler, a Baker and a Pharaoh

It is not quite clear what they did, but as things turned out, it is clear that the Pharaoh's chief butler and chief baker offended His majesty to the extent that they were both sent to the same prison with Joseph, on the grounds of Potiphar's estate.

One day, as he met with the captive butler and baker to inquire of their states of mind, Joseph discovered both of them even more morose and disturbed than they had been the afternoon they arrived at the jail. Both men had dreamed the night before and both were greatly agitated to know the meaning of their strange dreams. In those days, great stock was placed in dreams. And knowing this, God made full use of Joseph's close person-to-Person relationship with Him.

"Interpretations belong to God, butler," Joseph reminded the tall, worried gentleman. "Please tell your dream to me."

The chief of the butlers began to talk nervously. "In my dream I saw a vine, and on the vine, three branches. And no sooner did it bud than it blossomed, too, and its clusters ripened into grapes. Pharaoh's cup was in my hand and I took the grapes and pressed them into Pharaoh's cup, then gave the cup into his hand."

Joseph looked thoughtful. "This is its interpretation: The three branches are three days. Within three days Pharaoh will restore you to your position; you will hand him his cup as you have always done as his butler."

The tall, gaunt chief of butlers leaped to his feet and started to express his joy, but Joseph quieted him firmly, "Just one minute, butler. When all is well with you, please keep me personally in mind, and show your gratitude by mentioning me to Pharaoh. Help me get out of this jail! I was kidnaped in the first place from my native Hebrew country and certainly I did nothing to deserve being put in the dungeon here now."

Of course, the chief butler promised warmly that he would surely remember to help Joseph at the first opportunity. Sitting next to the tall chief butler, the round and rotund chief baker began to squirm hopefully. If Joseph's interpretation of the butler's dream was so encouraging, perhaps he should tell him the details of his dream also.

Joseph stood before the fat little man, who rubbed his heavy nose so hard it turned even redder. "Uh—I had a dream, too, you know. In mine I saw three baskets of white bread on my head and in the upper basket all sorts of bakers' delicacies for Pharaoh." The chief of the bakers shifted the middle bulk of his weight uneasily, tried to stand, thought better of it, due to the effort always involved, and went on frowning, so that his eyes were almost buried. "But the birds were eating the delicacies out of the top basket on my head!"

"Is that all, baker?" Joseph looked solemn as he did so often then.

"Why, yes. That's my dream." The frightened baker jerked impatiently on Joseph's rough prison garment, then gave up again on the idea of standing. "What does it mean? What does my dream mean?"

"This is the interpretation." Joseph was even more solemn now. "The three baskets are three days. Within three days Pharaoh will hang you on a tree; then the birds will eat the flesh from your body."

And it came to pass. All of it. The chief of the butlers was restored to full butlership and the chief of the bakers (obviously the guilty one of the two) was no more. He hung round and limp from a tree, just as Joseph had interpreted.

Two long years passed by, with no word from the chief of the butlers, now restored to full freedom and service to Pharaoh. Joseph was still in the dungeon, forgotten.

But one day Pharaoh himself dreamed a strange dream. A dream no one, not all the wise counselors and scholars in all of Egypt, could interpret. He saw himself standing by the Nile River, looking at seven splendid, well-fed cows which had walked out of the river and were grazing on the marsh grass along the bank. Then he saw seven other cows coming up from the river after them. These seven cows were ugly and lean, and as they stood with the other beautiful cows on the bank of the river, the hideous cows ate the seven splendid, well-fed cows! At this point Pharaoh woke up. Then—immediately, he fell asleep a second time and dreamed a second dream. This consisted of seven heads of large and full grain growing on a single stalk. He then saw seven lean heads of grain, wispy and blasted by the east wind, sprouting out after the full heads. And, as with the cows, the seven lean ears swallowed the seven large, full heads of grain!

Then Pharaoh woke up again. Woke up to a troubled spirit and a mind that would not rest and which grew more restless as every scribe and wise man failed to interpret his strange pair of dreams.

It was then that the chief of butlers remembered his promise! Joseph was summoned quickly, and as soon as he had shaved and bathed and dressed himself, he stood before Pharaoh, solemnly assuring the king that God would give the interpretation.

Gripping his rod in his brown, thick hand until the knuckles gleamed, Pharaoh detailed the dreams once more to Joseph. After a long moment of silence, while everyone watched him, Joseph began to speak firmly and confidently. "Pharaoh's dream is a unit. God has made known to Pharaoh what He is about to do. The seven fat cows represent seven years and the seven full ears represent seven years; it is one complete dream."

Pharaoh leaned forward in his great gold-encrusted chair as Joseph continued to tell him that the seven lean and ugly cattle and the seven lean and wispy ears meant seven years also. But in the symbolism was God's plan for the next fourteen years!

Joseph looked at no one as he spoke God's intentions with an authority that caused even Pharaoh to slump back in his chair in amazement. "This is my message to Pharaoh," Joseph's voice was loud and strong. "Take note! There are seven years of great abundance ahead throughout the land of Egypt, but following them there will come seven years of famine, and all the plenty in the land of Egypt will be forgotten; the famine shall exhaust the land."

The courtiers standing around the throne of Pharaoh began to mutter among themselves. But Joseph silenced them: "Now then, let Pharaoh look for an intelligent and prudent man and put him in charge of the land of Egypt."

Pharaoh and his courtiers listened intently as Joseph outlined his plan for collecting and storing one fifth of all the grain and other food in the entire land throughout the next seven years of plenty, in readiness for the seven years of famine which would surely follow.

Only about one minute passed after Joseph had finished before Pharaoh pulled his own signet ring from his finger and placed it on Joseph's finger. "You shall be in charge of my palace and as you give orders my people shall conduct themselves, Joseph. Only in matters of the throne will I be your superior. Observe! I have put you in charge of the whole land of Egypt."

Joseph was thirty years old when once more his life changed abruptly, from prison rags to fine linen, from prison bread and thin soup to the delicacies of the Pharaoh's table. He set out to travel throughout the land, giving orders to be followed to the letter in the new regime of Joseph! In his ears rang the glorious last words of Pharaoh: "I remain the Pharaoh, but without acknowledging you not one person in all Egypt shall stir hand or foot!"

With his new power came an end, also, to the grind of loneliness which had aged Joseph during his long years away from his beloved father in a strange land. Pharaoh married him to Asenath, the lovely and sensitive daughter of the priest of On, and before the famine years began, Joseph was the father of two sturdy sons.

And then the seven years of famine began. Not only in Egypt, but in all adjoining countries. Joseph's sleep was disturbed night after night as he wondered about his father, Jacob, and his brothers in nearby Canaan. But he went about his duties as superintendent of all Egypt and tried not to think of what they might be suffering.

"And all nations came to Egypt to Joseph to buy grain because everywhere the famine was severe."

Chapter 10

Joseph's "Third Degree" Tactics

Into the huge, high-columned chamber ten roughly clothed, unkempt, bearded shepherds shuffled across the awesome expanse of carpeted marble floor toward the great chair on which the potentate Joseph sat.

He raised one heavily ringed hand for quiet, as the ten men bowed all the way to the floor before him. There was a moment of silence, and in it Joseph remembered a dream of his own many years ago. "My sheaf rose up and stood erect while your sheaves surrounded it and bowed deeply to my sheaf!" Joseph rose slowly to his feet, forcing back sudden tears which stung his deep-set eyes.

His ten brothers had not looked at him yet. This was a private moment for Joseph to remember the past he thought was lost. What of his dear father? Was he still alive? Where was Benjamin, his own mother's other son? But a stir in the line of courtiers around Joseph snapped his reverie and he became once more the Egyptian potentate, his quick mind in action.

He spoke gruffly. "Where do you come from?"

Judah answered without raising his head. "From the land of Canaan to buy food, Sir."

Joseph's laugh was hard. "I believe you are spies! You have come to detect where the land lies exposed."

Three or four of Israel's sons protested at once: "Oh, no, Master, your servants have come only to buy grain for food. We are all the sons of one man. We are honest men. Your servants are not spies, Sir."

"I don't believe you. You come to find undefended places in the land. Have you any more brothers? Is your father alone?"

"No, our father kept his youngest living son with him, Master. His name is Benjamin." Simeon became spokesman for the group.

"Then, there are eleven sons altogether, providing your story is true, that is." Joseph's voice mocked them as skillfully as any Egyptian born potentate could have managed. "I don't for one minute believe your tall tale, but supposing it to be true, what a pity your illustrious father could not have had an even dozen sons! Especially if they were as splendid and manly as you ten appear to be, grovelling there at my feet pretending not to be spies."

Simeon's mind raced back to the deep pit where they had abandoned Joseph over twenty years ago, and he heard the pitiful cries of the boy for mercy. Was it over twenty years ago? Was it twenty dollars they received for him from the Midianite slave-dealers?

Joseph's hard, cultured voice crashed into his remembering. "What a pity, I said, that this illustrious father did not manage an even dozen magnificent specimens of manhood like yourselves!"

"Oh, he did, Master," Reuben answered nervously. "There was one other. He is not living now."

Joseph ordered them thrown into jail for three days. At the end of the third day, he brought them before him again. "Do this and survive! I revere God. If you are true, if you are not spies, then let one brother remain bound in prison here, and the rest of you convey grain home for your starving families. *But*, when you return, bring me your youngest brother, Benjamin, so as to verify your words. If you do this, you will survive."

The men began to talk among themselves, never thinking, since Joseph had spoken to them through an Egyptian interpreter, that he could understand every word they said!

"This is our punishment," Judah spoke first to the others. "We caused agony to Joseph's soul, now this agony is upon us."

"Did I not plead with you not to sin against the lad our father loved?" Reuben wrung his hands remembering. "But you paid no attention to me. Now, payment for Joseph's blood has come due for us all!"

"Our father's tears for him can now pour from our eyes," Naphtali, the more poetic of the brothers, wept openly.

"Look! The Egyptian potentate has left us. He has suddenly disappeared behind the heavy draperies around his throne!"

Joseph could face them no longer. The tender shepherd heart in him was still stronger than the potentate heart. Behind the thick, brocaded drapery, Jacob's favorite son, Joseph, tried to muffle his sobs in the folds of the curtain. Then he recovered his composure and reappeared once more, choosing Simeon to be retained in chains until the others should return with his mother's other son, Benjamin.

As the nine brothers hurried from the marble hall, Joseph felt his heart pull away, back toward his father's house.

The Silver Cup

Israel (Jacob) held his ancient, bony hands over his head and shook them frantically. "I am an old man! I cannot take this in at once. You say this Egyptian potentate demands that my Benjie be sent to him, too?"

Judah laid his hand on Israel's shoulder almost tenderly. "Yes, Father. Unless we bring Benjamin, he will not believe us. He accuses us of being spies."

"Why did you treat me so shabbily as to tell him that you had another brother? You bereave me of children! Joseph is gone. Simeon is in chains, and now you would take Benjamin! All this comes down on me so that I cannot bear it."

Judah was firm. "But, Father, we went through all this when we returned from Egypt the last time. This Egyptian potentate is a clever man! He vows he reveres God and now that we have all found our money returned by him in the tops of our sacks of grain we intended to buy, who can say what trick he will use next?"

Jacob moaned and clutched his breast. "But Benjamin is all I have left of his mother, Rachel. Must I pay for food with my own sons?"

"We must have food. That much I know. Our families, your grandchildren and our wives, are starving, Father. We have no choice!"

Reuben's voice had a note of finality as he spoke to his father after listening to Judah. "You may take the lives of my two sons if I fail to bring Benjamin home, Father. Place him in my charge and I will return him to you. Send him with me, Father, and we will get up and go. I will stand guarantee for him; demand him back from me. But let us go. We could have been back a second time and poor Simeon out of prison by now! Grief is one thing, Father, but it can turn selfish in the end."

Jacob's head dropped to his chest. God could ask no greater sacrifice of him now. The torment and conflict were too big for an old man's heart. He needed Rachel. He needed to talk with her. But Rachel had been dead so long. So long he had clung to

Benjamin, trying to cling to her. His thin old shoulders sagged. A man cannot cling to the dead. Not Rachel. Not Joseph. Not in Benjamin could he cling even to the memory of the slim, lovely shoulders and the flower-blue eyes of the girl who bore his two favorite sons. Not even in Benjamin.

"Not even in Benjamin," the old man muttered.

"What did you say, Father?" Judah was impatient to get started.

"Take my son Benjamin, then," Jacob's voice sounded flat and old. "If it must be, take him. But do this: Take along in your sacks choice products of our land for a present to the man who calls us spies. Impoverished as Canaan is, we still have some things Egypt does not produce. Take the man a bit of balsam, a little honey, some aromatic powder, some gum, and almonds. Have double payments with you, including the silver that was returned so strangely in your sacks. Perhaps it was a mistake." He straightened his bent shoulders then. "And take your brother, Benjamin, along, too, and get up and go back to this man. And may God Almighty grant you such favor with the man that he may let both Simeon and Benjamin come back. As for me—if I am bereaved of children, I am altogether bereaved."

Joseph sat looking down once more from his great chair into the coarse, bearded faces of his brothers. This time his heart ached to rush down from his majestic heights and embrace Benjamin. *Benjie, my own full brother. Son of my mother, Rachel. Son of my beloved father who thinks me dead! You've grown taller, Benjie. And broad-shouldered. You look frightened, too, or is it rebellious? Oh, Benjamin, my brother. My beloved brother.* These were his thoughts, but when he spoke his voice was the cool, calculated voice of the successful man who was second in command of all Egypt. He did not address his brothers at all, but gave orders to his steward. Simeon would be released and all these men would dine with him in his own luxurious house. When Joseph's steward explained to the puzzled brothers that their money had been intentionally placed in their sacks on their last visit, they were even more confused and apprehensive. What kind of man was this powerful young ruler of Egypt? Was he as hard as he appeared? As suspicious of them? What made them all squirm inwardly under his cool, penetrating glance?

And why, when they assembled at his home for dinner, did he suddenly rush from the room when he was introduced to Benjamin? "He seemed about to weep!" Naphtali whispered to the others.

"Not that one," Judah scoffed. "He never heard of tears!"

Joseph returned, hoping no one would notice his still moist eyes. He had washed his face to hide his weeping. And it helped his composure, too, to assume his dictatorial voice. So dictatorial that his steward jumped when Joseph shouted, "Serve dinner!"

In his heart, Joseph longed to know that his brothers had changed. Another little test entered his busy head. He would order Benjamin's portions to be five times larger than the others! Everyone ate and drank heavily. The brothers grew hilarious from their drinking, but no one showed the slightest sign of jealousy toward Benjamin's special attention. Joseph was hopeful.

The next day, he ordered his house steward to fill the men's sacks with as much food as they could carry and to put their payment back in the mouth of each sack as before. And then Joseph surprised his steward: "Place my favorite silver cup in the sack of the youngest, along with his grain payment."

As soon as the brothers had gotten a short distance from the city, on their way home to Canaan, Joseph sent a messenger riding hard after them. He even told the courier what to say: "Why have you repaid evil for good? Why have you stolen my master's silver cup?"

In the midst of hot denials, the messenger stopped searching the sacks long enough to hear one of them declare that if the silver cup was found in any man's sack, that man would gladly become Joseph's slave. It was Benjamin's turn to open his sack. Gleaming from its mouth was Joseph's silver cup!

"This is another trick!" Judah cried. "You have tricked my youngest brother in the name of that hardhearted Egyptian potentate."

Back before Joseph, the brothers fell to their faces in front of him once more. Judah offered himself and all the others as Joseph's slaves. "We know no way to clear ourselves. We are all your slaves, Master."

"Not so," Joseph replied. "I will do no such thing! The person with whom the cup was found—Benjamin—shall be my slave. The rest of you may return peacefully to your father."

91

Judah rose to his feet and moved a step toward Joseph, with his hands outstretched toward him for mercy. "With your permission, my master, your servant would tell you something intimate, and please, let not your anger blaze. This youngest of our brothers, Benjamin, is my father's only delight. He and Joseph, the dead son, are the only sons of my father's beloved wife, Rachel, for whom he still mourns after many years."

Joseph watched Judah carefully. He seemed to back up his words with his heart. Judah speaking from a tender heart? Joseph's hopes rose.

"When I return to my father and the lad, Benjamin, is not with us, he will die!" Judah wrung his hands as he spoke. "I beg of you, keep me, Sir, in the lad's place, a slave to my master, and let the lad go home with his brothers. I could not return to my father without Benjamin, Sir. I could not bear the grief he would suffer!"

Joseph's control was gone. "Have everyone withdraw from this place except these men from Canaan," he ordered, as the tears streamed down his smoothshaven cheeks. When they were alone, he rushed first to one and then another of his brothers. "I am Joseph! I am Joseph, my brothers! Tell me, my father is still alive, isn't he? Is he well? Does he still grieve for me? Listen to me. I am Joseph!"

For a long moment there was no sound but the sobs tearing at last from Joseph's throat. "Please come close to me, my brothers." Simeon first, and then Naphtali, Levi and Judah, and then the others edged closer, unable to speak. "I am Joseph, your brother, whom you sold into Egypt. God has worked everything out so that it is not to be regretted that you did as you did. He has used my position here in order that I may help all of you and your families and my father. There will be five more years of famine and I can feed you and keep you. Hurry now to our father and tell him. Tell him Joseph urges him to come quickly, and to bring all of you and your families. You will live in plenty in the land of Goshen, where grazing is best. Hurry and bring my father down here to me, so that I may see him again!"

Joseph threw his arms around his own brother, Benjamin, and kissed him and wept.

"Go now and bring our father, that I may be with him once more."

"They went up from Egypt and came to the land of Canaan, to their father, Jacob whom they told, 'Joseph is still alive and he is ruler over the whole land of Egypt.' Jacob's heart remained unmoved, for he could not believe them; so they repeated to him everything Joseph had told them, and when he saw the wagons Joseph had sent to transport him, their father Jacob's spirit revived and he said, 'Enough! My son Joseph is still alive. I will go and see him before I die.'"

Israel Dies and Israel Is Born

At the time He wrestled with Jacob, God had renamed him Israel. Israel, the ancient patriarch, lay dying in the pagan land of Egypt, but the old man was no longer morose. His beloved son, Joseph, stood beside him as he spoke of the future lives of his twelve sons gathered around him. On his happy journey to Egypt to join Joseph, God had once more spoken to Israel (Jacob) in a night vision. "Be not afraid to go down to Egypt, for there I will make you a great nation. I will go down with you to Egypt and I will without fail bring you up again. And Joseph will close your eyes."

Now, Israel lay dying, with his sons around him. And when he finished blessing each son from the oldest to the youngest, the old man drew his feet together upon the bed, breathed his last and was gathered to his people.

Joseph closed his father's eyes in death, weeping and kissing the dear, coarse, ancient shepherd's face he loved.

Israel, the old man, died and was taken back to Canaan to be buried. And when he died, Israel, the nation, composed of twelve tribes, named after Jacob's sons, was born.

Chapter 11

The Years of Moses

Miriam, his sister—ten or twelve years older than he—remembered the first forty years of her brother Moses' life. And her love for him kept the memory breathing through her like the Levite blood that pumped through her slim, vital body.

The First Forty Years of Moses

Miriam and Moses, along with their brother Aaron, were the children of Amram, a descendant of Jacob's son, Levi, Joseph's brother. Centuries rolled aimlessly by in the land of Goshen in Egypt, where Joseph had given land and herds to his father and brothers. Eventually the Israelites were hated, because Egyptians despised herdsmen. New Pharaohs lived, ruled and died. Joseph was forgotten. Almost no one knew just how it was that these strange, Hebrew herdsmen had come to be so numerous in Egypt. Too numerous to suit the Pharaoh who ruled the rich, pagan country in which Miriam's family lived with the others, confined to the area called Goshen, literally slaves to the Egyptians. Thoroughly despised slaves.

Slaves were good things to have, but this vicious Pharaoh who ruled in the near-by city of Raamses, feared the Israelites. All twelve tribes of them. Each named for one of Jacob's sons. Too clannish they were and far, far too numerous. What if Egypt were attacked? What would stop these fertile, headstrong Hebrew slaves from aiding the enemy?

Miriam remembered the gossip and the tears and the anxiety in the land of Goshen among her people the day Pharaoh issued the order that the midwives of the Hebrews should kill every male child. She remembered the shudder that tore through the minds and hearts and bodies of every man, woman and child among her people. A shudder that broke spirits and hearts. A shudder not unlike the gigantic storm of sorrow within the heart of old Abraham the evening he endured the Lord's prophesy concerning his descendants so many centuries before (pages 50, 51).

Children long to lean on their mothers. Wives on their husbands. Husbands on a leader who will breed hope. But there was no leader. And little or no hope. Even in the Lord God of their fathers. It had been so long. And they had suffered too much.

Miriam also remembered the second desperate decree of the Pharaoh who wanted to cut down the numbers of the chosen nation of God. It came just before their new baby came.

"Throw every newborn Hebrew son into the river and keep alive every newborn daughter."

The new baby at Miriam's house was a boy! A beautifully formed, healthy boy. Miriam was just a little girl, but all her long life she remembered her mother's quick work-hardened fingers weaving the reed basket, as she and her brother, Aaron, watched. She remembered the black under the broken nails, as Jochebed deftly punched thick pitch into each crevice. They were going to hide their baby boy in the River Nile, near where the Pharaoh's daughter bathed. Miriam remembered the long hours of waiting in the bulrushes nearby, keeping a grown-up eye on the baby bobbing in the ugly pitch-daubed basket at the river's edge. She would never forget how her legs cramped and how her throat tickled. She couldn't even cough for fear of being noticed.

In her less humble moments, Miriam thrilled for all her life at the courage she found to use the moment she came crashing on her half-numb straight child legs out of hiding and right up to the bejeweled Egyptian princess.

"If you like this baby, I'll be glad to get a nurse for you from among his own Hebrew people!"

The nurse she got was Jochebed, the baby's own mother. All through the long, God-guided life of Moses (the name the Egyptian princess gave her adopted son), Miriam felt that she had a special importance. After all, the boy was taught by their Hebrew mother about the one God. Early, Moses learned that God had promised to bring his people back to Canaan, where Abraham and Isaac, Jacob and his sons had lived. Moses was educated and trained in the philosophy and culture of pagan Egypt, too. By adoption he was an Egyptian nobleman. But God saw to it that the boy knew also of Him.

Moses grew up to be a thoughtful, serious young man. And he was lonely as only a man is lonely who belongs truly to no country. As the princess' adopted son, according to Egyptian law, which held that the throne was filled through the Pharaoh's daughters, Moses would likely have become a Pharaoh. His humanity reveled in the luxury of his life at court. But the conflict in his heart drove him one day to walk among his own Hebrew people to see for himself how they were being mistreated. He found old men and women and children too young to work bending their backs under the Egyptian cruelty of mind and whip from dawn to dark. He tried not to listen, but the cries of his people tore through Moses' heart and mind.

Dressed in the fine linen of his noble position in the Pharaoh's own palace, Moses walked alone one furnace-hot afternoon, along the hard roadway in Raamses beside which his people sweated and labored and groaned. Some of them looked at him and spat. Others looked and tried to smile. Especially the older ones. Tears streamed down Moses' face. Suddenly he was ashamed of his uncalloused hands and his linen clothes. Where was God in all this? If these were His chosen people, why did He allow them to be treated this way?

Moses couldn't look any more. He walked rapidly away down a lonely side road to think. The teaching of his mother about Abraham and Isaac and Jacob and Joseph—his own ancestors— stormed his mind. God had taken over for them in all cases, just in time. But where was God now? What was God really like?

The hot, empty afternoon split suddenly with a sharp cry of pain! Moses ran a few steps toward a bend in the road and what he saw stopped him motionless until a sudden vicious anger pushed up from his heart and catapulted the gentle, thoughtful young man headlong into his first violence!

Checking quickly to be sure no one saw him, Moses sprang at the throat of the Egyptian overseer who had brought the Hebrew slave to this lonely spot for a beating.

The bleeding Israelite man lay writhing in the dust as Moses, with his bare hands, killed his persecutor!

Miriam remembered the night Moses ran away, too. As soon as Moses found out that his murderous act had been seen, he ran away.

For the next forty years of Moses' life, Miriam remembered mostly her prayers for her beloved brother. Prayers for his safety, prayers for her people, prayers that God would send someone to lead them out of the horror of their slave lives.

Moses was gone, but Miriam never let go of him in her memory or in her conversations with the Lord God.

The Second Forty Years of Moses

Alone on the grassy hillside slopes of Mount Sinai above his father-in-law's flock of grazing sheep, Moses sat remembering the things that had happened during the long years since he ran away from Egypt. He remembered also the years in Egypt and no doubt he wondered, sitting alone on the hillside dressed in the rough nomadic shepherd's clothes woven for him by his beloved wife, Zipporah, what had been the purpose of his high cultural training in Pharaoh's court. What good did it do Moses now that he knew how to write Egyptian hieroglyphics, that he understood both Hebrew and Egyptian philosophy? Why was he seemingly destined to be a man without a real people?

The loneliness which had lurked always in the heart of the young boy growing up as potential heir to the throne of Egypt was still there, even among the warm-hearted, rugged desert nomads in the land of Midian (now Arabia) where he had fled. Old Jethro, the priest who gave Moses his daughter, Zipporah, for a wife, loved him as his own son. Jethro was the only father Moses ever knew, and much of Moses' quiet, deep wisdom he learned from his father-in-law, the desert priest who loved the Lord God. Moses was a part of a family, and his own sons by Zipporah were dear to him. But he had named his first son Gershom, which meant "I have become an exile in a foreign land." With the joys of a happy marriage and fatherhood, Moses was still an exile in his heart. And although he knew of the God of his fathers, He was not real to him as he sat alone that day, deep in the wilderness on the lower slopes of Mount Sinai.

Aloud, to ease the aloneness, Moses expressed his thoughts into the vacant air.

"If only I could ask someone about my people back in Egypt! Are they still cruelly treated? Are they still stumbling through the years of their lives scarred in their hearts and bodies by the Egyptian whip? What of my mother and father? My sister, Miriam? My brother, Aaron? Where is God? How has He forgotten those who are supposed to be His chosen people?"

Moses had been prepared, providentially, for a belief in one God, since the Pharaoh ruling Egypt during his young life had thrown over the established worship of many gods and adopted the sole worship of the sun god. Monotheism was not new to Moses at all. His mother taught him of the one God of Israel. His

Egyptian religious training centered on the one solar god. But Moses felt futile, sitting there alone on the hillside. Neither teaching had seemed to fulfill his life. To enlighten his inner darkness. To ease the tension of not belonging, which most likely brought about his life-long tendency to stammer when he spoke to other people. Sitting there alone that afternoon, though, he didn't stammer at all. He seldom did when he talked to himself on these lonely vigils.

Moses, now a man almost eighty years old, but still strong and quick of body and mind, sat remembering his people and Egypt and now and then he spoke his thoughts aloud.

"I am now an expert in these mountains. I know most of the trails and springs. Those I do not know, I know how to locate. I am a successful shepherd of my father-in-law's flocks. I am also, in my mind, a cultured Egyptian. And in my blood I am a Hebrew slave!" Sometimes he laughed aloud, too, out alone like this. He laughed now. But laughter was not a big part of Moses' personality. And this time, for certain, it was not a joyful laugh. It pushed from him, broken by old perplexities and choked off by new unanswered questions. It echoed flatly in the empty air.

"My father-in-law, Jethro, believes in the Lord God of my people. His faith has given him stability and wisdom. And he has been kind to me." Moses stood up and stretched himself, holding his arms open above his head a moment longer than a man does when he stretches. And in that moment, as he stood with his arms open to the wide wilderness, his heart opened, too. To what, he did not know. But it was in that moment that he saw the bright flame spring up in the center of a thorn bush a few yards away! The bush continued to burn, but not one branch burned away! Moses spoke aloud again, excitedly. "I'll go over there and examine this bush. It isn't burning up as it should with a fire like that blazing in it!" Moses started to run toward the burning bush, but a Voice jerked him to such a short stop he almost fell!

"Moses! Moses!"

"Here I am," Moses looked around him in dismay. Who spoke to him? He hadn't heard a human voice in days. Who was there?

"I am your father's God," the Voice answered. "Do not move nearer! Take your sandals off your feet, for the place on which you are standing is holy ground. I am your father's God, the God of Abraham, of Isaac, and of Jacob."

Moses' fingers trembled as he fumbled with the straps of his sandals. Then he covered his face, fearing to look at God Himself!

But God went on speaking. "I have seen the misery of my people in Egypt and I have heard their cry under the slave drivers; I know their sorrows. Now I have come down to deliver them from the Egyptians and to bring them up from there to a broad and good land, to a land flowing with milk and honey, to the country of the Canaanites. Moses, you come now, and I will send you to Pharaoh, so that you may bring My people, the Israelites, out of Egypt."

Moses couldn't have known, but the Voice was the same Voice which spoke reassuringly to the Egyptian slave, Hagar, centuries before, in another desert wilderness not unlike this one, and to Abraham and to Jacob.

Moses did not uncover his face, and his next words were unknowingly deep in the wisdom of humility. They revealed plainly what was really in Moses: "But who am I to go to Pharaoh and bring the Israelites out of Egypt?"

The Voice was quietly insistent: "*I* will accompany you. And this will be your evidence that I have sent you: When you have brought the people out of Egypt, you will serve God on this mountain."

Moses' next question laid bare his true ignorance of the God who spoke: "But when I go to the Israelites and say to them, 'The God of your fathers has sent me to you,' and they say to me 'What is His name?' then what shall I say to them?"

The Lord replied: "Thus you will speak to the Israelites, say that Jehovah, I Am, has sent me to you. Go and convene the elders of Israel and tell them that I have faithfully been with them and have observed their treatment in Egypt and that I promise to bring them up from their afflictions into Canaan, the land flowing with milk and honey. They will listen to your message, Moses, and you with the elders of Israel will call on the king of Egypt and tell him, 'The Lord, the God of the Hebrews, has met with us. Now, please let us go a three-days journey into the desert to sacrifice to the Lord our God.' "

Moses, his face still hidden, started to object. The Lord God anticipated his objection and went on speaking: "I am aware that the king of Egypt will not let you go except by a mighty hand, so I will stretch out My hand, after which he will send you away. And I will give My people such favor with the Egyptians that when you leave, you will not go empty-handed. There will be silver and gold and garments with which to dress your children."

Moses' hands clutched his staff until his brown knuckles whitened. He leaned heavily on the staff and yet he trembled. "But they will neither believe me nor listen to my appeal. They will say, 'The Lord has not appeared unto you.' "

From the turmoil of his half-pagan confusion, Moses dared to converse with this mighty Presence.

"What is that in your hand, Moses?" the Voice persisted.

"A staff." Moses still did not look up.

"Throw it on the ground!"

Moses obeyed and the instant he threw his staff on the ground, it became a snake and he ran from it, terrified. But the Lord said to Moses: "Put out your hand now, and catch it by the tail." The serpent turned at once into Moses' familiar staff!

For further proof to show the doubting Israelites, the Lord instructed Moses to place his hand to his bosom. When he removed it, the white, snowy disease of leprosy covered his entire hand! "Return your hand to your bosom now," the Lord said. And when Moses looked again, his hand was as brown and healthy as before. "Now then," the Lord went on, "should they still doubt after both of these signs, then take some of the river water and pour it on the ground. It will turn to blood."

Moses' doubts about God were gone! But his humanity took over this time. "Please, Lord, I am no orator now and I never was. I am slow of speech and of an awkward tongue."

"Moses, who has made man's mouth? Is it not I, the Lord? You, therefore, go and I will be with your mouth; I will teach you what to say."

Moses still pleaded, "O Lord, please send anyone else but me!"

Firmly the Lord reasoned with the tall, bearded man, trembling on his shepherd's staff. "I know Aaron to be a fluent speaker. He is your brother, and when you return to Egypt he will be coming out to meet you. He will be heartily glad to see you. Speak to him and convey the message, and I will sustain you both in your speaking. He shall be your spokesman to the people; for him, *you shall take the part of God*. Now, take hold of your staff, Moses, with which you shall work the signs."

The Lord's Voice was silent. The bush green and untouched as though no fire had burned anywhere around. Moses looked up at last and this time he stammered incredulously at the vacant sky, "I am to take the part of God? For my brother, Aaron, I am to take the part of God? I, who have never, until this instant, known faith in the living God? What manner of God is this to choose me to lead His people out of bondage?"

The Third Forty Years of Moses

Miriam remembered the day Moses came home, a strong, straight old man of eighty years. Somewhere in the deep eyes that looked out piercingly under the gray, shaggy eyebrows, she still found the gentle young brother she had loved almost fiercely.

And once more, great memories began to burn themselves into her mind, as she stood with the women in the crowd surrounding Moses and Aaron and the elders of Israel. When Moses had enacted his wonders which the Lord had given him, Aaron spoke brilliantly, saying all that Moses told him to say. And with the people of Israel, Miriam knew that the Lord had come to their very homes and she joined the others worshiping Him.

Through the troubled tragic days that followed, Moses, gaunt and tall, became a familiar figure both to the Israelites in Goshen and to Pharaoh and his court in the beautiful city of Raamses. Time after time, as Pharaoh refused to let his people go, Moses stretched forth his staff and plague after plague harrassed the entire land of the Egyptians. Disease struck down the people of Egypt. Hail storms so vicious that the crops were beaten into the ground and destroyed. And still Pharaoh's heart was hardened and he refused to let the Hebrews go. Over and over, Moses and Aaron appeared before the distracted king and one plague worse than those that had gone before came inevitably, hard upon his blunt refusals. Disease, and hail, and frogs and locusts, and the waters of the land even turned to blood! For three days, after still another stubborn refusal by Pharaoh, such a dense darkness fell upon the land that no one in Egypt could get up or move around.

Through it all, light and peace and protection from the plagues prevailed in the land of Goshen, where God's chosen people lived. In the face of even this proof of God's intentions, the stone around the Pharaoh's heart was not chipped until the worst plague of all struck his land. The first-born son of every Egyptian family would die!

On the tenth day of the month, at the beginning of spring, God instructed each Hebrew family to smear the blood of a freshly killed lamb on the doors of their homes. After that, they were to eat the roasted lamb with unleavened bread and herbs as a ceremonial feast. Once more God protected His chosen people. That night He passed over their homes, and not one Hebrew child died. But Egyptian history records that the ruling Pharaoh's first-born son did not live to inherit the throne.

Miriam remembered for all the days of her life the exact words Pharaoh had at last spoken in anguish to her brother. Moses repeated them to her that night as the Israelites were hurriedly packing to leave. "Get up and get out from among my people; both you and the Israelites," Pharaoh pleaded. "There is not a home in Egypt in which there is not loud wailing because someone is dead! Go and serve the Lord as you argued; take along your flocks and your herds and be gone. And—and ask a blessing for me, too." Miriam remembered every word, and her heart knew that even in the face of their oppression, Moses pitied the Pharaoh, as she did.

Moses had forewarned his people. They had baked unleavened bread and collected their belongings and perhaps if more of the Israelites had remembered, as Miriam remembered, the strange unexpected generosity of the Egyptians when they left, they would have exhibited greater faith in the God who had told Moses just what the Egyptians would do. Laden with gold and silver and garments and provisions, the Israelites' carts rolled and plunged through the gates of the city of Raamses and out and away; the old and the young transported by any available means, so their progress would not be slowed. Freedom pulled them like a giant magnet and the people were frenzied in their effort to put mile after mile between themselves and the hated Egyptians.

Miriam stood on the damp sand, leading the triumphant song. She was weary and excited at once. Something of the heroine in her which prompted her to approach Pharaoh's daughter in behalf of her baby brother, Moses, so long ago, sprang up again. She thoroughly enjoyed her role as lead singer and dancer with tambourine, as the people of Israel stood or danced or rested along the eastern shore of the Red Sea at the Straits of Suez. They sat or stood or danced according to their physical stamina or lack of it, but all of them felt the same way about what had happened. At least for the moment, while the miracle was still fresh, they all felt the same way: The God of Abraham and Isaac and Jacob had once more come to the rescue of His people. After all, even though Pharaoh changed his mind and sent Egyptian chariots in hot pursuit of the fleeing Israelites, Moses' lifted staff had brought such a wind to lash on the waters of the Red Sea that a wide path opened to permit each Hebrew man, woman, child and goat to cross the floor of the sea to safety! When the last Egyptian chariot disappeared under the giant rush of immediately returning waters, the Israelites stood speechless, almost unbelieving, for many moments. Only a goat commented now and then, or a confused child cried quietly. But when belief rushed over them as the waters over the Egyptians, Miriam grabbed up her tambourine from her family's cart and led the singing and the dancing and the rejoicing that lasted for hours among the homeless people spread thousands strong along the shore of the Red Sea.

There was a wide military highway which led directly northeastward from Egypt into the promised land of Canaan, but God ordered Moses to take the route across the Red Sea and into the rugged wilderness of Shur. Why had God chosen this route? Didn't He realize that the people would grumble and rebel at the lack of water and the extreme hardships which come up suddenly on a wilderness march? After all, the Israelites were accustomed to a humdrum existence in Egypt. They were down-trodden slaves, yes, but at least their problems remained the same, day in and day out. There was no particular need to adjust quickly and there were houses to live in and facilities for preparing food. In Moses' mind there was no real doubt of God's Presence. After all, the Lord God made His Presence known to all of them, every minute—night and day. In a cloud which hung protectingly over them by day, to lead them, and in a pillar of fire by night, which not only reassured them that God was with them, but kept their encampments safely illuminated against robbers and wild animals. No, Moses did not doubt God's Presence or intentions, but he was frequently confused by God's methods.

But one strange and magnificent day under extraordinary conditions, God's thinking began to clear up for Moses. The bearded old leader of the Israelites sat trembling under the physical strain of holding his now familiar staff high above his head for hour after hour. His trusted assistant, Joshua, was leading the straggling Israelites in their first military encounter. The land over which they traveled was by this time hilly and rough, and bands of native tribesmen began to attack them. The day the Amalekites rushed their camp, Moses stood on the top of a hill, holding his staff, in which the people believed, high above his head as long as he could stand. When he dropped it to rest his aging arms, the attacking Amalekites drove back his people! Their spirits fell when Moses' arms fell. But his brother Aaron and a friend named Hur began to hold Moses arms for him. They held them there above his head until the sun set. And during those long, trying hours, Moses began to understand why God had been feeding them on the strange, gummy, white manna each day. He understood why the manna spoiled if anyone tried to hoard a supply. There was no other way to teach the grumbling people to trust Him. Moses began to see something of God's methods. Of God's reasons for commanding that they have faith in Him. To take his mind off his aching shoulders as the men held his arms high in the air, Moses may have begun to see, at least dimly, that God was leading His people according to what He knew of their own vacillating, faithless, complaining natures. They needed to see Him rescue them along their hard wilderness journey. But to perform miracles for them was not an end in itself. He must *teach* them, so they would be able to live balanced lives in the future. He remembered, sitting in his cramped position, holding his staff over his fighting men, the times he had found water for them by striking a rock with this same staff. Gradually, Moses began to understand why God had allowed their thirst.

Moses' own faith was strengthened as his people received strength to fight off the Amalekites that day in the rocky gorges of the foothills of the Horeb mountains, some fifteen miles from the Red Sea. And his faith grew steadily as he kept leading the people across the rough Sinai desert toward Midian (Arabia) until the giant granite mountains rose around them, some as high as nine thousand feet. Into one of these narrow rocky passes, Moses led them, heading for the place where he had spoken with God in the burning bush. Back to the mountain (Sinai) where God had said He would meet them.

"Soon, Zipporah, we will be back where we met each other." Moses spoke to his beloved wife, the daughter the old priest Jethro had given him during the years in which he took refuge with Jethro's family in these same desert mountains.

Somewhere in a valley near Mount Sinai, where God was to meet Moses, the Israelites pitched camp. Many of the people had never seen such mountains. Egypt was a flat river country. And their hearts were stirred to a sense of expectancy and worship as they stood gaping up at the towering, barren crags around them. Here God gave Moses in detail the elemental laws needed to insure justice between man and man. Here He gave him the laws of sanitation and government for the people. Aaron was made their chief priest among those who would serve the designated ark of wood and the ten curtains of fine linen which Moses had been instructed to build. Wherever they went, this ark and tabernacle moved before them in their procession, as a symbol of the covenant God had made with their fathers: to make them a great nation and to return them to their promised land of Canaan. In fact, inside the veiled tabernacle was the holy place where they could be sure God dwelt.

Step by step, God was preparing His people to be the nation He longed for them to be. Step by step, He was caring for the people through whom the Redeemer of the world would come.

A great step in His preparation took place at Sinai about three months after they left Egypt, the day Moses went alone up into the great mountain to talk with God. God renewed His covenant with His people and told Moses to prepare them for His appearance in a cloud so they, too, could hear His voice. On the morning of the third day a violent storm broke over the great mountain and the people trembled with fear and expectation. Through the steep granite gorges, the wind roared and lightning seemed almost to snap the jagged peaks as the mountain itself trembled and swayed beneath the volcanic smoke pouring from its summit.

The people cowered and waited, as Moses stepped from their midst and called aloud to the Lord, who called back in a voice greater than the storm, "Moses, come up to Me on the mountain!"

There, in the presence of the living God, Moses received the laws known as the Ten Commandments. As God instructed him, he cut two slabs of stone and watched in awe and worship as the Lord God Himself wrote upon the stones!

Moses' step was firmer than ever as he slowly descended the mountain, his face shining. Not one doubt slashed his heart but that the people would be waiting expectantly and filled with awe, when he came down to them. He stopped to make a sacrifice to

God on his way back and although this took an even longer time, he strode down the side of the now quiet mountain, carrying the stone tablets, confident of God and his people.

Moses was learning about God, but human nature still fooled him! When he reached the camp, the pagan orgy he saw in progress among the Israelites brought his own human nature crashing to the ground along with the sacred tablets which he shattered in anger and disappointment at the obscene behavior of the chosen people of God.

Moses was gone too long, Aaron alibied. The people had put pressure on him, as their chief priest, to let them melt their ornaments and make a golden calf to worship!

Joshua, his young military leader, took no part in the orgy of dancing and pagan worship around the golden calf. Moses could talk to Joshua and trust him to understand.

"I had no right to break the stone tablets on which God Himself wrote our commandments, Joshua. My anger consumed me. But it is gone now. I must do something for the people."

"What will you do, Sir?" Joshua asked. "Only you know what was written on the tablets."

"I will pray for forgiveness from God, Joshua. I will plead with Him to forgive this ghastly thing they have done. And then I will just have to trust Him to do something about the Commandments."

Moses poured out his heart to God in behalf of His rebellious, blaspheming people. Although they suffered the inevitable consequences of disobedience, God heard him. In another trip to the great mountain, the Lord God wrote again, on a second set of tablets, the ten moral laws which would be the criterion for human behavior forever.

Under his arm, Moses carried the second set of tablets, and on his aging heart was graven the assurance that God would not clear the guilty, but that He is merciful and gracious, long-suffering and abounding in goodness and truth toward the repentant heart.

In Sight of the Promised Land

Joshua, tall, sturdy and solemn, stood beside the frail, but still erect, old man whom he had followed so faithfully. Moses was going to die. God had spoken with him about it. And as usual Moses was carrying out the instructions given him by the Lord he loved and obeyed.

Moses' voice was thin as he spoke to Joshua, but in spite of his 120 years, his vigor remained and his eyes were undimmed. "The Lord God told me, Joshua, that I am not to enter the Promised Land with you and the others."

"But this is not fair, Sir, you have led us so well and have taught us so thoroughly all that God has told you!" Joshua was not complaining at God, he was just reacting to his deep love and respect for Moses.

"I have no questions about God's will, son. My life has been a peaceful life from within because I have not questioned Him. This is not the time to start! Remember that well, Joshua. And remember, too, as I once more follow His command by laying my hands upon you to consecrate you as the leader of the people, that He has safely led us through every battle with every tribe and king during these last forty years since He gave us the Commandments. He will do the same for you. You are not to fear the enemies in wait for you in the promised land of Canaan, Joshua. You are to remember that the Lord God will fight for you, just as He always has."

Joshua was overcome with the deep emotions storming his own heart at that moment. Excitement and challenge for the future, new faith in God, and genuine grief at the coming death of his beloved old leader. He couldn't speak.

"When God told me I was going to die, Joshua, I prayed for a leader for the people. You are the one He chose."

With Joshua consecrated before all the congregation as the leader who would take the Israelites into the promised land of Canaan, God led Moses from the plains of Moab, where they were encamped, up into the mountain of Nebo (also called Pisgah). The city of Jericho in Canaan lay a few miles away across the Jordan River. Jericho was filled with clear fountains, fed by the hidden streams gushing from the mountains behind it. And beyond Jericho Moses could see the hills climb toward Jerusalem.

The old man stood looking away toward the bounteous land, as full of riches and fertility as Joshua and Caleb had reported to him when he had sent them spying. But also filled with fierce enemy tribes to be conquered. Moses' last breaths were prayers for Joshua and the people. Prayers for the people he loved and prayers of thanksgiving to the God he loved for having given him the strength to lead them up to the very borders of Canaan, the promised land.

Chapter 12

Rahab the Harlot and the Promised Land

The Israelites were no longer a disorganized, somewhat straggling band of escaped slaves. Through Moses, God had given them specific laws for the right regulation of human life in all its complex relationships. The judges Moses appointed to settle the knotty problems which come when people live together, were functioning wisely in their special areas. As Moses had done, Joshua, their new leader, handled the particularly difficult problems himself. And with great skill, Joshua had led the people victoriously through battle after battle, down from the mountainous region of Moab, where Moses died.

Now Joshua paced back and forth in front of his headquarters tent in their encampment in the Jordan valley, just north of where the river empties into the Dead Sea.

They were, at last, ready to enter the promised land of Canaan. In fact, their camp lay on the east bank of the Jordan, directly opposite the walled city of Jericho, and that heavily guarded city was the key.

Outside his headquarters tent, Joshua paced back and forth, waiting the return of his two spies sent to bring back more needed information about Jericho before he planned his attack. God had led them to the borders of the promised land, but they were going to have to fight for possession of it. Joshua's long strides up and down outside his tent matched the great memories which strode through his mind as he waited. Once he had been sent, along with eleven others, by his beloved leader, Moses, to spy in Canaan. Only Joshua and Caleb urged that they attempt to overpower the giants they found living in the fertile, luxurious land behind their great walled cities. The others were overcome with fear and weakness. And so, Joshua this time quite naturally chose old Caleb to go again. Caleb was tough-minded and he saw clearly. He knew what to look for. He would discover the actual temper of the citizens of Jericho. With Caleb, Joshua sent Salmon, a quick-witted young prince of Israel. And now he was waiting impatiently for them to return.

Joshua strode back and forth, and as he walked, he looked at the peaks of the steep mountains jutting up on either side of the Jordan valley, making the valley seem a great trench, at some places five and at others thirteen miles wide. And as he looked at the mountains, his memory continued to stride back through the years in which he had served as Moses' right hand man. No one had known the intimacy of Moses' friendship like Joshua. He had even been allowed to go with the great leader into the tent of meeting outside the camp where Moses communed with God. The people of Israel watched as the pillar of cloud came down upon the tent time after time. Many of those still alive knew that Joshua had access to these sacred times with Moses, and so he had the respect of everyone. No one still living actually remembered these times, because only Joshua and Caleb remained alive now, of all the thousands who had stumbled and hurried that day out of Egypt behind the sure steps of Moses. But their children and their grandchildren were there, respecting Joshua and eager to march at last into the land where Abraham had lived and covenanted with the same God who still hovered lovingly over His chosen ones.

Joshua knew the history of his people well, and some of his impatience was checked as his soul and mind and body thrilled to be a part of the actual fulfillment of God's promise to Abraham so long ago. He slowed his pace and by the time Caleb and Salmon stood before him to report their findings after their espionage mission to Jericho, Joshua was eager for the news, but quiet in his heart.

"Our reputation is the big news, sir!" Young Salmon cocked his head arrogantly. "The city is fully guarded—surrounded with a city wall wide enough to build houses on it. In fact, we had quite an adventure in one of them! And the men are giants, no doubt about that. But all the talk is about us, Sir! The word has gotten around all over Jericho that we are here and that God is with us. The big giants are trembling in their small souls because of the news of our strength which has gone before us."

Joshua smiled at Salmon's enthusiasm, then turned to Caleb for verification.

"Salmon's right, Master. But we must guard against over-confidence in ourselves. It is God who is our strength."

Caleb was a man of few words, but they stuck when he spoke. "In fact, we did have a narrow escape in one house built on the city wall. A harlot's house. And we committed ourselves to protect her and her family when we capture the city."

Joshua raised his eyebrows. "A harlot's house, Caleb?"

"Yes, Sir. A harlot's house. And we must keep our promise to her. She saved our lives."

Salmon couldn't bear to have the adventure treated so briefly and factually! "Oh, Master, it was a most unusual thing. You see, this woman—Rahab is her name—had heard so much about us that she knew almost to a man of our strength, and even more important than that, she knew of our astounding victories because God is with us."

"This woman knew all this?" Joshua was deeply interested.

"Yes, Sir. She knew that our God is greater than all the local gods called Baals. So, when we walked into her establishment we saw in a flash how we could make use of her information and she saw in a flash how she could make use of us, believing as she does that we will surely capture Jericho!"

Joshua turned to Caleb again for verification. "Is this the way it was, Caleb?"

"Exactly, Sir. When the soldiers of the King of Jericho entered suddenly, she slipped us upstairs and hid us successfully from their prying eyes. She is indeed a clever woman."

"And beautiful!" Salmon trembled with the wasted drama in Caleb's matter-of-fact report. "She sent us up to the roof of her house and told us to hide in the rushes she had drying there. We did—and mind you, she sent the soldiers right up and suggested that they pry among the rushes if they were so terrified of the Israelites! Oh, she is not only beautiful, this Rahab, she is clever, too. Of course, they would not humiliate themselves to do such an obvious thing and so they missed us entirely! Then—then, when we heard the soldiers march away, we crawled out from the bundles of rushes and had a marvelous look at the entire city from the roof of Rahab's house."

"And what did you discover about Jericho that we do not know?" Joshua looked to Caleb for the answer to this question.

"It is much as we had already learned from the caravan travelers, Sir, and from our previous mission there. Most heavily fortified. Its ample water supply is from the great spring near the gates of the city. Its climate is warm and mild. There are palms, fruit trees, flowering shrubs—it is like a bountiful garden sheltered by the towering battlements of the fortifications. Seen as we saw it from such close range, it is a formidable fortress. The city wall is continuous, more than two paces thick and built of stone and brick. Inside the great wall is a second wall. It is a strong city. God will have to take it for us."

Joshua turned back to Salmon. "What of this commitment with the woman, Rahab? What did you promise her in payment for saving your lives?"

"We promised her life to her, Sir. And the lives of the members of her family when we take the city. She will mark her house by hanging a scarlet cord from the window."

Caleb seldom volunteered information, but this time he did. "I asked her why she helped us, Sir. I was much impressed with her answer. She is helping us because she is in awe of our God. She claims she knows that He has given us the land already. One would almost think she believed in the Lord God. Although she does not know His Name. We must spare Rahab, Sir. And her family. She was valuable to us. She convinced me that the citizens of Jericho are weak with fear of us. This, I believe, is what you really wanted to know, Master. I do not believe they will fight fiercely. The Lord our God has gone before us to set their tempers."

"This is good news, Caleb and Salmon. But did you find any opinions among the people there concerning the other cities in Canaan and their kings? Jericho is only the beginning for us. God has given us the whole land."

"Yes, Sir. The other cities and their kings, while they are in possession of their lands, are depleted by the long years of Egyptian rule. They are not unified. They do not get along well together. The whole country is ripe for conquest. Our conquest, Sir! Under God. The big men of Jericho are no doubt still laughing over their wine cups at our boldness to draw up here on the east bank of the Jordan, but in their hearts they are quaking. And as the word goes out over the whole of Canaan, the others will quake, too!"

Joshua thanked the two faithful spies and stood thoughtfully for a long moment, looking at the mountains behind the encampment. The shadows stretched far down their slopes now, and although he said nothing more, his heart drew strength from remembering what God had said to him: "Moses, My servant, has died; so now arise, pass over this Jordan, you and this whole nation of Israel, to the land which I give them. Every place on which the sole of your foot shall tread, I have given you. Your territory will be from the Desert of Sin on the south east, and the Lebanon mountain range on the north, as far as the Euphrates River even to the Mediterranean Sea on the west. None will hold out before you all the days of your life. As I was with Moses, I shall be with you. I will never fail you and I will not forsake you. Be resolute and strong; for you will enable this people to inherit the land which I vowed to their fathers to give them."

A Dry River at Floodtide

Rahab paid even closer attention now to all the stories told about the Israelites by the travelers who stopped in her establishment. Within a few hours after it happened she knew first-hand, from a trader who saw it with his own eyes, that the moment the Levite priests bearing the ark of God set their feet in the overflow waters of the Jordan River, the waters were cut off. The water rushing downstream stood up like a wall! God had once more made dry land of a rushing body of water, so that His chosen people marched across safely, following the ark which assured them of God's presence with them. The story itself shook away what courage there was left among the men of Jericho, and as it moved from person to person across the whole land of Canaan, courage failed in its wake in every other city.

Rahab was excited and in awe of all she heard. Some of the men chided her for her neglect of their comfort. The once gay, cheerful hostess forgot most of the time now to swap stories with them and to keep their wine cups filled. Rahab was thinking strange, awesome, deep thoughts which she did not understand at all. Now and then she almost forgot to be clever as she questioned each man who came from the vicinity of the miraculous Jordan crossing. Her excitement possessed her, but she puzzled herself that she was not afraid. Not once did she doubt that these strange God-fearing Israelites would keep their promise to her. She checked often to be sure the scarlet cord was securely fastened to the window. Carefully, Rahab saw to it that her family stayed around her at all times. She did not neglect any of the preparations, but something was happening to Rahab's heart. There was no fear there. Instead, even with all the excitement, she was aware of a strange, new peace.

The Israelites were camped at last in Canaan at a place they called Gilgal, on the eastern edge of Jericho, and the entire city was closed in. No one entered or left it, and every citizen waited fearfully for what the Israelites would do next.

At Gilgal, outside the walled city of Jericho, the feared Israelites were keeping the Passover Feast, their first act in the Promised Land. They ate the lamb and unleavened bread, as God had instructed Moses so long ago in Egypt. The Israelites were now faced with settling down to co-operate with God in taking possession of the land of Canaan. They were no longer on the march toward it. They were there. And especially the women realized this sharply now, because for the first time since they had begun their long trip, there was no manna on the ground when they went out to gather it. They were in their own land and they would live off it from now on, even through the trying days ahead as the men of Israel followed Joshua in his every plan to capture the cities of Canaan.

Rahab knew none of this, but she knew that these nomadic Israelites were people of God and not her enemies. She was drawn to them by now, for more than just the safety of her own life.

Rahab didn't know what was going on at Gilgal among the excited, milling invaders of her land, but she trusted them. And waiting for their next move became more and more difficult for her.

At Gilgal, God Himself was appearing to Joshua as a man, and in detail He gave His trusted leader the strange plan for capturing Jericho. If Rahab had known this, her wonder would have consumed her. But she did not know. She could only watch and wait with the rest of the people of Jericho for the Israelites' next move.

The Great Silence and the Great Crash

Rahab's brother, Alman, was stationed to watch from the roof of her house, the same place she had hidden Caleb and Salmon

113

under the drying rushes. And as the hours dragged by, Rahab exhausted herself hurrying to the ladder at the roof's opening to question her brother. Between almost every customer who came to eat or drink, she called up to Alman for news.

Finally there was news. The Israelites had begun their march against the highwalled city of Jericho! Alman, from his rooftop lookout shouted down to Rahab, halfway up the ladder in her excitement. "They're coming! Hordes of them, Rahab. And about the middle of the procession men in robes are carrying a strange looking object, draped in heavy curtains. They carry it on two poles over their shoulders. These men are unarmed."

Rahab interrupted him. "They're all unarmed? All the Israelites?"

"No, those marching in front are armed with spears and arrows, but they are the only ones. The robed men carrying the strange looking object are not armed. But they're carrying something in their hands. Long, curved looking objects I can't quite make out yet."

Slowly with firm steps the long line of Israelites wound up from the encampment at Gilgal toward the walled city. Alman was not the only one watching. The locked gates of Jericho seemed somehow futile to almost every citizen trembling and watching from the wide, high wall. Everyone who could scramble up was there and the tension mounted as the strange line of conquerors came closer.

Rahab was on the roof of her house on the city wall, too, now, her dark, lovely eyes fixed intently on the swaying line of men. The swaying, steady, *silent* line of men. If only there had been some confusion in the ranks as they marched. Some sign of battle even! But there was only the steady approach of their sandaled feet and the swaying curtains of the ark and the silence.

"Those are trumpets—ramshorns those men are carrying, Alman." Rahab stared at the silent column and repeated herself. "Those are horns—trumpets. Seven men carrying seven trumpets." The dark-haired woman was awesomely silent herself now. Her brother's excitement seemed to miss her entirely. Rahab seemed only to be waiting.

Far enough from the wide city wall to escape a possible defender's jittery arrow or spear, the Israelites, led by Joshua and his armed men, bore the ark of God in the first of their strange marches all the way around Jericho. Not a sound did they make. Not a spear flew. Not an arrow left a bow. Not a man fell out of line. They just walked steadily and slowly all around the great walled city and then after a terrifying blast from the seven trumpets, (shophars) they returned as steadily and as silently to their encampment at Gilgal!

For six days the same eerie performance took place. Inside the locked city, the giant men quaked and some of them went berserk waiting. This was no ordinary attack. Their very minds were being broken. In the shadowy saloon of Rahab's inn, one massive young man, known the city over for his courage and his powerful body, sat sobbing over his wine like a terrified child. "They're fiends!" he sobbed at Rahab when she brought another bottle to him. "Those are not men, they are devils!" He grabbed Rahab's hand pathetically and looked up at her, his eyes full of fear and panic. "Look, Rahab—look at me! I'm a man, am I not? Everyone in Jericho knows I'm the strongest man of all the strong men here. You know that, don't you, Rahab? You know that, don't you?"

She smiled at him and there was only pity in her smile. Ever since the two spies, Caleb and Salmon had gone, Rahab had stopped flirting. And she didn't smile at all any more unless she meant it. This smile was one of pity and confidence.

"Yes, you're strong, but look at you now. And anyway, your strength is not the question. Those Israelites are no bigger than the men of Jericho. It is their God who is strong. It is their God you fear."

Day after day the solemn, silent line of Israelites had circled the city with no sound but the haunting blasts of the seven trumpeting priests. And on the seventh day, when some shallow souls in Jericho had begun to take their marching almost for granted, but when all those who thought at all were at the breaking point, the silent march began again. To all appearances the same as on the other six days. Up from their encampment at Gilgal, while the women and children waited behind, the same silent procession moved, out over the plain and up to within a safe distance of the high wall itself. Inside the high wall the old terror grabbed the citizens of Jericho as the almost fierce blasts from the priests' ramshorn shophars shattered their fitful sleep. This time there was a difference! Everyone felt it inside the city. For one thing, the Israelites were marching at dawn. It all looked the same. The shophar's scooping three-note wail was just as full of terror. But this time the strange invaders did not return to their camp. Instead, they circled the great city six nerve-cracking times, all the way around. Then, at one blast the terrible ramshorn trumpets stopped and a choking silence seemed about to smother all of Jericho! Even Rahab caught her breath and waited, trembling.

Then a great voice crashed upon the heavy air! "Shout!" And not a second squeezed between the command from Joshua and the terrible tornado of sound that tore from the throat of every Israelite! Like a victory shout imagined in the mind of the Creator God, their voices rose and clamored in the hot morning air, even above the violence of the blasting priest trumpeters who blew into their long, curved horns until their eyes bugged and their cheeks ached!

Rocking and cracking and groaning as though it stood toppling on the earth's own suddenly twisted axis, the great stone wall of Jericho—as wide as a city street—began to collapse! Now the citizens of the terror-ridden city shouted, too. Shouted in anger and screamed in mortal fear of what horror lay ahead for them. It was fear more awful than the fear of armed men invading. The city was being captured by the very God who had created its waving palm trees and who laid the streams that fed its beautiful fountains. Room was being made in the first city of the promised land for the chosen people of God. And as the impassioned, still shouting Israelites clambered over the flattened rubble of the city wall and into the streets and houses and market places of Jericho, there began a siege of death and destruction and ruin.

The houses and public buildings had crumbled as though they were built of dry bread crusts. Only one house remained and in it only one family. From the window of this house hung a red cord. And inside, when Caleb entered, panting from his conquest, huddled in the dark in a corner he found Rahab and her family. She sat a little apart from the others, apparently talking to herself.

"Rahab!" Caleb shouted over the din of the clambering, marauding Israelites in the ruined streets outside. "Rahab, hurry! We have kept our bargain. You and your family are to come with us back to our encampment at Gilgal. You will be one of us from now on."

The once proud harlot raised her eyes from her hands and looked at Caleb. "I am to be one of your people from now on?"

Her voice was wistful, but it could be heard somehow above the noise outside.

"Yes, that's what I said, Rahab.' Caleb stopped rounding up her family long enough to look back at her steadily. "What were you doing when I came in here, Rahab?"

"I was praying to your God. I don't know His Name, but I have been talking to Him often ever since you were here before."

When the "mopping-up" operations in Jericho were finished, the long line of tired but exhilarated Israelites turned once more back to Gilgal. The ark of the Lord had been carried victoriously into the first captured city of Canaan. And when the weary soldiers and priests straggled back into their camp, they still carried the precious ark proudly and steadily. The women of Israel welcomed Rahab and her family, and from that day on, the still beautiful but no longer wicked woman became one of God's chosen people.

The Land Secured

During the first few years after the Israelites entered the land of Canaan, Joshua proved his own military prowess and his faith in the God of his people. In a series of bloody but brilliantly executed military campaigns, the whole of the land which God had promised, from Mount Hermon in the north to below Hebron in the south, belonged to Israel. A few cities, like Jerusalem in the south and Megiddo in the north, Joshua by-passed; but when the major battles were over, he was able to divide the land as an inheritance among the 12 tribes as Moses had commanded.

The Israelites were a shepherd people and lived mostly in the hills, and except for an occasional minor skirmish, they had little to do with the Canaanites who still populated the valleys. Mostly there was peace under Joshua's firm, kind and generally wise leadership. More than four hundred years later, just as God had promised Abraham, his descendants were once more living in the fruitful land of Canaan.

But passing years often take with them the faith and ideals of a nation. Especially if the nation is prospering. Once more there was a turning among the Israelites. A thankless turning away from the God of Abraham and a turning toward the pagan gods of Canaan.

117

Joshua's heart was struck with sorrow. He was an old, old man now, but not too weak to call together the people, their elders, judges and leaders at Shechem. Old Joshua stood before them to remind them that they stood before the Lord their God at that moment: "This is what the Lord God of Israel says—" Joshua's back straightened, in spite of his years, and his voice rang strong as the Lord spoke through him to the idol-worshiping people. "Long ago your ancestors lived beyond the Euphrates River. Terah was the father of Abraham and Nahor, but they served other gods. So, I, your God, took your ancestor Abraham from beyond the river and led him through the whole land of Canaan, and I multiplied his offspring by giving him Isaac. . . . Then to Isaac I gave Jacob and Esau. I gave Esau the mountains of Seir to possess, but Jacob and his sons went down to Egypt. I have brought your ancestors out of Egypt and have given you land for which you have not labored; you have settled in cities which you have not built; and you eat of orchards and olive trees which you have not planted."

Joshua's voice rang more clearly as he added his own words to God's message: "You will choose now whether you will serve the gods of the Canaanites or the God of our fathers. As for me and my house, we will serve the Lord!"

The recently lagging spirit of the Hebrew people assembled before Joshua rose suddenly like a great wave pushed by the wind of his sincerity: "We, too, shall serve the Lord, for He is our God." The strength of their united voices quieted the old warrior's soul and gave him peace to die.

Joshua was gathered to his fathers at the age of 110 years, and Israel did serve the Lord for the rest of their leader's days. In fact, they continued to obey God for the remainder of the earthly lives of all the elders and judges who served under Joshua. And God honored them in battle. He even used the faith and cleverness of the first woman judge, Deborah, who with God's help managed victory for the Israelites when a heavy rainstorm bogged down the iron chariots of their enemy, the haughty Commander Sisera. God further showed that He didn't mind at all to work through a woman, in spite of her lowly place in the social structure of that day. The Israelites got rid of the contemptuous, cruel Sisera who hated God's chosen people—rid of him once and for all, in fact—through the daring of another woman named Jael. She may not have used God's highest methods, but she tricked Sisera into her tent and nailed him neatly to his bed with a mallet and a tent peg!

Good, bad, brave, fearful, interested and indifferent, the Israelites *were* the chosen people of God, and He worked steadily and carefully with them. Few seemed to catch on. Perhaps none clearly. But He went right on using the very human nature which defied Him, as a means of clarifying His own Nature. The Lord God worked with the people of Israel as they were using the sticks and stones of their uncertain, tension-filled hearts. And now and then He found a leader whose heart enabled Him to work with bronze and gold. One of these leaders was named Gideon.

There was peace in Israel for about forty years, but then the inevitable happened. The strange inevitable which dogged the generations of Israelites from the time Moses led them across the Red Sea. Their pattern seemed almost set. For a few years they obeyed and worshiped the God of Abraham. Then they forgot Him. And when they turned to worship false gods, they brought inevitable consequences upon themselves. During the years in which Gideon, the farmer son of Joash of the tribe of Manasseh, was growing up, the people of Israel had turned so utterly to other gods, that the lewd shrine to Baal was kept on his father's farm. Once more the vitality at the center of their entire culture seeped away. They became easy victims for the marauding bands of Canaanites still unconquered in the land. But by delivering His people yet another time through Gideon, God showed His consistent power and willingness to break through to anyone with an open heart. With a brilliantly executed plan given to him by God Himself, Gideon led 300 Israelites armed with pitchers, torches and trumpets, in a sneak attack at night and the heavily armed Midianites were almost annihilated.

After the astounding victory, the cheering Israelites begged Gideon to rule over them, but his answer was as firm as his strategy: "I will not rule over you nor let my son rule over you. It is the Lord that shall rule over you."

Back at his farming once more, Gideon lived out his life in peace. The peace that lasted among the Israelites for another forty years.

But it was a jagged peace, slashed with heartache and growing tension over the penetration inland from the coastal cities of a strange people known as Philistines. No one knew exactly where they came from originally, but there they were—tall, powerful, aggressive, and armed with iron weapons. Under their bronze helmets their strong, pagan minds seemed unacquainted with fear. And there was none in the hearts over which they held huge bronze shields in battle.

The tall "Sea People" or Philistines poured in hordes from the coast inland into southern Canaan, where the descendants of Judah and Simeon lived. They wanted the rich, fertile land God had given to the Hebrews and they became mortal enemies. Their warfare was not constant, but between the sporadic, fierce battles the peace was mostly built upon the fact that the Israelites traded with them. Once more, the chosen people of God began to turn from Him and to intermarry and worship with the Philistines, around their pagan gods. And once more, with the vitality gone from their faith, the Israelites fell into subjection to their enemies.

But there were some who still believed in the God of Abraham. And one among these was the strongest man in all Judah. His name was Samson, and his violent life was streaked with bold areas of high faith and infidelity; of great strength and great weakness; of legendary victory and pitiable tragedy.

Chapter 13

The Power of a Woman
and the Power of God

Samson, the most powerful man in Judah, was not merely a massive man with a freakishly strong body. He was a great man in body, mind and spirit. Single-handed, he killed a lion. When his own Hebrew people bound him with strong ropes to deliver him to their mutual enemies, the Philistines, Samson shook himself and snapped the ropes. And with the jawbone of a donkey, he killed hundreds of Philistines who were raiding the Hebrew villages in search of this man who, unaided, had foiled their every attack upon the Israelites.

The big man was wise, too. Shrewd, at times, and not afraid to use his cunning to avenge himself upon his enemies. Samson lived in the era when all that men saw as a way of life was an eye for an eye and a tooth for a tooth. God worked with the Israelites as they were, according to the light they had, and He honored Samson because Samson's heart was the Lord's.

He was a Nazarite, dedicated to the Lord's service from his birth. He kept the Nazarite vows faithfully. Samson never drank a drop of fermented liquor, never shaved, never cut his hair. The very strength of God flowed through him. Not because of these outward symbols but because Samson's heart was disposed toward God Himself. The stories of his prowess went the rounds of the campfires of Israel. He was more admired and feared than any man alive. To capture Samson became a national emergency among the Philistines! More so when Samson was made a judge in Israel. For twenty years he ruled the people and ruled them fairly and courageously, seemingly able to pour his own strength into them in battle. The Philistines simply could not best Samson, no matter what they did. After all, he had once uprooted two iron door posts and crumpled a city gate! Military might and iron bonds could not hold him. The Philistines had to find another way.

And they found it. Even Samson had one weak point. He loved women! Particularly Philistine women. And as the clever Philis-

tine princes hoped, the big, greathearted man of God met Delilah, a Philistine beauty, and fell hopelessly in love with her!

Big Samson laughed happily, tossing his heavy long hair like a
freed stallion. His day's work was finished. It was night and he
was alone in the shut-away freedom of a lover's world—with Delilah. Time after time he had come to her now, with his great heart
full of love and his big arms aching to embrace her firm, fragrant
shoulders. Delilah talked of many things as she leaned away from
him at the other end of the silk-covered rug pile in one corner of
her house. She talked of too many things to suit Samson.

"Delilah, I love you," his thick, long hair fell over hers as he
tried to stop her chatter long enough to pull her to him for a kiss.

The Philistine woman laughed and Samson's hurt creased his
broad, bearded face. "Why do you laugh at me, Delilah?"

She checked her laughter and smiled quizzically. "I'm not
really laughing at you, dear Samson. I'm puzzled, that's all."

"Puzzled? My heart is as open as a young boy's heart. I may
puzzle your people and even some of mine, Delilah, but I should
be no puzzle to you. There's nothing I wouldn't do for you."

She slipped from his grasp and stood above him still smiling.
"It's my womanly curiosity, Samson. You are so magnificent a man,
I must know if anything could bind you so you would be like
other men!"

Samson laughed, relieved. "Is that all? I'll be glad to tell you
how I can be reduced to the weakness of other men. If you would
bind me with seven fresh, wood fiber cords—not yet dried—then I
shall become weak and like any other man."

Delilah signaled, and a Philistine prince brought the fresh
wood fiber cords as soon as they could be secured. She tied the
laughing Samson securely, stepped back, and cried mockingly,
"The Philistines are upon you, Samson!"

Samson, too much in love to consider treachery, shook himself
and snapped the strong cords as a strand of rope snaps when it is
exposed to fire!

When Delilah once more begged to know the secret of his
enormous strength, Samson went on playing his little game. This
time he broke out of a tough bind of new unused rope as though
it were twine!

But Delilah was far from through. The Philistine princes, who hid behind her drapery hoping to capture Samson, had promised her 1100 pieces of silver if she could discover the secret of his strength. Delilah loved money more than she could ever love any man.

Time after time Samson visited her simply because he could not stay away.

"Samson, you have made a fool of me with your lies! And yet you profess to love me." Delilah held her face close to his and her breath was like night-flowers. His large deep eyes twinkled behind the shaggy brows. "This time I'll tell you the truth. Weave my seven locks of hair into that cloth you're making there on your loom and I'll be helpless!"

This time she didn't signal the hiding princes, but she knew they were waiting. Instead she kissed Samson and cradled his big head on her shoulder until he fell asleep. Then she wove the seven locks of thick brown hair into the cloth on her loom. Her shout woke him with a start: "Samson, the Philistines are upon you!"

He jumped to his feet, tearing loose the very pin from the loom with the cloth! Delilah rushed at him in anger and then thought better of it. She fell into his arms instead. Having her in his arms was suddenly all of life to him! Reason left the great and mighty judge of Judah. He forgot even the Lord his God and blurted his secret to the woman who had done what a thousand Philistines had failed to do. "I'll tell you the secret of my strength, Delilah. It is from God. I am a Nazarite from my mother's womb. I have vowed to God never to cut my hair. If I do, I lose God's strength. If razor touched my head, I would be weak like any other man."

This time Delilah was as careful as she could be with him. Her woman's instinct knew this *was* the secret. As the princes watched from behind their drapery, she stayed close to Samson and vowed her love for him. She held his massive head in her lap and lulled him to sleep with soft words and kisses on his long, thick hair. When he was sleeping soundly, she signaled a man to shave his head.

As soon as his hair was gone, Delilah could feel the strength leave his big arms. Even she could control him!

The rough bronze chains dug gashes across his big back and around his thick, muscular ankles. The harder he strained to turn the heavy gristmill in the prison yard, the more his open wounds pained him. But the pain of the chains was nothing compared to the pain in his soul. Even the ache in his empty eye sockets was dimmed by the searing torment in his heart because he had forsaken his vow to God.

Samson was a captured mass of pain and despair. Still huge, still heavily muscled—but sightless now, and instead of the soft swish of his heavy hair against his bare shoulders, there were the chains which bound him to the endless dragging round and round, and the endless grinding of the two giant millstones one against the other. The Philistine princes had sprung upon him that night from behind the drapery in Delilah's room. Her cruel cry: "Samson, the Philistines are upon you!" had come painfully true. Grindingly, painfully, tormentingly true. And he loved her so much. With all his big, generous, loyal heart, Samson loved Delilah. Delilah whom he would never see again, because her princes had dragged him—helpless with his hair shorn—to the prison yard and before hooting, cheering mobs, had gouged his eyes from their sockets. He remembered losing his balance when one eye was gone—all but the hot pain. He remembered one quick, desperate last look to see if she was there before the heated iron gouged into the other eye. Twice the pain. Then all pain. Samson was all pain and guilt and torment.

He was an ox now. Blind and harmless. An object of ridicule and jeers and rejoicing for the Philistines who never seemed to tire of their cruel amusement as they watched the once great man of Judah stumble in his new darkness and groan heavily, dragging the big timber which controlled the two mammoth millstones, round and round and round and round. No end. No destination. No light. No strength. No sense of God's presence. Only agony.

At night Samson lay on the damp stone floor of his cell and covered his shaven head with his big hands. He wept inside, because eyes that were not there could not weep.

Delilah had her 1100 pieces of silver. The Philistines had Samson, helpless at last. Praises to their pagan gods rang through the entire area of Judah. Their once feared enemy was now a groaning, weakened, beast of burden. What the Philistines did not know, as they beat gongs and banged big harps in their frenzied joy, was that Samson was still a man of God inside that stooped, weakened, bleeding body. The months dragged by as endlessly to Samson as the big, oblong ring around which he dragged the grinding stones, but in his heart Samson communed again with God. He had broken his vow to the Lord God, but slowly, slowly each night when he rubbed his bristly head, he could tell his hair was growing again! And with it grew Samson's new and deeper dependence on the God of his fathers.

The Philistines' desire to celebrate their victory grew, too, and the day approached when the whole area rang with harsh shouts and hurried plans, and orgy followed orgy as the temper of the people rushed toward the day set aside to offer the special sacrifice to their god, Dagon, in the huge temple.

Samson would be the main "attraction!" A small boy was sent to lead the big, blind man to the center of the temple floor. The fever of the crowd was pitched for the show they would enjoy with all the cruel darkness of their pagan hearts.

Three thousand Philistines crowded the roof and a thousand more packed the temple itself to watch and laugh and jeer. Samson's faith in God was high. He knew little of the love of God (few men did then) but he held what he knew in his heart and God honored him for the light he had. Samson's God was a God of vengeance and power. And as the boy led him to the center of the jeering, mocking mob, the huge, stumbling man asked to be allowed to lean against one of the two main pillars between which they had stationed him. What harm could that do? After all, he was weak now and helpless and blind. He was less than any other man. And as Samson's work-hardened hands groped for the smooth surface of the pillar, the people roared their delight at his helplessness. But in his heart he was in direct contact with God! He gripped one pillar, but his hand felt flabby and weak. He gripped the other one and stood swaying a moment, both arms outstretched, clutching the pillars, while the laughter crashed around him. Perhaps the boy beside him heard him cry out, but surely no one else could hear above the din.

"O Lord God, remember me, I pray Thee; do strengthen me only this once, O God, that I may now wreak vengeance upon the Philistines for both my eyes!" Samson felt the old power fill his big body again. His hands were like vices now around the two central pillars which held the building. His big neck arteries bulged and he shouted to the Lord God: "Let me die with the Philistines!"

And as he shouted, he bent his huge body forward. Hundreds of startled eyes looked up when the temple roof began to crack! Down from the roof came mammoth, broken timbers and with them the hurtling bodies of the three thousand people who had come to gloat over God's man. The men fought each other to get outside, the women screamed and Samson stood straight and motionless, his sightless face raised toward heaven.

For one long, deep moment, Samson, the mighty, stood in the power of God again, greater than any man. And when at last he crumpled beneath a huge stone gargoyle which thundered down upon his shaggy head, he had killed more of the enemy in death than in all the years of his earthly life.

All Samson knew of God was His great power. And God honored Samson with what he knew of Him.

Chapter 14

A Love Story

All Samson saw of God was His great power. In fact, most of Israel's moral culture was built on this half-seeing. But, as with Samson, God worked with His chosen people according to what they saw of His true character.

Now and then, however, the *love* of God broke through. Not in so many words, perhaps, but in the inner-natures of a few people.

One of the great love stories is the story of Ruth, not an Israelite at all, but a Moabitess. The Moabites were hated enemies of the Israelites, and with reason. Because when Moses was leading them on their long journey from the Wilderness of Sinai to the promised land of Canaan, the king of Moab had refused to let them pass through his land. They were forced to take a long and difficult route around Moab's borders. "An eye for an eye and a tooth for a tooth," motivated the Hebrew heart, so they did not forget this unkindness. Israelites just did not like Moabites. They fought periodically, in fact, both sides attacking across the Jordan River as the notion struck them.

But during a truce period, when there was a severe famine in Judah, a Hebrew man named Elimelech from the village of Bethlehem, a few miles south of Jerusalem, took his family across the Jordan into Moab, where there was plenty of grain for food.

With his beloved wife, Naomi, and his two sons, Elimelech settled in Moab. When he died, his body was buried there in the foreign land. His two sons married Moabite women—one named Orpah and one named Ruth. The two couples lived contentedly with old Naomi for about ten years. Then both sons died and their bodies were also buried in the land of the people who had once been their national enemies. A unique love-pattern, most unlike the times, was somehow being woven into the lives of these simple farm people.

Ruth and Orpah, the young widows, sat alone with Naomi, after they buried their men, each sharing the other's grief.

Naomi covered the young women's hands with her own. "I have just learned, my daughters, that there is once again plenty in my land of Judah, across the Jordan. We will go back together."

But on the way, Naomi sensed Orpah's added grief. "Orpah, you are bowed low with a heavy heart. It is not right that you two young women should leave your mother's homes and go with me back to a strange land where my people hate your people. You go back, each of you to her mother's house! May the Lord treat you kindly as you have treated those who have died and myself. The Lord grant that you may find rest, each in her husband's home." Naomi took both women tearfully in her arms and kissed them. The young widows wept audibly and clung to her.

"We are certainly going back with you to your people," Ruth insisted, and Orpah nodded, weeping too much to speak.

But Naomi said, "Go back, my daughters! Why should you go with me? Do I have any more sons within me, who could become your husbands? Go back, my daughters—my beloved daughters, go your way."

Orpah kissed Naomi and left her and went back to her mother's house in Moab, but Ruth clung to the older woman, weeping.

Naomi held the girl at arm's length and tried to reason with her. "Look, your sister-in-law has gone back to her people; you return after her, Ruth."

"Do not urge me to desert you by turning away from you; because wherever you go, there I will go; wherever you lodge I will lodge. Your people are my people, and your God is my God; Wherever you die I will die, and there I shall be buried. Thus may God do to me and worse if anything but death separates you and me!"

Ruth had stopped weeping and her voice was strong and determined. Both women walked toward Bethlehem together, arm in arm. Heart to heart. And the love of God was in them both.

Back in Naomi's hometown of Bethlehem, Ruth was experiencing the confusion and hurt of intolerance. She was a Moabitess, therefore a victim of prejudice and scorn—particularly from the women of Judah. But her heart was quiet, and her loyalty and devotion to her mother-in-law, Naomi, only grew as the gossip and criticism among Naomi's old friends shut the two women away even more closely in their love for each other.

They arrived in Bethlehem at the beginning of the barley harvest, and Ruth offered to join the other women gathering the heads of grain dropped by the harvesters in the fields. This was a custom in Israel among women who had no other support.

Quite by accident, on her first day out, Ruth was gleaning in the fields of Boaz, a rich relative of Naomi's husband. Toward late afternoon, after she had worked all day long in the hot sun, stooping to gather the excess grain, Ruth stood up to watch as Boaz himself strode into the very field where she was gleaning.

He was tall and extremely handsome, but more than that, she saw real gentleness in his face and kindness not often found in the voice of a man in his position. Especially not when speaking to employees! But Boaz smiled at his men as he passed by and called out warmly, "The Lord be with you!" Ruth's heart pounded with joy when the workers called back, "The Lord bless you!" This kind of friendly greeting between employer and employee in Bethlehem where the people had been so unkind to her? What manner of man was this Boaz anyway? Admiration flowed from the slender, quiet-faced Moabitess and more than she realized at that moment, her heart responded to this man named Boaz.

One night she told Naomi about him, and the old woman's face brightened. "Boaz is a near relative of my dead husband, Ruth! God must have guided you to his field. No wonder your baskets are so full of grain! Boaz probably ordered the men to drop extra heads just for you."

Ruth smiled. "Naomi, you're too romantic! But he did stop to speak to me. And so kindly, too. He told me I could stay right in his fields and assured me he had ordered the young men to leave me alone! He also said when I got thirsty, I was to drink from the vessels his men provided."

Naomi slapped her hands together. An idea had struck! "Ruth, Boaz winnows barley tonight on the threshing floor. So should I not look for a resting place for you so that you may prosper? Boaz is a fine man *and* a relative. See here! Take a bath, anoint yourself, dress up and tonight step down to the threshing floor."

Ruth was blushing and her laughter was full of good-natured protest. "But Naomi, my mother, he is such a great man!"

"Hush, daughter." Naomi would not be stopped, and she knew Ruth would obey her. "Remember, don't let him see you until he is through eating and drinking. When he lies down to sleep beside his grain to protect it, watch carefully the exact spot where he lies down; then you slip in, raise the covering from his feet and lie down. He will let you know what to do next."

Ruth was excited and embarrassed, but she did as Naomi told

her to do. When Boaz had eaten and drunk and was sound asleep, she moved near his pallet, turned up his footcovering and lay down quietly.

At midnight, Boaz awoke, startled, and of course surprised to find a woman lying at his feet!

"Who are you?" He was sitting straight up now, looking at her shadowy face peering up at him from the foot of his pallet.

"I am Ruth, your servant girl. Spread your covering over your servant girl, for you are a near kinsman." Her voice grew steadily more certain, but she was not audacious. Just natural. She felt unbelievably natural with this man!

Boaz did not light a lamp. He wanted no gossip. He was a man of God and knew not only his intentions toward Ruth but also the condition of his heart toward her since that first afternoon.

"I'm glad you're here, Ruth. May you be blessed of the Lord, my daughter." His voice was so kind she wanted to cry. Instead, she bowed at his feet and thanked him.

"My heart goes out to you for your kindness to my kinsman's wife, Naomi. Love like that is not often found, Ruth. And you have kept yourself from flirting with any of the young men—rich or poor. You are a Moabitess, but you are also a woman of the Lord God."

Boaz reached for one of her strong, slender hands. "Ruth, do you know that when a woman lies at a man's feet like this, it is the custom in Judah to marry?"

She was glad it was dark. A woman needs to blush sometimes. "I suspected my mother-in-law of knowing this, Sir."

"I have admired your willingness to work so hard in my fields, Ruth. I have known how poorly the women of Bethlehem treated you, too. And how sweetly you bear your persecution." He was silent for a moment. Then he covered her hand with both his hands so warmly and with so much gentleness that Ruth began to weep quietly. "I have noticed many things about you, Ruth. But above all, my heart has taken notice of you. I am glad you have come to me like this."

He waited a long moment, hoping she would say something. She did. "Boaz, I am glad, too."

"Now, my dear, you must feel at ease about everything. I love you. Everything you suggest, I will do for you. It is true, I am a near kinsman, but there is one kinsman nearer. Before I can claim you I must handle him. I will do this tomorrow. You see, it is a Hebrew custom that the nearest kinsman must buy up anything sold by a widow in order to keep it in the family. I will go to the nearest kinsman before me and offer him the chance to buy Naomi's one remaining field and to take you with it as his wife."

Ruth clung to his hand. "If he accepts, must I marry him, Boaz?" Her horror filled her voice.

"I don't think he'll accept, Ruth. He's full of prejudice against foreigners! I must make the offer to him, but I'm counting on his stuffy soul to make our life together possible! Now, lie down until morning, beloved Ruth, and rest. Be sure to leave before anyone sees you. It is hard for people to believe the best about anyone!"

Back at Naomi's house, Ruth told her what had happened. Old Naomi was more delighted with the news of Boaz' plan than the sight of the six pecks of barley he had poured into Ruth's shawl as a gift for Naomi.

Ruth's excitement ran high. "Do you think Boaz will remember to see the nearest kinsman today, my mother?"

Naomi wagged a brown old finger and grinned. "Just wait quietly, Ruth. That man Boaz will not stop without completing the whole matter today!"

Seated at the city gate in the presence of the nearest kinsman and ten city elders, Boaz made his proposition. He offered the man the right to buy the field, which he accepted at once, figuring he could sell it back to Boaz at a profit. But when he discovered that Ruth went along with the field, Boaz' prediction came true. The nearest kinsman turned it down, with all the people around the gate and the ten elders as witnesses. When Boaz rose to go to Ruth with his happy news, he could scarcely get away from the people who crowded around saying, "May the Lord make the woman who will come into your house like Rachel and like Leah (the wives of Jacob), who jointly built up the house of Israel."

Boaz and Ruth were married and with their child, Obed, old Naomi praised the Lord, who did not, at last, leave her without a family to love. Even her gossiping neighbors said, "Praise be the Lord, this daughter Ruth means more to you than seven sons!"

Love had won a total victory.

Chapter 15

A Tall King With a Small Soul

The old prophet Samuel was the last judge of Israel. Hannah, his mother, had given him to God before his birth and he served Him faithfully all his long life. But it was a confusing life, even for a man so close to the Lord God. Samuel's own heart was sure, but his temper flared and his patience ran out again and again during the long years of his judgeship. He was not a warrior like Samson. Samuel was a mystic, who followed God so adamantly in his own heart that he seemed strange much of the time to the people he served. They seemed odd to him, too. In fact, Israel was in a strange, mixed-up era during Samuel's time as judge and chief prophet. The Israelites had never been able to take all of the promised land of Canaan. In fact, the pagan inhabitants still in the land began to take over Israel! Even the ark of the covenant stood in the Philistine temple of Dagon where Samson had died in the last mass slaughter of his enemies. The temple was rebuilt now and there beside the half man and half fish image of Dagon, their god, stood the holy ark of the covenant of the Lord God! The very inner strength of Israel belonged to the Philistines.

And so the elders of Israel came to Samuel demanding that they be united into one kingdom and be given a king. They wanted to be like other nations. They were tired of the tribal life where their only bond was belief in the one God. This was no bond of any real value to them, since their obedience was so spotty and their faith so shallow.

Samuel was hurt by their request. It made him feel a failure. But he was old and none of his sons followed the Lord God, so he went to God for orders, and under these orders anointed a tall, handsome, eccentric man named Saul to be the first king of Israel.

Saul was God's choice for king over Israel, but time after time he acted on his own will rather than the will of God. Saul was black of beard and hair and eyes, arrogant, proud, courageous in battle—in fact, he won many decisive military victories—but his kingly bearing did not include a kingly heart. A brave heart in battle, yes. But during the two years after his coronation, it became more and more evident that Saul ruled for the glory of Saul —or at least for the gratification of Saul's ambition—not for the general good of the kingdom. Saul was not a bad king, as kings go, but he was a self-centered king, with an erratic, brilliant mind and great emotional instability.

King Saul, in fact, was the antithesis of his son Jonathan. In Jonathan the currents of wisdom ran deep. His was a practical, open heart. Perhaps Jonathan was like his mother. Certainly he was not like his moody father.

King Saul's loyalties rocketed this way and that throughout his life, and his headlong actions were tempered almost insanely with moments of desperate repentance before God. But no one, perhaps not even Saul himself, and certainly not Samuel, the old prophet of God, could attach much value to these times.

Samuel was growing old and feeble, but he was still strong in spirit. Once when Saul took matters in his own hands after he grew tired waiting for the old man to arrive to make a sacrifice to God, Samuel raised that prophetic voice and cried: "Saul, what have you done? Making the burnt offering yourself in my absence! You have acted foolishly. You have not observed the instruction of the Lord your God, which He charged you; else the Lord would have established your kingship over Israel forever!"

Saul towered above the bent old prophet. "I *am* the king! What right have you to speak to me like this?"

Samuel stood as straight as his bent old back would permit and faced the haughty, troubled king. "Your kingship will not last. The Lord has sought out for Himself a man in harmony with Him, whom the Lord has already appointed to be His people's prince because you have not obeyed what the Lord commanded you." The king and the prophet of God never saw each other again. Samuel grieved long and painfully over Saul's failures. He grieved so deeply that the Lord finally said to Samuel: "How long will you grieve over Saul since I have renounced him as king over Israel? Fill your horn with oil and go; I am sending you to Jesse, the Bethlehemite, for I have selected a king among his sons."

The old man's heart quavered at this word from God. "But, Lord, how can I go? If Saul hears of it, he will kill me." Then God gave Samuel a plan. He was to take a heifer with him to Jesse's house and invite Jesse and all his sons to the sacrifice. Most im-

portant, the Lord promised to point out to Samuel just which son
He had chosen from among the sons of Jesse to be the next king.

The Secret Shepherd King

Standing in the group of tall, well-built young men, Jesse of
Bethlehem (a descendant of Ruth and Boaz) looked puzzled
when Samuel asked if these were all of his sons.

"Yes, all of my grown sons. There is one more, David, the
youngest—a mere lad. He's out tending the sheep."

But young David was God's choice. Samuel knew it the minute
the ruddy-cheeked, bright-eyed shepherd boy ran toward him up
the hill. And as Samuel anointed the surprised lad with the oil
he carried, Israel had a new, secret king—chosen of God.

Perhaps it was at the very moment the oil ran down over
David's bright, curly head that Saul began to lose his slim hold on
sanity. He knew nothing of what Samuel had done in the Name
of the Lord. But a dark mood possessed the king and everyone
feared what he might do next. In spite of his impetuous disobedience, Saul loved Samuel, and after the break between them the
king continued to suffer periods of deep melancholia. In his way,
Saul revered the Lord God, and when Samuel saw him no more,
he feared God had withdrawn His spirit, too.

Part of the time, Saul carried on his kingly office in a reasonable
manner. But as the days wore away, his confidence in himself
seemed to wear away, too. He would sit for hours in full retreat
from reality. Retreat from anything was a pitiable state for a man
of Saul's courage, and he seemed helpless against the black moods.
Sometimes he stood tall and dark and vacant, leaning for hours
against the center pole of his tent pavilion, staring at nothing.
Alone and lost in the deepening shadows of his tumultuous mind.
Even Jonathan could not rouse him. And it was during one of
these times of torment for Saul and for all those who served him
that someone suggested sending for the shepherd lad, David, the
son of Jesse.

It was said that David played his harp so sweetly even the
trees responded to his melodies.

Jonathan stood alone outside his father's tent the night before
David was to come and prayed that the Lord God would quiet
his father's troubled spirit through the music of this young man
who was as yet a stranger to Jonathan.

Quiet in the Valley of the Shadow

Jonathan led David to his father's headquarters. And before the shepherd boy stooped down to crawl through the opening into the outer enclosure of the huge canopied tent, Jonathan laid his hand on David's arm. No word passed between them, but David's sensitive heart received Jonathan's message of love and concern for his father. As David crawled along the grassy plot toward the inner entrance to Saul's own room, a new desire sprang to life in his heart. An overwhelming desire to be God's messenger of love to the mentally ill father of the clear-eyed, handsome young man he had just met.

It was dark and shadowy inside the inner room of the tent. David blinked a moment, adjusting his eyes from the glare of the desert sun outside. Then he saw the king. Tall, shadowy, leaning against the center pole of the four cornered tent. Doing nothing. Just leaning there—vacant of thought, almost vacant of spirit. Staring. Big and disheveled and vacant. The king of Israel gone blankly into a mood so dark the shepherd boy's tender heart weakened for a moment. He wanted to run back outside. Anywhere to get away from the huge agony before him. But he remembered the plea in Jonathan's eyes, the confidence in Jonathan's touch still on his arm from a moment ago. He remembered the Lord God. And David began to play softly on his harp. He played the little tune his sheep knew so well. Quietly, slowly, sweetly, his young fingers moved across the sensitive strings, meeting their sensitivity with his own.

There was no movement from Saul whatever. No sign that he even knew David was there. The boy breathed a prayer to the Lord God and played the same little melody again. Halfway through, Saul groaned. David did not stop playing. Nor praying. The third time through the same tender tune, the big, troubled king raised one hand to his rumpled hair. Clumsily, unfeelingly, he seemed to be trying to smooth his hair. David played the delicate, simple melody again. And again. Saul held his pounding head in both hands and wept. Not violently this time. His weeping was quiet and deep. When David began the same melody once more, this time he ventured to sing along with it. A song he himself had made up out on the hillside near Bethlehem, alone with his God and his father's sheep. A song David understood, as he

135

understood God and the needs of the sheep under his care:
"The Lord is my shepherd, I shall not want;
He maketh me to lie down in green pastures, He restoreth my soul."
Saul stopped weeping and looked around. His tear-brimmed eyes
found the slim figure of the boy with the harp. David finished his
song and sat quietly, holding the strings of his harp silent with
his strong young hand. He prayed. In a moment, Saul stooped
down and picked up his crumpled turban from the ground.
Lamely he put it on his head, and tried to stand erect and kingly.
His sanity was returning. David's sweet music had quieted his
heart. The storm was over for that time. And Saul was grateful. He
walked from his tent out into the bright sunlight with one arm
around David's shoulder. Jonathan was waiting outside. And the
look of love and gratitude which passed from Jonathan to David
when he saw his father, stirred David's heart to respond to Jonathan with the first whole love the lad had ever known for anyone
outside his own family.

Saul insisted that David be kept on at court to play for him and
so he made the boy his armor-bearer. Jonathan was glad.

The Giant Killer

Saul's general condition improved to the extent that he led his
armies in a few victorious battles, and David continued to serve as
his armor-bearer. The boy was honored to serve his king, but he
missed the quiet little hills outside Bethlehem and the life he
loved there alone with God. And when his brothers had to go
with Saul on one particular campaign against the Philistines, David returned to his shepherd life with joy in his heart. There was
some sorrow, too, because he had come to love Saul deeply and
he knew his beloved friend, Jonathan, would be in the fighting,
too. "I will fear no evil, for thou art with me," David sang, back on
the grassy hillside alone, attempting to still the fear in his heart at
the thought that Jonathan or Saul might be killed in battle.

But this was a strange campaign. An actionless campaign, in
fact, though David knew nothing of this out there on the hills beyond Bethlehem. The Philistines were massed in force at Sho-
choh, in Judah, south of Jerusalem and Bethlehem. And the Israelites under Saul were stationed in the Elah (Oakdale) valley
below, only a shouting distance away. In fact, the Philistines' "attack" so far had been all shouting. They were trying a new tactic.

In their ranks was a giant named Goliath who rattled his armor and his brawn every day down the sloping hill toward the valley, at the same time shouting: "Why draw up in battle formation? Am I not a Philistine and you Saul's slaves? Choose a man to represent you and let him challenge me. If he is able to fight and kill me then we shall be your slaves. But if I beat and kill him, then you will be our slaves and serve us. I defy the ranks of Israel today, to furnish me a man so we can fight each other!"

Goliath's voice rolled around the valley and not one man among Saul's troops dared to show himself. Goliath stood nine feet tall. His big bronze helmet would have fallen to the shoulders of the biggest Israelite. His bronze coat of mail weighed two hundred pounds. His massive legs were swathed in bronze leggings and the shaft of his bronze javelin which he balanced easily on his big shoulder was the size of a weaver's beam.

"He's bigger than Samson, I'll wager," one of David's brothers said in disgust after Goliath had rumbled his challenge once more across the valley to the silent army of Saul. "Who among us could stand against a man like that?"

For forty tension-filled, monotonous days, Goliath took his position and made his boasts and his challenge, and everyone, including Saul himself, was dumbfounded. No one had an answer. The Israelites could not attack up the hillside, they would all be slaughtered for sure. And the Philistines would not come down in open battle. They only kept sending Goliath, whose anger mounted with each trip down the hillside because it must have seemed to him that no one else in the whole Philistine army was doing any work but him!

After awhile only a few of Saul's troops paid much attention to the giant's shouting, until the day young David arrived at the Israelite camp with food for his brothers. The lad stood fascinated as Goliath roared his threat into their ranks.

He was fascinated and shocked at the same time. Not at Goliath so much as at the cowardice of his fellow Israelites!

"Is Jonathan not among you?" David asked his brother, Eliab.

"Jonathan is not here. He is back at court in Gibeah. What is that to you, little brother?" Eliab was still annoyed in his heart that David and not he had been anointed by old Samuel that day at Jesse's home.

"It is nothing to me, Eliab, except that if Jonathan were here, he would fight Goliath. And since he is not here, I will fight him myself." David was not boasting. He was simply stating a fact.

The general hubbub among Saul's troops reached the ears of the king himself and he stood smiling in amazement and affection at young David.

"I killed a lion once, Sir, when he got after my father's flock. I held him by his chin whiskers and killed him. I have also killed a bear. This pagan Philistine will go as they went, especially because he has defied the drawn-up army of the living God."

David was more than three feet shorter than Goliath, and he didn't weigh nearly as much as Goliath's coat of mail. But his voice reached Saul's inner being and the failing king caught some of David's faith. "The Lord who rescued me from the paws of the lion and the bear will rescue me from this Philistine, Sir."

Saul smiled at the slender boy who stood before him clad in his shepherd's skin garment. The king's voice was deep with admiration and affection and faith. "You go, David, and the Lord be with you."

Saul spoke words of encouragement to David as he dressed the boy with his own hands, in his own coat of mail. Over David's head, Saul placed his own heavy, bronze helmet. Obediently, David buckled on Saul's long sword around the awkward coat of mail and tried to walk. Some of the men laughed.

"I'm not used to this, Sir. I'll go as I am. Thank you."

Saul watched him walk away briskly, unarmed and unprotected, toward the brook that ran through the valley near the foot of the hill where the Philistines were encamped. Goliath stood a few hundred feet from the spot in the brook where David stopped to pick up five smooth stones and drop them into his leather pouch. For a moment, Goliath just stood there and stared at the boy's slim back. Then he roared:

"What kind of insult is this? A stripling boy coming to me with a shepherd's stick in his hand?" David walked straight toward Goliath, his sling in one hand and his staff in the other. His steady approach infuriated the giant! "You come to me, you Hebrew slave, and I'll feed your skinny body to the birds of the air and— and - -" Goliath spluttered in his fury. "I'll feed your skinny body to the birds of the air and the beasts of the field! By Dagon, I'll smash you straight into the ground!"

David kept on walking, but now he too shouted toward Goliath as he walked: "You are meeting me with sword and javelin, but I meet you in the Name of the Lord of hosts, the God of the armies of Israel, whom you have defied. Today the Lord will hand you over to me, and I will slay you and cut off your head."

Goliath's laugh roared across the valley and kept on roaring. But David was still shouting, too. "Today I will feed the corpses of the Philistine army to the birds of heaven and the beasts of the field, so that the whole earth may know there is a God in Israel."

Goliath hoisted his heavy girdle, adjusted his bronze helmet, and made ready to attack the shepherd boy. David moved nearer, still shouting: "This whole gathering, too, shall know that the Lord does not save through sword and spear; for the battle is the Lord's and He will hand you over to us."

Suddenly David began to run toward Goliath, quickly dropping one smooth stone into his sling. One, two, three times he swung the gray knit sling and Goliath fell forward heavily on his face, the small stone from the brook drilled into his forehead between his eyes. David's aim was perfect. This was the only chink in the bronze helmet and his little stone found it! The giant writhed on the ground alone, but not for long. David had been running toward him from the moment the stone left his sling! He grabbed Goliath's own sword and cut the massive head free from the hulking body. Their giant was vanquished and the Philistines fled before the pursuing Israelites.

Saul had been genuinely fond of David before this amazing thing took place. Now, he was genuinely interested in him as a person. He sent for David the next day, and Jonathan brought him to his father.

"By the time David was through talking with Saul, Jonathan's soul was in unison with David's soul. Jonathan loved him as himself. On that same day, Saul retained him and did not let him return to his father's home. Because he loved him, Jonathan made a covenant with David; he stripped himself of the robe he had on and gave it to David; also his armor with sword, bow, and belt. David went out wherever Saul sent him and enjoyed success, so that Saul put him in charge of troops; he was in favor with the people and with Saul's servants."

Chapter 16

A New King Coming

When old Samuel died, all Israel mourned for him. Saul, in his better moments, must have grieved, too. But Saul was on his way out. God had not been able to speak clearly to His people through Saul. As long as Samuel lived, God had a voice. But He would have another voice (human, nonetheless) when the new king, David, would ascend his throne.

David grew to manhood in the service of Saul. It was not always a peaceful service, because Saul continued to be erratic and moody, even violent at times. And from the day after Goliath's death, when David was cheered in the streets above Saul, the tall tumultuous king alternately loved and hated his new captain, the son of Jesse.

Even as Saul's son-in-law (after he married his daughter, Michal) David knew no peace with the king. Certainly his deep, enduring friendship with Saul's son, Jonathan, had not smoothed the rough way between David and Saul. Now and then David's music smoothed it, as Saul's ugly moods melted into tenderness and love for him. But more than once Saul hurled his javelin at David as he sat singing and strumming his harp for Saul's pleasure.

So violent grew Saul's jealous attacks on David that Jonathan, who loved David as he loved himself, helped him escape. And he became, in fact, an outlaw—a sort of Robin Hood, leading a courageous band of men who fought the enemies of Israel, plundered the land for their very existence—even eating the holy shewbread from the temple in order to stay alive! David was already anointed by God, through Samuel, to be the next king of Israel. He had to stay alive, but time and an ugly fate also had to work through their design before David could become king.

The tragic design ended in another bloody battle with the Philistines, when both Saul and Jonathan were killed. Saul, in his last black hour of desperation, rather than be humiliated by defeat, fell on his own sword.

Few knew it, but God had already anointed the new king.

David the Beloved King

David, the new king, was a man with a heart so tender it broke itself into a song of grief at the death of Saul, the man who had tried so many times to murder him. No one was surprised that David grieved for Jonathan. But for Saul? Shouldn't he have been glad that his path to the throne was open at last? Surely David was ambitious, but the great paradox that *was* the man, David, held throughout his life. As a young shepherd boy, he sang sweetly to his fathers sheep and killed wild animals and a giant singlehanded!

The paradox grew as David's life matured, and quite simply, he was great enough to contain within himself strong contradictory characteristics more potent than six average men could contain!

He was a poet and yet he was practical. As the revered administrator of the new government in which he had more power than Saul, he could not resist dancing in the streets with his subjects when the ark of God was returned. He composed beautiful music and designed a complex political system. The paradox that was David reached farther than the facts of his brilliant and bloody military victories executed simultaneously with tender, deep understanding of human problems. In fact, the paradox reached to the extreme predicament of a carefully planned willful sin against the God whose heart he saw more clearly than any man alive in his time!

In David's great soul was the insight and wisdom of God Himself. But in frequent conflict with the Lord's wisdom, gigantic human desire did battle not only with the Spirit of God, but with David's own longing to be God's faithful servant. In one sense, David was the victim of his own greatness.

The gentle singer of the psalms which sprang from his own creative mind and heart led his forces into battle after battle until the fertile land of Canaan was strewn with the corpses of his enemies. David "killed his ten thousands" and still sang his sweet songs. Even Joshua had failed to capture the heavily fortified city of Jerusalem, but David succeeded. And when, after seven years as King of Judah, in the south of Canaan, the northern tribes asked to be his subjects, he moved his capital from Hebron to Jerusalem. David, the military genius, became David, the peacemaker, be-

141

cause the north and south of Israel had been in competition for years. With his palace at Jerusalem, David reasoned that neither north or south could complain, since this city had never before been conquered by the Israelites.

The old loosely knit tribal confederacy had become a new nation, and at its head was David, the king—winsome, brilliant, fearless, gentle. He managed to keep himself free of enemies in the surrounding countries and he used his personal charm as well as his military might to accomplish this. The Philistines were driven from the land once and for all, and his empire stretched from the Lebanon mountains to the very borders of Egypt, from the Mediterranean Sea to the Arabian Desert. Israel never again rose to higher political power.

Reaching these heights had kept David busy all his life. From his early days as Saul's armor bearer, to his own throne at the head of a united kingdom, David had been in constant action. He was a man's man, in spite of his handsome appearance and poetic nature. And in spite of the fact that women clamored after him, he had had little time to think of them personally. True, he had a harem of beautiful women and during his life, a total of eighteen wives—but the very fact that he chose to surround himself with a number of wives and concubines, instead of giving his devotion to one as Saul had done, proves that David had never really been in love. After his beloved friend, Jonathan, was killed in the last battle under Saul, David had written that Jonathan's love surpassed the love of women.

His life as the all powerful ruler of the united kingdom of Israel was heavy with responsibility. Life in the court of David was anything but quiet. After all, there were not one but many wives scheming and conniving to win favor for their various sons! But the kind of activity around him did not use up David's energies. He was still only in his forties and being forced to stay at his magnificent cedar palace (built for him by Hiram of Tyre) was a frustrating thing to this man who had been a shepherd, a guerilla chief and a warrior king.

He still played his lyre and he still sang. Now and then he composed a new song, fitting the beat of the lyrics together with the haunting oriental music that seemed present in endless supply in his creative heart and mind. David's songs were directed to the Lord God. He composed and sang them consciously in

His presence. And they laid bare the deep wonderings about himself in the heart of the poet king:

"Thou hast searched me, Lord,
And Thou knowest me.
Thou hast me in mind when I sit down
and when I rise up;
Thou discernest my thoughts from afar.
Thou hast traced my walking and my resting,
and art familiar with all my ways.
For there is not a word on my tongue,
but Thou, Lord, knowest it perfectly."

He was a powerful king now, shut away in his splendid palace, and so he played his lyre and fitted strong, swift poems into his melodies. And each day, when his work was done, David walked. And thought.

Only as a shadow each man walks about;
truly, in vanity they are greatly disquieted;
each stores up riches, not knowing who shall gather them.

One day a great urge came upon him as he walked alone on the east terrace of the palace. He was suddenly ashamed that the ark of the Lord was still housed in a tent, and David burned with a desire to build a temple more magnificent than any in the world to house the ark of God. Surely this would be the crowning achievement of his life!

But David's heart dropped when he told his plan to the prophet Nathan. The old prophet had heard directly from the Lord God, and the message was that not David, but his son would build the temple of God. David had shed too much blood in his life. Which son would build the Temple? Was he born yet? The king's heart was heavy over the refusal of God, but the ark remained in a tent and David remained obedient. Ambition was not an easy thing to surrender. Not in a man of action like David. But his heart was fixed on the Lord God, and so he obeyed Him.

No man loved God more than David the king. No man longed to obey God more than he. The years passed and David governed Israel wisely, but in middle life his energies still ran high and although he had not built the Temple, neither had he found an outlet for his restlessness. None, that is, except the steady flow

143

of poetry and music as he revealed the deepening love for the
Lord God in his strong, full heart.

"Thou dost make me know the path of life;
in Thy presence is fulness of joy;
in Thy right hand are pleasures forevermore."

David ruled and prospered and poured forth his love to God
in his quiet moments away from the hubbub of court life. And
in the evening, he walked back and forth alone on the palace
terraces overlooking Jerusalem.

The songs David wrote came from his heart, and as they took
form, their words of devotion to God dropped into his subcon-
scious mind. They came from David and they went back to David.
They were a part of the man himself, as his devotion to God was a
very part of his life.

But one evening, as he walked on the wide terrace, a new violence invaded the great heart which had dared to go in the
strength of the Lord God to meet the thundering Goliath!

David stopped walking, stared across at a near-by rooftop and
felt his soul leap out and across the space between! There on the
roof, leisurely bathing herself, was the first woman whose exqui-
site beauty struck David's heart as swiftly and surely as the deadly
stone from his shepherd's sling had struck the giant's forehead.

A Great Love and a Great Sin

King David gripped the cedar balustrade along the terrace
where he stood staring at the woman on the roof nearby. His heart
had hurtled courageously through the blood and terror of a hundred battles. It lost no beats as he walked as a lad up the hill toward Goliath, armed only with five smooth stones and a woolen
sling. No lion, no bear, no enemy forces plunging toward him at
battle-heat had disquieted the heart of David. He had gone "in
the strength of the Lord God" all his life, and his heart had
stayed quiet and in his possession within him.

Now, as though wounded in battle, David reeled and gripped
the cedar railing more tightly. The woman on the roof top took
the towel from her slave girl and dried her lovely body slowly,
unaware that the king watched. A warm breeze ruffled the sheer
robe she slipped into and brought the scent of her spice oil to the
king. His heart's quiet vanished. He forgot the Lord God—quickly
learned her name and sent a servant to bring her at once to the

palace! She was Bathsheba, wife of Uriah, one of David's own soldiers, away at that moment fighting for his king.

Standing before him, the woman was more beautiful than ever. "Bathsheba," David spoke her name, not as a king might speak it, but as a man. David, the man, slipped suddenly from God's control. On his own! Pagan in his desire, aware only of the woman before him and of his own hunger.

"Bathsheba!" Two steps and his arms held this woman who had unknowingly shattered his inner strength.

Night after night David sent for her and night after night she came to him willingly. After all, she was a subject for him to command; and surely it was a singular honor that he wanted her as he did. Women were not new to David, but Bathsheba was unlike any other woman to him. He showered her with gifts and his passion for her became his life! He was restless and irritable all through the day until just before dark, when he knew she would be brought to him again. The giant soul of David was lost in the warmth and fragrance and beauty of the first woman who had stirred him in the deeps of his heart where he loved the Lord his God. Beside her at night, David might never have known of the Commandments given to Moses on the smoking mountaintop. And he seemed not to remember them for himself even at noon as he handled the affairs of the kingdom of God's chosen people.

David lived for the hour of her arrival each night and his heart sang with the joy of her love for him. Their idyllic hours held him captive. He seemed not to think at all. Nothing got through to him even to slow his pace, until one night when Bathsheba seemed different. She was not cool toward him. But his sensitivity toward her warned him that this night he must be unusually gentle with her. With Bathsheba, David's poet heart had kept him always tender. He had grown to love her. The pagan desire did not lessen, but neither did it smother his poet heart.

He held her from him and looked at her, his deep-set blue eyes searching hers with immense love and caring.

"I must tell you something, my master." Bathsheba looked steadily at him, too. "I am going to bear your child."

Like a sudden thunderclap, David's dream-like days came to an end! No other oriental king of his time would have been disturbed by this news. But the moral standards of Israel were above those of the surrounding lands. It was acceptable for a man to have a harem, but on the stone tablets, brought down from the mountain in the arms of Moses, God had written: "Thou shalt not commit adultery." David's problem was grave. Bathsheba's husband, Uriah, had been away for many months with David's army beyond the Jordan. It was the Hebrew custom to stone to death any woman who had been taken in adultery! As soon as Bathsheba's condition became apparent, her blood would be mingled with that of hundreds of other women at the place of execution outside the city wall. There was the dried blood of many men spattered there, too, since the partner in adultery was equally guilty.

David's quick mind sprang into action. He sent for Uriah, fighting beside Joab, the king's commander, a few days' journey away. With Uriah home—presumably spending a night with his wife— he could be sent back and the taint of Bathsheba's child by David would be wiped out. No one would know.

Uriah was not a clever man, but he was a good soldier, and he was not pleased to be brought home in the midst of the fighting. Like his wife, however, he was a subject of the king, and forced to obey. With Uriah before him—ostensibly for a military report, David felt confident of his plan. The battle-stained Uriah stood quietly, giving a detailed account to David of all that had taken place under Joab's command in their fighting with the Ammonites. When he had finished, David, attempting to be casual, urged the faithful soldier to go home and refresh himself. Implying, of course, that he could spend the night with Bathsheba, his beautiful wife.

Uriah bowed out of David's presence, but he did not go home. Instead he lay down outside the palace with the king's soldiers stationed there, and slept. Uriah could not bear such comfort for himself when he knew the hardships beyond the Jordan among his comrades.

Standing before David again the next day, he declared in his slow, determined speech, "The ark of God stands in a tent beyond the Jordan with my comrades in battle. Could I go to my house and eat and drink and be with my wife? I swear by your life, by the life of your soul, my king, I shall do no such thing!"

Ordinarily a king would have been delighted with such discipline and honor in a soldier. David was frustrated. He ordered Uriah to remain one more day and be his guest at dinner. Uriah's concern for the ark of God in its battle tent beyond the Jordan had not touched David's heart nor made him remember the Lord his God. He was a man driven now by another passion; he had to protect the woman he loved and himself! Uriah was plied with drink at the palace feast the next night. But even though he was quite drunk when he left, he still refused to visit Bathsheba. Instead, he slept again with the soldiers outside the palace gates.

Once more Uriah stood before his king, ready to return to the Ammonite fighting beyond the Jordan. David had little to say to the strong, simple man before him. There were heavy lines in David's face, and his handsome mouth twitched nervously as he handed Uriah a sealed note.

"Give this message in person directly to my commander, Joab, immediately upon your arrival." David turned his back on Uriah, and waited for his loyal, strong-hearted subject to leave the throne room.

The note in Uriah's pouch as he started away read: "Put Uriah in the front line of the heaviest fighting; then withdraw from behind him so that he will be struck down and killed."

David, the beloved king, for love of a woman, had broken another commandment of his God. Faithful Uriah fell in battle—on orders from David the king! After a proper time of mourning, Bathsheba was brought to David to stay. She bore him a son, and David rejoiced that she would never have to leave him at dawn again.

The Finger of God

The king once more went about his daily affairs of government with his old calm. Bathsheba was his wife. She lived every day and every night now under his own roof. The child she bore David was his joy. Life could go on now, only with more happiness than David had ever known. His conscience seemed well under control. At the end of the day, on a certain day some months after his son was born, the king rose from his throne and prepared to visit Bathsheba and the child. He was more than annoyed when old Nathan, the prophet, asked for a hearing.

Nathan seemed almost unmindful of the king's irritation. He stood before David sturdily refusing to budge, his bent, heavily robed figure authoritative, from his thin gray hair to his sandaled feet. Something in Nathan's manner caused David to sit down again, slowly, a little puzzled.

147

"I have come to tell you a story, Sire." Nathan's voice made this strange mission sound as grave as it was. David gestured and Nathan began to speak.

"There were two men in a certain city, one of whom was rich and the other poor. The rich man had flocks and herds in great numbers; but the poor man had nothing at all except one little live lamb which he had bought and nurtured, so that it grew up with him, along with his children. It ate its part of his little food, drank out of his cup, and lay down in his arms; it was like a daughter to him. Then a traveler came to the rich man who, unwilling to take an animal out of his own flock or herd for the use of his traveling guest, took the poor man's lamb to prepare for his visitor."

David stood up greatly angered at this injustice. "As the Lord lives, Nathan, the man who has done this deserves to die! He must also make that ewe lamb good four times over, because of this thing he has done and because he has shown no pity!"

Old Nathan's long nose seemed to point directly at David.

"My king, you are the man!"

David stepped back as though the old prophet had struck him. And as Nathan pointed his own bony finger at David, it was to David's suddenly guilty heart the finger of God Himself: "I, Myself, anointed you as king over Israel. It was I who rescued you out of the hand of Saul. . . . Why have you despised the Lord's commandment by doing what is wrong in His sight? Uriah, the Hittite, you have struck down with the sword, and his wife you have taken to be your wife; you murdered him by the sword of the Ammonites!"

David stood for a long moment, staring into the black, accusing eyes of God's old prophet. The long, bony finger still pointed at David's heart. For the first time in months, David's heart ached with loneliness for the Lord his God. The loneliness was no sharper than the guilt that burned through his whole being. The guilt no sharper than the loneliness. In spite of what he had done, David loved the Lord. His broken heart moved within him from sheer longing for the God he loved. Through his tormented mind stray lines from one of his own poems flicked his agony like a long whip: "My soul thirsts for Thee; my flesh longs for Thee in a dry and thirsty land where there is no water!"

The tortured king twisted into his tall, ornate chair and hid his face in his hands. Nathan had delivered the Lord's message, but his own eyes filled with tears of compassion as he looked at David, the beloved king, hiding his face like a criminal, but suffering the pains known only to those who have wounded a loved one. David loved the Lord his God and he had wounded Him. His gold crown glistened in the rays of the afternoon sun as David's head swayed back and forth, his handsome face drawn and hidden in his hands. Could one man contain so much guilt? Could one man bear the grief of so much guilt?

Nathan wanted to comfort him, but he stood true to God.

David the king would have to humble himself of his own accord before the Lord. He would have to repent out of the shame of his own heart. Many slow, tortured moments squeezed by between the prophet and the suffering king. Then David raised his head from his hands. At first, he seemed unable to stand. But his heart was still strong within him and one slow, agonizing movement followed another as the tall king got to his feet. Tears streamed down his tormented face, lifted now toward God alone. His voice was thick and old, older than David was in years, but no older than his soul at that pain-pressed moment. His words pushed slowly up from his heart, one at a time.

"Have mercy—upon—me, O God, according to Thy—loving kindness. According to the greatness of—Thy—compassion—blot out my transgressions!" David was aware only of the Lord God now. Aware of Him *again*, but not yet with the peaceful communion of the other times which now seemed years instead of mere months ago. He was calling directly to God now, almost shouting: "Against Thee, Thee only, have I sinned, and done what is evil in Thy sight! Hide Thy face from my sins and blot out all my iniquities. Create in me a clean heart, O God, and renew a steadfast spirit within me. Cast me not away from Thy presence . . . O, my God, cast me not away from Thy presence!"

David's sobbing filled the big room. The two men stood before the living God. Nathan felt moved to assure his king: "The Lord has taken away your sin; you will not die. Nevertheless, because you have provided by this action such an opportunity for the enemies of the Lord to ridicule, the son born to you must surely die."

Old Nathan had scarcely had time to return to his house when David's son by Bathsheba became ill. The king was inconsolable

149

while the child lay sick. But when the little boy died, his father accepted the tragedy as from God and he stopped his mourning. David and God were friends again. Although his life bore the scars of his great sin, David was forgiven. Once more he could live in the strength of the Lord God.

When Bathsheba bore David another son whose name was Solomon, David proved that in spite of his torment after his sin against God, his love for this woman was real. Without question, Bathsheba was the one wife David loved.

"Will you make me a promise, my beloved king?" Bathsheba whispered as David knelt beside her and the child, Solomon.

"Anything you ask in the name of our love, I will do."

"Then let this son of our love, Solomon, be the one to follow you to the throne. For me, do this for me!"

David smiled at her and holding one of her hands and one of the baby's hands in each of his own he promised that Solomon would be the next king of Israel.

The Last Years of David

The Lord God restored David to friendship with Himself, but the last years of the beloved king's life were scarred with tragedy and bathed in tears. David continued to love with the deep energy of his great heart, and because of this capacity to love, he suffered in equal measure.

One son, Absalom, the child of his wife Maachah, brought double torment to his father for this very reason. Absalom was another David in appearance—tall, handsome, a mighty warrior. David loved him fiercely, in spite of Absalom's ambition and treachery. Double grief struck the king's heart when Absalom had another of David's sons murdered and then in an attempt to snatch the kingdom from his own father, was killed in the process. Joab, David's commander, killed Absalom to protect the throne. But so wild was David's grief over the death of his beloved son that David and Joab had strong words over the king's continued mourning.

"Absalom was a traitor, Master! He has caused trouble now within the kingdom by convincing the northern tribes that you favor your own tribe of Judah. For the people to see you grieve over this scoundrel will cause more trouble. The northern tribes will believe him! For the kingdom's sake, you must stop this mourning!"

David's reply was the same cry he had carried in his heart ever since Joab had killed the handsome prince. "Would God I had died for you, O Absalom, my son, my son!"

Joab's fury ran high. "Absalom is not here! It is I, Joab! I have served you long and well, Sire. We have extended the boundries of Israel beyond anyone's dreams. Now get up and speak encouragingly to the people and to the servants here—or not one of them will stay with you!"

David was forced to give up his public mourning, but another scar lay across his great heart. And day after day, tension grew in the palace as David's wives and their sons built intrigue upon intrigue anticipating the death of the old king. Each wife coveted the crown for her own son. No one seemed to know that David had already promised Bathsheba that her son, Solomon, would succeed him. No one but Nathan, the prophet, who agreed that Solomon was God's choice. As with David, while Saul still reigned, there was already another secret king. Solomon had not been anointed in secret by the prophet, but even as a teen-ager he began to show marks of superiority. He was not a soldier like his father, but his unusual wisdom set him apart from his brothers and caused David's other wives to hate Bathsheba more than ever. David had not only one wife—he had eighteen wives, and all jealous of the king! All jealous for their sons. Seventeen of them united in only one questionable trait—hatred for Bathsheba, whom David loved.

The king was growing feeble and the reins of his government often tangled in his hands as his own personal griefs bewildered and confused him. David's heart remained the same. All his life he had only meant to love. It was David's love of God that caused him grief over his sin with Bathsheba. Men were punished because of the law for such acts, but few felt real grief in their hearts. It is not David's sin that is the amazing fact of his life. It is his tender conscience toward God in a day when man felt only the pinch of the law and not the grief of repentant hearts! The wonder is not that David sinned and brought grief into his later years. The wonder is that he experienced the sting of guilt in his own heart and cried out to God for forgiveness!

David had always loved above the norm of his day. When there is love, there is pain, and pain came again to David when another beloved son, Adonijah, tried to grab Israel from the failing king.

More pain came to David when his commander, Joab, threw in his lot with young Adonijah. David was becoming so weak with age that Joab feared the kingdom would break apart without a strong king on the throne. And it was then that the prophet Nathan and Bathsheba joined forces to persuade David to make Solomon ruler at once over the united kingdom.

In his heart, David knew his own death was near. He was old in years and weary at last. Bathsheba was beside him.

"Call our son, Solomon, and tell him his father wants to speak to him." David's voice was weak and raspy with age. His lyre and his songs had been put by as he was now putting by his life and his throne.

But as his strong, dark young son, who would take over the throne, knelt beside the old king, David's young dream came back to him and he began to speak to Solomon about it and to prepare him for it.

"Hear me, my son. I am about to die. You must be strong and behave like a man. You must observe the charge of the Lord your God by walking in His ways, by observing His statutes, commands, judgments, and testimonies, as it is written in the Law of Moses, so that you may succeed in everything you do and in everything to which you may turn; and that the Lord may confirm the word which He spoke to me: 'If your sons watch their steps, so as to walk before Me devotedly, with their whole heart and soul, there shall never be wanting for you a man upon the throne of Israel.' " The old king blinked back tears from his sunken eyes. With all his failing heart he longed for Solomon *not* to follow in the footsteps of his father and mother by breaking God's commandments. Then he brightened a little and spoke directly of his dream. "I myself had in mind to build a temple as a resting place for the ark of the Lord's covenant and for the footstool of our God. But God told me I was not to build the temple in His name because I had been a man of wars and bloodshed."

Young Solomon bowed his head in reverence to his father and to God, as David went on speaking to him. "The Lord has chosen you, my son Solomon, to sit on the throne and to build the house of the Lord." The old king touched his son's hand. "The Lord God has chosen you to build a house for the sanctuary. Be strong, Solomon, and do it!"

Chapter 17

The Great King Solomon

Nearly 500 years after Moses led the slave children of Israel out of bondage in Egypt, King Solomon strode—tall, splendidly robed, proud—up the ten wide, white stone steps of the magnificent newly completed Temple.

The people stood in awe of him, as he mounted the Temple steps. All of Jerusalem was there for the dedication and inspection of the Temple which would house the ark of God in a gold-lined room behind the golden altar. Solomon had begun the building of the Temple in the fourth year of his reign. It was finished in seven years, and they were years of wonder and some rebellion for the people. Wonder at the elaborate and breathtaking plans for the amazing structure and rebellion at Solomon's decree that they must give one third of their time as slave laborers to him in order that his dream might become reality. Literally thousands of skilled craftsmen were brought in from Tyre and surrounding countries, but the manpower of his subjects was needed, too. And although the king was ready to employ force if necessary, the people had worked, and now they stood in awe of their striking king standing before his Temple lined with hand-carved cedar wood from Lebanon and built of expensive white stone.

The people were allowed to look at the golden vessels, candlesticks, snuffers, censers, tongs, bowls and even handwrought hinges, and their hearts swelled with pride in themselves, and in their wise king. Solomon took a chance on rousing the people against him by conscripting them to such hard labor, but in the first four years of his reign he had won their admiration by his uncanny wisdom. He was not a "beloved king" as his father, David, had been, but Solomon had pleased God by asking only one thing for himself at the beginning of his rule—wisdom to rule his people well. While he was still a young man, he was being consulted constantly by potentates and rulers from countries all around Israel and Judah, the united kingdom.

With all his heart, Solomon meant to serve God. His human

weakness was his brilliant mind, into which God poured His own wisdom. Solomon's wisdom was from God, but when a man's mind is greater than his heart, wisdom alone is not enough. David's devoted heart kept him strong in his belief and depending on the Lord God, in spite of his enormous talents. All these talents and more were passed on to his son, Solomon, who was an authority on trees, animals, birds, reptiles, fish, and whose speech was studded with such wisdom that he is known to have been the author of literally hundreds of proverbs. Like his father, also, he wrote beautiful poetry. Unlike David, though, Solomon wrote love poetry to women as well as to God. But even this was of such a poignant spiritual nature that his Songs were included in the Holy Bible. His philosophy recorded in the Book of Ecclesiastes reveals the inner reaches of this man who demanded more from life than even his genius could discover, in his twilight age before God had fulfilled His plan to show Himself in the Redeemer who would come through David's lineage.

In the excessive energy of his movements as he strode up the ten wide stone steps of the Temple that day, Solomon betrayed his inner restlessness and carefully harnessed nature. Everything he did, he did enormously. Even to the number of his wives and concubines.

And standing on the Temple steps, the people seemed to sense their king's heart was at the bursting point with all it contained of pride and confidence *and* the almost contradictory desire for dependence upon the Lord God.

Wherever Solomon appeared, the crowd was caught up in the gigantic energy of his mind and emotions. So that by the time the priests and Levites bore the beloved ark of God from its tent dwelling to the magnificent Temple, the crowd was in a frenzy of excitement. Unlike his father, Solomon did not dance in the streets with the people. He lived behind his royal calling, never once becoming one of them.

The priests and Levites carrying the ark and the two stone tablets given to Moses, mounted the ten wide, white stone steps, entered the carved cedar doors, and disappeared from the people's sight to place the old ark in the gold lined room Solomon had prepared for it at the far end of the Temple. For a time there was almost silence in the crowd as the priests and Levites inside ministered to the Lord with the ritual instituted by David.

Suddenly, out upon the wide platform between the two great pillars of the Temple rushed the priests, their eyes wide with a kind of holy terror! And from the open doorway to the Temple there poured a thick cloud which had so filled the interior that they could no longer continue their ritual. The glory of the Lord had filled His house!

Solomon stared for a moment and then proclaimed: "The Lord said: He dwells in a heavy cloud. I have indeed built a lofty abode for Thee; a house for Thee to dwell in forever."

The people fell quiet. Solomon turned toward them in silence. Then back to the altar. Kneeling with his face turned toward the wide, high sky, he spoke slowly and steadily to God: "Blessed be the Lord God of Israel. . . . I have built the house for the Name of the Lord God, and I have made here a place for the ark wherein is the covenant of the Lord which He made with our fathers when He brought them up out of the land of Egypt."

Still kneeling before the altar of sacrifice in front of the whole congregation, Solomon spread out his arms toward heaven. "O Lord God of Israel, there is no God like Thee in heaven above or in the earth beneath, who loyally observes the covenant with Thy servants when they walk before Thee with perfect devotion." His prayer poured from his heart for many minutes, filled with petitions for the people he ruled, and the Spirit of the Lord laid hold of the heart of the king as he called upon God to fulfill the promise that the descendants of David would always sit upon the throne of Israel and Judah.

It took seven years to build the Temple of God, but thirteen years of slave and skilled labor went into the magnificent palace which Solomon built for himself. And still another splendid house was built for the Pharaoh's daughter, the wife Solomon took in a diplomatic move with the weakened throne of Egypt. In fact, this Egyptian wife began what has been called Solomon's "united nations," composed of strategically selected wives from surrounding countries.

His wealth grew to a fabulous figure. He received about 20,000,000 dollars a year, beside mercantile taxes and the profits from the lucrative trade with the Arabian kings. His throne was made of ivory, overlaid with pure gold. All of his drinking utensils were solid gold. In short, "King Solomon surpassed all the kings of the earth in wealth and wisdom." And as representatives from all the known world came to consult him, their lavish gifts swelled his wealth.

At this period, less than five hundred years after the Lord God led the children of Israel out of Egypt, their king and their kingdom were the most famous and most powerful in the world.

It was into the splendid, towering realm of Solomon that a queen from a far away, primitive land rode one day at the head of a long caravan laden with still more gifts for the wise king of Israel. There was nothing unusual about her visit, generally speaking, but there *was* something unusual about the Queen of Sheba, herself.

The Queen with a Curious Mind

When the Queen of Sheba arrived at the court of Solomon, she presented him with great quantities of rare spices never before heard of in Israel, and 3,500,000 dollars in gold!

She also brought silk-lined caskets of precious gems. But to Solomon, the most interesting thing she brought was her unusually curious mind. The dark-skinned queen did not make the tiresome 1200 mile journey from her southland of Sheba (part of Arabia) merely to obtain ordinary advice from Solomon. True, they did make an important trade alliance, so that her land could share in the rich gold transport from near-by Ophir, but her visit had a unique feature. Unique enough for Solomon to request that it be written down by the court Chronicler. No other visit from any other potentate was detailed in the Court Book (Chronicles) which David had instigated during his reign. The account of Sheba is there, though, and obviously she made a marked impression on Solomon himself.

At the time of her visit, Solomon had so many wives and concubines (final official count 700 wives and 300 concubines!) that a woman's company was surely not novel to him. But Sheba was different. Being Solomon, he was not unmindful of her dark beauty, and yet the long hours they spent together apparently were marked by a provocative meeting of minds. At first, she asked him riddles. All of them he answered to her entire satisfaction.

From there, their conversation must have moved to more serious subjects.

"I confess I have come, Sire, with some skepticism about all that I have heard of your great wisdom and understanding. You are generous to have answered my riddles with such patience. Now, would you explain to me about your God?"

The queen and her subjects worshiped many gods, with Attar their chief god. But the queen's question was not asked in antagonism. She was not argumentative, and Solomon sensed it.

"Your question gladdens my heart, my Queen. I believe you are seeking more truth than can be found in the array of pagan idols you worship."

"I do seek truth, Sire. Wherever truth leads me, there I must go. I beg you to tell me of the God who has so prospered you and filled you with more wisdom than any man on earth!"

Hour after hour they talked, and Solomon told the Queen of Sheba about the Lord God. How He had called his forefather Abraham out of the pagan city of Ur and had established and protected the nation of Israel all the way down through almost five hundred years to Solomon himself, upon the throne of his powerful nation. The intelligent queen listened thoughtfully as Solomon impressed his great knowledge and intellect upon her.

Apparently nothing in her talk or her manner caused Solomon to think she was not fully impressed—with him. The actual thoughts of this strange, pagan woman were kept locked in the depths of her ample mind. There is no hint of her true reaction as she watched Solomon offer his lavish burnt offerings to the Lord God in the Temple. Considering, however, that Solomon numbered his wives in the hundreds (and surely she had been invited to stay!) it is evident that the queen saw through the superficiality of the man, Solomon, and realized that his wisdom and success came from a Source outside himself. This queen went home! Apparently not tempted at all to become another member of Solomon's feminine "united nations." She managed her trade alliance by her wits alone. Without doubt she was full of wonder at the riches and splendor and power of Solomon's dynasty, but she *did* go home. Her parting speech to the king did not praise Solomon the man, if one looks carefully beneath her well-phrased comment: "The report about your understanding and wisdom that I heard in my land was true; I did not believe it until I came and my own eyes saw it. Truly the half had not been told me; your wisdom and wealth exceed the report I heard. *Blessed be the*

Lord your God who was pleased to give you the throne of Israel.
Because the Lord loved Israel eternally, He made you king to rule
justly and righteously."

Not only did the perceptive Sheba give God the glory, she
tucked in a challenge to Solomon in the process! "He made you
king to rule justly and righteously."

Solomon's God impressed the foreign queen more than Solomon himself. She left the king and his splendor, but obviously
she took with her a living faith in His God. Because some 950
years later, "After Jesus had been born at Bethlehem in Judea during the reign of King Herod, there arrived wise men at Jerusalem
from the east (Sheba) inquiring, 'Where is the newborn king of
the Jews? For we saw his star in the east and we have come to worship him.' "

Women and the Kingdom's Downfall

"You must not cohabit with them, nor they with you, for they
will certainly turn your hearts to their gods." Over and over
Solomon had heard this warning of the Lord God. And yet his
harem swarmed with beautiful foreign women who had apparently no trouble at all persuading the king to follow the oriental
custom of building shrines to whatever pagan god the women
worshiped! The Temple of the Lord God of Israel was surrounded by lewd shrines to the goddess Ashtoreth, for his Sidon-
ian wives, and to the gods Milcom for the Ammonites and
Chemosh for the Moabites. In spite of two personal warnings to
Solomon himself from God, the wealthy king, in his old age, fell
into blasphemy because he could not resist the women he loved.

True to His promise to David, God did not tear the kingdom
away from Solomon during his lifetime. But as He had done during the closing years of Saul's reign, the Lord chose a new king.
The man's name was Jeroboam and he was one of Solomon's best
servants. In fact, the king had shown his appreciation for Jeroboam by making him overseer of all the conscripted laborers
from the house of Joseph. God made known His choice to His
prophet, Ahijah, who met Jeroboam one day alone in a field outside of Jerusalem. The amazed Jeroboam stood staring while
Ahijah tore his new robe into twelve pieces. This carefully done,
the prophet spoke to Jeroboam: "Take ten pieces for yourself,

for thus says the Lord God of Israel: I am tearing the kingdom out of the hands of Solomon, and I will give you the ten tribes, but he shall retain one tribe for my servant David's sake and for the sake of Jerusalem, the city I selected from all the tribes of Israel."

Also like Saul, when David had been secretly selected king, Solomon tried to kill Jeroboam, but he fled to Egypt and stayed there until the death of the king whose soul was not great enough to contain his wisdom.

The logical successor to Solomon's throne, his arrogant, shallow son, Prince Rehoboam, ended up with only the tribes of Benjamin and Judah, both of which refused to make war against the ten tribes of Jeroboam. The union between the north and south had never been any stronger than Solomon himself, and here, because Jeroboam weakened also and made idols for his people, began the disintegration of the once mighty united kingdom of Israel and Judah.

There was never again a united kingdom.

Chapter 18

A Pagan Queen and a Prophet of God

Jeroboam's failure to lead his people of the northern kingdom back to a firm faith in the Lord God brought generation after future generation into all manner of strife, including one bitter civil war. And it was out of this general chaos in northern Israel that a strong, ruthless military general named Omri brought the warring factions together by sheer force and made himself king of the north. He set up a rival capital to Jerusalem in Samaria, located in the highlands north of the City of David.

To protect the heavily walled city he built, Omri made an alliance with the Phoenicians on the northern coast, and as was customary, sealed it with the marriage of his weak-willed son, Ahab, to Jezebel, the strong-willed, ruthless daughter of Tyre's king.

When Jezebel came to Samaria, she brought with her much more than a lavish dowry. She brought a kind of satanic power of mind and purpose unlike any before unleashed against the faith of the Israelites! Jezebel's father, a priest of Astarte, the goddess-wife of Baal, had taught his daughter well. She burned to crush all faith in the Lord God and make Baal and Astarte the gods of Israel. Even before the death of her powerful father-in-law, King Omri, she had used her influence to have most of the priests of God killed. And when her weak-minded, pleasure-loving husband, Ahab, took the throne, Jezebel had the king himself taking part in the wild, lust-filled rites of Baal and Astarte! In no time, King Ahab bowed to her wishes and built an altar and a temple of Baal within the walls of Samaria.

It had never been too difficult for the emotionally unstable people of Israel to give in to pagan worship, and so it is no wonder they followed their king and his beautiful, evil queen.

But there was one man in Israel who feared God and who did not fear King Ahab or his pagan queen! His name was Elijah and he appeared one day in the midst of court proceedings and stood before the surprised king—tall, stern, and hard of body. Wearing a hair cloak, a leather girdle around his loins, and fixing the flabby king with his black, piercing eyes, Elijah cried: "As sure as the

Lord God of Israel lives, before whom I stand, there will be neither dew nor rain in these years except by my word!"

There was famine in the land and although the easily influenced King Ahab trembled at what Elijah blurted out in the Name of the Lord God, the prophet's warning was only insolence to Queen Jezebel. From that moment, the lean, heavily bearded prophet of God became her mortal enemy!

To protect His prophet from Jezebel's assassins who had murdered so many Israelite priests, God sent Elijah into the hills to live by the brook Cherith, from which he drank. Elijah was a rough, muscular man, well accustomed to life under the wide sky, and God sent ravens morning and evening to bring him meat and bread.

Then, when the famine had been in the land for three more years, God directed Elijah to go back to Samaria and show himself to King Ahab.

"Is it you, O troubler of Israel?" the king shouted at Elijah.

Elijah folded his strong, hairy arms and fixed the king once more with his stern eyes. "I have not troubled Israel, but you and your father's house have by forsaking the commandments of the Lord and going after the Baals."

The soft-faced, lightly bearded king shrank back in his big gilt throne chair and looked helplessly toward Jezebel who now stood defiantly giving Elijah stare for stare. The big-boned prophet took a step toward the two thrones and shouted an order which caused even Jezebel to sink back into her chair: "Now send for and assemble to me all Israel at Mount Carmel together with the 450 prophets of Baal and the 400 prophets of Asherah, who eat at Jezebel's table."

Even the Queen could not prevent her frightened husband from obeying the command of this rough mountain man. There was so much of God in Elijah that a king obeyed him without a murmur, and when all the people were assembled before Elijah, he walked up near the crowd and demanded: "How long will you lean to both sides? If the Lord is God, follow Him, but if it is Baal, follow him!" The people said nothing at all. There was only heavy silence, except for Ahab's nervous cough. Elijah walked up and down in front of the crowd. Then he shouted:

"I alone remain as a prophet of the Lord, while the prophets of Baal number 450 men." The people and their splendidly robed king and all the lavishly gowned prophets of Baal stared at the long-haired, sun-tanned man in his worn leather girdle. Not only did he look ludicrous in such regal surroundings, he looked— alone. But Elijah went on shouting his proposition to the assembled multitude. "Let the prophets of Baal provide two bullocks for us; then let them select one of the bullocks, cut it up, lay it on the wood, but set no fire to it. I, too, will prepare one of the bullocks, put it on the wood, but set no fire to it. You must call upon the name of your god, and I will call upon the Name of the Lord. The God who responds with fire is the true God!"

As soon as his daring broke over the crowd, the silence broke, too, and the people shouted, "The plan is excellent!"

From early morning until noon the next day, the 450 prophets of Baal, their bullock prepared and laid on the wood of the altar, called upon the name of Baal with all their strength. In relays, the 450 took turns beseeching their god to set fire to the altar. Elijah stood by enjoying the spectacle hugely, his big arms folded, his heavy eyebrows low above his black eyes which were darting here and there missing nothing that went on among the perspiring, pleading prophets of Baal. When they had grown almost too hoarse to shout, "O Baal, hear us!" they began to hop wildly around their altar, flinging their arms frantically in supplication to the god who remained absolutely silent and sent not one wisp of smoke near their sacrifices!

The foolish hopping was too much for Elijah, the man of wide spaces and deep silences before his God; and he began to tease the frantic prophets of Baal: "I suggest you shout louder, for he is a god and far away. Or maybe he's in conversation or has gone out!" Elijah walked among them, arms still folded, and still taunting, "I know, your god is on a trip! Or maybe he's asleep and must be awakened!"

By early afternoon, Elijah stopped his taunting and stood staring hour after hour at the growing panic among the frenzied priests of Baal, as they tried to shout louder in their efforts to rouse the silent god. Soon they were cutting their arms and legs with lances, so that their own blood flowed upon the ground where they stamped and hopped and jumped and raved like men gone mad, until the time for evening sacrifice.

Still there was no sound, no answer, no recognition.

In the evening, Elijah called the people to him, where he stood before the old unused altar of the Lord, now in ruins. Carefully he repaired it with 12 stones corresponding to the number of the tribes of the children of Jacob whom the Lord named Israel, so long ago. He then dug a trench around the altar a yard wide, arranged the wood, cut up the bullock and laid it on the wood. Next he amazed the people by ordering them to fill four jars with water and pour it over the sacrifice and over the wood! "Now, do it again!" Elijah shouted. They did. "Now, do it a third time!" And water ran all around until the trench was filled, too.

This done, the gaunt, bearded man raised his eyes to heaven and cried: "O Lord God of Abraham, Isaac and Israel, today let it be known that Thou art God in Israel, and that I am Thy servant, and that I shall have done all this in accordance with Thy word!"

The people fell back, gasping at what happened next!

Fire in abundance from the Lord came down and burned up the sacrifice, the wood, the stones, and the dust, and blazed and crackled over the ground until it had licked up every drop of water in the trench!

Elijah continued to look silently toward heaven, as the people fell on their faces and shouted, "The Lord, He is God! The Lord, He is God!"

All the prophets of Baal were seized and slaughtered, and before Elijah returned to the hills to pray for rain to end the famine, he had faith to say to the pale and trembling King Ahab, "Get up; eat and drink, for there is the sound of a downpour of rain!" Elijah intended to prove that the Lord, not the so-called "fertility god," Baal, controlled the weather conducive to fertility.

After climbing to the top of Mount Carmel, Elijah began to pray for the rain he had promised would come. Six times he sent his servant in vain to look toward the sea for a sign of the coming rain. The seventh time, there was a cloud the size of a man's hand, and soon the heavens were pouring rain in torrents from the wind-beaten, dark clouds gathered there.

Once during the three years of wandering under God's protection, before the mighty defeat of the prophets of Baal, Elijah had even been able to use the power of God to raise a widow's son from the dead. He had faced the 450 prophets of Baal with a faith that had no chink in it. The same faith gave him courage to promise rain to Ahab even before he had prayed for it. But when her frightened husband reported to Jezebel that all 450 of her

163

prophets were dead, she sent a message to Elijah which chilled the strong man's heart!

Jezebel threatened to kill him, and Elijah ran for the mountains! He traveled on foot for forty days and nights, all the way to Beersheba and beyond it to the wilderness of Sinai, where he took refuge in a cave on Mount Horeb, where God had given Moses the Ten Commandments.

Sitting alone and dejected, as the darkness already filling his cave home crept over the whole mountain of God, Elijah heard the Lord speak to him: "What are you doing here, Elijah?"

And the big, rough man with a suddenly weak and human heart began making high-sounding and quite unnecessary explanations to the God he had served so faithfully. "I have been most zealous for the Lord God of hosts; the Israelites have forsaken Thy covenant, Thy altars they have wrecked, Thy prophets they have slain with the sword, until I alone am left, and they are attempting to take my life!" God needed none of these obvious explanations. He already knew. But He also knew his prophet's human nature, and so He began all over with Elijah, as though he were a child who needed encouragement.

"Go out and stand on the mountain before the Lord."

Elijah crawled out of his cave and outside he was suddenly almost unable to stand on his strong legs. Such a mighty wind rushed by that it tore off portions of the mountain on which the prophet stood. Surely the Lord would speak out of that roaring wind! But no. When it passed, there was only silence. And immediately there was an earthquake which dashed huge boulders in pieces and tossed them down the black mountainside. Then, more silence. No word from the Lord. Elijah had scarcely regained his balance when the whole mountainside roared with a raging fire. He rushed for his cave and huddled there trembling. But when the fire was gone, the prophet knew God had not spoken in it either.

Then out of the thick silence around him inside the cave, he heard a whisper. Automatically, Elijah threw his coat over his face and stood at the cave's entrance, listening again for the whisper. It came. God repeated His question: "What are you doing here, Elijah?" And Elijah gave the Lord exactly the same explanation, ending with the same note of self-pity: " . . . I alone am left, and they are trying to take my life now!"

God did not explain in words that His voice is a still, small voice, a whisper, but He trusted His loyal follower to have learned the lesson. Neither did God sympathize with Elijah. He merely showed His caring and confidence by giving some specific orders: "Go back by the desert road to Damascus and when you arrive, anoint Hazael to be king over Syria; anoint Jehu son of Mimshi to be king over Israel; also anoint Elisha son of Shaphat from Abelmeholah to be prophet in your place. I will spare 7000 in Israel, none of whose knees have bowed to Baal and none of whose lips have kissed him."

Because He spoke in the stillness by a whisper, and not in a whirlwind or a fire or an earthquake, the Lord God showed Himself to be *more* than a "nature-god" or a "fertility god" as Baal was believed to be. He controlled the elements, but His word was to men personally, to Elijah and to 7000 Israelites whom He would preserve. And from the revolutionary orders He gave Elijah, He showed Himself also to be a God who acted within the framework of human history. Elijah's communion with the still, small voice of God did not turn him into a recluse or a mystic; it pried him out of his cave and sent him into action!

Elijah continued his semi-nomadic life, taking to himself young Elisha as a helper and preaching to the people, when any would listen, that they were to turn from worshiping pagan gods and revere only the Lord God of their fathers.

The big, bearded prophet had escaped Jezebel's threat successfully, but with Elijah gone on his preaching tour, King Ahab fell once more under her spell and sinned again against the God he had never had the courage to follow.

Miles apart, Jezebel and Elijah were still locked in combat for the soul of the king.

The Vineyard That Produced Blood

Weak, spoiled King Ahab shuffled like a pouting schoolboy past the alert guard at the entrance to his bed-chamber and threw himself on his luxurious bed, refusing to eat.

Two guards winked as Jezebel swept through the bed-chamber door a few minutes later and demanded to know why her king kept his face to the wall!

Ahab still did not turn toward her as she spoke, but his queen had long since given up trying to force royal manners from this ill-tempered weakling she married.

"I forgive you for not rising in my presence, *little* Israelite king," Jezebel's voice would have cut him deeply if he had not been so preoccupied with his own pitiable self. "But I do demand to know why you behave like this! What is so wrong, Ahab?"

The foolish king mumbled with his mouth half-hidden in a silk cushion. "I want that vineyard of Naboth's, Jezebel! It adjoins my land and I have my heart set on an herb garden where the vineyard stands." The king was whining now. "But Naboth has refused all my generous offers! He won't sell it to me!"

Naboth, as an Israelite, had a right to refuse even the king, since by law all the land belonged to God and each man could keep his own inheritance and not be forced to sell. None of this impressed Jezebel, however. Her training was purely commercial and she pounced on Ahab accordingly: "Do you not exercise the kingship over Israel? Look at you, snivelling there like a whipped dog! Rise, eat and be of good cheer. I will give you the vineyard of Naboth the Jezreelite!"

Being Ahab, he went along with Jezebel in her murderous plan. She found two wastrels who agreed to vow they had heard that good citizen, Naboth, curse both God and the king! According to law, the people stoned the hapless man to death, and Jezebel swept arrogantly once more into the king's chamber where he still pouted with his face to the wall.

"Rise now, and take over the vineyard—Naboth is dead!"

Ahab kissed her hand and gave her a quick hug on his happy way to the vineyard he now owned.

Elijah had always had a way of appearing suddenly when least expected. And certainly nothing could have jarred Ahab more than to have been confronted at the far end of a lush row of grapevines by the tall, accusing figure of the wandering prophet of God!

Ahab's shoulders slumped and the smile sagged on his face, as he mumbled, "Have you found me again, O my enemy?"

Elijah's voice caused the heavy grape clusters and Ahab to tremble: "I have found you because you have committed yourself to do evil in the sight of the Lord. The Lord has told me to warn you that He will bring calamity upon you and your house. As for Jezebel, the dogs shall devour her in the valley of Jezreel!"

In his heart, the weak king had always meant to worship the God of his fathers. But he was no match for Jezebel, and as he listened to the words of the prophet, his heart was crushed with shame. Jezebel tried, but this time she could do nothing when Ahab tore his garments, put on sackcloth, fasted—even slept in sackcloth, and went about with a sad countenance. She taunted and teased, but not one woman trick brightened poor Ahab's face. And God gave the stupid king and Elijah a deeper look into the true nature of His own heart when He said: "Do you see how Ahab has humbled himself before Me? Because he has humbled himself before Me, I will not bring on the calamity in his lifetime."

No calamity struck Ahab in his lifetime, but Jezebel met her prophesied end, and the dogs devoured her beautiful body, when, in a later uprising among the people, she was thrown from the palace wall and died in the street below!

Elijah's departure from the earth was as dramatic and unusual as his sudden appearances had been during his long and ruggedly faithful life. He was taken up in a whirlwind by the Lord God, in the presence of his loyal successor, Elisha, who became a staunch prophet of God in the hectic years to follow.

Elijah's strange supernatural exit from this world, by way of a visible chariot and horses, which swept him from the sight of his beloved helper, Elisha, in no way showed God to be contradicting the factual way he had worked through Elijah right in the main stream of human history. In fact, it merely presses home the reminder that even though He moves in the everyday events of daily life, God is not limited by time. This same Elijah was going to stand some 900 years later on the Mount of Transfiguration, along with Moses, and talk with Jesus of Nazareth in the presence of three stunned fishermen!

God's ways are so much higher than the ways of man that He *can* move with and in spite of the tide of human history and remain true to His overall purpose to redeem His beloved world.

Jezebel had met her predicted tragic end, but she had left her fatal mark upon the Northern Kingdom through her son. And as the increasing pressure from Assyria began to weaken the Hebrew nation, God was forced to begin to work more and more through individual prophets. In order to continue His loving outreach toward His chosen people, through whom He was going to bring the Redeemer.

Chapter 19

Judah and Israel Are No More!

On tablets of baked clay, and gouged into stone obelisks, is the silent but unmistakable proof that the Assyrian people to the north left a record of cruelty and ruthless ferocity. Their conquests were massive and they disrupted whole populations which had been in existence for centuries. Among these was the once powerful Northern Kingdom of Israel. Weakened from within once more by their persistent return to idol worship, the people heard the prophet Amos cry: ". . . a basket of summer fruit is my people. The end is come upon my people of Israel, and the songs of the temple shall be howlings."

The Assyrians were a haughty race of strong warriors, bearded, long-haired, and boastful of their conquests. During David's and Solomon's reigns the nation lay fairly dormant, but soon after, Assyria became more and more of a threat to the Northern Kingdom of Israel. King Omri escaped destruction by paying a high tribute to the Assyrian government. Weak King Ahab had managed to turn them back with the help of Phoenicia and Syria, but when Tiglath Pileser III (called Pul) came to the throne, the Northern Kingdom was in grave danger. Pul and his maurading hordes beat their way steadily southward, conquering all the Northern Kingdom except a small amount of land around the fortified city of Samaria, which held out on its mountaintop for a short time and then fell to Sargon II.

More than 27,000 people living in Samaria were carried off to Assyrian cities. The ten tribes of the Northern Kingdom quickly disappeared into the Assyrian empire and into Egypt, and were never heard from again! God had told Elijah and Hosea that the Northern Kingdom would fall because of its idol worship and internal decay and that prophecy came true.

Judah, to the south, was left standing alone, shrunken to a pitifully small size. Even so, it was richer than the Northern Kingdom, Israel, had been. Its main cities—Hebron, Bethlehem, Gaza, Beeroth, Gibeon, Gibeah, Jericho and the capital at Jerusalem—were still flourishing. King Hezekiah made a sincere effort to turn the people back to the Lord God, as did a later king, Josiah. The Temple, which had been allowed to fill up with rubbish before it was closed altogether, was opened and cleaned out, and for the first time in centuries the Israelites once more found the scroll containing the Law given to Moses. Not only had the inner resources of the people dwindled during the preceding years of idol worship, but the discarding of the sanitation laws alone brought lower living standards and an outbreak of disease.

Both Hezekiah and Josiah made valiant efforts in behalf of the Lord God, but Josiah was killed in battle, leading his small forces against the raiding Egyptians.

The Assyrian kingdom had meanwhile been divided between the Medes in the north, and farther on down the Euphrates River, the Babylonians. It was only a matter of weeks until the ruthless and powerful Babylonian king, Nebuchadnezzar, captured Jerusalem. His forces stripped it bare and took away into captivity some 5,000 people and the cream of the young men from among its nobility, among them the young prophet Daniel. And when the puppet king, whom Nebuchadnezzar put on the throne of the fallen Judah, dared to rebel against the Babylonian cruelty, the beautiful city of Jerusalem was leveled to the ground, Solomon's temple was gutted by fire, and most of the people sent away into captivity in Babylon.

In spite of God's efforts to protect these people whom He loved, the once powerful, united kingdom of Israel and Judah had ceased to exist anywhere on His earth.

169

Chapter 20

A Twig Shall Shoot Forth

During the last chaotic years of Judah, God raised up a prophet with a message shot through with a strong, bright shaft of positive enlightenment. Whereas Amos had described the judgment as "thick darkness with not a ray of light in it," Isaiah could see "a great light" breaking upon the "land of deep darkness." True, the prophet Isaiah, who ministered during the short, choppy reigns of five kings of Judah, did not fail to exhort the people concerning their sinfulness before the Lord God, but a new note flashed within the message of Isaiah: "A twig shall shoot forth from the stump of Jesse, and a Branch from his roots shall bear fruit. The Spirit of the Lord shall rest upon Him . . . . Comfort ye, comfort ye my people, says our God. Speak heartily to Jerusalem, and shout to her that her warfare is completed, that her iniquity is pardoned, that she has received from the Lord's hand double for all her sins."

Through the reigns of Uzziah, Jotham, Ahaz, Hezekiah and into the reign of Manasseh, the clear voice of the poet-prophet, Isaiah, would not be stilled by any apparent disintegration in Judah. He had heard the direct word of the Lord. He had been permitted to see into the very heart of the God of his fathers—surely more clearly than anyone had ever seen before! Not once did he fail to remind the people of their sinfulness, and of God's punishment (through the gentile Assyrian nation), but Isaiah had seen more. He had glimpsed, however dimly, the sure image of a shepherd God who would guard the small remnant who had never worshiped a false god.

"He will feed His flock like a shepherd; He will gather the lambs in His arms, carrying them in His bosom and gently leading those that are with young."

Isaiah's message shouted the glorious news that this same God is also a Redeemer God. "For your true husband is your Maker, the Lord of hosts is His name, and the Holy One of Israel is your Redeemer; He shall be called the God of the whole earth."

170

The people heard, but few really listened. Their ears had been banged too long by the brassy, dark rhythm of pagan idol worship. The Creator God a shepherd? Speaking tenderly to His people?

And more amazing than all this, Isaiah dared to speak of a strange Suffering Servant who would bear the guilt of the people for their sins! Perhaps not even Isaiah understood why he spoke of this Suffering Servant. Why he said that "He was pierced for our transgressions; He was punished for our iniquities; (that the) punishment which procured our peace fell upon Him, and with His stripes we are healed."

It was not a new message from a prophet of God that "All we like sheep have gone astray . . ." but it was new and strange and cloudy in the minds of the few devout ones who heard that " . . . the Lord has laid on Him the iniquity of us all!"

Who was He? Who was this Suffering Servant of the Lord? Was it Israel itself? Surely all Israel was suffering, but Isaiah's message seemed to point to one representative Israelite who would come from the line of David, from the root of Jesse to be Immanuel (God with us)! Someone who would come as a child: "For to us a Child is born, to us a Son is given; the government shall be upon His shoulder: and His name shall be called Wonderful, Counselor, Mighty God, Everlasting Father, Prince of Peace."

A strange, yet unknown Child would be called the Mighty God? And would there, could there be *peace* for the rebellious, suffering, seemingly cast-off children of Israel?

Isaiah did not predict a coming kingdom which would be merely an improved age of David. Rather he wrote of a return to the harmony and bliss of the Garden of Eden! "The wolf shall live with the lamb, and the leopard shall lie down beside the kid . . . the nursling child shall play over the asp's hole, and the weaned child shall reach its hand in the snake's nest. They shall not hurt or destroy on all My holy mountain; for the earth shall be full of the knowledge of the Lord as the waters cover the sea."

One day man would know God as He really is, and there would be peace on earth!

No details were given, but the new note of joy and hope throbbed steadily through the message of Isaiah: "There shall be no end to the increase of His government or to the peace upon the throne of David and upon His kingdom, in that it is firmly es-

171

tablished and supported in justice and righteousness from now on and forever."

No wonder few listened as Isaiah poured out his strange, prophetic message throughout the reign of five kings. Some must have thought him mad! Wasn't the Northern Kingdom already gone? And wasn't Judah being weakened by its enemies every year? How could this man cry that the throne of David is firmly established?

The throne of David was gone! And the throne of Solomon! And when at last some time after Isaiah's death, Judah also collapsed and was no more, who but a few thoughtful ones could have taken the message of Isaiah seriously?

Surely Isaiah himself must have wondered in awe and confusion at his own theme. No Child had been born upon whose shoulders the government could rest!

Isaiah's prophetic message poured itself relentlessly into the time of the final decay of Judah, like a Bach fugue coloring its main theme with the bright counterpoint of new motifs. His main theme cried that God was not limited to human history! That human affairs are not governed ultimately by historical events, fate or chance, but by God. He saw the whole stream of history through God's eyes, with Redemption as much a part of God's responsibility as Creation! Isaiah saw history in the bright light of divine purpose moving steadily from beginning to end. He saw that the Creator is the Redeemer and the Redeemer the Creator. "The everlasting God" was still in charge to Isaiah, and around and through the main theme of the fact that God would send an Anointed One to inaugurate His own kingdom, coursed other strange new motifs whose meanings could not have been clear even to Isaiah. A voice, he said, would cry: "Clear the way for the Lord in the wilderness; make straight in the desert a highway for our God . . . ." To whom would this voice belong? Did Isaiah think it was his own? There is no indication that he did, but how was this to happen? This way-clearing? And when?

Another mysterious motif sang through the main theme of God's coming kingdom at a time when it must have made no sense at all. "Silently listen to Me, you islands; let the peoples renew their strength . . . .Who raised him up from the east, whom righteousness called to service? Who placed nations in subjection to him, and made kings submit to him? . . . " Of whom did Isaiah prophesy here? During his lifetime, Judah had not yet been taken captive into Babylonia. Judah had not yet fallen! God was planning to influence even a gentile king (Cyrus) to rescue His people from their captivity, but who could have realized this before the captivity had taken place? Isaiah died before the crushing out of the remaining two tribes of Judah, having seen none of his message come to pass, but he had declared it with a clear voice because he heard it from the Lord who was moving His divine purpose along to bring redemption and release through His still beloved children of Israel.

To the chaotic, scarcely enlightened minds of the people who listened to Isaiah in the wilderness of their pagan worship and crumbling national events, voices crying in a new wilderness about a Child yet to be born, cried almost in vain. But among those who were taken into Babylonian captivity under King Nebuchadnezzar were some who had remained faithful in their hearts to the God of their fathers. Whether or not they understood the meaning of what Isaiah had said, their faith was still alive.

And God had spoken truly through Isaiah of what would occur, so there could never be a suspicion in anyone's mind that God had been taken by surprise!

Chapter 21

God Worked Through a Pagan King

Because of their persistent idol worship, God had allowed the powerful Assyrian nation to overrun all of Israel. Moving within and yet controlling even the flow of human history, He broke up their false existence as a kingdom in order to bring in His kingdom according to what He alone knew of lasting reality.

Assyria was a pagan nation. And God did not hesitate to use a pagan king, Cyrus of Persia, to rescue His small remaining remnant of faithful ones from the captivity in Babylon. But before the words of His prophets came true, the people of Judah learned an entirely new way of life in Babylonia where they had been taken captive when Nebuchadnezzar overran Judah.

The Babylonian captivity was at once a time of suffering and education into a new and more progressive way of life. The Israelites (who had now come to be known as Jews, because they came from Judah) were farmers and herdsmen by tradition. In the prosperous, splendid city of Babylon, they learned new trades. There were teachers, craftsmen, shopkeepers and bankers among the captive people. The citizens of Babylon wondered how some of the Jews could be suffering as they seemed to be in the midst of such apparent comfort and security. Instead of the spare, rugged hills of Judah, were fruitful plains. The waterways and roads of the great empire swarmed with traffic. Irrigation canals were fringed with willow and palm and fruit trees. Babylon was a magnificent city of high walls and towers and hanging gardens; of colossal temples with tall, regal portals. But it was not home to the Jews. True, some who had never really worshiped the Lord God adjusted quickly and made the most of the situation materially. Still, many of the people felt forsaken of God. Jeremiah the prophet, writing from Judah, reminded them that the Lord had loved them with an everlasting love. He declared that the Lord would build their nation again, but most important that He would forgive their sins and that they would return to their own land one day.

Some clung to this letter from the shy, gentle prophet Jeremiah, but most of them could understand little of it. After all, their beautiful Temple had been burned to the ground. The ark had not accompanied them on the tragic day they filed miserably through the ruined gates of Jerusalem into pagan captivity. How could their sins be forgiven without the Temple and the familiar blood sacrifices offered by their priests? The faithful among them gathered by the beautiful Babylonian waterways to sing the dear, familiar songs of their homeland, but usually they wept and hung their harps on the willow trees, unable to sing.

Among those in captivity was another prophet named Ezekiel to whom the people turned with their question: "Look at the magnificent Babylonian temples in which they can worship. And we have none at all. Does that mean their gods are greater than the Lord God?"

Ezekiel struggled for words adequate to express the majesty and greatness and holiness of the Lord. He reminded them that it was their own wickedness that brought their downfall and captivity. "The gods of Babylonia are nothing! And Babylonia will one day suffer for its sins. Read what the prophets have said."

Together the unhappy Israelites read and studied the words of Amos and Hosea and Micah and Isaiah. Each one had spoken like Jeremiah, declaring that their doom was due to disobedience. Realizing this, they felt only more doomed. But Ezekiel told them that if they would return to the Lord and ask forgiveness, He would forgive them fully.

In captivity, with Solomon's Temple destroyed, God managed to get them to a place of new insight about Himself! They found they could study their Scriptures together and worship Him in their hearts even without a Temple. Instead of offering sacrifices in the Temple, they fasted to atone for their sins. In this personal sacrifice, Ezekiel's words became more real to those who believed. A great desire for obedience possessed them! And some of them began to see that God did not choose them because of their merit but because of His love. Here the Scriptures of Isaiah became suddenly vital. The Israelites received some peace in the face of their gnawing questions about their great suffering. Isaiah had said that it was not only because they had sinned that they suffered in captivity. Some came to see that whoever would be God's servant would suffer in a sinful world, and that somehow that kind of creative suffering would bring other people nearer to the true God. That through suffering, the faithful would somehow learn obedience. With Isaiah's writings they comforted themselves in the thought that the Lord had a great and surprising plan up ahead. A plan that concerned a Redeemer-King. That God would not desert them, any more than a mother would desert her child.

They were comforted, but their questions burned within them because nothing had really changed. They had read what Isaiah wrote concerning the fact that the Lord would use Cyrus the Persian as His instrument to free them and restore them to Israel, a respected people once more. But there was no sign of anything like this anywhere!

True, God was giving local signs for their encouragement, along with the words of the prophets. Daniel, a faithful prince of Judah, had refused to worship in Babylonia except in the tradition of his fathers. For his act of disobedience, Daniel was sentenced to die in a den of lions. But when the king went to the den, he found Daniel safe and the mouths of the lions sealed by the Lord whom Daniel continued to worship! Even before this direct sign from God that He was still in charge of His own, three Jewish young men, friends of Daniel, had been sentenced to death in a fiery furnace by Nebuchadnezzar. Their sentence came because they also refused to worship the golden pagan idol. As the king and his counselors watched, they saw inside the roaring furnace—not three, but four figures! And Shadrach, Meshach and Abednego, the three Jewish young men, were not even scorched. Once more the Lord God Himself, in the form of a man, had appeared to save His loved ones!

These signs and wonders were some consolation to the homesick Jews in captivity, but understandably their hearts were heavy most of the time. Heavy with loneliness for their homeland and heavy with questions concerning when God would once more rescue them from a plight into which they, as a nation, had plunged.

But what they didn't know was that already the power of Babylon was being undermined. During the reign of Belshazzar, the king who succeeded Nebuchadnezzar, a strange and terrifying thing happened which once more showed that God was in charge, even of human history! As the king and his drunken guests drank from the golden vessels stolen from the Temple in Jerusalem, a man's hand began to write on the wall in large letters! Only Daniel could interpret it, "And this is the interpretation: God has numbered the days of your kingdom and brought it to an end. You have been weighed in the balances and found wanting; your kingdom is divided and given to the Medes and the Persians."

Even then the Medes were taking over Babylon!

When Cyrus the Persian became king, the seventy years of captivity ended. Just as the prophets had said, he released the Jews in Babylon, returned the golden vessels and all the other furnishings stolen from their Temple, and told them they could go home! Some of the Jews by that time preferred the already established wealth of Babylon, but most of the faithful went back to Judah and began the rebuilding of their land. The Temple they built this time was not as magnificent as Solomon's Temple, and some of the older Jews wept the day it was dedicated to the Lord God. But it was theirs and the people were grateful. Perhaps this time Temple worship meant more than at any other time in their history. In exile, at least some had learned the potential of a personal relationship with the Lord God, and leaders like Ezra and Nehemiah helped them to continue seeing more and more of God's plan for them.

Because many Jews lived too far from the Temple in Jerusalem for regular worship, synagogues began to be built throughout the land—smaller meeting places where the people could worship and be taught from the Scriptures concerning the Word of God to them, given through the years by their faithful prophets. More and more curiosity was aroused concerning the message of Isaiah that one day an Anointed One would come, on whom the Lord would lay all their iniquity! He would be gentle and humble and would do no wrong. They puzzled among themselves because the prophet said they would despise and reject Him. With all their hearts they longed for a mighty Messiah who would set up His own kingdom—their kingdom! How could He be put to death like a common criminal as the prophet said? Some of the more devout truly yearned over the part of Isaiah's message which assured them that this Suffering Servant would make up for all the sins of the world and that through Him God and His world would be reunited. At least they longed for their own sins to be blotted out. There is no sign that they were much concerned about the sins of the whole world.

Jeremiah said the Messiah would be "a Man of sorrows and acquainted with grief." Hadn't they known enough sorrow? How could their coming King be sorrowful if they were going to be restored as a powerful nation on the earth?

The prophet Zechariah had said another confusing thing. He declared that the One who was coming would be just and meek. To make his statement more graphic, Zechariah had even cried: "Look! our King comes to you, riding upon an ass . . .!"

This was not the kind of King they could accept. After all, David and Solomon had been majestic kings and powerful rulers. But there *was* the hope in their hearts. Someone was coming! And life wasn't too unbearable under the Persians, and they were at home once more.

In their semi-darkness and confusion, some even found themselves attracted to one particular saying of the old introverted prophet, Jeremiah, who wrote: "Behold, the days come, when the Lord will make a new covenant. He will put His Law in your inward parts. In your *heart* He will write it!"

Perhaps gloomy Jeremiah saw more clearly than anyone else that no hope lay in a national kingdom. God would have to do it another way!

Four Centuries of Silence

Little is known of the actual history of the Jewish people over the next four hundred years. But through the years in which Israel lived under Persian rule, the Temple rites were carried out with solemn faithfulness. No matter how far a Jewish family lived from Jerusalem, where the new Temple stood, the members of that family were united in worship with all Jews each morning and evening through the burnt offering on the altar in the great inner court of the Temple. The offering was a lamb, with flour and a libation of wine. Before dawn each day, a solitary priest made his way toward the altar where a fire was kept burning. Aside from the flickering altar fire and his slow sandaled step, there was no movement in the high-vaulted sanctuary other than the long, stretching shadows laid slant-wise by his robed body along the side walls of the silent room. In his hands he carried gold implements to remove the ashes piled up during the night. Then the Levite priests entered the Temple, chanting psalms, as still others trimmed the lamps, divided the lamb to be sacrificed and placed it on the stone grid which covered the sea of fire upon the altar. Finally, the prescribed prayers and benedictions were intoned in the Temple, empty of everyone except priests.

To most Jews, these sacrifices were only form. To the devout, they were gifts to God. All across the Jewish area around Jerusalem, in their homes, the people read psalms of penitence and thanksgiving as the silent priests carved and offered the sacrificial lamb in Jerusalem on the Temple altar. Not infrequently whole families would travel the long, dusty miles from their homes to Jerusalem, feeling closer to God because they were nearer His Temple. Some longed to have His law engraved on their hearts, as Jeremiah had said. Others thought only of the Temple when they thought of God, and in their materialistic minds, prosperity was the desired result of worship. Still others swayed between the two viewpoints. But all Jews, at least, were taught that one day God would send the Messiah. In this they were united.

In fact, for the first time in her history Israel was held together mainly by her outreach toward the God of Abraham and Isaac and Jacob—regardless of the motive. But in the twilight time before the promised Redeemer came, soon even the sacred Temple worship took on an idolatrous flavor. The priests and Levites and Temple servants saw to it that every rule regarding Temple worship was obeyed with care. In fact, they went so far as to write scores of new rules and regulations. On the theory that it is better to do more than God requires than too little, they began sorting the wood used for the sacrifice piece by piece, tossing out any piece with even one wormhole in it! If a priest had a temporary blemish of any kind on his body, he could not serve in the Temple until he was healed. Their attention to correct regulations caused many to forget the heart of the prophet's teachings.

Large groups of learned men known as scribes (lawyers) spent their time studying religious law and explaining it to the people. Everything was majestic and intricate and elaborate and meticulous—but it required so much time and attention most of the people sank back into semi-confusion and spiritual dullness.

The prophets had tried to show them that God was the Creator and Lord of the whole world. But the exclusive Israelites found this difficult to believe. At least to act upon.

One man named Jonah was ordered by God to preach repentance to the pagan people of Nineveh, the capital city of Israel's long-time enemy, Assyria. Jonah, like so many other Jews, was not interested in his enemies. He followed the God of Abraham!

He was all for that God, and he was convinced that the God he followed was all for him. Or at least, all for the Israelites. Reasoning that the Assyrians had caused God's people to suffer so much, Jonah got on a ship and sailed in the opposite direction! In a violent storm, he was forced overboard and was swallowed up by a huge fish God had maneuvered to the scene. There sat Jonah in the stomach of the mammoth fish—as captive as the hearts of the Israelites who shared his self-righteous, exclusive philosophy! He did repent, was coughed up on dry land, and went to Nineveh after all. But he didn't expect any good to come of his preaching there. God had not acted at all the way Jonah preached! "You will be punished for your crimes!" the disgruntled servant of God thundered at the citizens of Nineveh. Instead, they repented and turned to God and were not punished at all.

Jonah's mood was black when God spoke to him, as he sat under a withered gourd vine, steeped in self-pity and loathing for the heathen to whom he had just preached. "Jonah, do you have a good reason to be angry about the withered gourd?"

"I have good reason to be angry, enough to die!" Jonah complained irrationally. God admonished him for feeling grief over a vine too withered to give him shade, when Jonah had nothing whatever to do with the vine's growth! "Then should not I feel grief over Nineveh, that great metropolis, in which there are more than 120,000 persons who do not know the difference between good and evil?"

Some of the Israelites recognized themselves in Jonah's story. But their solution to national pride and prejudice was merely to revise their already complicated laws! And there sprang up among them a cult (the beginning of the Pharisees) whose sole aim in life was to see to it that everyone obeyed every jot and tittle of the law.

Under the cruel King Artaxerxes Ochus, toward the end of the Persian rule, more devastating trials came to the Jews. Various parts of the empire rebelled against him and hundreds of Jews were killed in the uprisings. Those who prided themselves on their strict observance of the law complained to God that they had suffered enough as a nation! Others called to Him for continuing mercy.

When Alexander brought his huge armies east and defeated the Persians, the High Priest surrendered Jerusalem, and although

Alexander spared the land, Palestine might as well have been under Greek rule. The vested-interest, high priestly faction (known later as Sadducees) were so influenced by Hellenistic thinking that they no longer believed in life after death. Judaism was threatened from within by its own priests! Some Palestinian cities became Greek in population and government, and many Jews moved to all parts of the known world. Judah was ruled as a sub-province of near-by Syria, but the High Priest and his senate governed it, and in time Greek gods were worshiped in the Temple itself!

A few believers remained true to the Lord God, however, and when the inevitable conflict came, the bloody, guerilla rebellion was led by a believing Jewish Priest named Maccabeus (the Hammerer). For a short period (166 to 63 B.C.), the victorious Maccabees ruled, but the independent Jewish state soon fell to Rome, the new world power. A brilliant, erratic, brutal non-Jew named Herod was forced, by the last of the Maccabees, to be circumcised and to embrace Judaism. The Roman Emperor, Augustus, made Herod King of the Jews, and Rome seemed about to absorb the small Jewish remnant and its faith in the God of Abraham. But the new threat once more forced the people to return to the Scriptures concerning the Anointed One, who would come to bring God's own rule to the world. The few faithful had never stopped reading, but now the learned materialists, impatient for Hebrew supremacy, reread Isaiah's promise that "a twig shall shoot forth from the stump of Jesse, and a Branch from his roots shall bear fruit."

In the city of Jerusalem the scribes and Pharisees sat reading the most important prophecy Micah ever made and wondered about the small neighboring town of Bethlehem, where David was born: "As for you, Bethlehem Ephrathah, little as you are among the thousands of Judah, from you shall He come forth to Me, who is ruler over Israel . . . and He shall be peace."

Some hoped for a warrior king—others for a mighty being from on high, who would come on the clouds of heaven, to establish an everlasting kingdom on earth. At any rate, when the Messiah came, He would surely be the King of the Jews!

In the desperation of daily life under Herod and the tyranny of Rome, the Jews clung more and more to everything that made them different from the other peoples of the earth. They further

181

complicated their rules and regulations for Temple worship, added to their food laws, their ritual cleansings, and even excluded all non-Jews from their daily lives. If they would continue their strict observances of their law and their worship, God would surely one day bring glory to Israel!

A party known as the Zealots (Jewish nationalists, regarded as traitors by the Romans), worked night and day for converts to their cause. They were not content to wait. The Zealots were enraged by the double taxation—tax to the Roman government as well as their own Temple tax. They took it for granted that God would prefer them to die rather than live under a foreign power. They saw that their Hebrew high priest, along with the other hereditary priests and the whole Greek-influenced party of Jewish Sadducees, was more and more swayed by Roman customs and thought. Even their modest Temple, built after the Babylonian exile, had been torn down by ambitious King Herod, who insisted upon "pleasing" the political-minded Jews with a magnificent new one!

The scribes and the Pharisees were constantly annoyed with the Zealots. But in their way—although it was a way of appeasement and bargaining with Caesar's government, they, too, confidently believed in God's judgment upon Rome and the ultimate triumph of Israel by a mighty act from on high.

Outwardly, since Rome ruled the world, there was peace. But a new kind of idolatry was abroad among the chosen people of God and it could well be called religio-political intrigue!

No one had worshiped Baal in Israel for more than four hundred years, but under the polished, silk-robed, religious exterior of the times, a serpent of godless self-seeking bit its way deeper and deeper into the heart of the true religion of Abraham. The Jews in power seemed no longer to worship the Lord God; rather, they worshiped their "exclusive religious approach," and they made frequent use of it in their connivings with Rome.

In small houses on outlying farms, and herding flocks of sheep on the rocky hillsides outside the large cities, were still to be found the true followers of the Lord God. But the Romans worshiped Caesar and the metropolitan Jews worshiped their religious laws! The end result was a society prospering from without and rotting from within.

It was a civilized time. Art flourished. The silversmiths and goldsmiths were stunning craftsmen. Government was systematized and firm. The palaces, gymnasiums and sports arenas were more magnificent than even Solomon could have dreamed.

It was also a bloody time. In the huge sports arenas the Romans introduced the chariot race and although it was a social event of high color, mangled bodies of hapless charioteers were dragged for miles along the blood-caked ground of the wide track over which high-bred horses pounded for tortuous lap after lap. The savage chariot races were held in the architecturally splendid stadia and arenas built by Herod the First—a monarch whose psychopathic obsession with his throne smeared his entire reign of 41 years with not only the blood of priests and small children, but with the blood of his own family, including his most adored wife and three of his own sons.

It was a bloody time in another way, too. A slow, quiet, agonizing way. Criminals were nailed to heavy wooden crosses thudded into deep sockets in the ground and left to stand until the gaping crowd had watched the last drop of living blood drain away.

2000 years before, God had made a covenant with Abraham alone under a wide, quiet desert sky. The Lord God told the sensitive, thoughtful, faith-filled man that He would make of his seed a great nation. Six hundred years later, He reaffirmed His covenant through Moses, to the descendants of Abraham gathered on the rocky side of Mount Horeb. And the covenant still stood for the Jews who milled busily about their own affairs through the narrow, crowded streets of Jerusalem during the reign of Herod. And especially for those who lived in quiet faith on the hillside farms and in the villages beyond the intrigue-riddled city, in the year 5 B.C.[1]

---

[1]Since the birth of Jesus Christ divided not only history, but time as well, it would seem to be confusing that the date generally designated for this birth is 4 or 5 B.C. However, "the calendar which most of Christendom observes is known as the *Gregorian*; it was established by Pope Gregory XIII in 1582 and adopted in England and her American colonies in 1752. Its initial date, 1 A.D., was supposed to have been the year in which Jesus was born. This system of reckoning time originated with Dionysius Exiguus, a Roman abbot, who worked it out during the sixth Christian century. But the good abbot, using fragmentary knowledge of his time, erred by somewhere between four and six years" (*Story of the Bible World*, Nelson Beecher Keyes: Hammond, p. 123).

Chapter 22

In Bethlehem of Judah

The three dusty, sun-tanned travelers walked rapidly up the long stone staircase at the court of Herod the Great, who was called by Rome the King of the Jews. They had traveled to Jerusalem over the same 1200 hot, desert miles Sheba's curious queen had traveled more than nine centuries before to visit another Israelite king. There were differences, however. The queen's caravan was loaded with gold and silks and spices and other lavish gifts for Solomon. The three excited travelers who approached the inner court of Herod's magnificent combination home and fort left outside a small caravan, and they did not come to visit the present King of the Jews. They were only stopping at Jerusalem, hoping to find someone who could give them the directions they needed to get to the One who had just been *born* King of the Jews!

One of the three travelers spoke for the others. His voice trembled with anticipation and excitement, in spite of the weary miles of travel. These men were seeking Something so important to them that even their bodies were energized by the thought of it.

"Where *is* the newborn King of the Jews?"

Herod's chief counselor stood before them, frowning. "Herod is the King of the Jews, by appointment of Caesar Augustus. We know of no other king!"

The spokesman for the three travelers leaned toward him eagerly. "But we are astronomers and we have seen and followed the new King's star from the east. We have followed it over 1200 miles and we thought surely we could find exact directions here in Jerusalem. You see, we have come to worship Him!"

The skin whitened on the old counselor's face. If Herod knew there was another threat to his throne, anything could happen. While he was still in good health, his monstrous jealousy had driven him to murder the members of his own family who laid claim to the throne. Now, Herod was fatally ill of a disease no physician could control. He was in constant agony and these days the violence within him spewed forth against anyone who crossed him unintentionally. The situation was one even the wise old counselor refused to handle. And so the three travel-stained men were taken quickly to ask their question of Herod himself.

All three men knelt before the king, their heads to the marble floor at the foot of his throne. Herod sat slumped to one side of the big, ornate, gold chair. His face was bitter and drawn with suffering.

The spokesman for the astronomers from Sheba lifted his head from the floor to ask the same question again. As he spoke, the other two raised their heads also. These were the truly wise men of Sheba, but there was an almost childlike eagerness about them. A simplicity and authority that struck terror to the tormented heart of Herod.

"We saw and followed His star in the east and we have come to worship Him. Can you tell us where we may find this newborn King of the Jews?"

Herod struggled to his feet, his pain-filled body twisting with fear and fury. Forgetting to keep their heads bowed, the three excited travelers looked steadily up at him from their kneeling positions at his feet. The courtiers and attendants around the throne room stood more rigidly stiff than protocol demanded. They were terrified. Each one knew Herod's vicious nature to be capable of any action he felt might protect himself. And in his dying state, he would not hesitate to vent himself on the people of Jerusalem in general.

For a moment there was such a quiet in the big hall that everyone heard one traveler's sandal scuff sharply on the marble floor, as he thoughtlessly shifted one leg in his kneeling position.

Then Herod surprised everyone, except the three astronomers who had no idea what to expect. The ailing king swayed, steadied himself on the arm of his throne, and then sat down again quietly. For Herod, even his voice was quiet as he addressed them: "So you followed a star all the way from your land."

"Yes, Sire, His star—and if you can tell us where we might find Him, we want to go at once to worship Him."

Herod knew that any show of fear on his part could bring new uprising against him among his people. Herod was not a Jew by birth, but he had adopted the Jewish faith for political purposes and perhaps he reasoned that should there be a child king born by divine will, as the prophets declared, it would make good sense that a heavenly star might appear!

A plan began to form in his sick but still active mind. He sent the travelers away to be refreshed and called the Jewish chief priests and scribes to appear before him at once. When they were assembled, he demanded to know where the promised Messiah was to be born.

A short, well-fed scribe unrolled the scroll in his hand and read from the prophet, Micah: "And you, Bethlehem, in the land of Judah, are by no means insignificant among all Judah's rulers, for out of you a leader shall arise who will shepherd My people Israel."

"So the Messiah will be born in the little neighboring town of Bethlehem, eh?" Herod dismissed the scribes and priests impatiently. His mind was on other things now. And he managed to be quite civil to the three travelers, whom he summoned once more to his throne.

"You will be glad to know that I have found out for you where this Messiah is supposed to be born." Herod leaned toward them confidentially. "I have emptied the room of people, so that we might converse alone. I intend to ask a favor of you. But first, I have a question. Just when did this strange star appear in the sky?"

The men thought a moment, then their spokesman said: "We have been traveling for many months, Sire. But we have observed the star for no longer than two years."

Herod leaned toward them confidentially. "Very well. Now, I have learned that the child is to be born in Bethlehem—just a few miles away. It should be easy for you, who have traveled so far, to find him in a town as small as that. Go and find out every particular about the child and when you have learned this, report to me so that I too may come and do him homage."

If Herod had not emptied the room, he would never have dared to make such a rash statement. But the three travelers had not been in Jerusalem long enough to get the full picture yet and so they thanked the scheming king, bowed again, and set out immediately for Bethlehem.

By nightfall the star moved steadily ahead of them, as it had done for all the 1200 miles, and then it stopped in the sky directly above a small, one-roomed, dried brick cottage, with scattered shoots of grass growing on the flat, mud-covered roof.

The three visitors dismounted from their tall camels, took the ivory inlaid boxes handed them by their servants, and each carried a box in his hands as they walked slowly toward the doorway of the small, modest house over which the star stood. Their steps were no longer strides. They were men approaching a holy place and a holy thing.

The doors of these Palestinian houses were never closed in the daytime, but at night they were locked from the inside when the family went to bed on the mats piled across the rear of the upper level.

Inside there was a stirring among the few animals kept always on the ground level at the front of each home. One cow lowed softly, half asleep. A few nervous sheep complained. And then in answer to their firm knock, a man's voice called to them from inside the house. They would have to identify themselves clearly. No one took a chance in the black Judean night. The hill country was full of robbers.

In answer to the man's question, the spokesman for the three called out: "We have seen the star of the newborn King in the east and have come a long way to worship Him. Pray, may we see Him? We have come far for this moment!"

A few minutes passed, the men too tense with excitement and awe to speak even among themselves. The animals stirred and complained more loudly and then they heard someone unbolting the wooden door from the inside. When it creaked open, there in the flickering light of the olive oil lamp the travelers saw the sleepy face of a big, gentle looking workingman, with tousled graying curls covering his head and the lower part of his face. He smiled at them, as though he were not at all surprised to see them. It was not the first time anyone had come like this to find out about the new Baby.

"If you will be kind enough to wait until my wife is ready, we will be glad to have you come up to our quarters to see Him." Joseph's voice was low and as gentle as his eyes.

The three men stood in the earthy smelling animal enclosure, holding their gifts. From upstairs they could hear the kind of soft mother talk which keeps a just awakened child quiet. There was nothing unusual about rousing a simple workingman's family from sleep, except that their hearts pounded and their hands trembled, holding the boxes of costly gifts. They might have been asking directions and this same scene could have happened anywhere in Judea. But their hearts did pound and their hands did tremble and they knew themselves to be approaching the Great Moment of their entire lives.

The Baby responded to His mother's soft talk in the language only mothers understand, and in a moment, the big, bearded, kind man rejoined them and gestured hospitably toward the narrow stone steps that led to the upper quarters where the little family lived.

At the top of the short stair, the men stopped in amazement. Not so much at what they saw—a small, round-faced Hebrew woman standing almost shyly beside a rectangular cradle, surrounded by the meager comforts of her tiny one-roomed home. They were amazed because their weariness dropped away the moment they stepped into the room where the Baby lay, wide-eyed and watching from the cradle.

Their host walked to his wife's side and smiled at them warmly. She smiled, too, then.

"I am Joseph, a carpenter," he said simply. "And this is my wife, Mary. And here is the Baby you have come to see."

Holding their gifts of costly spice and incense and gold, the three travelers knelt before the cradle and worshiped. And no one in the room thought it incongruous that three highly educated scientists would be worshiping a tiny Baby in a carpenter's house in the dark of that night. Strange, yes, but not incongruous.

When the men had laid their gifts on the wooden floor, something in Mary's smile and Joseph's words made them feel it was the natural thing to do to sit down as guests in their home. Joseph assured them they could ask any questions they wanted to ask. "We'll try to answer them. There is still much we do not know. Mary and I are simple people."

"Two years ago we first saw His star in the sky. We are astronomers."

Mary, modest, but impressed that men of such high learning should visit her, bowed in acknowledgment of their rank. But a small smile made her large, oriental blue eyes light up in spite of her modesty. And she spoke for the first time.

"Joseph, did you hear? They saw His star!"

"Twelve hundred miles away, in the far off land of Sheba, and we have traveled here to find the One we knew to be born King of the Jews."

No one asked how they knew this, but one of the men did say: "Many years ago, the Queen of Sheba made the same long journey to visit another king of Israel, named Solomon. She came back believing in the Lord God."

Mary's blue eyes grew wider. "Oh, yes! I remember hearing the story of her visit. And here now, you have come to see my Son." It was more than she could take in. "And it is so far, too." Her soft, breathless voice trailed off, and to hide her intense wondering, she turned and adjusted the Child's covering. He had gone back to sleep.

Joseph helped Mary bring honey, leben (a kind of yogurt), parched grain, cheese and flat thin loaves of barley bread to their guests for refreshment. The men sat cross-legged on the floor and the conversation was amazingly easy in spite of their guests' educated minds and foreign culture. Somehow the presence of the sleeping Baby made them comfortable together.

"Will you tell us about His Coming?" the men asked of Joseph. It was customary for the man to do the talking, but it was also customary for the man to order his wife to prepare food for his guests, and Joseph helped Mary. "I believe these circumstances are such that my wife should tell the story, gentlemen. Certainly you deserve to hear it, you have come so far."

Story in the Night

Mary sat on a small pile of cushions beside the cradle, always within reach of the Child. She smiled and then looked away from the visitors, back into the strange, holy events of the past months. No one could miss her great serenity now, but it had not always been this way.

"Joseph, shall I tell them about Elizabeth, too?" The young woman's large eyes turned dependently toward her gentle, bearded husband, who sat cross-legged on the floor beside her. "I cannot tell about His Coming without telling about Elizabeth, too. They are so bound up together." She turned politely back to her guests and explained, "Elizabeth is my cousin."

"By all means, Mary. You tell it as it happened to you."

Anyone could see the depth of Joseph's love for her. And yet, he seemed to be not a part of the Event, as a woman's husband would be. He was *in* It, with his whole heart. But somehow *outside* the Event Itself. His big calloused hand reached for her hand as she started to talk.

The visitors listened eagerly as Mary began her simple, reverent telling of the heavenly invasion of the lives of the God-fearing, humble folk involved in the strangest story ever lived out in human history. She spoke slowly and almost shyly at first, but then more easily. Mary was at home in her story, in spite of her wondering heart. The parts she did not understand came as simply as the few she understood. When it all began, she had felt walled away in a high-turreted, unfamiliar heavenly enclosure—alone. Now, as she looked at the Baby asleep beside her, the awesome unfamiliarity of what had happened to her seemed somehow grounded and made bearable. He was her Baby. She was fulfilled as mothers are fulfilled the world over, and although she never forgot who He was, His very Baby humanity put her at ease with life. At ease even with these three distinguished visitors by night in her humble home.

"It began before my husband, Joseph, and I were married. We lived in Nazareth of Galilee, I with my family in my father's house not far from Joseph's carpentry shop. I was betrothed to Joseph, and excited as only a young girl can be, who looks forward to the day she will belong to the man she loves as I love him. I sat alone one spring evening in front of my father's house, grinding barley for the bread my mother and I would bake the next day. I thought of nothing in particular. But I was singing a little psalm of thanks to the Lord God for my blessings to come, when suddenly I knew Someone else was there!"

Mary's words came more quickly now. The holy excitement of that Moment remained with her. "I looked up from my grinding into the face of the kindest and most beautiful Creature I had ever seen! He smiled at me before he spoke. I sat holding the handle of the mill in my hand. His voice was clear and quiet. 'Greeting, favored lady! The Lord is with you.' I was frightened to the depth of my soul! He seemed to know this, because he went on talking even more gently to me. 'Have no fear, Mary, for you have found favor with God. And observe, you will conceive in your womb and give birth to a son and you shall call Him Jesus. He shall be great and shall be called the Son of the Highest, and the Lord God shall give Him the throne of His father David. He shall be King over the house of Jacob forever; there shall be no end to His kingdom.'"

As she talked, Mary clasped her hands tightly together, remembering the confusion and perplexity and awe in her young heart at such news!

"It was a lovely spring evening. I remember I heard a redstart sing in the olive tree above my head, and then I caught my breath enough to ask: How shall this be, since I have no husband yet? Still smiling at me to show me he understood my confusion, the Angel said: 'The Holy Spirit shall come upon you, and the power of the Highest shall overshadow you and therefore that holy Offspring shall be called God's Son.' When he said this, I covered my face with my hands. The message was more than I could bear! He was silent awhile, and then he helped me greatly by telling me about Elizabeth."

Mary paused a moment and straightened the covering on the Baby, who had stirred slightly in His sleep. This quieted her and she went on.

"The Angel took a step toward me as though to reassure me further. 'Your cousin Elizabeth is to be mother of a son in her old age, and this is her sixth month, who was called sterile. For nothing is ever impossible with God.' My ears did not quite believe what they heard, but my heart did. Suddenly, my heart knew this was no dream of a young girl! I bowed before him and said all I could say: "Here I am, the Lord's servant girl. Let it be with me as you say.""

Joseph sensed the emotional strain on Mary and helped her along quietly. "The Angel left her then, gentlemen. And the next day—without being able to tell me why, my Mary left for the hill country in Hebron, where her cousin Elizabeth and her husband, the priest Zacharias, lived."

Mary went on. "Until then I had known nothing of Elizabeth's miracle. And indeed it was a miracle. But the moment I walked in the door of her house and greeted her, the old woman began to speak to me in a strong, clear voice, as one filled with the very Spirit of God! 'Blessed are you among women and blessed is the fruit of your womb. And how did this happen to me, that my Lord's mother should visit me? Just think, when the voice of your greeting reached my ears, the babe leaped within me for joy! And blessed is she who believed that the things told her by the Lord shall be accomplished.' My own heart leaped for joy, too! Surely the Lord Himself had told Elizabeth. She could have known no other way. And she had called my Baby—her Lord! My own lips broke into praise, too. My soul magnified the Lord and my spirit was glad in God my Saviour, for He took notice of the lowliness of His servant girl. I knew that from that moment on, all generations would call me blessed, for the Almighty had done great things for me. He had sustained Israel, in remembrance of His mercy, as He had promised our fathers, from Abraham through all his descendants forever."

Joseph laid his hand on Mary's shoulder, sensing the weight of her emotion. "Mary stayed with her cousin, Elizabeth, for three months after that. I was greatly puzzled that she did not come back to Nazareth. I missed her so. And I knew nothing of what she has told you. But God sustained me and the time she spent with Elizabeth was a holy time."

Mary was quiet for several minutes, remembering the good, deep hours spent with Elizabeth. Hours of holy sharing and wonder at what had happened to two simple women. Hours in which the old woman found solace and peace after the terrifying ordeal of facing childbirth at her age. Elizabeth's prayers for a son were answered, but her years bore down upon her as her time approached, and with Mary, the burden lightened. The joy of God's direct action in their lives took over for them both. The high-walled exhilaration in which Mary had lived before Elizabeth knew of her miracle became all quiet joy. The suspense was bearable and the loneliness and distraction vanished.

One of the visitors spoke for the first time. "What had occurred with your wife's cousin, Elizabeth? Can you tell us that, Joseph?"

"Oh, yes!" The big carpenter's eyes shone. "Her cousin's husband, the priest Zacharias, went into the Holy Place to offer the morning incense upon the golden altar. Suddenly, he was not alone there! An Angel stood with one hand resting on the altar and promised Zacharias that the old man and his wife would have a child. They had both long ago given up hope of such a thing. Zacharias was stunned, and more so when the Angel told him that the child would be no ordinary child, but that he would have a special role in the coming Redemption! That his birth would herald a new era for all men everywhere. Of course, every Jew who trusted God believed that the awaited Messiah would not come until the prophet Elijah first returned to the earth to announce His coming and to prepare the people to receive their King.

"The old priest Zacharias heard the Angel say that his son would be the expected forerunner of—of the Christ, the Anointed One." His voice vibrated with perhaps a still deeper realization of Who it was who lay in the cradle beside Mary. "Zacharias could not truly believe it, though. It was too much for him to believe that his son would preach in the power of Elijah, with the power of God upon him from before his birth!

"The Angel told him to call the son John, and to rear him in the strictness of the Nazarite law. Old Zacharias wrung his hands and stared in disbelief. And until the day of the birth of the baby, he could not speak a word! He had to write when he wanted to talk. The miracle of his lost speech brought belief to his heart, though. Their son was born, just six months before Mary's son, and the moment Zacharias wrote that he should be called 'John,' God loosed his tongue."

The big man looked in open adoration at the Baby, sleeping soundly in the cradle he had made in his own shop.

"Mary returned in three months from visiting her cousin and told me of her condition. Of course, I was shocked. Frightened, too, because the law calls for death by stoning for an unmarried woman with child. My heart was torn in every direction. I knew Mary did not lie to me, and yet it was so strange."

Mary interrupted shyly. "Dear Joseph wanted to give me a letter of divorcement and put me away privately, so no one would know or accuse me of a shameful thing. But Joseph *believed!*" This seemed all important to her.

"Then I had a dream," Joseph said quietly. "An Angel of the Lord appeared to me also and said, 'Joseph, son of David, be not afraid to marry Mary, for what is conceived in her is from the Holy Spirit. She will give birth to a son and you will call Him Jesus, for He will save His people from their sins.' When I awoke, I remembered the words of our prophet, Isaiah, who had said, 'The virgin shall be with child and shall bear a son and they shall name him Immanuel, which means, God with us.' That prophecy was about Mary! Then I began to see that the Lord God had done all that needed to be done to give simple folk like us the certainty we needed. We didn't understand very much, but we knew the

Lord God was acting. Mary and I were married, and it was my joy to conserve her virginity until He came."

Joseph and Mary both smiled at the Baby. "His Coming was difficult for Mary. You see, Caesar Augustus had decreed that all the world should be taxed and that meant a complete census had to be taken. Everyone had to go back to the city of his birth. Mary and I are of the line of David, born here in Bethlehem. It was the hardest time of my whole life, that trip from Nazareth. She was brave and did all she could to keep me from worrying myself to death before we got there! Seventy miles on a donkey with the Baby due any time would have been too much for most women. Not for my Mary. And not for Him. But by the time we reached Bethlehem on that last night, everyone else had reached it first, it seemed. I ran all over the town trying to find a place where Mary could at least lie down and give birth to her Baby."

"Finally I found a stable dug into a cave in the hillside behind one of the big inns here in town. At least there would be straw for Mary to lie upon, and the time had run out! I carried her into the stable, elbowing cattle and donkeys out of my way as I went. We felt strange, and my heart was breaking for her—but she was magnificent. And—and——"

Joseph's voice broke with the memory and Mary took the story tenderly again. "And—we were not alone. God was with us, and His Son was born into the world. It was even warm in the stable with all the animals around. I wrapped Him in the swaddling clothes we had brought along and then laid Him in the clean straw Joseph piled in a manger."

The three visitors from Sheba looked at the sleeping Child and bowed their heads to the cleanly swept floor of Mary's house in Bethlehem. Joseph and Mary looked at Him too, and their hearts also worshiped Him.

After awhile, Mary once more picked up the story with tenderness and wonder. "You gentlemen will want to know this, too. There were, in the fields outside the city, some shepherds keeping watch over their flock that night. As though by another miracle, these men came straight to the stable where we were with the Baby. They looked as though they had seen a vision as they tiptoed in to look at Him. We were so surprised to see them! Joseph and I didn't know anyone knew we were there. And the shepherds were followed by several townspeople, too, who had become curious.

"We all marveled at what they told us had happened to them just at the time He was being born! An angel of the Lord had appeared to them, too, out in the field, and the glory of the Lord shone all around them. Of course, they were frightened. But the Angel said to them, 'Have no fear, for behold, I announce to you the good news of great joy that shall be for all the people; for today there is born for you in the city of David a Saviour, who is Christ the Lord. And this is a token for you: You will find the Baby wrapped in swaddling clothes and lying in a manger!' Then they told us that suddenly there was right there with the Angel, a multitude of the heavenly host, praising God and saying, 'Glory to God in the highest and on earth peace among men of His favor.' Oh, you should have seen their faces when they went back to the field that night, glorifying and praising God for everything they had heard and seen, just as it had been told them. I remember Joseph remarked that these were simple men, who had taken time always to worship and to believe the Lord their God. But none of us understood His Coming in such a humble way."

For a brief moment Mary seemed almost to hope for some enlightenment and help from the three educated visitors. "Oh, I have so much I am pondering in my heart! So much." When she said no more about it, Joseph went on with the story.

"After eight days, according to Hebrew law, we had Him circumcised and we named Him 'Jesus,' as the Angel had told us to do. Then, after the 33 days set aside by law, we went—the three of us—to the Temple in Jerusalem, for Mary's purification and to present Him to the Lord."

Joseph saw that Mary wanted to tell this part of the amazing story. She was young, and now and then excitement caused her to forget her natural shyness.

"As Joseph and I were walking into the Temple for His dedication, an old man of Jerusalem, named Simeon, hurried up to us and took the Baby Jesus in his arms and began to speak to the Lord God loudly and tearfully. He held Him close to his old breast and cried: 'Now Thou lettest Thy servant depart in peace, Lord, in agreement with Thy word, for mine eyes have seen Thy salvation, which Thou hast prepared before all the nations, a light for revelation to the gentiles, and a glory to Thy people Israel.'

195

Joseph and I couldn't grasp it all then. This pious old man recognized Him! He called Him the Lord's *salvation*. God had prepared his heart, too. He was looking for Jesus! And he knew Him at once. Joseph spoke at length with him about it."

"Yes," Joseph said, "Simeon told me the Holy Spirit had told him that he would not see death before he had seen the Lord's Messiah! The old man recognized Him all right. He certainly did."

Mary's eyes clouded then and her voice showed its first anxiety. "He blessed us before he left the Temple, and said more strange things which have left us wondering greatly. To me he said, 'See, this Child is appointed for the falling and rising up of many in Israel and for a sign that shall be *contradicted!*' Then his old eyes which had bored into me, turned tender and filled with tears. I just stood there, holding the Baby and waiting for him to speak again. He said, 'And a sword shall pass through your soul, so that the reasonings of many hearts may be revealed.' What he could have meant by a sword that will pass through my soul, I cannot think. And how it will reveal the reasonings of many hearts, I do not know." She shook her young head wonderingly. "There are so *many* things I do not understand!"

Joseph laid his hand on Mary's head to comfort her. "Yes, there are many things we do not understand. But one thing we know. The Lord God did not allow Him to be born unannounced. That same day in the Temple, an old widow—in her eighties—also approached us. In her youth she had only known seven years of married happiness when her husband died. The rest of her life she never left the Temple, worshiping day and night. She too lived close enough to God so that she recognized Him and gave thanks to the Lord and talked about Jesus to all the people standing around!"

Joseph was thoughtful for a moment. "Many know about Him already. They are all simple folk, but many know already."

"I confess I am anxious because so many know about Him," Mary murmured. "Joseph understands better than I, but King Herod-"

"Herod!" The visitors looked at each other and for the first time remembered the promise to the strange, vicious man Rome called King of the Jews. "We told Herod we were searching for the new King! We asked directions from him."

Joseph stood up alarmed, not quite sure why he felt as he did, but instinctively he knew he must protect Mary and her Baby from hearing more. Covering his fear, he offered the men shelter in their small home, but they refused and after opening their gifts of gold, frankincense and precious myrrh, they gratefully took their leave.

That night the three men were warned by God in a dream that they should not return to Herod to tell him of the newborn King, as they promised they would do. So, they went back to their own far-off land of Sheba by another route.

Another Dream for Joseph

Joseph and Mary sat watching the Child sleep for a long time after their distinguished visitors left. Mary seemed engrossed in the Child and her thoughts. What on earth would they do with such costly gifts?

Joseph was noticeably disturbed, still not able to put Herod out of his mind. He didn't know the three travelers had broken their promise to Herod and had gone home by another way. He only knew of Herod's violence and that he would stop at nothing—not even the murder of his own sons, if he feared for his throne.

"I believe I'll sleep now, Joseph." He held her in his arms a moment and then helped her spread the soft pile of mats where she slept. Mary was tired. The telling was almost like reliving for her.

Joseph slept fitfully, and long before dawn he sat bolt upright, rubbing his eyes to hurry the return of full consciousness. He had dreamed again! This time a dream of intense urgency. An Angel had once more appeared to the great-hearted, trusting man, saying, "Rise! Take the Baby and His mother and escape to Egypt. Stay there until I tell you, for Herod is about to search for the Child in order to murder Him."

Before dawn broke pink and gold and gray-gold over the bleak Judean hills outside of Bethlehem, Joseph and Mary and the Baby were on their way south, fleeing toward the Judean border into Egypt.

When Herod discovered he had been outwitted by the three astronomers from Sheba, his anger flamed into a blood and tear bath for the parents of boy babies two years old and under in all the city of Bethlehem and its outlying areas. They were all murdered by order of the king. Hebron, where Elizabeth and Zacharias lived, was not included in the cruel edict, so the baby John was unharmed.

In a few months, the ruthless, hate-filled life of Herod the Great twisted painfully to a close. And once more the Angel of the Lord appeared to faithful Joseph in Egypt in another dream, saying, "Rise! Take the Child and His mother and cross over into the land of Israel, for those who were seeking the Child's life are dead."

Back in Israel, Joseph apparently wanted to settle in Bethlehem, instead of returning to Nazareth. In all ways his great heart was open to his beloved wife, Mary, and her Son, and he feared the gossip back in their home town. When the little family returned from Egypt to Bethlehem, however, Joseph, whose heart was open in all ways to God, too, once more experienced a divine warning that the Baby would be safer in Nazareth. Herod's son Archelaus had succeeded him to the throne, and his reputation was as bloody as his father's had been.

With his usual obedience to God, Joseph took Mary and the Baby and began the journey back to Nazareth, trusting God to handle everything. The trip was a happy one this time. It was spring, and they traveled leisurely north from Bethlehem, along the Joppa road as far as the great caravan route crossing at Lydda, then across the plains of Sharon and Esdraelon, spread riotously with wild flowers.

Mary sang to her Baby, and Joseph smiled and made plans for their life together in the little Galilean hill town. From His mother's arms, as she rode atop the same faithful donkey which had carried them both to Bethlehem for the census, the Child, growing steadily more aware, watched the sky create its moving cloud-world, blue and white and gray above Him. And His mother hugged Him gently every time she heard a redstart sing— remembering the other spring evening when she first learned of His Coming.

Chapter 23

Childhood in Nazareth

No one paid much attention to the little northern town of Nazareth in Lower Galilee. People laughed at it mostly. Especially did the intellectuals down south in Judea scoff at the colloquial speech and unscholarly piety of its people. In fact, no one ever expected anything good to come out of Nazareth. Much of Galilee was Hellenized, but along the streets and roads of Nazareth, on its little hill cupped in the lower slopes of the Lebanon Mountains, lived the simple, faith-filled country folk of Jewry. They were earthy people and, unlike the self-conscious, arrogantly pious Judeans, most Galilean Jews were healthily aware of their beautiful countryside and of God.

There was far more than a negative reason for Joseph and Mary to return to Nazareth. Bethlehem, in Judea, would have offered only rigidity and confinement to the growing Boy. In Galilee, people took time to be normal. In sharp contrast to the gray and barren Judean hills, the very landscape of Galilee tossed joy and adventure and discovery into the hearts of growing boys and girls. There were green hills to climb and blue lake water where a boy could fish to his heart's content. According to the rabbis, it was easier to rear a forest of olive trees in Galilee than one child in Judea! A boy would discover things in Galilee, and learn all he could contain, growing up among the warm-hearted, generous-spirited, country folk. There were good and bad people in Nazareth, as in any other town, but they took time to enjoy life according to the promptings of their hearts—right or wrong. They were not people poured into a stuffy mold of their own making, like the Judeans.

Among the naturalness of these people in this flower-spangled countryside, Jesus spent the longest period of His earthly life. Here, in the earthy normalcy of Galilee, He was free to be True Man. Here He learned to fish, and to laugh when one of His brothers lost a big one or caught one bigger than His own.

Here He found out about seed-time and harvest, so that He could express life in terms simple enough for anyone to understand. On the sloping farms of Galilee He discovered that a grain of wheat must fall into the ground and die before it can spring out of its hull into a full head to be ground for bread. Here, watching His mother bake Joseph's favorite flat barley loaves on the hot sides of a big earthen jar, He learned the sacred value of bread itself.

Playing around the lush vineyards, He watched the hard green grape swell to purple because it was attached to its parent vine. He thought about the grapes which could have matured on the branches the husbandman cut off and burnt in a crackling, fragrant fire outside the vineyard. The workmen liked Him and one of them explained carefully that the remaining grapes would be bigger and juicier for better wine because some of the branches had been pruned.

One day He laughed along with the other children when, by accident, a workman poured some new wine into a row of stiff, old skins. The explosion made an exciting sound to a boy's ears, but His active mind also grasped the loss to the vineyard's owner.

He spent a lot of time sitting on the side of His favorite hill across from the city, where He could see Nazareth sprawling briefly on its own little hill; and He was proud of it because it was His home town. Travelers passing by were bound to see it. It was a city set on a hill and it made His boy heart glad that it could not be hid. To a growing boy it was an exciting city, too, because the hill on which it was built had the advantage of being honeycombed with caves and ancient tombs. An arrangement to delight any boy's love of mystery. And of course, the caves and tombs made good hiding places.

Like every other boy in the devout Jewish home of Galilee, He started school when He was six years of age. But His training had been going on since infancy by example and the patient, loving explanations of Joseph and Mary. As soon as He was old enough to toddle, He followed His mother around the house as she performed her woman's religious duties—preparation of the Sabbath meal, kindling the Sabbath lamp, setting aside a portion of the dough from the bread. And even before He could walk, His alert child eyes must have been attracted to the bright metal case of the *Mezuzah*, attached to the doorpost and inscribed with the Name of God. Mary's duty also was to keep the *Mezuzah* in place and polished, and as soon as He could listen, she must have begun to teach Him that it was the symbol of the divine guard over the homes of Israel. As soon as He could reach it, He too touched the little metal case containing the folded parchment Scripture and then kissed His fingers, as He had seen his parents do every time they went in or out their front door.

Jewish parents kept their children entranced hour after hour with the romance and adventure of the true stories of their ancestors, the chosen people of God. And long before His first day at school, He was intimately familiar with the traditional rites and festivals of Israel. Joseph, His earthly father, was bound by the Torah to teach Him, even if it meant missing a meal. So by school-age learning was a part of His life.

Seated on the ground in the synagogue, alongside other boys His age, in a semicircle around His teacher, He was taught the Law, how to avoid vice, how to learn gentleness, how to see all sin as repulsive. Jesus and His classmates were never taught to avoid sin merely to avoid its terrifying consequences.

From six to ten years of age, His only textbook was the Bible. From ten to fifteen, He was taught the Mishnah, or traditional law; after fifteen, Rabbinical studies.

During the time Jesus was being taught the Mishnah, when He was twelve years of age, He had an experience of high adventure for a boy from the country town of Nazareth. For a year He knew He was going to be allowed to go with His parents to the annual Feast of the Passover in Jerusalem, almost a hundred miles away! The carefree, normal Galilean days rolled slowly toward the great day. He attended school, helped His mother grind the barley, went with her to Mary's Well for their daily supply of water, watched the crocuses, then the cyclamen, then the blooming flax and other lilies of the field come and go, and when the winter wheat was ready, so was the Boy. It was His twelfth year and the big journey was up ahead!

The day before Jesus and His parents left for Jerusalem, He slipped away from His brothers and two sisters and walked alone to His favorite spot on the side of the hill north of Nazareth. Naturally, He was excited about the trip to Jerusalem, and He had worked fast that morning helping to pack. Before He left for the hillside, He stopped in Joseph's carpenter shop to sweep up the piles of sawdust and the fragrant curls of wood under the work bench. This was never a chore for Him. He was intensely interested in learning Joseph's skill. Something in Him responded enthusiastically to the idea of creating beautiful and useful things with His hands.

"They're good hands, Son," Joseph said often. And never too often to please Him. Invariably, He smiled broadly and stretched His even, broad-nailed fingers as though to get them ready for the day He could work there, too. Beside that, He loved to please Joseph, and the two seemed closer sometimes than Joseph and his own sons.

"You do a good job of being the oldest one, Jesus. I watch You with the others when You aren't aware I'm watching."

Jesus' smile came quickly and it was a grateful smile. He loved Joseph deeply.

He rounded the last turn in the narrow, steep path and sat down on the hillside to think. It was a habit of His to work fast and finish His chores in time to do this. Sometimes His brothers thought Him strange. He fished well, and He could climb trees, and already He could handle the sawing of the rough lumber for Joseph. But He did like to sit alone and think, and His brothers laughed at Him for this. In reply, He merely smiled. Or sometimes He looked so serious they ran away.

On the day before the big journey to Jerusalem, He did a lot of thinking, sitting there on the little grassy plot He loved, stretching down from the base of a big rock that made a fine back rest.

To the south, He could see the plain of Esdraelon, and His well-taught mind raced back through the centuries, picturing the armies of Israel battling their hated enemies along its rolling floor. His thoughts of the bloody slaughter which had taken place over the flower-filled valley did not rouse Him to want to be a soldier and exhibit His prowess by "slaying his ten thousands" as David had done, however. His thoughts of strong-bodied young men dying in their own blood and the blood of their enemies filled Him with revulsion and pity. He did not think of whole armies moving magnificently under their high-colored banners. He thought of each soldier as a human being, with flesh and bones like His own, and a heart to be torn open uselessly by an enemy spear, and healthy, red blood to be spilled. His eyes grew moist as he thought of the families who mourned the death of these men.

He thought of each one of His own Hebrew ancestors who had died there, but He also thought of every Egyptian and every Assyrian who had pitched headlong from a rumbling iron chariot like a helpless doll, to roll and writhe and eventually to die in the mixed blood of the nations who hated each other for hatred's sake. He thought also of those who spilled Philistine and Bedouin blood on the same beautiful plain. Hebrew, Egyptian, Assyrian, Philistine, Bedouin—all living parts of God's beloved world!

Still looking at the plain of Esdraelon, His human heart swelled with the strange nearness He felt for David, and He pictured him leading his outlaw band back and forth over the same plain, trampling the flowers and flattening the soft, wild grasses. He experienced, as though it had been His own, the sharp grief David felt when his beloved friend, Jonathan, and King Saul fell in death somewhere on the same plain.

It was a clear day and He turned His deep eyes toward the west. There was the great, sturdy ridge of Carmel, where Elijah challenged the prophets of Baal to prove whose God was the true God.

Eastward, He could make out the white marble walls of the cities of the Decapolis, glimmering witnesses to the strange, fierce new civilization which had come to His country with the Roman conquest. On His way home that evening, He stopped to watch a not uncommon sight—a Roman legion, pounding along the rocky Galilean road toward a Decapolis city. The sun was dimming for the day, but at least half of the Roman gold eagles flashed incongruously in the quiet country evening.

He walked slowly toward His home, looked for and saw the light of the flat oil lamp already flickering through the high window just under the roof. He thought of His beloved mother, preparing supper. He thought of Joseph, closing the shop with the quiet carefulness of a good man who loved his work. He thought of David again. He was descended from the line of David. David was a great man. A great king. But He had killed so many men in battle that God could not allow Him to build the Temple. Even David.

The twelve-year-old Boy shook His head and wondered about many things as He quickened His steps now, remembering there would still be much to do before the big departure tomorrow for the Feast of the Passover in Jerusalem.

It took a week to make the journey from Nazareth to Jerusalem. The slow-moving line of friends and kinsmen from Nazareth grew in length and laughter and song as it wound happily over the rough roads, south through the otherwise forbidden land of the Samaritans toward the Jordan, which they would cross east of Jericho, and begin the long fourteen-mile climb to Jerusalem.

Mary laughed and waved and indulged in lively woman talk with the friends and distant kinsmen who joined them from this town and that on the way. Except for the annual trip to Jerusalem for the Feast of the Passover, most of these simple folk had no way of seeing each other. All up and down the straggling caravan of travelers ran waves of the latest gossip and the familiar remarks of inevitable surprise that this boy or that had grown so much!

"Yes," Mary smiled, watching Him stride up ahead with the other boys, "Jesus is twelve now." She always seemed to infer so much more than she actually said about Him. And gently, uncomplainingly, beneath her joy in Him, she carried the old perplexity in her heart.

Joseph swung into step beside Him, and encircled His broadening shoulders with his arm, affectionately.

"Well, Son, how does it feel to be one of us now?"

The Boy smiled up at the gray-haired man. "It feels fine, Father. I'm very grateful to you for letting me come."

He was growing tall. His brown head reached to Joseph's shoulder as they walked along together, singing with the others, psalms of praise to the Lord God for what the greatest of all the holy festivals really meant—the exultant commemoration of the day Moses led the Hebrew slaves to freedom out of Egypt. Jesus felt a part of every Jew on his happy way at that moment, from all parts of the known world, toward Jerusalem. His young heart beat faster with the passing of every day. For the first time, He was a part of the pilgrim throng, marching to the Holy City of God. He would actually see the walls and towers of Jerusalem. He would pass through her gates and walk up and down her ancient streets where prophets and priests and kings had walked, and He would listen carefully for the sound of every sorrow and hope which had ever beat their way through the strange, glorious, tragic history of His people in the Holy City.

They arrived in Jerusalem the day before Passover, and Jesus walked and walked for hours along the narrow, stone streets. At twelve, He was an accomplished scholar and He gave His fine, young mind time to roam back through the centuries with His people.

His heart filled to the brim with a strange, ancient emotion as He stood on the gentle slope of the Mount of Olives, and looked and looked across the brook called Kidron, toward the great, gold encrusted dome of the Temple of God.

In that Temple, He knew the elaborate rites, enacted in thick clouds of incense and smoke from the sacrificial altars, had appeared variously to God through the centuries, according to the hearts of the people. Jesus was well trained in the intricacies of the law. He thrilled at the sight of the sun slanting its last evening light off the gold of the Temple dome. He knew that to that very day, the details of the law were strictly kept and rightly so. But His sensitive heart was troubled and He frowned with the weight of His thought. He had memorized the Scriptures in school, and up into His conscious mind as He stood there looking over the Holy City, exploded the words of the old prophet, Jeremiah: "After those days, saith the Lord, I will put my law in their inward parts, and write it in their hearts. . . ."

He repeated the words aloud several times and they rang with truth in His innermost being. He was a superior student. He had learned His lessons at school and learned them well. But watching the sun leave the gold dome of the Temple, He knew as though the knowledge came from within Himself, that there was another more important law—the law of the love of God which would make strong the human heart from within!

When the great festival day came at last, "at even, at the going down of the sun, at the season that thou camest forth from Egypt," every Jewish family kept the solemn ritual of the Passover meal. The Boy Jesus ate the Paschal lamb thoughtfully, with Mary and Joseph.

When the time came, the caravan of friends and neighbors from Nazareth and Jericho and other towns along the way met at an appointed place and started the trip home.

Neither Mary nor Joseph saw Jesus when they began the return journey, but no one was alarmed, since the group was large and usually the younger members ran along at the front of the caravan. Sometimes they went on with the *dragoman,* the person who went ahead to prepare a place for the people to rest that night and then came back to lead them there.

The day passed by, Mary talking happily with her friends, and Joseph with his. But in Mary's heart, as the evening shadows stretched toward them, an uneasiness began.

She found Joseph and asked, "Where is He? Have you seen Jesus today?" Joseph wrinkled his broad brow.

"No, Mary. But the Boy must be up front. He's so helpful, He may have gone on with the *dragoman* to help prepare a resting place for us for the night."

Mary wasn't satisfied with this. "I'm worried, Joseph. The *dragoman* must have come back an hour ago. Look, the sun is setting fast. Will you ask if anyone has seen Him? Please?"

Joseph asked person after person. He walked the length of the long line of travelers. There was no sign of the Boy.

In real alarm, Joseph and Mary left their friends and began the long climb back to Jerusalem. When they arrived on the second day, both of them were deeply worried. It was not like Him to cause trouble. Not at all like Him.

They set out early on the third day to make the rounds of all their friends' homes in Jerusalem. Mary was almost ill with worry. "He's such a gentle Lad, someone may have harmed Him!"

Joseph was not successful at consoling Mary. He was too worried himself. "I wish I could say something to make your heart rest, Mary, but I don't know where to look! We've visited all our friends."

Mary clung to his arm. She seemed about to faint under the stifling load of her anxiety. He steadied her, his arm around her.

"We'll go to the Temple, Mary. That's the only place He might be we haven't looked. The Temple holds a real fascination for the Boy. Let's try it."

The educated, scholarly members of the Sanhedrin, the highest governing body of the Jewish faith, subject only to the Roman Governor, sat in formal session in their splendid, special hall high in the Temple, all through the Passover festival. At the close of the festival, however, it was customary for the esteemed members of the court to descend to the lower levels of the Temple, where the public was permitted to gather to ask questions of the distinguished teachers.

Joseph held Mary's arm firmly as he steered her through the jostling, curious crowd clustered around the Sanhedrin, seated a little apart in a circle of richly brocaded robes and jeweled turbans.

Standing on his tip-toes. Joseph peered over the heads of the people and there, quietly sitting with the Sanhedrin—not standing with the rest of the mob, was Jesus! He spoke intelligently and calmly with the learned men, and Joseph gasped in astonishment: "Mary! There He is."

"Where, Joseph? Where? I can't see over the heads of these people. Where is He?" She jerked helplessly at Joseph's robe, straining to see.

"He's sitting right down with the teachers, Mary! Talking with them like a grown man! They seem to be paying attention to Him, too. You wait here, Mary. I'll get Him at once."

When the Boy stood outside the Temple gates before His parents, He was not ashamed. He was not rebellious. He in no sense seemed to fear a reprimand from them, and yet neither was He brash about having caused them worry. He simply stood there, looking squarely at them, and waiting for them to speak first.

After she had embraced Him, Mary took Him by the shoulders, and, choking back tears of relief, asked: "Child, why have you treated us this way? Your father and I have been anxiously looking for you."

Joseph couldn't resist his pride in the Boy. "We've found Him now, Mary. Anyway, you should have heard the respect they were giving Him! Why, when I got through the crowd to where I could hear, I could see plainly that everyone—including those high and mighty teachers—was astonished at His understanding and His answers!"

"Nevertheless, Joseph, you and I were worried sick about the Boy! Child, why did you treat us this way?"

He didn't smile. Nor did He frown. He just looked at her and asked in His steady boy's voice, "Why were you seeking Me? Did you not know that I ought to be about My Father's affairs?"

Mary started to make another gentle reprimand and checked herself. Joseph said nothing. Both parents looked at the Boy and then at each other. He was still neither frowning nor smiling. Mary and Joseph were both as confused and helpless as they looked. This serious-faced Boy of twelve might have been their parent. Neither of them understood what He had said; but neither of them said anything more.

He went home with them obediently and cheerfully, and back

in Nazareth He passed the remainder of his youthful years submissive to them.

As He grew in wisdom and stature and in favor with God and men, Mary His mother watched Him often, still patiently carrying the old perplexity beneath her pride in Him. He became a skilled carpenter in His middle teens, and the totally responsible head of the house when Joseph died a few years later. His voice changed, His beard grew, His shoulders thickened, His slender hand grew strong around the saw and the hammer and the plane.

He was in no sense maudlin or soft, but His kindness was so consistent it made some of the citizens of Nazareth uneasy. In every good way, He tried to be one of the people, and even appeared to be trying to make up for the fact that He sometimes seemed different, by being kinder and more understanding than ever. Only the children never misunderstood Him.

One morning, the widow Mary watched her Son, born of the Holy Ghost, stride from their modest one-roomed house toward the carpenter shop a few hundred yards down the narrow village street. There were no tall, "goodly cedars" in the foothills of the Lebanon Mountains where Nazareth sprawled. But Mary had heard them praised in the Scriptures. A Lebanon cedar was a king among trees to the simple woman who watched her tall Son walk briskly away carrying a heavy wooden beam over His strong shoulder. Mary had never seen a Lebanon cedar, but she thought of one as He strode out of sight down the narrow street.

The next day, as He had done every year since Joseph died, Jesus would take His mother to Jerusalem for the Passover Feast. She thought of a Lebanon cedar that morning as she watched Him leave for work. She also remembered the serious-faced twelve-year-old Boy who seemed somewhat surprised that she hadn't thought it perfectly natural for Him to be about His Father's affairs in the Temple at the end of His first Passover Feast in Jerusalem eighteen years ago, on that frightening day when they thought He was lost.

"What did He talk about to those learned members of the Sanhedrin? What did He mean by what He said to Joseph and me?"

The still simple, blue-eyed, middle-aged woman scooped up some barley flour He had ground for her before He left, shook her graying head wonderingly, and went inside the house, pondering all these matters in her heart.

Chapter 24

A New Voice in the Wilderness

After four hundred years of silence, another prophet of God stalked out of the wilderness of Judea, clad in camels' skins and leather girdle, gaunt and formidable, his soul ablaze with but one passion—to confront his people in the awful light of the righteousness of God.

Not far from Jerusalem, by the fords of the Jordan River, this strange, intense man drew enormous crowds of people, all hopeful that he was Elijah returned to announce the coming of the Messiah to Israel. He was indeed like Elijah, not only in appearance, but in the sharp singleness of his purpose. Up and down the muddy Jordan River his voice pierced the ears and hearts of those who came to be baptized in the brown waters by this man who preached the baptism of repentance for the forgiveness of sins. In a voice like an outraged trumpet, he declared himself to be the one written of in the messages of Isaiah, the prophet of old—"A voice of one shouting in the desert: Prepare the Lord's way; make His paths straight." The passion of his dedicated life poured from his great throat in torrents of condemnation upon the people until hundreds begged to be told what to do. He was a man with a fevered hold on a truth which had shaped his life from before his entrance into his mother's womb.

"Viper brood!" he thundered across the cringing crowds. "Who forewarned you to flee from the coming wrath? Then produce fruits in harmony with your repentance, and do not begin to say within yourselves, 'We have Abraham for a father,' for I tell you that God can raise offspring to Abraham from these stones! The ax is lying ready at the root of the trees, so that every tree that fails to produce good fruit will be felled and thrown into the fire."

His words struck suspense and fear into the hearts of the people and many followed him and were baptized. Excitement and curiosity and a holy awe gripped those who heard him cry: "He who comes after me ranks ahead of me because He was before me."

Was he announcing the coming Christ, the Messiah for whom all Israel had been waiting?

Not only the common people thronged to hear him, but the priests and Levites from Jerusalem came on orders from the cult of the Pharisees to find out if perhaps this strange, ember-eyed desert prophet could himself be the promised Messiah!

"Who are you?" they demanded of him as he stood perspiring and exhausted from the physical effort of his fiery sermon.

"I am not the Christ!" he retorted.

"Then who are you? Elijah?"

"No, I am not!" the prophet snapped, facing the pompous priests stolidly, his feet apart, his arms folded across his bare, hairy chest.

"Then why do you baptize, if you are neither the Christ nor Elijah?"

He stood his ground, fixing them with his fierce gaze. His voice vibrated with conviction and humility as he said a most surprising thing! "I baptize with water. He who comes after me stands among you, whom you do not recognize, the strings of whose sandals I am not fit to untie."

This was in the fifteenth year of the reign of Tiberius Caesar. Judea had, humiliatingly, been made a Roman province. A series of governors had ruled there, and now the governor was a calculating man named Pontius Pilate. The tetrarch of Galilee was Herod Antipas. Annas and his son in law, Caiaphas, were the high priests. Political chicanery maneuvered its evil way hand in hand with the vested interests of the Temple itself. Even the Sanhedrin had been packed by Rome. The prophet from the wilderness shouted his message of repentance to a Jewish nation rotten almost to its ancient core.

But around the countrysides of the land were still the faithful remnant of believers who hoped and prayed and participated in Temple worship and festival days with their whole hearts turned toward the God of Abraham.

In Nazareth, Jesus had already begun to speak in the synagogue. And wherever people gathered to discuss the burning question of the day—the coming kingdom of God, He listened intently and then He weighed what He heard against what He knew in His heart. Of course, He had heard of the blazing prophet who declared himself to be the herald of the coming Messiah. He

210

knew the desert preacher was His cousin, and that His mother, Mary, and the prophet's mother, Elizabeth, were cousins—and had been, before Elizabeth's death, close friends.

In the sputtering yellow light of their olive oil lamp He stood behind His mother one night, as she sat in a smooth wooden chair He had made for her. His strong, senstive hands rested on each of her slightly bent shoulders.

"He is six months older than You, my Son. His mother and I were close in those days, when we were both carrying our sons in our bodies, under our hearts. John was born to my cousin, Elizabeth, when she was far too old to bear a child. He was a miracle, too. A gift of God. Not like You, yet a miracle. It was all so strange. So beautiful. So hard for us to understand. Now, you tell me Elizabeth's son, John, is preaching to great crowds of people. And that You are going to find him. Must You go, my Son? Must You leave your home here in Nazareth? You have been such a support to me since Joseph has been gone." Mary clung to His hand resting on her shoulder.

After a moment, He stepped around in front of her, lifted her half-frightened face and smiled. He had never been more certain of His identity. Never closer to Mary, and yet never so removed. Then He stopped smiling, touched her bowed head gently, as though to bless her.

When she looked up, Her tall, serious first-born Son was gone.

This Is My Beloved Son

Jesus laid down His carpenter's tools in the shop at Nazareth and walked away into the beloved world of His Father in heaven.

It was not a beautiful world. It was not a world in which true religion flourished. It was a world gone mad for power. There was no absolute right. Might was right. And the pagan religion of Rome permeated most of the civilized world with the decadent moral stench of deified human beings, a power-crazed government and unmitigated superstition. Human nature had advanced far in the field of art, but in the main it was a corrupt art which pandered indecency among its lovers. The sanctity of marriage had ceased. The idea of human conscience was almost unknown in the thriving, complicated, moral decay which was devouring the very heart of God's beloved world.

211

A line chiseled into the tomb of a mere child screamed its silent description of the darkened world orbiting independently of its Creator: "To the unjust god who robbed me of life!"

Half of Rome's two million people were slaves. These unfortunates were exposed to nameless cruelties which nourished a bitterness and hatred that marked every life their lives touched. Many of these slaves were tutors whose lives scarred the hearts of children who would grow up to further distortion of spirit.

Rome had been transformed from a city of brick to a city of gleaming marble, but the injustice of its society forced the people to live in abject poverty or incredible luxury.

In contrast to the necessity to care for the poor, which marked the true Hebrew religion, the pagan world into which Jesus walked the day He left His home in Nazareth ignored its poor, feeling alms to be a means of extending a life which was already worthless.

This Man who had worked with His hands, constructing useful implements and furniture, and whose heart responded to His work with interest and joy, now entered a society bitten deeply by the loathesome insect of prejudice. In fact, all manual labor except agriculture was looked upon with real contempt.

The great minds of the day longed for change to come, but they ended their earthly lives in despair. Seneca, the philosopher, longed for "some hand from without to lift him up from the mire of desperation." Cicero tried to picture the enthusiasm which would greet the "embodiment of real virtue" should it ever appear on earth. Tacitus called all human life a farce and believed the Roman world lay helpless under some evil curse.

Into this violent, ugly world walked Jesus of Nazareth, His whole heart set on the fantastic mission of showing the almost oblivious world the love of His Father!

In the face of the political cruelty and sordidness of all the known world, when even the Messianic hopes of Israel dimmed and wavered, rugged John the Baptist admonished the people to prepare themselves for the coming of the kingdom of God!

The self-seeking, intellectual rabbis stood arrogantly for the outward *form* of such a kingdom. And in the hearts of the simple, devout Jew, the *hope* remained. But through two simple small-town women with trusting hearts, God had begun to move in a completely unexpected way into the chaotic field of human history. Elizabeth's son John was heralding the coming of Mary's Son Jesus!

The hopeful voices of the ancient prophets had been silent for so long that John's big voice roused Jewish men and women from all walks of life—all eager, for whatever their individual reasons, for the coming of the kingdom of God at last. The people of Israel had become Hellenized, self-centered; even their priests bartered with pagan Rome, but the flicker of hope for the Messiah still glowed at the scattered national heart, like the eternal lamp which burned in the shadows of the synagogue in front of the heavy veil that hung over the sanctuary. And so, Pharisees and Sadducees and Nationalists and Zealots, and farmers and fishermen and housewives and children, flocked to hear the Baptist.

With the same true humility with which Mary carried her perplexity in her heart, John carried his. He had been convinced during the years in which he lived alone in communion with God that He *was* to announce the coming King and the kingdom of God, but John did not know the Name of the King! With all the strength of his dedicated heart, he knew what was expected of *him*, but He made no pretense of knowing beyond that.

"He who comes after me stands among you, whom you do not recognize," John cried, "the strings of whose sandals I am not fit to untie."

The crowd, milling twenty deep along the reedy banks of the Jordan River, muttered, and everyone craned his neck to see who might be among them whom they did not know! For a moment the Baptist peered over the crowd, too. He stopped speaking as though he needed to wait for some sign. A few people laughed nervously and others looked frightened.

John began to preach again and the attention of the crowd returned to him. Then he called for those with repentant hearts to form a line to his left for baptism in the river. Slowly a few people moved out from the crowd toward John. Others took courage and followed more rapidly. As the Baptist waited, one or two more came and stood reverently, some weeping, in the long line to his left. There were a few Pharisees, even one or two scribes, half a dozen notorious nationalist and Zealot agitators, five obvious women of the streets, countless plain, decent women, workingmen, fishermen, the poor and one or two of the rich. But

213

all stood in the same line with their hearts bowed before the same God. John began to baptize them, one after another.

The ritual had continued for over an hour, when, almost unnoticed, a Man of average height, with brown hair and beard and deep-set eyes, moved unobtrusively into the crowd of bystanders. He watched and listened a few moments, then walked directly and quietly to the end of the line of those waiting their turn to be baptized.

He did not stand apart. But something set Him apart, and a few people commented about Him. He was a stranger in Bethabara, as far as anyone knew.

It was late afternoon by the time the line dwindled to three persons. The first of the three was a prostitute, well-known to some of the men who had been ahead of her in the line of penitents. She emerged from the river with her lined face lighted from within and she lifted her hands in praise to God as she walked away, alone.

Two remained to be baptized. One, the quiet Stranger, and the other an elderly leather craftsman. He had spoken to the Stranger as they waited.

"I was brought up in the faith of our Fathers in Israel. I have always believed He would send us our Messiah. But I wanted to be ready when He comes." The old man's eyes smiled. "I want this man to baptize me so I'll be ready for the kingdom when it comes."

When John called the old man, he waved a warm greeting to the last Man in the line. His greeting was returned. After his baptism, as the elderly man re-laced his sandals, the young Man walked slowly toward the Baptist.

For a moment, neither spoke. John stood looking at Him with an expression close to reverence.

"I am Jesus, of Nazareth. Our mothers were cousins."

John remembered little about old Elizabeth, who died when he was a child. His manner as he exchanged courtesies with Him was not that of a kinsman. He was like a man seeing a light so bright he almost feared to look. He gripped his leather girdle with both hands and his speech came haltingly.

Jesus came quickly to his rescue. "I have come that you might baptize Me."

John stepped back. "I—I need to be baptized by You! Why should You come to me?"

Gently, but firmly, Jesus replied, "Allow Me now, John, for so it behooves us to fulfill all the divine requirements."

Then, fulfilling all divine requirements in a way only He fully understood, Jesus was baptized like all others, by John, in the shallow Jordan River. When He came up out of the river, the heavens were opened and the Spirit of God descended like a dove, lighting upon Him.

John backed away, up the river's bank, in worshipful awe, because as Jesus stood praying, a Voice from heaven said, "This is my Son, the Beloved in whom I delight."

Those who stood gaping on the sidelines heard John speak out in a strong but quiet voice as Jesus walked toward him a few moments later: "Behold the Lamb of God that takes away the sin of the world. *He* is the One of whom I said, 'After me comes a Man who ranks ahead of me for He was before me.' I did not recognize Him, but I have come to baptize with water so that He may be made known to Israel. I saw, and you saw the Spirit descend and remain, and I testify that He is the Son of God."

John and the people who still lingered along the banks of the Jordan watched Jesus walk away then, alone. His step was resolute, but there was nothing in His manner which indicated that He considered His baptism experience to be superior to that of the others. He walked as a Man motivated from within by a terrible certainty. A certainty no longer unfamiliar to Him, but now so definite that He had no choice but to move with it, toward its inevitable end.

Jesus disappeared from their sight and headed for the desolate wilderness country to the west of the Dead Sea.

Victor in the Wilderness

To the right and to the left of Him as He walked, the brown, burned-out, treeless wilderness stretched—vast, monotonous, empty. There were no birds, because nothing grew to feed them. No small animals scampered about the coarse, cracked earth. For forty days and nights He was alone, as a Man wandering on the deeply seamed surface of a still undiscovered planet.

By day the unbroken rays of the desert sun burned His feet and face and hands, and by night the darkness was dense and silent as a tomb, except to be slashed now and then by the paralyzing scream of a hyena, before the lunge of a giant prowling desert cat.

Empty day followed empty night. He sat and walked and slept in a motionless sea of emptiness. He took nothing with Him to eat. And as the arid hours crept by, His inner being became so sensitized that every thought sifting through His mind was sharp, and etched with more reality than ordinary men could endure.

Just as physical hunger sharpens the senses, so emotional hunger whets the soul. Jesus was emotionally hungry, too. He was human as well as divine, and His humanity craved the familiar sound of another human voice. Under the strain of fasting, the spirit mounts. Communion with God becomes a necessity.

The Spirit of God had guided Him to his place of aloneness for a reason so vast one can only partially comprehend. As with much of His earthly life, the veil of divine mystery is lifted here only at one corner. But it is lifted enough to reveal a Man entering into and willingly involving Himself with all earth-bound human nature.

Alone in the hard atmosphere of the wilderness, this Man from Galilee entered into the condensed darkness of human egocentricity. During these forty days alone, Jesus *was tempted*. Nothing He saw in the human heart surprised Him after that. With all His being He identified with all human temptation and the suffering that stalks it.

Jesus was utterly human, and in the midst of the gnawing, aching aloneness of these forty days alone, His humanity was "tempted by the devil." As with man from the beginning, He heard the "voice" of the often plausible lower choice whisper insistently, straining for His attention. He knew His mission on the earth. Deliberately He had set Himself to begin the public life for which His Father had sent Him. His years of waiting in Nazareth, working to support His mother and younger brothers and sisters, had served Him well. His goal was clear. The human impossibility contained in it was clear. He *was* God's invasion of human history and with full respect and adoration for the advance work of John the Baptist, He knew in His heart that His would be a lonely mission. God's beloved, sin-twisted world lay all around Him, and He had made Himself aware of its political and social and moral evils.

He now knew all His mother knew of His identity, and more. He had experienced thirty earthly years of sinless, unbroken communion with God. Knowing this, the Spirit had still motivated His forty days of wilderness temptation. Once and for all, His humanity must know itself to be in tune with the divine. If He had not experienced the visitation from the tempter in the brown, lifeless stretches of the solitude that surrounded Him there, His humanity would have been incomplete.

Jesus was the Son of God, but He was also a Man. And His human heart heard the "voice" of the "easy way" suggest first that in the enormous public work which He must now begin, the best way to win the allegiance of the people would be to supply their material needs!

"If you are God's Son, tell this stone to become bread!" His own physical hunger was acute by now. How much of His emotional and physical pain from the days of fasting would vanish if He did what He knew He could do—turn even one of the smooth stones around Him into a fragrant loaf of nourishing bread! Nothing in Him questioned His ability to do this. After all, He was One with the Father who had created the stone and the wheat in the first place! And how quickly would the multitudes follow Him if He fed them by what they would call "miracle."

Jesus' answer was firm and steady: "Man shall not live by bread alone; but on every expression of God."

He had learned this in the Scriptures at school. His whole being, divine and human, took its truth up at that moment, to use! Those who followed God for what they could get would never understand His nature. They must first seek God and His Kingdom, and *then* all other things would be added to them.

That settled, His tempter squared himself for another attack. Standing on a high hill in the wilderness, Jesus' mind went to the spread-out, conquered, wretched world below Him. His own people cried out for a military Messiah! One who would justify Israel and make her powerful on the earth again. One who would shake her invading hordes forever. Every Hebrew chafed under Roman rule.

The tempter voice of personal ambition rushed at His hungry body and His eager, seeking mind: "All the power and splendor of these will I give you, for it has been handed over to me and I bestow it on whomever I please; so if you will kneel before me, it shall all be yours."

He heard the offer, but something deeper in His spirit answered, once more experiencing and making His own the truth of the Scripture He had learned well: "It is written, 'You shall worship the Lord your God and serve Him alone.'"

This settled, His mind went to the Temple in Jerusalem, which He loved and hallowed in His heart. If He had rejected the suggestions of material supply and military might, and if He were determined to stake the entire outcome of His life's work on nothing but the power of the Spirit, then surely God would protect Him and defend Him, and keep His earthly life from harm!

His tempter spoke again: "You stand on the pinnacle of the Temple in Jerusalem. If you are God's Son, throw yourself down from here, for it is written, 'He will give orders to His angels on your behalf to protect you,' and 'They shall carry you on their hands so that you may not stub your foot against a stone.'"

He had been struck with the cleverest suggestion of all! But standing there alone in the vast empty waste, He squared His wide shoulders and the thing was settled forever: Aloud, alone, He spoke with a strong, clear voice: "It has been said, 'You shall not test the Lord your God.'"

The vacant wilderness echoed His words. And when the last faint echo was no more, neither was the voice of His tempter. In fact, the tempter himself was gone, at least for that time.

He had not even dared put the condition of divine protection upon Himself along the way of the difficult, dangerous mission stretching ahead. He refused to allow His faith in His Father's purpose to be touched by what might happen to Himself.

Now the mind of the Man from Nazareth was a unit with the mind of the Father. He had been ready to begin, but now He had cleared the way of its negatives. He saw what He must *not* do, regardless of the pressures which He knew full well could cost the last drop of human blood in His body!

He had been ready to do His Father's will, but now He had settled the manner in which He would do it.

Jesus walked out of the wilderness back toward Galilee, alone.

Chapter 25

Follow Me!

On His solitary journey north, near Bethany, Jesus once more found John the Baptist, standing with two of his disciples, John, the son of the fisherman, Zebedee, and Andrew, another fisherman. It was about four in the afternoon, the baptizing was over for that day and the crowd was almost gone. When the Baptist caught sight of Jesus coming toward them, he exclaimed:

"Behold the Lamb of God, that takes away the sin of the world!"

Jesus and John and the two disciples talked awhile, and when Jesus left, John and Andrew the fishermen followed Him.

"Well," He said pleasantly, "what are you two looking for?"

John, the more impetuous of the two, spoke first. "Rabbi, we want to know where You stay."

Then Andrew repeated eagerly, "Yes, Teacher, where do You live?"

"Come and see." His smile made them welcome.

John and Andrew spent the rest of the day with Him at the small caravansary where He was staying. That night Andrew could scarcely wait to reach his brother Simon. The small clay oil lamp fastened to Andrew's right foot slowed his pace through the darkness, but it kept him from stumbling over the coils of rope and the folded nets. He and his brother Simon were staying with fishermen friends who also were disciples of John the Baptist.

Andrew burst into the dimly lighted one-room house shouting, "Simon! Simon—we've found the Messiah! John and I have found Him. We've found the Christ!"

Simon was a huge man, with a thick thatch of light curly hair and beard. The sandy hair on his big, bulging forearms curled, too. Unlike Andrew, Simon was rough of body and voice and manner. He was as much at home with an oath as he was with a net in the blue waters of the Lake of Galilee, back home. But Andrew's excitement didn't faze the big man that night. Not at first. He had hoped with all his heart that John the Baptist was the Messiah. When John denied it, Simon lost interest. And when he was uninterested in something, it was as total as his huge enthusiasm could be when he was interested. He lifted one shaggy eyebrow at Andrew and said nothing.

"Simon, John and I met Him with the Baptist late this afternoon. We've been with Him ever since. It's Jesus of Nazareth!"

Simon jerked his big head toward his brother. "What?"

"I know He's a cousin of John and James, but that doesn't alter the truth, Simon. This Man is the Messiah."

Simon was whittling. He slammed his knife down and laughed.

"Forget it, Andrew. We've got to stop this rabbi business and get back to fishin'! I'm not cut out to be anybody's disciple."

Andrew knew Simon well enough to say nothing for awhile. So he just waited, knowing his big, burly brother would talk himself into finding out anyway.

"Every other week somebody turns up who claims to be the Messiah. Maybe someday He'll come. Don't sit there grinnin' at me like I'm a fool! You know I want to find Him as much as anybody else. But—" Simon exhaled noisily. "All right, where is He?" Before Andrew could tell him, he bellowed, "I said where is He?"

Andrew actually had big Simon by the hand, hurrying him along like a stubborn child, the next day when they found Jesus. The big man had been protesting half-heartedly all the way, and he was still swearing mildly when his own bright blue eyes caught His. Andrew let go of Simon's coarse, calloused hand.

Jesus looked at the huge fellow steadily for a long time. Simon tried to grin, then thought better of it. He shifted his weight clumsily from one foot to the other and then just stood there. Jesus smiled at him. Simon relaxed a little, scratched his head once, tried to grin again, and then went back to just standing there.

Andrew spoke first. "This is my brother, Simon, Rabbi. Remember? I told you about him."

Jesus seemed to be seeing in the big, rough fisherman all that no one had dreamed was there. He smiled warmly then, and said, "You are Simon now—the son of John. But you will be called Cephas."

Simon blinked. "Cephas, Master?"

"Yes, Cephas, translated 'Peter.' You know, in Hebrew that means 'rock.'"

He had recognized the potential of Simon's faith in Him, even before Simon knew it.

"I'm going to follow Jesus," Andrew said simply, to his brother.

"You are?" Simon asked, for want of something more suitable to say.

And in his heart, he knew, as Jesus knew, that he, Simon, was going to follow him, too—as Peter, the rock.

The three walked north together. At Bethsaida, Peter's and Andrew's home town, another disciple joined them. A clear-thinking, earnest young man also a fisherman, and a friend of Andrew and Peter, named Philip.

As the four spoke together, Jesus suddenly interrupted the conversation by His first spoken call to any man: "Philip, follow Me!"

In this thoughtful, long-time friend of His first two disciples, Peter and Andrew, He had again found the potential of faith which He sought. Knowing all human nature as He knew it, He sensed that His call would find immediate response in the heart of Philip. It did. And Philip's discovery led at once to sharing.

Before they left Bethsaida that day, the newest disciple went to another close friend, a deep-thinking, strong believer in the Lord God of Israel. A scholarly man of prayer and faith named Nathanael, whose home was in Cana, twenty miles away. Philip found him at prayer, in the privacy of the low hanging branches of the fig tree in front of Philip's home where he was a guest. The two men were close friends, close enough so that Philip did not hesitate to interrupt Nathanael's prayers. He had known his friend's deep longing for the Messiah. This was the moment for which Nathanael prayed! Philip's words tumbled over themselves in his excitement.

"We have found the one of whom Moses wrote in the Law, and the prophets did, too! He is Jesus of Nazareth, the son of Joseph."

Nathanael was a true scholar. Philip knew better than to make his announcement to him without backing it up with Scripture. Nathanael looked at his friend for a moment, and then smiled tolerantly. He loved his friend, Philip. He respected his sincerity. But Nathanael said all he could have said after what Philip had blurted about the son of Joseph from Nazareth!

"Philip, Philip—can anything good come out of Nazareth?"

Philip also knew Nathanael. There would be no point in trying to argue with him. He knew the Scriptures better than Philip knew them. Philip, however, knew Jesus, and so he wisely answered, "Come and see!"

As the two friends approached Jesus and Peter and Andrew, they overheard Jesus say, watching Nathanael walk toward Him, "Now, there, truly, is an Israelite without deceit in him!"

Nathanael smarted from embarrassment remembering his remark about the backward country town of Nazareth. But suddenly his heart longed for the simplicity of direct truth, and he could only ask of Jesus, "How do you know me?"

"I saw you under the fig tree before ever Philip called you, Nathanael."

There was no accusation in His voice. Nathanael knew that he was known! Jesus' quiet answer left no doubt whatever that this Man knew him as he was. Nathanael's remark about His home town of Nazareth would have sounded caustic to any other man. This Man had called him an Israelite without deceit! This Man realized his educational background. This Man knew and was not one bit ruffled by the fact that the world of scholarship scorned the simple people from Nazareth. This Man was Himself without prejudice and therefore prejudice could not upset Him. This Man realized that Nathanael really had believed nothing good could come out of Nazareth!

Did He also know that Nathanael no longer believed that? Did He also know that in the space of the last passing moment, Nathanael *knew*?

For once, scholarly Nathanael could not wait for his questions to be answered. He had come and he had seen and he did the only thing he could have done. He gave himself to this Man, and found the deepest longing of his own heart met in the truth of his own whispered words: "Rabbi, you are the Son of God; you are the King of Israel!"

Was He the long awaited King?

The four new disciples stared at Him, trying to cope with the moment. Here, He gently began to show Himself as He was, in contrast with the sometimes terrifying message of John the Baptist.

The Baptist and these four men could see only the awesome Kingship of the Messiah. They could look only from the past *toward* Him. During His wilderness temptation, He had set Himself to reveal the kingdom in its total reality, *but* to place it at the disposal of ordinary, frightened, confused, hungry-hearted human beings like these who stood staring at Him. He *was* the King, but He wanted more than their awe-struck obedience.

The Lord God, Himself, had come down from the Jews' awful mountaintop to live among the sin-damaged, helpless people of His beloved world!

Nathanael's words still hung in the clear, sun-filled Sabbath afternoon: "Rabbi, you are the Son of God; you are the king of Israel!"

Jesus began His careful invasion of their hearts. His voice was quiet. Unlike the zealous Baptist, He knew men's hearts must be quieted before they can be truly opened.

"Nathanael, do you believe because I told you I had seen you under the fig tree?" The men shuffled and relaxed a little. "You will see greater things than that. Truly I assure you all, you shall see heaven opened and the angels of God ascending and descending on the *Son of Man.*"

He damaged not one word of the truth to which John the Baptist was giving his great life. He shook no tiniest leaf from the tree of their faith in the prophecies of the kingdom or its king. He shattered no hopes. Firmly, gently, directly, He led them out of the need for hope toward the necessity for realization. Their hopes were now reality. He had come. He was there among them, as the Son of God, but equally as the *Son of Man.* He was God's, but He was also theirs. No one of the four really understood, but all four were compelled to follow Him.

With Simon Peter, Andrew, Philip and Nathanael, He walked along the familiar waterfront at Bethsaida the next day. The three fishermen knew everyone they met, and Peter, especially, made it a point to wave conspicuously. Perhaps only the Master knew that he did this for two contradictory reasons: He was proud of his new Master, but he was also self-conscious before his brawling, joking fellow fishermen. He was boasting and he was covering up. Peter was big enough to contain both complexities and play them both to the hilt!

When they approached the fishing boats belonging to Zebedee and his two sons, James and John, Peter was really in his element. They were his partners, and Peter's own boats lay at anchor just beyond theirs. In answer to Simon Peter's lusty greeting, John, who had already talked with Jesus the day he and Andrew followed Him, ran happily to meet them. Old Zebedee's temper flared as usual, but his shouts and curses slung from long habit after his son John made no impression on anyone. When his other son, James, walked curiously after John a few minutes later, the old man's thundering finally dwindled to an angry grumble as he went on mending his nets.

John had not been able to forget the afternoon he and Andrew spent with Jesus. He had thought of nothing else. He had talked of nothing else to his brother James. The few moments on the lake shore were deep ones for all seven men. John took his eyes off Jesus only long enough to see for himself that James felt the same pull toward Him. It was as though they had forgotten He was their cousin, that His mother Mary was their mother's sister.

For the time being, James and John would stay with their father. But they would be waiting eagerly for Him to return.

Chapter 26

Water Into Wine

Regardless of the amount of understanding in the minds of Nathanael and the other three disciples, Jesus had put their hearts at rest. They felt *natural* with Him. And the next thing they did was the natural thing to do.

Nathanael's home was in Cana, a lovely small village spread on the gentle slope of a hill, a few miles from Nazareth, on the road to the Lake of Galilee. Since Jesus planned to return to Nazareth, at least briefly, before moving his mother and the other members of his family to the bigger town of Capernaum, it was the natural thing for Nathanael to invite Him to stop on the way at his home in Cana. Peter, Andrew, and Philip went, too.

Soon after they reached Cana, Nathanael learned of the marriage of a local girl whose family had been close to Mary and Joseph. Jesus was delighted when He learned that His mother would be a guest at the wedding. He was already well known as a rabbi. There was nothing unusual about His invitation to the wedding, and His invitation would naturally include His disciples traveling with Him.

He launched no conspicuous "campaign." His ministry had begun, but He began it as the Son of Man living naturally among people. Jesus greeted His mother at the wedding feast with the same joy any devoted son would feel at such a pleasant surprise.

With the other guests, He entered the spacious, lofty dining room in the home of the wealthy bridegroom. It was brilliantly lighted with lamps and candlesticks, and the guests reclined around the tables on couches soft with tapestry-covered cushions. The bridal blessing was spoken, and the bridal cup emptied, according to Hebrew custom. The feast began. Laughter and songs and the usual merriment of such a time filled the room, but there was a deep sanctity about a Jewish wedding which kept the behavior of the guests in good taste. The wine flowed, but even if the bride's family and relatives had not been devout people, the presence of a rabbi would have controlled the hilarity.

These were simply happy people enjoying the chance to share

in the joy of the bridal party. Mary, especially, was enjoying herself. She loved the young couple in whose honor the feast was held, but her happiness was greater because her beloved Son was there!

Jesus reclined, as was the custom, with the other men at one group of tables. Halfway through the happy evening, His mother slipped through the crowd of merrymakers and touched Him on the shoulder. "Jesus, I have just learned that they are out of wine!"

One thing Mary had discovered about Him during the years in which He lived with her in Nazareth was that she could absolutely depend on Him. Perhaps she had no idea whatever about the next thing to do, but the first thing that came to her when she learned of their host's dilemma was to tell Jesus! Perhaps her mother's inclination was to remember that her Son and His four friends had been last minute guests. At any rate, with the simplicity of a child, Mary rushed to tell her Son about the difficulty.

Just as it is hard to remember a bright, sunny day when the skies have hung for weeks with rain-clouds, so Mary may have found the long years since the Birth of Jesus obscuring her sure knowledge of His calling. After all, only twelve years had passed when she fell into a typical mother's anxiety and confusion with Him in the Temple the day He had been about His Father's business. Now it had been thirty years. She rushed to Him when the wine ran out, as any proud mother would turn to her son, believing he could do something.

His voice was kind when He spoke these strange words to her, whom He loved so deeply, as she stood expectantly awaiting His answer. "Woman, what is that between Me and you? My hour is not here yet!"

With all His sensitive being He felt her pain. Mary both understood and did not understand. From the beginning she had both understood and misunderstood so much about her Son Jesus. Still, there remained the absolute confidence in Him, and although she had no way of knowing that the time had come for the end of their mother-son relationship as she had known it, Mary said simply to the waiters standing beside her, "Do whatever He tells you!"

He had not humiliated her, nor did He refuse to help. Immediately He ordered the waiters to bring the six water jars used for the Jewish rite of purifying and fill them with water. They did—

in their excitement, all the way to the brim. Then Jesus instructed them to dip some of the contents of the jars and take it to the table manager. The disciples must have enjoyed the look on the manager's face when he tasted the sudden supply of excellent wine! There had been the embarrassing emergency, and now there were six stone jars, holding from eighteen to twenty-four gallons, filled with superb wine! The surprised manager (who knew nothing of what had been done) exclaimed to the bridegroom: "Everyone serves the good wine first, and the poorer when men have drunk freely; but you have retained the good wine until now!"

The feast went on, and His disciples believed in a new way. Perhaps Mary did not realize the end of the old relationship with Him, nor the beginning of the new. Their tender bond remained. Following the wedding at Cana, He took her with Him for a few days to look for a home in Capernaum. Life went right on, with Jesus participating in it. But He had now begun to live among them all, both as Son of God and Son of Man.

Eventually, it would become more and more evident that from that time on, His life relationship was *first* "My Father and I."

Chapter 27

Revolution in the Temple

During the months following the wedding at Cana, Jesus' mother and brothers moved their homes from Nazareth to Capernaum. His married sisters remained in Nazareth with their husbands and families and from that time on, Capernaum was to be known as "His own city."

Nazareth had served Him well during His youthful years. He had drunk of its clear, clean water, eaten its fruit and grain, and His mind and spirit and body developed naturally and healthily in the simplicity and seclusion of the country town.

Now He must live more in the turbulence that was the daily life of most of the men and women of the world. He must be where the need was most evident. He must live among the victims of the ugly time. The twisted, tormented, clangorous time of collapsing ideals and human beings in moral and iron chains. He must live among the breadless poor and the boil-infected beggars. He must love and move among the heavy-hearted, the over-taxed, the sick, the dying.

Capernaum (now Tell Hum) was a busy little lake port on the northwest shore of the Lake of Galilee, about two and a half miles south of where the Jordan empties into the Lake. Its harbor was always crowded with fishing boats, and all along its sturdy stone quays, laughing, cursing, perspiring fishermen packed fish for shipment, from daylight to dark. Capernaum was also a Roman military post along a highway which ran north from Damascus to Galilee and south to Jerusalem in Judea.

Life at every level was lived out in the city which bustled up the gentle slopes, away from the baroque and elegant white limestone synagogue close by the lake shore.

Jesus' family moved to Capernaum, but He had no actual home of His own. During His sojourns there, He stayed for the most part in Simon Peter's house, because when Jesus chose Capernaum for His headquarters, the disciples made plans to move their families there, too.

In the spring of 27 A.D., when it was Passover time again, the disciples joined him on the journey south to Jerusalem, and attended the Feast with Him. He had walked quietly along the busy shore of the Galilean Sea, calling one after another of the waiting men—Simon Peter, Andrew, Philip, James, John, and Nathanael, who joined them from Cana.

Jesus' arrival in Jerusalem did not go unnoticed this time. Following the miracle at Cana, His fame had spread over all the countryside. He had preached in many synagogues, and the people who heard were amazed at His authority. There was already much talk about the Man from Galilee who had some connection with the fiery desert preacher, John the Baptist.

The whole land of Palestine seemed in a chaos of preparation, because the numbers of Jews making the pilgrimage to Jerusalem for the Passover lived in all parts of the known world. A month before the feast, bridges and roads were put into repair, and sepulchers whitened to prevent accidental contamination to the pilgrims. Along the roads to Jerusalem the money-changers opened their stalls a month before the Feast. All Jews and proselytes—except women, slaves and minors, had to pay the annual Temple-tribute of a half a shekel, and the money had to be paid in exact half-shekels of the Sanctuary, or ordinary Galilean shekels. Since, besides Palestine silver and copper coins, Persian, Tyrian, Egyptian, Grecian, Syrian and Roman money was in circulation, the money-changers did a huge business.

These busy places of profit remained open in the rural areas for ten days, until their greedy and industrious owners would bundle them up, move them by cart, and re-open until Feast time within the precincts of the Temple in Jerusalem. Here their trade really thrived, since many of the Jews from foreign countries wanted to shop in the Holy City, as well as make huge votive offerings at the Temple.

But the booths of the money-changers were not the only profitable businesses within the sacred Temple enclosure. Countless other schemes were carried out in the bazaars where sacrificial animals were sold to the pilgrims who did not bring their own. Here the men who hawked their "sacrificial" wares crowded around wooden cages of doves, and unfragrant stalls, into which sheep and lambs and young calves were packed together in noisy and painful confusion. The priests and Levites came in for their share of the profits, since the public could be sure it bought "duly inspected" animals.

The rich were charged exorbitant prices and the poor were squeezed of their copper coins, in the bawdy and profane businesses which boomed through their "unholy seasons," year after year, within the Temple of God. The people resented it, but being people, they followed the line of least resistance, traveling miles each year to spend a few hours near their revered Temple, knowing full well that the Temple officials reaped big dividends.

One of the most thriving of these business ventures was openly called the "Bazaars of the sons of Annas." Annas was the High Priest, and his booths were manned by servants who actually had been known to beat the people with sticks to keep the evil traffic moving!

Into the midst of the bustle and activity of the Bazaars of the High Priest, Annas, strode Jesus of Galilee. When a rabbi raised his cummerbund (sash) above his head in a gesture of righteous anger, it signified total condemnation upon those around him. The Rabbi from Galilee was a poor man. His sash was made of twisted rope. Even His disciples backed away with the crowd when He began to remove His sash. There was a swift moment of near silence in the Temple's Court of the Gentiles, as He stood in a tall, aroused majesty, with His rope sash held high over His head!

Then He broke the silence, moving quickly from one money changer's table to another, turning them over with no regard for the confusion of spilled out foreign coins, or the anger of the changers. The people fell back to give Him room to act! And He required room, because ahead of Him He drove the sheep and oxen and other cattle all the way outside the Temple precincts. The doves He released from their wooden cages, and for several violent moments the Temple was filled with frantic birds, cursing men and stampeding cattle. Over His head, the Rabbi who called Himself the Son of Man held His rope sash in a gesture of divine condemnation upon the desecration of His Father's house!

Some of the doves and pigeons were still caged. "Take these outside!" He commanded the men who cowered behind the cages. And when the bedlam had quieted somewhat so He could be heard, His voice rang throughout the high enclosure: "Do not make My Father's house a sales shop!"

John, His disciple, stood with the others a little apart from Him, wondering at the energy and holy anger of the Man he had only known to be quiet and gentle. Finally John leaned near Peter and whispered, "It is written in the Scripture, Passion for Thy house shall consume me."

Big Peter could only nod in agreement. Mostly they stood gaping at Him, impressed by His actions, but not understanding His real motive. In the most elementary way, He was once more "about His Father's affairs" in the Temple.

Not a hand was lifted against Him for what He had done. No move was made to arrest Him. His Presence awed the people. His words awakened their consciences. They knew He was right in what He did.

Even when the Temple officials came forward to speak to Him, no one dared touch Him. It was not His time. In front of the sympathetic crowd, they would not have dared harm Him. Anyway, wise policy dictated quiet within the Temple enclosure, since the Roman garrison was close by, in Fort Antonia. Nothing would have pleased the Roman military more than disorderly conduct among the Jews in the Temple!

But even stranger than these curbs on their conduct was the fact that when they gathered courage to speak to Him, no one reproved Him for what He had done. No one even intimated that His behavior had been improper!

The spokesman for the Temple officials sidled near Him, his fat, white hands crossed over his ample paunch, and inquired:

"What sign will you show us for your authority to do these things?"

It was a cunning question, and it made a clear, sudden map for Him of their future attacks. They would not attack Him head-on. They would attempt to cut His authority from under Him, slyly, in ways that caught the interest and sympathy of the multitudes.

Jesus stood looking down at the fat little priest who, after an embarrassing silence, repeated his clever, calmly worded question: "What sign will you show us for your doing these things?"

There was no scorn in Jesus' eyes toward the priest himself. None toward the people. The dignity of His Presence in the midst of what had occurred scorned their conduct. He had everyone's attention at that moment, and their combined and varied reactions to His Presence were no mystery to Him. Momentarily He

231

seemed to shake Himself free of His realization of all their hearts, and then He answered firmly and slowly:

"Destroy this Temple and in three days I will erect it."

Deftly, one Temple official after another smothered his anger at Jesus' seeming impudence. At least He might have answered in words related to their question! The people muttered in surprise and then fell quiet again, when the Temple spokesman said sarcastically:

"This temple has been in the process of building for forty-six years, and will you erect it in three days?"

No one, not even His disciples, could have known that He spoke of His bodily temple. Just as they could only "see" the coming of a powerful, materialistic, earthly kingdom, so they "saw" only the tall marble columns of the magnificent building in which they stood.

While He was in Jerusalem, He preached and performed signs and miracles which seemed to bring hundreds of people to a place of faith in Him. But He also saw their hearts, and knew they were convinced only outwardly by His "sign." He could not "commit Himself to them." Still, He did not withhold Himself. He continued to preach and perform wonders when constructive opportunities were at hand. And even though He knew most of the people were merely impressed, He also knew some were stirred in their depths by His message that the "kingdom is at hand." It had not been the people who demanded a "sign" to hide their contempt of Him in the Temple that day. It was the Temple officials. And so He gave the people "signs," but in Himself He knew of the few who were truly stirred.

As yet there was little to encourage Him.

Chapter 28

Visitor by Night

The disciples James and John were not rich men, but they had been successful fishermen, and no doubt they were happy to be able to rent a small house so that Jesus could live with them during their stay in Jerusalem in April and May of 27 A.D.

The spring wind swept up the narrow streets of Jerusalem, and banged at the window of the low ceilinged guest chamber. A Man sat alone in the chamber, built on the flat roof of the house James and John rented for their stay in Jerusalem. The olive oil lamp was still burning in the little roof-top room, and its light streamed out into the darkness in broken patches of yellow, where the whipping top of the fig tree broke it, as the quixotic wind blew this way and that.

Jesus had not retired for the night. He was just sitting on the pile of mats, which would be His bed, His elbows rested one on each knee, and His hands hung, loosely clasped. He was thinking.

The fig tree scratched the wooden window slats, and now and then He heard a snatch of excited conversation from downstairs. The disciples were trying to speak softly so He could rest. But Peter was there visiting with James and John, and when Peter was dead certain of something it was impossible to keep him quiet.

"They're as different as day and night, the Master and the Baptist! As for me, I like the Master best!"

Jesus could picture Peter pounding one big fist into the other open palm to punctuate his statement. He heard James say something in a voice too quiet to be understood, and then impetuous John forgot about Jesus' need for rest and shouted, "The Master will win the people a hundred times over because He mixes with them! The Baptist is a great man, but the Master is greater. The Baptist makes me want to run from him in shame, and the Master makes me want to run after Him!"

Jesus stood up, His head almost touching the low, flat ceiling of the guest chamber. He must speak to His men about criticizing

John the Baptist. But He couldn't resist smiling at their enthusiasm, and their reasoning—half-truth, half-emotion. He loved James and John and Peter.

Downstairs they must have remembered Him at that moment, because they lowered their voices again. And for another few minutes, He stood looking out over the Holy City, through the narrow window near the ceiling.

It was then He heard the slow, stealthy footsteps outside. Someone was climbing up the narrow wooden stairs from the ground to His chamber on the rooftop of the small house. Jesus remained at the window, His back toward the narrow door which was standing open to the top of the stairs. Whoever it was, he carried a light, which now filled the room. His visitor was in the doorway. Jesus turned to look at him, and nodded courteously, gesturing for him to come in.

The gray-bearded man who entered the guest chamber was elderly and obviously well-to-do. Over his straight, well-tailored tunic, he wore a cloak of fine, deep blue wool; his turban and cummerbund were of rich silk. His elegant attire and proud bearing marked him as a Pharisee of the Pharisees, but his eyes were kind and he lacked the haughtiness Jesus had come to expect when He was addressed by a ruler of the Jews.

"My name is Nicodemus."

Nothing in the manner of the young Man who faced him showed the smallest surprise that he had come. And yet the wealthy old Temple official had done an unheard of thing! Socially and economically, a man in Nicodemus' position would never have made a personal visit to a Man in the roof-top guest room of such a humble house. More than that, at least outwardly, every finicky Pharisee in Jerusalem was suspicious of the (to them) unorthodox, itinerant preacher. But most amazing of all—Nicodemus was an elder member of the mighty Sanhedrin—the Jewish supreme court! He was a ruler of Israel, and it was from men in his position that Jesus saw the sharp-edged opposition begin.

"I was among those who confronted you in the Temple the day you—ah, upset things, Rabbi."

Nicodemus was a direct man, even though he was paying a secretive visit under cover of darkness. Even the windy, spring chill had protected him. On a night like that, he was less likely to be seen by loiterers on the dark Jerusalem streets. The epitome of courtesy, the dignified old Sanhedrinist felt no need to apologize for the lateness of the hour he had chosen to make his surprise visit. It would have been superfluous. Jesus showed no excitement, no shock, neither did He show any special deference to His distinguished guest. The same calm which kept Him from depression over the superficial faith the crowds showed, held here. He was kind but not eagerly polite. Nicodemus observed all this, knowing the normal reaction of a comparatively unknown young country preacher would have been one of anxious deference toward a "prize" potential convert such as himself.

Jesus was quiet and in full control of the interview. He was neither eager nor dogmatic. He was interested and attentive and gave Himself freely and earnestly, in spite of His weariness and the lateness of the hour.

Nicodemus was cautious, even in his directness. He had stood silently in the group of Temple officials who confronted Jesus that day in the Bazaars of Annas, but without doubt he had been thinking deeply. Jesus sensed the extent and the limit of the old man's interest. Anyone who thought at all knew that a deadly feud between Jesus and the Jewish authorities had already begun. Jesus knew His guest was well aware of this. Nicodemus' wisdom and experience as a member of the ruling body which could sentence a man to death for religious infractions increased the drama of the meeting. Both men knew that the other had all the facts.

The older man sat on the one straight chair in the guest chamber. His full, gray beard fell to his waist. He leaned on his walking stick, looking directly at Jesus, who now sat once more on the pile of mats.

"Rabbi," Nicodemus began, "we know that you are a teacher who has come from God; for no one can work the signs you work unless God is with him."

Evidently the Sanhedrinist had been in the crowds around Jesus outside the Temple, too, and had seen His demonstrations of the power of God. Had Nicodemus recognized the startling difference between the works of Jesus and the usual "miracles" claimed by many of the spiritually decadent rabbis of the time? Had he noted the authenticity and balance invariably present in the miracles of Jesus? How much of the clear light of the Lord God had reached the heart of the old ruler? Was his comment from his heart? Did he really believe Jesus was a teacher sent from God, or was it merely a diplomatic compliment? Could it have been both?

Obviously, Jesus knew the answer and more. Without insult or lack of graciousness the strong, quiet young Man went straight to the heart of the matter. He did not ignore Nicodemus' generous comment, but neither did He reply to the actual words the old man spoke. Rather, He *answered* the unspoken but vital question which He knew turned itself provocatively in the old ruler's mind.

"Truly I assure you, unless a person is born from above he cannot see the kingdom of God."

As always, Jesus considered the individual to whom He spoke! Nicodemus had been "born" to an exalted position. He not only possessed material wealth and prestige, but he was exceedingly proud of his birth into the ranking class of the Jewish race. His natural birth had given him everything. And yet, here he was— an old man suddenly aware of his empty heart! Knowing all this, Jesus gave him the answer He knew Nicodemus needed.

"But how can a man be born when he is old?" Nicodemus fingered his beard nervously. "Can he enter his mother's womb a second time to be born?"

Jesus' guest was not being clever. He was attempting to conceal his rising emotions and at the same time get at the heart of the thing.

Jesus replied, "Truly I assure you, unless one's birth is due to water *and* Spirit, he cannot enter the kingdom of God." His face was the mirror of His heart at that moment. He cared deeply about this old scholar. And when Nicodemus did not comment, He went on earnestly, "What is born of the flesh is flesh and what is born of the Spirit is spirit."

Still Nicodemus did not speak. He was thinking, and Jesus' manner gave him liberty to be still and think.

The young Man leaned toward him, identifying with the old scholar's confusion. "Do not feel surprised because I tell you, you need to be born from above." He gestured toward the windy night outside, "The wind blows where it pleases, and though you hear the sound of it, you neither know where it comes from nor where it is going."

Nicodemus nodded, still silent.

"You see, it is the same with everyone who is born of the Spirit."

The old ruler frowned. "How is that possible? How is it possible for a man to be born of the Spirit? What does a man do to enter the kingdom of God?"

Jesus showed no impatience. His voice was kinder than ever. "You are a teacher of Israel. Are you still ignorant of this truth? I truly assure you that we speak of what we know and we testify to what we have seen; but you (even though you are a materialist at heart) do not accept our actual evidence. If you do not believe in earthly matters I mention to you, how can you believe the heavenly things I might tell you?"

At that point, Nicodemus brightened a little. Perhaps he saw, however faintly, that even he, with his scholarly background, needed an invasion by the Spirit of God before his mind could be enlightened to understand what this sincere young Man was saying. Still, he said nothing, and Jesus went on talking to him.

"No one has gone up to heaven except He who came down from heaven, the Son of Man whose home is heaven."

Nicodemus looked at Him sharply. Was he looking at the Son of Man whose home was in heaven? Jesus knew the moment was reeling for the old man and, graciously, He began to speak in terms He knew Nicodemus knew well.

"Just as Moses lifted up the serpent in the desert, so the Son of Man must be lifted up, so that whoever believes in Him may not perish but have eternal life."

Nicodemus stood up. Jesus sensed this was all he could hear for one time.

As the old ruler turned to Him in farewell at the door of the guest chamber, the very voice of the Lord God of Israel seemed to speak to Nicodemus. *"For God so loved the world that He gave His only-begotten Son, so that whoever believes in Him should not perish, but have everlasting life."*

Had the young Man spoken these words to him? Nicodemus seemed not to be sure. He slipped away into the night, as silently and stealthily as he had come, his old heart struggling with the new light crashing painfully against all he had been taught. Did people love the darkness more than the light? Had the Lord God sent His Son into the world, not to condemn the world, as he a Sanhedrinist, was called to do—but that the world, the whole world, could be saved through Him?

Old Nicodemus walked rapidly back to his luxurious home, gripping his walking stick as though to clutch with his will the old concepts of which he had been so proud. He had come to no final conclusion as he talked with the Galilean, but all the way home, along the dark, narrow Jerusalem streets, he found his attention going again and again to the trees bending this way and that in the wind above him.

The wind which he could not see.

Chapter 29

The Woman at the Well

By January of 28 A.D., Jesus and His disciples had moved from Jerusalem, north to the banks of the Jordan River within the province of Judea. Jesus preached and His disciples baptized, as the Baptist continued to do some miles farther north at Aenon Springs, near Salim in Perea province.

Though he was still preaching with his old, zealous fire, John the Baptist was not drawing his customary crowds. The Pharisees took full advantage of John's decreasing ministry by taunting him with the numbers who thronged to hear Jesus and to be baptized by His disciples.

When Jesus heard this, He stopped His disciples' baptizing, and left at once for Galilee. He loved the great-hearted, rustic preacher and wanted to avoid hurting him. Neither did He want to play into the wily hands of the ruling Jews who were attempting to make trouble within what they called the "new movement."

The road through hated Samaria was the shortest route to Galilee, and to escape quickly from the certain trouble He saw up ahead from the priests in Judea, Jesus and His disciples took the Samaritan road in late January.

No sharper hatred existed between two peoples as between the Jews and Samaritans. True Israelites considered them pagan, even though most Samaritans were mixed-blood descendants of the ten tribes of Israel which were scattered after Solomon's kingdom fell apart. Their religion was a form of politically perverted Judaism—twisted and altered with the passing centuries to satisfy the bigger nations in power. They did believe a Messiah would come from their midst, like Moses, who would eventually convert all nations to Samaritanism. They also had their holy mountain, Mount Gerizim, on which they had built their own temple. The Jews, of course, believed Mount Moriah to be the Mountain of God.

A true Israelite would take the long road around Samaria merely to avoid any contact with its despised people. None of this bothered Jesus, but His disciples were far from immune to the prejudice. However, He was gradually convincing them that His heart was in no way an exclusive heart, as theirs had always been. This appealed to Peter and his fellow-followers, even though it was difficult to understand. That Jesus struck them as being more like the God of their Fathers, who could rejoice with His people in their prosperity and encourage them to give thanks for the plenty of the land He provided, was a great relief to them. Jesus plainly enjoyed good meals and the laughter of other human beings. John and James, Peter and Andrew, Nathanael and Philip leaped quickly to His side here! But it was another thing when He also seemed eager to eat and live and minister among the hated Samaritans.

They stood grouped around Him on the top of a long ridge north of Shiloh, and watched His deep, dark eyes drink in the beauty of the wide sweep of the Shechem Valley, enclosed seven miles or so northward by the twin snowy peaks of Gerizim and Ebal. Samaria, although it resembled Judea, was not barren. Around the little band of men on the hillside, the tender, green, wild anemones waited only for the February rain to turn them pink and blue and purple and yellow and red.

Jesus looked for a long time down the narrow Shechem Valley, and smiled at His men when they showed their discomfort at entering the land of their national enemies. They were feeling more relaxed with Him every day, and Peter whistled nobly, hoping to show the Master that even if it was Samaria, he too thought it was a beautiful sight.

Down the hill and along the narrow, olive-shaded road they followed Him, to a place where several ancient Roman roads met, about half a mile from the Samaritan village of Sychar. At this intersection was a welcome sight. One they had been eager for—the Well of Jacob. They had walked a long way across difficult terrain and they were tired and thirsty and hungry.

Jesus dropped down wearily on the low stone wall at one side of the ancient well. His disciples trudged the other half-mile to Sychar for food and a well bucket.

The well was deep and full of clear, cold water. Jacob had dug it through solid limestone. But until the disciples came with a bucket, Jesus could not drink. The water they had brought in their goatskin bottles was warm and tasteless. No one from the village was likely to come for water at noon. He would have to wait.

But, in less than a half hour, down the stone steps from the common road to the well, a middle-aged woman came with her water jar balanced easily on her dark head. She moved rapidly and seemed oblivious of the beautiful countryside and the warm winter sun. The little tune she was humming broke off and she stopped abruptly when she saw Jesus.

He stood up and smiled. Too many thoughts whirled in this ignorant countrywoman's head for expression, and so she lowered her jar into the well without a word or a sign of recognition. After all, He was obviously a Jew, and His smile was so clearly kind she had no way of coping with it.

When her freshly drawn water appeared from the depths of the ancient well, Jesus stepped toward her and asked, "Will you let Me have a drink?"

At once He had put Himself in a position of asking a favor of a mere Samaritan woman! If she gave Him a drink, He would then be able to say, "Thank you."

The woman stared at Him in amazement. "How is it that you, a Jew, should ask me, a Samaritan woman, for a drink?"

Jewish men asked nothing of Jewish women in public, unless necessary. For a man to address a strange woman courteously in public was unheard of! More than that—a Samaritan.

Jesus looked at her rough hands. Her dress was the ordinary dark blue homespun, but around her waist she wore an inappropriate bright silk girdle, and on her head an even gaudier headdress—neither of which accomplished what the woman intended. Her voice was strident, almost coarse. She would not have been comfortable at the well with the average mild-mannered Samaritan housewife. He sensed the reason she came to the well at noon instead of in the cool of the morning or evening, when other women were there, too. Men sometimes stopped at noon to fill their skin bottles, but women made their trips for the family water supply in the cooler hours. Even in January, the sun could be hot at noon.

She did not give Him a drink but stood looking at Him with open woman-curiosity, her hands on her hips, her sandaled feet in a wide, somewhat impudent stance.

Jesus looked into her heart, and did not ask again for water.

The woman shifted her position self-consciously. Now she stood like an ungainly girl, and one dusty foot rubbed the dusty instep of the other.

"How is this that you, a Jew, should ask *me* for a drink?" The outsized string of coins around her headdress clinked as she spoke, this time less defiantly.

He was extremely careful and direct with her. What He had to say was so important, He took great care—even with one bawdily dressed Samaritan woman. "If you knew God's gift and who really asked you for a drink, you would have requested of Him and He would give you living water."

She laughed sarcastically. "Sir, you have no rope and bucket and the well is deep. Where do you get that living water?"

He stood looking at her with a kind of compassion she had never seen in a man's eyes.

She pressed her point, nervously. "You surely are not superior to our father, Jacob, who gave us the well!"

He answered her immediately. "Whoever drinks from this water shall again be thirsty. But whoever drinks the water I shall give him shall not thirst eternally—the supply is plentiful forever. The water I shall give him shall become a well of water within him that bubbles up for eternal life."

Her hands had dropped from her hips as He spoke. Her thoughts never ran deep, but her instincts were well practiced. Thirst was a common bondage with every living creature! Instinctively she took a step toward Jesus.

"Sir, give me this water, so that I will not get thirsty nor have to come all the way for drawing water again!"

She was interested only in an easy way out of her daily drudgery, but while He had some of her attention, He shocked her into more reality.

"Go, call your husband and come back here!" His voice was still gentle, but firm.

The woman cocked her head in surprise and the string of coins around her headdress jangled. "I do not have a husband!"

Before He delved into her conscience more deeply, He took time to praise her for her honesty. "You say correctly that you have no husband. You are frank and forthright."

She relaxed a little.

"You have had five husbands and the one you are now living with is not your husband. In this you told Me the truth."

The Samaritan woman was at once stunned and comforted. Who was this Stranger at the Well of Jacob on an ordinary January day? How did He know so much about her? Who was He? Who was this Man who gently forced her to think? To be so honest with Him?

He waited quietly for her to speak next. Her voice was no longer strident. It was little more than an awed whisper. "I perceive, Sir, that you are a prophet."

For a Samaritan to say this meant she had recognized some great authority! They believed in no prophets after Moses. But did she know what she had said? He still did not speak, wanting her to think it through for herself.

"Our fathers worshiped on this mountain," she gestured toward Mount Gerizim. "But you are a Jew, you say that Jerusalem is the proper place to worship." Was she really thinking, or was she stalling—trying to divert His attention from her personal life to the centuries old controversy between the Samaritans and the Jews concerning Mount Gerizim and Mount Moriah?

He knew she was stirred to her untouched depths by both interest and the desire to evade His knowing. He knew her ignorance and the half superstitious religion which had warped her life. She had never heard the whole truth of God, and so He was more direct with her than He had been with the learned Nicodemus. He helped her think.

"Believe me, woman, the time has come when you shall worship the Father, neither merely in this mountain nor merely in Jerusalem. You worship what you do not know; we worship what we know, for salvation comes from among the Jews. But, the hour comes—and is now—when genuine worshipers shall worship the Father in spirit and truth." His voice was gently urgent now. Entreating. "The Father is *looking* for such as His worshipers. God is a Spirit and His worshipers must worship in spirit and truth."

Her inner being moved toward Him in a way she did not understand. "I know that the Messiah, called Christ, is coming, and when He arrives, He will make everything plain to us." She spoke quietly now, almost wonderingly.

Standing a few feet from this half-awakened woman, with a reputation which made her fear to come to the well in the company of other women, He said what He had not yet said to anyone.

"Woman, I, talking to you now, am He."

She had no chance to speak. Laughing and joking like noisy schoolboys, the disciples invaded her sacred Moment. They were back from the village with a water bucket, dried fish, bread and cheese.

Their laughter stopped abruptly, as they all stopped a few yards from Jesus and the Samaritan woman. Each man among them was shocked at what he saw. Their Master in earnest conversation with a creature like that! But their respect for Him ran so deep no one said a word. The silent Moment hung there, wordlessly. She felt the disciples' scorn, but she also felt Jesus' presence.

She did the only thing she knew to do. Quickly, she handed Him a drink of water. The one she had forgotten to give Him when He asked for it. Then, leaving her water-pitcher on the rim of the well, she ran down the narrow road toward Sychar.

When she was out of sight, the disciples began to chatter again, somewhat uneasily. To cover their discomfort, they made too much of the ordinary lunch they had purchased.

Peter blustered the most. "Look at this fish, Master! Isn't that a nice one? Wouldn't be surprised if I hadn't caught that one myself!" He laughed too much at his feeble joke.

Jesus said nothing. He was still looking down the dusty road in the direction the woman had run.

John, who loved Him so much, knelt beside Him on one knee, offering His lunch to Him. Jesus looked at John, also with great love, and sorrow for the loyal disciple's lack of understanding, but He did not take the fish and cheese.

"Rabbi, eat! Please eat." John was genuinely disturbed.

"I have nourishment of which you have no idea." He did not withdraw His attention from them, but neither did He join them.

Nathanael turned to the others. "Perhaps someone has brought Him food already."

"No," Jesus answered. "My nourishment is that I do the will of My Sender and completely do His work." He looked out over the rolling, fertile wheat fields stretching away toward the two tall mountains. "Do you not say, 'Still four months and the harvest is here'?"

"Yes, Master." Peter was trying to understand. "That's right.

This is the end of January. In four months it will be harvest time."

Jesus looked beyond the still green wheat fields of Samaria. "Look, I tell you, raise your eyes and observe the other fields, how they are white for harvest. Already the reaper receives his wage and gathers the crop for life eternal, so that the sower and the reaper may be jointly glad. For the saying, 'One sows and another reaps' is verified here."

"Here in Samaria, Master?" Nathanael asked incredulously.

"Here in Samaria, Nathanael," He replied, looking toward the woman's village of Sychar. "Here I will send you to reap a crop on which you have not worked. Others toiled and you step in, to benefit from their work."

The disciples finished their lunch in silence. All of them thoroughly perplexed at His words.

In the little village of Sychar, the woman was running from one man to another group of men, excitedly telling them about Jesus. "Come, see a man who told me everything I have done! Is not this man the Christ?"

Most women would not have dared approach a group of men in public. This woman had no such qualms. Nor would her newly released heart permit them, if she had! "Come to the Well of Jacob, and see this man who told me everything I did! Surely, He is the Messiah!"

The disciples spread their rough woolen cloaks and stretched themselves on the grass beside the road to rest after lunch. Jesus lay resting on the cool ground, too, watching the flat winter blue sky.

Suddenly, John, who lay near Jesus, sat up. Dozens of men were running along the road from Sychar. The "harvest fields" were coming to them! Because of the woman's story, the men of Samaria urged Jesus and His men to stay awhile with them in the village.

Their journey back to Galilee was delayed two days. And during those two days, many Samaritans believed in Him.

The day the travelers left to continue their trip north, Jesus listened gratefully to those who said: "We no longer believe only because that woman told us her story. We believe in You now because we have personally listened and we know You are the Saviour of the world."

Chapter 30

Back in Galilee

Things were changed in Galilee by the time they returned, after almost a year of travel and work in Judea. The Galileans who had watched Jesus in action in the Temple at the Passover Feast last spring were no longer unimpressed with the Son of the Galilean widow, Mary. They flocked to hear Him this time, and He was treated like a famous, favored Son!

Word spread like a fire gone out of control concerning the second miracle He performed during a brief visit to Cana, where He had turned the water into delicious wine at the start of His ministry. This time, a courtier who had seen Him perform His many signs and wonders recently in Judea traveled until he found Jesus in Cana, and begged Him to come back down to Judea and heal his son. Jesus merely said to the man, "Go your way; your son lives!" Before the courtier reached home, because he believed Him, his servants ran to tell of the miraculous healing of his beloved son.

His disciples walked proudly after this Man who was now being lauded by everyone.

In the early spring He decided to visit His home town, Nazareth. As was His custom, He went to the synagogue on the Sabbath, and because His fame had followed Him even to the obscure little city of Nazareth, He was asked to read and speak in the service. The book of the prophet Isaiah was handed to Him, and He began to read from Isaiah 61.

"The Spirit of the Lord is upon Me, for He has anointed Me to preach the Gospel to the poor; He has sent Me to announce release to the captives and restoring of sight to the blind; to set free the downtrodden; to proclaim the year of the Lord's favor."

When He had finished reading, Jesus rolled up the scroll and handed it back to the custodian. The congregation of familiar faces sat somewhat smugly, but quite unmoved. It was a nice diversion, having a native Son speak to them. Most of them took Him for granted. Some were even antagonistic at the idea of being taught by a home-town "boy."

One member of the congregation nudged another and whispered, "Imagine Joseph's son sitting down to teach us in such a high and mighty fashion!"

His manner was not high and mighty. In fact, His sisters, who still lived in Nazareth, sensed how really glad He was to be home again. They smiled tenderly at Him as He looked up and down both sides of the congregation—one side lined with women who had been His mother's friends—the other with the men of the town.

Jesus sat down to teach them, His last words read from the Scripture still hanging electrically in the close air of the synagogue. "The Spirit of the Lord is upon Me, for He has anointed Me . . . to proclaim the year of the Lord's favor."

As the congregation began to stir uneasily under His quiet scrutiny, Jesus put aside His human desire to keep their friendship. His voice startled them as much as His first words: "Today this Scripture is fulfilled in your hearing!"

On the men's side of the synagogue there was displeased coughing. The women jerked themselves to show their annoyance at such audacity from a carpenter's son!

He went right on relentlessly, reading their shallow hearts.

"You will doubtless quote for Me this proverb: 'Physician, heal yourself.' Do in your own country of Nazareth what we hear you did in Capernaum and elsewhere."

The tension deepened in the sudden silence of the sanctuary. The people had stopped nudging each other, and no one coughed.

"But I assure you that no prophet is acceptable in his home town. I tell you truly, in the days of Elijah there were many widows in Israel, when for three years and six months the sky was closed up and a severe famine visited all the land; but to none of them was Elijah sent! He was sent only to a widow outside of Israel—at Sarepta of Sidon."

The custodian and the rulers of the synagogue rose angrily. The people, too, began to get up as He spoke. Who was He to dare address His elders so! Until they grabbed Him by the arm and began to shove Him out of the synagogue, Jesus kept on speaking in a firm, unruffled voice. "There were also many lepers in Israel, too, in the time of Elisha the prophet but none of them was cured. Only the outsider, Naaman the Syrian!"

Their smoldering suspicion of Him as He had begun to speak was now open hostility! No one could have prevented what happened. The elders and all the congregation—men and women, pushed Him along the familiar streets of His beloved Nazareth to the outer edge of the city, toward the high bluff He had loved so much as a Child. The disciples grabbed first one person, then another, in their panic to save Him. They fought their way toward Him in the angry mob and were forced back again and again.

Peter caught a glimpse of Jesus' face once, and never forgot that it remained unangered. Sorrow, yes, but no anger at all. And He walked along, without resisting.

As they neared the precipice where obviously they meant to push Him to His death, the yells and curses of the crowd decreased. There was only the scuff of their sandals and then that died, too.

John wanted to run to Him, standing there with His back to the great drop below, but there was a majesty upon Him, and a great calm. John could only stare along with the other disciples and all the angered, murderous mob.

No one moved, but there was a feeling that the crowd shrank into its own exposed nature. Jesus stood motionless for the passing of those stark, tense moments, then He began to walk toward the people, away from the high precipice at His back. No one even muttered as one by one, and in groups, they fell back to let Him pass through.

One by one John, then Peter, then James and Philip and Nathanael left the crowd to follow Him down the familiar mountain road and away from His beloved Nazareth.

Jesus and His disciples traveled all of Galilee, teaching in the synagogues, announcing the good news of the kingdom, and healing all kinds of disease and illness among the people, who came for miles around to see Him. Rumor about Him spread to all Syria and they brought men and women to Him who suffered from every kind of ailment. There were demoniacs, epileptics and paralytics, and He healed them all. Great throngs followed Him out of Galilee, Decapolis, Jerusalem, Judea and from beyond the Jordan.

Peter and James and John and Andrew and Philip and Nathanael scurried about attempting to keep the crowds under control. And always they were proud of their Master. Even arrogant at times because they were close to Him. He loved them all deeply, but as the busy days went by Peter and James and John grew to be His closest personal friends.

Jesus realized the cost to these men of discipleship. After all, they had left their profitable businesses and their families to follow Him. He was grateful, and although He had no delusions about any of them, He was glad for their personal loyalty to Him. Glad for the way they cared for His physical needs. He never ceased to be touched at the sight of young John—eager, enthusiastic—running toward Him with the best of the fish, and his own woolen cloak to spread on the ground for his Master's rest. Jesus knew John and James had both left a well-to-do home, where servants had waited on them since childhood. Now John, particularly, wanted to wait on Him hand and foot. And with such open love and loyalty.

After the trouble in Nazareth, they went to their new city, Capernaum, and Jesus taught in the beautiful white synagogue there, and healed a fear-ridden demoniac. All Capernaum was agog over this, but Jesus took it in His stride, wishing in His heart that He could do something to alleviate the trouble Peter was having at home because he chose to follow Him.

The same day Jesus healed the demented man in the Synagogue at Capernaum, He went with James and John to the small stone house where Peter and Andrew lived with Peter's wife and mother-in-law. Peter's quiet, plump little wife met them at the door.

"My mother is sick, Peter. She's had a high fever since the day after you left for Nazareth! Nothing the doctor can do seems to help her."

This was almost four hundred years before the Greek physician, Hippocrates, had set up his sensible system of medicine, and Peter's wife had been following the local doctor's orders by giving her ailing mother prescribed doses of pulverized horse teeth, mixed with a little scraping of mouse fat, ashes of a charred wolf's skull, and crab eyes!

Peter's life would have been simpler without his mother-in-law, but a new kind of love was invading the big man's heart these days. Even though most of the trouble between them was over

Jesus, Peter couldn't let the old lady suffer and die with the Master just outside the house.

"Master, will You heal her?"

Jesus nodded, but said nothing as He walked past them and up the narrow stone stairs to the old woman's quarters.

She lay tossing on her pallet in an agony of fever and pain, her face turned toward the stone wall. When she heard His footsteps, she jerked her head to look at Him and in her glazed old eyes there was only hostility when she saw who it was.

Jesus did not try to speak to her. He took her hand in His and just stood there by the bed. Involuntarily, the bony old hand pulled back, then nestled itself suddenly in the warmth of His strong palm. One of her withered fingers wrapped itself around His, as a baby's might do. And she rested.

In a matter of seconds, Jesus lifted her up. All the way up, so that she stood on her own feet! The hatred in her had melted so quickly and her strength came back so fast, she felt dizzy for a moment. Dizzy, then embarrassed, then grateful. Jesus smiled at her and standing there in His Presence she saw her resentment of Him as all selfish. She had thought He was stealing her daughter's husband. She had thought He was ruining Peter's career. Tears ran down her wrinkled, brown cheeks, but for once Peter's mother-in-law couldn't talk.

She couldn't even thank Him, but she did the only thing she knew to do. Right into the kitchen she went, and cooked dinner for them all, and served it to them. To Him she gave the best portions and hovered over Him all through the meal to be sure He had everything He wanted.

The old woman stayed as near Him as possible all that strange, exhausting, glorious evening, too, when it seemed that every person in Capernaum gathered at the door of Peter's home. He healed them all of their physical and mental diseases. And when Jesus was at last able to retire, the old woman had prepared His bed lovingly with her own hands.

His own nature kept Him giving Himself freely to the crowds of diseased and crippled people. He healed them patiently, one after another. But knowing His mission was to proclaim the new kingdom and to teach men that a personal relationship with the Father was now possible—with the law written in their hearts—

He was forced at times to escape the crowds who pressed for physical healing.

The day after He healed Peter's mother-in-law, Jesus got up before dawn and went to a quiet place alone, to commune with His Father concerning His next move.

As soon as the sun was up, back at Peter's home, the crowds were once more gathering outside for healing. When they didn't find Jesus, Peter and Andrew went to hunt for Him.

They knew how tired the Master was, but this was a big day for Peter, having the whole town at his front door again!

"They're all calling for you, Rabbi."

Both disciples sensed His answer before He spoke to them. They must not stay in one place too long. There was so much still to be done. And so, without returning to Capernaum, they left for other neighboring Galilean towns, where He preached in their synagogues and healed the sick and cast out demons.

One day He healed a leper, but sent him off with the stern injunction, "Be careful to tell no one; but go and show yourself to the priest, and, to assure others, offer what Moses has prescribed for your purification."

Jesus did not want to be known merely as a miracle-worker. Too much talk of this kind swamped His real message from God to His world. But the leper spread the news of his healing far and wide. From that time on, Jesus could no longer enter a town openly and unobserved. For many weeks He had to preach in far-off, lonely spots. Even so, from everywhere, the people crowded the roads on their way to find Him.

Chapter 31

"Your Sins Are Forgiven"

Late on the first night Jesus and His men returned again to Capernaum, Peter and James and John sat talking on the roof of Peter's house. They had just finished repairing the damage to the roof as a result of the strange incident of that afternoon. Jesus was asleep in the house on the floor below. It had been an exhausting, exciting and somewhat disturbing day for everyone. Disturbing for everyone, seemingly, but the Master Himself.

"I looked in on Him when I went down for water just now," John said. "He's sleeping soundly, as though He didn't notice the faces of those bigoted scribes today!"

Peter stretched his long, muscular legs and lay back flat on the roof. "He noticed all right. I think He actually read their thoughts!"

"He must have, Peter." James stroked his short, fine beard and frowned. "He came right out and asked them, 'Why do you argue this way in your hearts? Which is easier, to tell the paralytic that his sins are forgiven, or to tell him to pick up his mat and walk off?' "

Peter laughed. "The Master really had them cornered! I thought that one hawk-eyed scribe would burst a blood vessel, he looked so furious."

"Forgiveness of sins is for God alone." John was not laughing. A great truth was sinking into his young, impetuous heart, but as yet he seemed not to know what to do with it.

Jesus had performed another miracle that afternoon in Peter's house. As soon as the people of Capernaum learned that He was back, they crowded the house, inside and out, so that four men had to do a most unorthodox thing in order to get their sick friend to Jesus for healing.

The houses along the streets of Capernaum had adjoining roofs. Actually, people took the "roof road" frequently instead of the narrow streets of the city. When the four men found their way blocked to Jesus, they took the "roof road" with their paralyzed friend, removed a section of the roof of Peter's house and lowered the sick man down through the hole—in a shower of falling tile and dry mud—to the feet of Jesus!

The faith of these four friends touched the heart of the Master. He stopped teaching, looked at the drawn, immobile limbs of the paralytic and said, loudly enough for everyone to hear, "Son, your sins are forgiven you!"

Sins? Among the well-dressed scribes (lawyers) there to spy on Him was an angry stir. No one spoke, but their faces registered shock and horror at what to them was out-and-out blasphemy! Only God could forgive sins; and, according to the scribes and Pharisees, God would do it only if all the Temple regulations were met in the minutest detail.

The sick man lay still paralyzed on his mat, but as he looked up at Jesus, there was hope in his eyes. Jesus looked straight at the row of frowning scribes. It would be bad psychology if they openly attacked Him before all the admiring crowd. This was no secret to Him, and He asked them point-blank, "Why do you argue this way in your hearts? Which is easier, to tell the paralytic, 'Your sins are forgiven,' or to say 'Rise, pick up your mat and walk off'?"

The lawyers were trapped and they knew it. No one answered Him. So He put Himself on record publicly, giving them still more ammunition to use against Him.

"To let you know that the Son of Man *has* power to forgive sins on the earth (He turned again to the sick young man on the mat at His feet), I tell you, son, rise, pick up your mat and go home!"

Movement flew back into the boy's face first. He half-laughed and half-wept. The possibility seemed too good to be true—but he tried it, and up on his feet he sprang, shouting to his friends! Jesus watched the faces on the angry lawyers as the boy rolled up his mat and walked triumphantly through the way opened for him by the crowd of gaping people. There were shouts of joy and men and women praised God and said, "We never saw anything like it!"

Jesus left the house shortly after that, and went out to the seashore to teach. All the people who had seen Him heal the paralyzed boy went along, and hundreds more came from other parts of the city.

The agitated scribes hurried back to the Pharisees to report the "blasphemy" they had seen and heard.

The Man All Men Hated

Levi, the son of Alphaeus, was a customs officer—a despised tax collector—in the service of Herod Antipas, the ruler of Galilee. His post was at Capernaum, beside the sea, on the border between Judea and Galilee.

A tax collector was always a hated man. He could stop a traveler anytime on any pretense and tax him for his cart, the wheels on his cart, his donkeys, the load he was carrying—there was no limit to his authority. And no limit to the hatred he received from the people, usually with good reason. The Jews especially loathed the tax-collector, since the devout Jew believed only God had the right to the offerings of man. More than that, the tax-collector was a Jew turned traitor to work for the Romans. Customs officers were considered open criminals by society, and along with murderers and harlots, were social outcasts.

Only men whose personal lives were twisted by their own evil natures or circumstances ever applied for a job such as Levi held. Tax-collectors were men given up by society. Men lost to shame, devoid of any possibility of honor. Men so distorted in their souls that the hatred heaped daily on their heads could not lessen them. They were the least among men already!

Before Levi's tax-booth, Jesus stopped one day on His way to the seashore to teach.

He had seen Levi time after time as He went to and from the shore. Levi had seen Him; he had heard Him speak, and had seen Him make whole men and women out of physical and mental wrecks by the touch of His hand. Most important to Levi, however, was what Jesus had to say about the kingdom of God. A seed of hope had sprung to life in his embittered, defiant heart.

Year after year, Levi had added layer after layer of bitterness and resentment around his heart—hoping for nothing more than a thicker crust of protection against the hatred which he saw in the eyes of those forced to stop at his despised place of business. He had learned to hate those who hated him. It was his way of survival.

Jesus spoke of the love of God! More than that, He *lived* the love of God among the very people who hated Levi. Still more than that, there was an energy about Jesus—a conviction which Levi could not forget, even at night when he lay down to sleep in his empty, lavish house.

Now, this Man about whom everyone was talking stood at Levi's tax-booth looking directly at the hated, slightly built, balding collector. For that moment, Levi had the full attention of this famous Man! And for the first time in all his lonely, embittered, adult life, someone was smiling at him.

His acquaintances smiled wryly at him, hoping for favors. He entertained lavishly, using his power and his position to buy the company of those who felt it expedient to cater to the wretched little man; but he had never received a smile like this one. He felt his whole being throb almost unbearably with a strange emotion which he did not recognize at once as *encouragement*. He wanted to plunge and run from his tax-booth and never return!

Levi was unable to speak to Jesus. He could only sit hunched behind his counter and stare at the tall, compelling young Man with the deep-set eyes, and brown hair and beard.

A small crowd of people began to gather behind Jesus as He stood looking at Levi, but for this cherished moment there might have been only two persons in all the world—the despised tax-gatherer and the One who was about to become his Master.

Jesus spoke now, and one life ended and another began for the outcast man behind the counter.

"Levi, follow Me!"

Like a man coming out of an ordeal which he thought would never end, Levi pushed himself slowly to his feet, left his booth, and followed Jesus.

In his enthusiasm for his new Master, Levi entertained his questionable friends at dinner, with Jesus as guest of honor. Except for the other disciples and some Pharisee lawyers, all the guests were tax-collectors and sinners—Jews who refused to pay their Temple tax or keep the law. Not one of the Pharisaic lawyers would have attended a banquet at Levi's home among such despised guests had not their curiosity about Jesus over-ruled their snobbery.

The Master reclined comfortably with the others, enjoying His meal and delighting in Levi's excitement and joy. Jesus and His men ate often with people like Levi's friends, so only the haughty scribes were ill at ease.

Halfway through the magnificent banquet, one of the lawyers—a tall, angular man with a matching nose—could contain himself no longer. He nudged Peter, who reclined beside him, enjoying himself to the full, and asked with great disdain, "Why do you and your Master eat and drink with common tax-gatherers and sinners?"

Jesus Himself answered the question.

"Healthy people do not need a physician. Those suffering from illnesses do. I have come not to call the upright, but sinners to repentance!"

A sudden quiet fell across the room. He had done far more than answer a two-edged question posed by the clever lawyer. Reclining at dinner among His disciples, His new friends, and His enemies, Jesus announced His reason for coming to His Father's beloved world!

Perhaps no one around Levi's table really understood Him, but the pompous lawyer ignored His answer, and posed still another double-edged question. Rubbing his angular nose which matched his angular body, the scribe asked in a voice which matched both, "Tell us then, Rabbi, the disciples of John the Baptist fast and pray frequently, as do those of the Pharisees. But you and your disciples eat and drink right along—day in and day out. Why is this?"

Above the luxury and intended joy of Levi's banquet, Jesus could see the still distant cloud of opposition rolling toward Him.

He was eating an olive when the lawyer asked his question. Jesus finished the olive, placed the seed on His plate, and replied quietly and steadily, "Can the wedding guests be made to fast while the bridegroom is with them?"

In his eagerness to learn and to please his new Master Levi exclaimed, "Why, no, naturally not!"

No one rebuked Levi. He was the host; and Jesus was glad for his loyalty and enthusiasm.

"But the time will come." Jesus went on, looking directly at the lawyer, "when the bridegroom shall be taken from them, and in those days they will fast."

One of the guests, another tax-collector, spoke out of both ignorance and interest in what had happened to his host, Levi,

"You scribes and Pharisees don't understand about the Rabbi's teaching! Neither do I, for that matter, but I know it's new. Too new for your old scholarly heads!"

Some of the guests laughed uproariously. So did Peter. Jesus waited a moment, and when He began to speak again, the laughter stopped.

"No one patches an old garment with a patch taken from a new one. If he does, he will tear the new, and also the old. Furthermore, no one pours new wine into old wineskins, else the new wine will burst the skins and run out and the skins will be ruined. New wine should be put into fresh wineskins!"

His voice was kind, even sympathetic with the darkness of the scribe's mind, steeped as it was in the ceremonial law.

"I understand your suspicion of Me, Sir," Jesus went on. "No one used to drinking old wine wants new wine right after, for he says, 'The old is preferable'!" Jesus spoke directly to the lawyer, who represented those whom He now knew were His enemies.

That night before Jesus and His men left Levi's home, He gave the despised ex-tax-collector a new name—Matthew, which means "Gift of God."

Chapter 32

Another Stand in the Temple

In the summer of 28 A.D., Jesus went alone to another Jewish Feast at Jerusalem.

On the way, He heard the news from other pilgrims of the arrest of John the Baptist by Herod Antipas, Tetrarch of Galilee. John had lashed out publicly against Herod for taking his brother's wife, Herodias.

"You have no right under God to have your brother's wife!"

Herod feared John's influence anyway. So much talk of the coming kingdom had kept Herod in fear of an insurrection among the people. The Baptist's arrest was inevitable. His public condemnation of Herod's private life only precipitated it.

Still shouting his message of repentance and kingdom of God, the craggy-faced young preacher was seized on the banks of his beloved Jordan River, and dragged off as an insurrectionist to the dark and loathesome prison at Machaerus Fortress.

Jesus and John had never actually worked together, but the news of John's arrest darkened the outline of Jesus' aloneness among men. The differences in approach and personality between the two men were sharp. John was a rigid purist who could not stand the presence of evil. Jesus associated freely with sinners. John slashed them with scathing invectives. Jesus showed warm interest and understanding. John drew back from sin. Jesus walked to meet it. Still, the bond between them was of God, and Jesus was deeply hurt by the news of His cousin's arrest.

John had said with a humility that stabbed and strengthened Jesus' heart, "He must increase and I must decrease." Jesus knew His was to be a way of aloneness, but His humanity caused Him to feel walled off in a deeper way when He knew that John was no longer able to raise his piercing young voice "in the wilderness" of the people's darkness.

The lone Man from Galilee, who had chosen to make this pilgrimage to Jerusalem without His disciples, climbed the steep fourteen miles from Jericho through Bethany to the Holy City, deep in thought and communion with His Father.

He loved the Temple at Jerusalem. It was His Father's house.

As a Boy of twelve, its holy meaning had laid hold of His heart and mind, so that He could not leave with His parents at the close of His first Passover Feast. At the outset of His public ministry, He had acted on His knowledge of the holiness of His Father's Temple by physically upsetting the cheap commercialism within the Temple court.

Jesus was in no way antagonistic to Temple Law and ritual. His pilgrimages were regular and devout. Still, the superficiality and glitter and pomp displayed by the ruling Jews stifled Him. As one needs to escape from a stuffy, heavily draped room into the cool air, Jesus needed to escape the airless, unnatural confinement He saw choking the clear breath of God from Temple life. Empty tradition hemmed Him in and saddened His heart.

Back into His native climate walked Jesus on the Sabbath day of the Festival; up and down the streets of Jerusalem, among the suffering, ignorant, troubled people. He strode away from the smug "great ones of Israel," sorting and sifting their Law, sure that by their subtle analysis of its every letter they would possess for themselves eternal life.

Jesus could not remain long among those who struggled pompously with the belief that God offered Himself only through *their* channels. They were not able to believe His message and He knew it! They would find eternal life through their own understanding of the Law! The fresh air of the kingdom message of Jesus, which offered a man eternal life through a surrender to the will of the Father, irritated them. *They could not believe it!*

Jesus could not waste valuable time among them, knowing their highly trained minds had locked and bolted their hearts. And so He walked the streets of Jerusalem where the full needs of men helped them to believe.

No more pitiable sight could be found in all the Holy City than the regular gathering of invalids of all wretched descriptions beside the Pool of Bethesda, near the Sheep Gate in the north course of the wall of the Holy City. Suffering drew Him inevitably, and so He joined the crowd of onlookers at the pathetic display of human agony among those who crawled and hobbled and were carried to the pool, where superstition held that an angel stirred the waters at certain intervals. The people believed that

259

the first invalid to get into the pool after the waters had been disturbed would be healed.

There were five entrances to the pool, all crowded, and Jesus walked among the crowd, unnoticed, until He found the most wretchedly hopeless invalid. The man lay motionless on a dirty mat, able to move only his head. Someone evidently brought him there every day, but left him to the frustrating agony of trying to reach the pool. Looking at him, Jesus could see no hope in the man at all, except that he was there again that day.

He stood beside the shriveled body of the paralyzed man who had become such a familiar sight, no one had even questioned him for years.

"Do you *want* to become well?"

The man's wrinkled, bitter face tensed; he squinted up at Jesus, blinking his small, sunken eyes. The question was finding its mark. It landed in a tangle of miserable self-pity! The invalid stretched his neck toward Jesus, literally demanding sympathy.

"I have no one, Sir, to put me into the pool right after it has been disturbed! You have to get in the water at once. I have no one to help me. Every time—for thirty-eight years while I am trying to get to the water, another gets to it ahead of me!"

Jesus wasted no words of unnecessary sympathy. He did not preach to the man. He merely said, "Get up, pick up your mat and walk!"

Instantly the man was on his feet, picking up his dirty old mat, and exclaiming to everyone around!

Running up and down in sheer delight, in the crowded area, he bumped into a silk-robed Pharisee!

"This is the Sabbath, and you have no right to carry your mat on the Sabbath! The law says a man cannot carry any burden on the Sabbath Day."

The man whom Jesus had healed was totally unaware of any "burden" so great was his joy, and much more than Pharisaical rebuke would have been needed to dampen his spirit. It was "Sabbath" in this man's heart!

With the childlike faith which had enabled him to obey Jesus' command to walk (as though it should be enough for the Pharisee), the man replied, "But the one who healed me told me to do it! He said to me, 'Pick it up and walk'!"

"Who is the person who told you to do this on the Sabbath?"

The Pharisee pressed his question sharply. "Tell me his name!"

The man grew somewhat nervous. "I do not know who it was who healed me, Sir. I honestly do not know his name."

He looked around for Jesus, who had slipped away in the crowd.

Later, wanting wholeness of spirit as well as healing for the man, Jesus hunted until He found him in the Temple enclosure.

"You are now enjoying health," Jesus said to him. "But you must quit sinning or something worse will happen to you."

There was no threat involved, merely a careful warning that a man's heart turned against God in self-will can harm his whole body. The man may or may not have grasped Jesus' words, but he was so excited over both his healing and the admonition of the Pharisee, he ran straight back to him and identified Jesus!

When the Jews found Jesus in the Temple and questioned Him for causing a man to desecrate the Sabbath, He faced them squarely and set up Himself what would be both lines of their opposition to Him! He well knew they could oppose Him to the death on two charges: His views on the Sabbath and His claimed relationship to the Father.

"My Father works till now—on the Sabbath—and so do I work."

No one was ready yet to attack Him openly on either point, but Jesus was ready to be attacked. In the Temple at Jerusalem He had once more been forced to light the fuse of their anger.

There was no other way.

Chapter 33

Report to the Disciples

Back in Capernaum after the Feast in Jerusalem, which He attended alone, Jesus attempted to tell His disciples about His encounter in the Temple with the Pharisees. He wanted them to understand that when He chose the Twelve who would be His close companions and fellow-workers, they would be placing themselves in the same line of fire.

Several of His men sat or lounged on the sand of a secluded rocky cove on the Lake of Galilee, near Capernaum. They were glad to have Him back.

As He explained to them about His experience in the Temple in Jerusalem, John in particular seemed to weigh His every word.

"Master, did they accuse You of not following the Scriptures?"

"Yes, Rabbi," Peter broke in before Jesus could answer. "You teach from the Scriptures! Oh, I admit our interpretation is Your own. But after all, You've a right to interpret them. If they have a right, so have You!"

"Is it a matter of a 'right' to interpret the Scriptures, Master?" John's eagerness kept him talking.

"Certainly the Master has a right to interpret Scriptures!" Peter was about to take over the conversation again when Thomas, a newer disciple, with a factual, inquisitive mind, said, "It seems to me it would be well if the Master had a chance to talk. Just what did You say to the Pharisees, Rabbi, concerning the Scriptures?"

Jesus told them that He had said, "You investigate the Scriptures, because you suppose that you have eternal life in them! But they are the testimonies for Me. Yet you do not want to come to Me in order to have life."

Judas Iscariot had been pacing, as usual, up and down the wet, packed sand of the shore. He was a rabid follower of Jesus, but impatient with what he considered His leisurely approach to most problems.

"This is where I am lost, Master," Judas complained. "Where is the coming kingdom in this 'life' You speak of? And did the

Pharisees accuse You of bigotry when You spoke of Yourself as giving life?"

More than anything, Judas wanted to be chosen as one of Jesus' permanent disciples. He knew he took a chance by showing so much impatience, but no matter how hard he tried he could not resist prodding the Master into more definite answers and more action.

Jesus did not answer Judas' question about the kingdom that day. Judas and the others would be exposed to all His kingdom teaching in the days to come. But He did tell them what He had said to the Jews at the Temple in regard to His constant personal reference.

"I said to them, whatever you may think, I reach for no human fame. Still I know you Pharisees. You do not have the love of God in you!"

"Whew!" Peter smacked his broad, muscular knee with his open palm. "The old boys must have been furious at that!"

John sat beside Jesus, thinking deeply. How did the love of God come into a man? Was God Himself the same as love? If a man had love, did he have God? And if a man had God, did he have love?

Jesus got up from the thick coil of rope on which He had been sitting as they talked. The men jumped to their feet, too, waiting for Him to say the next word. He seemed finished with His account of the experience in the Temple. The next thing was to go home. They were all tired.

The crowds had been so enormous that day by the Lake of Galilee that He had used Peter's small boat launched just offshore as a pulpit from which to teach.

"Hold Out Your Hand!"

The next Sabbath day Jesus once more met opposition on the issue of human need and the Sabbath. He was teaching in the synagogue, as usual, under the watchful eyes of a group of silk-robed Pharisees.

This time they had brought along a man with a withered arm. If Jesus healed this man on the Sabbath, they would have another charge against Him. Their law forbade the act of healing on the Sabbath except in a case of life and death. This man had been handicapped by a paralyzed arm for years. Jesus, they reasoned, could have waited until the next day.

The man did as Jesus directed.

The heart of God never wants to wait to alleviate human suffering. Jesus acted invariably in harmony with His Father. He knew their plan, but He met it with His usual clear motives and calm courage.

Turning to the man with the crippled arm, He said, "Stand up and come here to the center of the group!"

Then He turned to the Pharisees and said, "I want to ask you, Doctors, if it is allowed to do good or to do evil on the Sabbath?" He pressed His question. "Is it allowed to save a life or to destroy it?"

The Pharisees stood silent, answerless, and angry, attempting to appear aloof.

Jesus looked leisurely around at all of them. Then, turning back to the man with the withered arm, He said, "Hold out your hand!"

The paralyzed arm reached quickly toward Jesus and everyone present saw that it was completely healed.

No one among the group of Temple officials could answer His question concerning the legality of doing evil or doing good on the Sabbath. But angered by what He had done, they stalked in a pompous, frustrated body out of the white stone synagogue to discuss together what they might do to be rid of Jesus!

Chapter 34

Calling the Twelve

His entire life was geared to bearing the truth of the reality of the kingdom of God to the people of the world, but Jesus was still a Man with an enormous capacity for friends. In one sense, He was destined to be alone except for His constant communion with His Father. But unlike John the Baptist, who thrived on the lonely life, Jesus was sociable by nature, and obviously enjoyed being with people. He needed a few loyal men to travel and work with Him until they could go out to preach the good news of the kingdom. But He also needed them as friends, and He seemed never to try to hide this need in Himself.

His choice of the Twelve who would come to be known as His Apostles seems a strange one. They were all men from the middle to lower economic classes—blustering, warm-hearted, impetuous; or shy, uncertain—and in the case of Matthew, socially frowned upon. But Jesus' message centered in the tremendous potential, inherent in *any* human life, when that life is linked with the life of God. It would have been ludicrous for Him to have chosen men who fit the human standards of the Pharisees and Sadducees!

Much more than an intellectual conviction was Jesus' heart-determination to live among His disciples in the new relationship of the kingdom. What He *was* Himself, was always more important than what He said, and so He set about *being* His message among the odd assortment of men whom He chose to share His work.

In His attitude of heart, His teaching and His healing, He entered deeply into the lives of others. No problem in the life of any disciple (or of any person anywhere) was too small for His interest. He would be taking upon Himself the sorrows, the sufferings, the perplexities and the joys of these men whom He chose. His prayers rose to the Father that in the hearts of this collection of ordinary men whom He loved would be born the desire to learn to live together in harmony. Harmony which could only result from the invasion of the love of God in their lives.

Every rabbi had a group of faithful followers, but here the similarity ended. The rabbis and their disciples concerned themselves with the study of the Scriptures and interpretation of the Law. Jesus always taught against the background of the Scriptures, but His was a message *announcing* the arrival of the kingdom of God!

"Repent, for the kingdom is at hand!"

He spoke to the multitudes of the characteristics peculiar to kingdom living; alone with His disciples, He taught them in as much detail as they could comprehend that the deepest meaning of the kingdom can be understood only as each man encounters the supreme, personal rule of God for himself. Not once did He attempt to explain what the rule of God *is*. He related the kingdom and eternal life with Himself! If men would follow Him, they would know. He recognized their blindness, and the terrible contradictions they must overcome. Contradictions between His teaching and what they had grown up believing as Jews who waited for an earthly kingdom which would once more prove that *they* were the chosen people of God! Patiently, bit by bit, He allowed them to find their own way to the dynamic of what He taught.

He seemed to be preparing them (not in so many words at first) to carry on His work for Him. This was difficult for them to understand. Jesus was just past thirty years of age.

Some of the disciples were older than their Master. Each man among them had some understanding and some confusion concerning His teachings and His purpose; but each shared one common certainty—an attraction to the Person of Jesus which caused them to forsake their work and their families when necessary, in order to follow Him.

Many more than twelve had been following Him periodically. Now He was ready to choose from among them those who would share most intimately His daily life and mission. The men sensed that the time had come for the choosing.

One Sabbath He suggested that they leave Capernaum and try to find a place deserted enough for a special meeting together away from the ever-present crowds.

As they walked away from the seashore, toward the mountains on a bright June day, they took a short cut through the rich grainfields which stretched between the city and the hills beyond.

There was no apparent way to avoid the persevering Pharisees, because even on this private journey one of their paunchier lawyers puffed along unable to keep up with their vigorous strides. No one tried to avoid him, he just couldn't keep up.

He caught up, however, when the disciples grew hungry and stopped to pick some grain to eat. Their walk would be long and to conserve their food supply, they rubbed the grain in their hands to loose it from the big, full heads, and ate it. Since they all had healthy appetites, the men showed a great amount of delight in what they did.

Gaping in horror at the casual Sabbath behavior of the disciples of a man who claimed to represent the Lord God, the scribe demanded (after he had caught his breath), "Why do you practice what is not allowed on the Sabbath? Picking grain is a labor not allowed by the Law!"

Jesus Himself answered so pointedly that His men stopped crunching the grain and pondered the strange viewpoint He advanced:

"The Son of Man is Lord of the Sabbath. The Sabbath was made for man, not man for the Sabbath!"

When they had at last shaken the troublesome scribe, Jesus did what He loved to do. He taught His disciples out of the immediacy of what had just happened. He wanted no one to think that the Sabbath was for man to use for his own selfish ends.

Carefully He explained that the Law was given originally by God to provide for man's need of guidance for life on earth. If the Law of the Creator God were followed by His creatures, their lives should be full and righteous and their needs should be met.

His disciples never thought of doubting the Creator God. The faith (whatever its degree) of all Jews presupposed the reality of God and His sovereignty over His created world. So they understood that God's laws for man would, according to the very nature of God, be given to fill the *needs* of man. The laws were given not to restrict people, but to serve them! Now the Jews had reversed God's order to the extent that men were slaves attempting to serve the letter of the law! Jesus' men were hungry, they needed food for their long walk. To Him the letter of the law was not involved here.

The men listened intently.

"What did You mean, Master, when you said, 'The Son of Man is Lord of the Sabbath'? Did you mean us, as men, or did You refer to Yourself?" Judas Iscariot's question was in all their minds.

Jesus answered him with a reminder. "I also said, the Sabbath is made for man, not man for the Sabbath."

"You always include Yourself with us don't You, Rabbi? I will never grow accustomed to this, I guess."

Matthew's heart kept him reminded of his life in his tax booth as a social outcast who stopped at nothing to gain his own selfish ends. It was always fresh and important to Matthew that Jesus had wanted him.

John walked silently beside Jesus. In his mind an idea turned and turned. The one idea that haunted and possessed him these days. His Master must have some special authority to be able to make such practical heart-sense of the Law! How did He see depths in it which no learned man had ever seen? They believed in their hearts that He was the coming King of Israel, and yet He had never once acted like a Messiah! What was His authority? What lighted the Master's mind as no other human mind had ever been lighted? When would He proclaim Himself to the world?

Judas Iscariot was thinking deeply, too, but his innate impatience forced him to voice the questions which turned in his practical, energetic mind.

"Master, You have an ability to understand all of life which sets You apart from other men! When will You declare Yourself to be who You are? When will we set about establishing the kingdom of God? What are we waiting for?"

Jesus smiled at Judas, but the conversation was closed for that time. He had explained to them what they needed to know then about the incident in the grainfield. There was something else to be done now.

They were well up the side of the mountain. It was growing dark. Jesus left them and went off alone to spend the entire night in prayer with His Father.

The next morning the crowds had found them, but He called His disciples to Him and told them He was now ready to select twelve from among them. He did not exclude the others. Jesus excluded no one. These He would simply be commissioning to forsake all and follow Him daily to the end. Once more their hearts stirred uneasily within them. What did He mean by the end? Where would He be going?

The moment had their attention, though, because none knew for certain whom He would choose.

Jesus moved a little farther up the gentle, flower-cluttered slope, a few yards away from the group of disciples, and began to call the names of those He had chosen to ordain as His special followers.

The first name the waiting men heard was Simon Peter!

Peter scrambled to his feet and ran like a happy school-boy up the hill to stand by Jesus.

"Andrew!"

Peter's brother Andrew ran, too. It was characteristic of Andrew that although he had brought Peter to the Master, he did not seem to mind being second. His name had been called. He could go up the mountain to join Jesus. Nothing else mattered to Andrew.

"James and John!"

The two "Sons of Thunder," as Jesus nicknamed them, started up the mountain together. When they had almost reached the Master, John found an extra burst of speed. His heart had always hurried him to Jesus' side. It hurried him even more that morning.

"Philip!"

"Nathanael!"

Up the side of the hill still wet and green from the night strode the two friends, their faces as full of hope as the new day breaking clear now across the quiet sky.

In the group of men waiting at the foot of the hill, a slender, sharp-featured young man with a dark, straight beard, had been pacing nervously. Every movement of his quick, agile body showed his inner tension. Waiting was the hardest thing this feverishly energetic young man ever had to do!

Another waiting disciple, Thomas, grew impatient with the constant pacing of the sharp-featured, intense young man who now picked up stones to throw at the ground as he kept up his nervous activity.

"Sit down, Judas! Don't you think we're nervous, too? Do you think you're the only one who isn't sure he will be called?"

Judas whacked the innocent grass with another pebble and frowned. There was so much to be done! Why did the Master always take the slowest way to accomplish things?

Once more the voice of Jesus broke the silence.

"Matthew!"

The balding ex-tax-collector rose to his feet. He hadn't dared believe that Jesus would actually call his name! Before Matthew had gone very far, another name was called: "Thomas!"

The two walked up the hillside toward Jesus as though a magnet drew them.

"James, the son of Alphaeus!"

"Simon, the Zealot!"

Jesus waited a moment as these two also came toward Him smiling, grateful for their call.

Judas stopped pacing abruptly. Ten men had walked up the hillside. The Master would be calling two more names!

"Judas—son of James!"

The nervous young man's disappointment was so sharp he did the only thing he could bear to do. He began to run away—down toward the city. The Master had called the name of "Judas," but He didn't want *him*. He wanted Judas, the son of James!

"Judas Iscariot!"

Jesus' voice reached after him as he ran, found him, stopped him!

"Judas Iscariot!"

For a moment, while his heart realized what his ears had heard, the angular, fanatic disciple could only stand where the Master's voice had stopped him on the slippery grass. He still faced toward the city, his back to Jesus and the others.

Slowly Judas Iscariot turned around and began to walk toward the Master in whom he believed so urgently. Judas was too despairing of life to smile as he climbed deliberately up the hillside again, clenching and unclenching his slender fists to release some of the excitement which built with every step he took toward Jesus.

He was going to be a vital part of the kingdom after all!

Chapter 35

Teaching on the Mountain

Jesus sat on a large, flat rock jutting from the side of the mountain outside Capernaum. Beside Him was John. The other eleven sat—some at His feet, their arms locked around their knees—some stretched on the grassy slope of the gentle Galilean mountainside.

Below, in the valley, the crowd still lingered, but this time the people kept their distance. They knew this was a sacred time for both Jesus and the men whom He had called. Interest ran high among those gathered below in the valley. Some were friends of the Twelve who sat now with the Master on the side of the mountain.

Jesus conducted no elaborate ordination ceremony. He gave them no pep talk. They knew well enough the seriousness of the moment. To the twelve men, it was so serious they were relieved and grateful that Jesus remained natural and relaxed with them. Having been chosen by their beloved Master brought more joy and excitement than they could contain. Understanding their emotional state, Jesus simply began to teach then as He had done so often during the past months.

What He had to say this time, however, focused in a new way the nature of the kingdom He came to announce. Jesus waited a moment, looking with deep affection at each man.

Suddenly Matthew blurted, "Master! How is it that You have chosen *me?*"

"Or me!" Peter's big voice boomed brokenly.

"Or me, Rabbi!"

"Or me!"

All the men caught Matthew's awe, and Jesus said, "Blessed are they who sense spiritual poverty, for theirs is the kingdom of heaven."

He stopped there, realizing that the men needed time to comprehend.

"*Ours* is the kingdom if we know our worthlessness, Master?" John asked incredulously.

"Yes, blessed are they who sense spiritual poverty, for theirs *is* the kingdom of heaven," Jesus repeated slowly.

Judas Iscariot was deeply perplexed. This was not the kind of kingdom he longed to see come!

Jesus spoke again.

"Blessed are they who mourn, for they shall be comforted."

Judas frowned. He was the only Judean among the Twelve. His life had been brittle and barren like the Judean hills. He hated the superficiality of the Temple officials in Jerusalem, but Judas had little interest in mourners. The eleven others from among the warm-hearted Galilean people understood weeping far better than Judas. His heart was in turmoil over the condition of the world under the hated Roman rule, but he had little sympathy for tears.

Peter was thinking hard. Then he brightened.

"I get it, Master! We are more apt to know God is comforting us if we mourn."

Jesus nodded, pleased with Peter's comment.

"What a way to get God's attention!" Judas snorted.

"Be still, Judas!" Peter roared, forgetting his new insight.

Jesus cut into the pending dispute.

"Blessed are the *gentle,* for they shall inherit the earth."

Peter hung his head.

The Master's voice was quieter now. "Blessed are the hungry and thirsty for righteousness, for they shall be satisfied."

Peter looked up sheepishly, without raising his head. He needed righteousness all right. But how did the need make him *blessed?* Was it because he knew he was not righteous? But Judas could be so irksome!

Once more the Master's voice and words pricked their hearts.

"Blessed are the merciful, for they shall obtain mercy."

Peter jerked his head up now. "Say that again, Master, please!"

"Blessed are the merciful, for they shall obtain mercy."

Peter turned around toward Judas.

"I'm not very merciful to you, Judas."

The big fisherman had gotten the point. So did the others. God's mercy was not experienced by obeying the letter of the law. He was a merciful God, but man only knew that mercy at its fullest when his own heart showed mercy.

"Blessed are the *pure* in heart," Jesus continued, "for they shall see God."

Matthew clenched his hands tightly.

"Master, how could my heart ever be pure? You know what it has been like all my life! You know the people I have cheated—the poor I have over-taxed. I long to see God, Master—but I have been so sinful."

"No more than I, Matthew!" Judas Iscariot snapped.

Nathanael of Cana, the scholar among them, commented thoughtfully, "For that matter, Judas, according to the Scriptures, 'All have sinned and come short of the glory of God!'"

"Some more than others, I'm sure," Matthew was still troubled. "And I am the worst."

John, still sitting on the big stone beside Jesus, laid his hand on the Master's knee.

"Could it be, Master, that what You mean is, if a man *wants* to see God, as Matthew certainly does—that man is on his way to purity of heart?"

Jesus smiled and Matthew's troubled face began to relax.

"When a thing is *pure*," James mused, "it means it is not mixed with anything else, right? So maybe this means that a man's heart is pure if his motives are right down one line. Not mixed with helping himself or dodging something he should be doing for the Master."

Each one got some of what He said, and His way was to let them think things through for themselves.

Before He spoke further, Jesus looked around the strange band of men with Him. Men who, for the most part, could never have gotten along together at all.

There sat Matthew, the once hated quisling Jew, who collected from his own people outrageous taxes to be paid to the Roman conquerors. Sitting next to Matthew—expressionless and silent, but quietly listening, was Simon the Zealot, who, until he began to follow Jesus, was a member of the most vengeance-filled nationalistic party in all Jewry!

Simon would have murdered Matthew on sight before he met Jesus of Nazareth. Now he was Matthew's brother in the work of announcing the kingdom of love! Matthew's deeply repentant heart had helped make peace with Simon the Zealot, who hated everything Roman.

Jesus looked at Matthew, who He knew never missed an opportunity to do a favor for Simon, and then taught them again.

"Blessed are the peacemakers, for they shall be called God's sons."

Matthew rubbed his bald head happily and smiled at the Master, then at Simon the Zealot, who nodded briskly.

Knowing full well that these twelve men whom He loved would face real persecution before their earthly lives ended, Jesus' face was at once full of tender love and great strength as He further said: "Blessed are those persecuted on account of righteousness, for theirs is the kingdom of heaven."

Once more Judas was deeply disturbed.

"Master, I am trying to understand You, but for the life of me, I can't see how we, who are to be a part of the powerful coming kingdom of heaven, can be 'blessed' in persecution! Have not our fathers been persecuted enough? If we act in strength and faith in God, will not the real kingdom, when it comes, be one to free Israel forever from persecution?"

Jesus looked at Judas, loving him, understanding his misplaced fervor. Not answering Judas' question, but looking straight into the dark, fiery eyes of this intense young man, Jesus said: "Blessed are you when they slander and persecute you and falsely accuse you of every wrong because of Me."

Judas turned away, unsatisfied.

"Be glad," Jesus went on, "and supremely joyful, for in heaven your reward is rich, for they persecuted previous prophets the same way."

Thomas was a man who had difficulty living with an unasked question.

"Master, You say we are to be supremely joyful, knowing that they persecuted *previous* prophets. Does this mean *we*, Peter and James and John and Andrew and all the rest of us are prophets, too?"

Jesus grinned at Thomas and his question.

"Prophets, Thomas? You are the salt of the earth!"

No one thought of anything to say in response to this surprise the Master tossed them, until Peter said, "Oh, well—salt is pretty important! After all, food isn't worth eating without salt."

Simon the Zealot had been characteristically silent. Now he spoke. "For that matter, salt is a preservative, too."

Jesus was unusually pleased with the Zealot. It was good when a man's violence turned thoughtful. He nodded good-naturedly at Simon.

"But if the salt has lost its quality, with what shall it be salted? It is thereafter good for nothing but to be thrown out and walked on by the people."

Then He threw them a challenge.

"You are also the light of the world. A city built on a hill cannot be hid. Neither do they light a lamp and place it under a peck measure, but on a stand; then it shines for everyone in the house. Similarly, let your light shine among the people so that they may observe your lofty actions and give glory to your heavenly Father.

"Do not suppose that I came to annul the Law and the Prophets . . . but I tell you that unless your righteousness surpasses that of the scribes and Pharisees, you shall not at all enter into the kingdom of heaven.

"You have heard how it was said, 'An eye for an eye and a tooth for a tooth,' But I say to you, Do not resist the injurer, but whoever strikes you on the right cheek, turn to him the other as well. And if anyone wants to sue you for your undergarment leave him your coat, too. And whoever forces you to go one mile, go with him two miles. Give to the solicitor and do not refuse the borrower."

They could scarcely believe their ears! All of them were dumbfounded and bewildered that Jesus spoke as He did.

"Forgive me, Rabbi, but to my mind this is madness!" Judas exclaimed. "What kind of kingdom would it be if every man gave to every solicitor who came and never refused a borrower? Believe me, I am trying to follow Your line of thoughts, and my whole heart is in following You, but there would be economic chaos in a kingdom set up as You have just described! I'm a practical man. If a kingdom is operated on the basis of going the second mile and giving away your clothing to anyone who sues you, it will collapse! A man who sues you is your enemy. He must be treated as we have all been taught. 'An eye for an eye and a tooth for a tooth' is just good business!"

Jesus gave no sign of surprise or disapproval when Judas finished his tirade.

"You have heard that it was said, 'Love your neighbor and hate your enemy.' But I say to you, Love your enemy and pray for your persecutors. In this way you may become sons of your heavenly Father, for He makes His sun to rise on the evil and the good and He pours rain upon the just and the unjust . . . You then, are to be spiritually mature, as your heavenly Father is perfect."

The men looked at one another and then at Jesus. No one spoke for several minutes.

Then Peter said, "How can ordinary men like us be that good, Master? You know we want to be what You want us to be, but how can we?"

"Maybe from now on we can be, since we're going to be with You most of the time!" Matthew's sincerity was consistent as always. "I don't seem to have as much trouble when I'm actually with You, Master."

Philip agreed, and so did Andrew and Thomas. All the men nodded except Judas Iscariot and Simon the Zealot. Both disciples longed to please Jesus, but neither could follow Him where His concept of the kingdom was concerned. Simon was too nationalistic and Judas too practical. Both men were impatient for action they could see and in which they could participate. They were not in disagreement about the fact that they were better men in Jesus' presence. They were just not thinking about being better men. They wanted to get to work in the promised kingdom!

"We can be with You, Master, but what about the millions who can't be?" John asked. "How will we convince them of these things You have taught us?"

Thomas chose only one of the many questions twisting in his mind. "How can *we* convince the Israelites that the Pharisees are wrong in sticking to the letter of the Law without something more concrete to use in our arguments?"

"Remember, Thomas, I have told you, I did not come to abolish but complete the law. You, as My disciples, are to be careful not to perform your good works publicly to be noticed by the people. When you do benevolence, do not blow a trumpet as the hypocrites do in the synagogues and in the streets to gain glory from men. When you practice charity, your left hand must not know what your right is doing, so your charity will be in secret. And your Father who sees in secret will reward you.

"And when you pray, do not be like the hypocrites, for they love to pray standing in the synagogues and on the important street corners to be seen by the people. When you pray, enter into your inner room and with your door closed pray to your Father, the Invisible, and your Father who sees in secret will reward you.

"When you pray, do not repeat and repeat as the pagans do, for they imagine that for their much talking they will secure a hearing. Be not like them, for your Father knows your need before you ask Him."

"Master, I for one do not know how to pray! Will You teach us to pray?" Andrew asked.

"Yes, Master, how should we pray?"

All the men shared a common interest here. Jesus was quiet a moment and then He said, "This is the way you should pray:

"Our Father, who art in Heaven, Thy name be kept holy. Thy kingdom come. Thy will be done on earth as in heaven. Give us today our daily bread. And forgive us our debts as we forgive our debtors. And lead us not into temptation, but deliver us from the evil one. For Thine is the kingdom and the power and the glory forever, Amen."

Jesus spoke to His Father in a quiet, natural voice. Then He explained one important part of His prayer to the men.

"If you forgive others their trespasses, your heavenly Father can forgive you, too; but if you do not forgive people, neither can your heavenly Father forgive your trespasses."

"You are to ask and it will be given you. You are to seek and you will find. You are to knock and it will be opened to you. For every supplicant, if he seeks first the kingdom of God, *receives*. The seeker *finds*, and to him who *knocks* it is opened."

He taught them for many hours that day on the mountain near Capernaum, and as they finally came down into the valley together, they found a huge crowd had been listening. Everyone looked at Jesus in a new way. His popularity among the people was already great. Now they seemed more amazed than ever. No one had ever heard teaching like that! Unlike their scribes, who quoted other teachers as their authority, He taught them as with His own authority and they followed Him back toward Capernaum.

The Faith of a Roman Officer

The crowd fell back from Him only long enough for Jesus to

heal a leper, and to marvel that He did not mind touching the unclean man.

When they reached Capernaum, a captain in the Roman army ran up to Jesus, pleading, "Lord, my servant lies paralyzed at my house. He is in great agony."

James nudged his brother, John. "The captain called Him 'Lord'!"

Jesus replied to the officer, "I will come and heal him."

The Roman officer surprised everyone around by saying, "Lord, I am not fit to have You come under my roof. If You will only speak the word, I know my servant boy will be healed! You see, I am personally under authority and have servants under me. To one I say 'Go!' and he goes. To another, 'Come,' and he comes, and to my slave, 'Do this!' and he does it. If you will but speak the word, I know he will be healed!"

It had been a long day of hard teaching for Jesus, but as He listened to this gentile officer whom He had never seen before, He marveled, and said to those with Him, "I assure you, I have not found anyone in Israel with so much faith! And I tell you that many such as he shall come from east and west—outside of Israel, and will be reclining with Abraham, Isaac and Jacob in the kingdom of heaven, while the sons of the kingdom (Jews by birth) shall be expelled into the outside darkness!"

Turning to the captain, He said, "Go home! As you have believed so shall it be for you."

At that exact moment the servant boy was healed.

Jesus and His men went home, too, the Master to sleep, the disciples to toss and wonder at what lay ahead.

In the crowd stood the usual spies from the Pharisees, who scurried off to report as blasphemy what He had said about the gentiles who would "come from the east and west" to be with Abraham, Isaac and Jacob in the kingdom of heaven!

Chapter 36

"Are You the Coming One?"

The formidable fortress-prison of Machaerus stood in Peraea (now Jordan), on a mountain overlooking the northeast shores of the Dead Sea.

In a small, shadowy cell hewn out of the solid rock of the mountainside, John the Baptist sat day after day, shut away from the open sky and the bright Palestinian climate which had energized his body as his message energized his mind.

Now his face and hands were pale, his body weakened from inactivity, his mind weary with waiting and wondering. At first he planned vigorously, paced the short length of the damp cell, and believed God would answer his prayers for freedom to continue his beloved work. As the empty, silent days inched by, the gaunt, frustrated young man spent more and more time just lying on the dirty pile of rags on which he slept.

Where was Jesus? Certainly He knew of his arrest. Why had He not used His power to free him? John's guileless mind could only turn itself endlessly in childlike confusion.

There he lay, apparently abandoned, except for an occasional visit from a few of his faithful disciples. Such visits were not normally permitted in the high-walled prison, but Herod, although he had John arrested, stood in awe of the desert prophet. He wanted him out of the way, but Herod had listened to John preach many times. Believing him to be a dedicated and holy man, he allowed his disciples to visit him, and did not order his execution.

No one seemed to be doing anything about John. He felt utterly alone. For a man of action, this was torment.

One day, late in the summer of 28 A.D., two of John's disciples sat hunched in the tiny cell with their teacher.

"I confess I am confused about Jesus of Nazareth. Does He know I am here?"

"Yes, Master, He knows."

"If I could only be sure He is the Messiah!" John buried his shaggy head in his hands.

"We thought you were sure, Master."

"You were right. I was. But, except for the episode in Nazareth, when He was almost killed by His own people, I have heard of no other time when He has declared Himself to be the Anointed One of God."

"Word reached us sometime ago that Jesus declared Himself to be the Christ in the small Samaritan village of Sychar, and many believed on Him. Now, all Judea and Galilee hum with the report of what He did in Nain just a few days ago!"

John brightened. "What did He do?"

"He raised a poor widow's son from the dead—brought him to life right on his bier as the funeral procession passed down the street where Jesus was! We've been told that the people were overcome with awe, and that they gave God the glory, believing that a true prophet had been raised up in Jesus."

John's heart was filled with wonder at what he had heard. Still, there was a nagging doubt.

"I want you to go to Jesus—find Him, and ask Him this question for me: 'Are You the coming One, or should we look for someone else?' "

The Baptist's disciples found Jesus in the center of a throng of people on a missionary journey in southern Galilee.

He was healing one person after another, as John's disciples pressed through the jostling crowd to ask their question.

Peter saw the two forcing their way past the line of crippled, demented and blind people, and tried to stop them.

"Can't you men see the Master is busy? Who are you?"

When they told him, Peter led the two men through the hot, shoving, complaining crowd to Jesus, who gave them His immediate attention.

"Our teacher, John the Baptist, has sent us to ask You if You are the Coming One, or should we look for someone else?"

Jesus answered them, pointing to the crowd around Him, "Go and tell John what you see and hear. The blind see; the lame walk; lepers are cleansed; the deaf hear; the dead are raised; the poor are evangelized."

Jesus knew John would understand from this message that He was actually the Messiah. Knowing the Scriptures as John did, he would remember that Isaiah had written many centuries before of the Coming One who would be sent to lead Israel back to God:

"Then the eyes of the blind shall be opened, and the ears of the deaf shall be unstopped. Then shall the lame man leap as a hare, and the tongue of the dumb sing."

Jesus knew the Baptist would make the connection with His own ministry.

John, who had been so outspoken, could not understand why Jesus chose to *act* His Messiahship rather than proclaim it. Sitting alone in prison, John had not thought far enough about the temper of a crowd. Jesus did not want an intellectually or psychologically convinced people. If He had either declared Himself openly or freed John from prison by a miracle, He would be setting His own material power and authority against that of Herod and Rome. Instead, Jesus had come to establish the new kingdom *in men's hearts.* But because He loved John and wanted to comfort him as much as possible, He added this message: "Tell John also that I have said, Blessed is he who does not feel offended by Me."

He could not free John from prison and remain true to His mission, but He wanted John to know He was sorry.

As John's disciples were pushing their way out through the crowd, Jesus began to talk to the people about the Baptist.

"When John the Baptist was preaching in the desert country around the Jordan, what did you go out to gaze on? A reed swayed in the wind? What did you really go out to see? A man dressed in soft clothes? Wearers of soft clothes live in palaces! Why, then, did you go out? To see a prophet? I tell you, John is far more than a prophet! He is the one about whom it is written, 'See, I send My messenger before your face who shall prepare the road ahead of you.'"

John's disciples hurried back to their teacher at Machaerus prison. He accepted the message from Jesus, and contented himself as best he could, knowing now that he must stay there.

Before He returned to healing the long lines of people that day, Jesus took the opportunity to make use of the unexpected visit of John's disciples to further clarify the true meaning of the kingdom He had come to announce.

"I assure you none has arisen among those born of women, greater than John the Baptist. Yet, the least in the kingdom of heaven is greater than he! From the time of John until now, the kingdom of heaven has been rushed! The impetuous have seized it by force—repenting only from the wrath to come as John preached."

Coming onto the scene, as he did, between the era of the law and prophets and the coming of the Christ, John preached repentance of sins in order to escape "wrath." Jesus was now among them to establish the truth of the desire in the Father's heart to *give* eternal life to His beloved world for the sake of His own heart. The Father did not intend to browbeat and frighten lost human beings into the kingdom! He wanted to *give* them the kingdom.

Over and over His disciples heard Him say, "Do not fear, little flock, for your Father is pleased to give you the kingdom."

The people listened and their hearts were drawn toward this One who had come to reveal the Father's heart to them, but so few responded that He accused them of being like children playing games! They came in large numbers to hear Him preach, as they had done when John poured His message of the Coming One up and down the banks of the Jordan. But there was no appreciable heart response to either of them among the people.

"John came, neither eating nor drinking, nor attending weddings and feasts, and people say, 'He has a demon.' The Son of Man comes eating and drinking—being in your midst as one of you, and they say, 'Look at a glutton and drinker, a friend of tax collectors and sinners.'"

As Jesus reproached the unrepentant cities where most of His wonders had been performed, His own heart was spontaneously lifted to His Father, as He cried, "I thank Thee, Father, Lord of heaven and earth, for hiding all this from the learned and intelligent and revealing it to babes—to children, to the uneducated people. Yes, Father, for thus it was pleasing in Thy sight."

Jesus held no prejudice against the scholars. His heart was lifted in thanks to His Father merely because He knew eternal life was available to *everyone*. A scholarly Sanhedrinist and an illiterate shepherd boy shared an equal opportunity to discover the gift of the kingdom of God.

When He had finished His prayer of thanksgiving before the multitude, He looked around at the crowd and said with the energizing force of the love that motivated His entire being,

"Everything has been handed over to Me from My Father, and no one understands the Son except the Father, nor does anyone understand the Father except the Son, and he to whom the Son wishes to reveal Him."

The Pharisees standing near Him whispered angrily to one another. Jesus ignored them and held out His hands toward the lines of troubled, demented, crippled and blind men and women who waited for His touch.

With characteristic daring, He had declared that no one could understand the Lord God of Israel, His Father, except those to whom He, Jesus of Nazareth, chose to reveal Him! But at once, He added:

"Come to Me, *all* you who labor and are heavily burdened and I will rest you! Take my yoke on you and learn of Me, for I am gentle and humble of heart, and you will find rest for your souls. My yoke is easy and my burden is light."

Those who had ears to hear that day, heard the Carpenter from Nazareth claim that *anyone* could understand the Father by learning of *Him*! And that His "yoke" was easy compared to the "yoke" of the Law.

A few hearts began to glow with faith in Him, and the embers of antagonism among the Temple officials were fanned almost into flame.

Chapter 37

Broken Alabaster and a Mended Heart

In the Galilean city where He was ministering when the Baptist's disciples found Him, Jesus was invited to dinner at the home of Simon, a leading Pharisee. The invitation in no way meant interest on the part of the Pharisee. It was merely courtesy to the visiting Teacher and His men. Courtesy, and a chance to check personally the rumors now spreading rapidly among his fellow Pharisees all over Galilee—that this Man was a heretic!

Reclining at Simon's table in his luxurious home that evening were several other Pharisees, along with Jesus and His disciples. Simon was an impressive man, elegantly clothed, and the lavish meal was served with impeccable taste. It was no mere oversight that the feet of Jesus and His men were not washed when they arrived. They were admitted politely and the food was enough to make the disciples glad they came. But the social snub was intentional. It put them in "their places" in a civilized manner—typical of Simon, their host.

Conversation ran well, though casually, as the guests reclined on the soft couches, one elbow on the table and their feet turned toward the polished, wood-paneled wall of the dining hall.

A shadow fell across the lamp-lit table, lengthened, and then stopped, as a woman appeared up the veranda-step from the open courtyard, and stood behind them at Jesus' feet, weeping.

Jewish men did not converse with any woman in public, no matter how noble her character. No one spoke to this woman, but too many of the richly robed, reclining Pharisees recognized her, although none would admit it.

She was no longer beautiful or young. Her long, dark hair was threaded with gray. The sordid life she had lived clung to her, pulling deep lines in her face and bending her body, so that she stood at Jesus' feet like a woman bearing a cruel burden.

She seemed to drag the strained silence with her from the shadows outside.

Every guest at the table stared at her—except Jesus.

The woman seemed aware of no one but the Master. That afternoon she had been among the crowd when He spoke of the *rest* He offered. His voice and His words still rang through her heavy heart:

"Come to Me, all you who labor and are heavily burdened and I will rest you. Take my yoke on you and learn of Me, for I am gentle and humble of heart, and you will find rest for your souls."

Twice she had lost Him in the crowds on the way back to the city. Then she found someone who knew He was having dinner at Simon's house. That was enough! The prejudice against public conversation with women might not have existed for her, as she ran through the darkening streets hunting Jesus.

Now she stood near enough to touch Him! She could not speak. There would have been no words. He had said He would give her *rest* if she came to Him, and somehow she was depending fully upon His understanding of her weariness. He had said she could learn about Him. That if she learned about Him, she would understand the Father! He had said He was gentle and humble of heart.

The broken, disillusioned, sinful woman stood at His feet weeping—unaware of the gaping men around the table—depending on Jesus to know of her weariness, and the burden of her wretched life.

The disciples watched their Master, confident that He would know just what to do. Simon and the other Pharisees watched Him too—watched her and watched Him. Perhaps the wretched woman had given them the opening they wanted, to trap Him. How would He handle this awkward situation? What would He do?

Jesus did nothing. He knew she was passing through the shattering moment of seeing herself as she was—in His presence! He could not spare her the shame and guilt of that moment, but *in it* with faith like hers, He could begin to heal her heart!

The woman dropped to her knees and covered His feet with her tears! Still there was no sound in the crowded room but the sound of her weeping—agonized, tight-throated sobs at first. Then with her tears still bathing His feet, the weeping grew quiet. Quiet and grateful. Quiet and grateful and relieved. Aware of a new kind of love.

With eager, joyous movements, she wiped His feet with her long hair, and kissed them tenderly over and over, still unaware of anyone in the room but Jesus.

Around her neck she wore, on a thin chain, a small alabaster vial of perfume. Impulsively, she broke it open and anointed His feet!

Simon, the host, had said nothing, but his clever Pharisee's mind was busy with what he believed to be private, personal observations.

To himself, Simon said, "If this Jesus were a prophet, He would know what kind of woman is touching Him—this woman is devoted to sin!"

Jesus broke the silence in the room.

"Simon, I have something to tell you!"

His voice roused His host to polite attention. "By all means, Teacher, speak up!"

Jesus turned so that He faced Simon directly.

"Two men were in debt to a money-lender. One owed him five hundred dollars and the other fifty. As neither had anything to pay him, he generously canceled the debt of both men. Which of them will love him more?"

Simon stroked his black, coarse beard, and replied cautiously, "Why, I suppose the one for whom he canceled the larger debt."

Jesus nodded. "You have judged correctly."

He turned toward the woman, who still knelt, kissing His feet, but went on talking to Simon. "Do you see this woman? As I entered your home, you supplied no water for My feet. But she has washed My feet with her tears and wiped them with her hair! You did not give Me the customary kiss of welcome, but she has not stopped tenderly kissing My feet."

Simon shifted his position slightly, and raised a patronizing eyebrow, not at all apologetic. Merely listening.

"You did not anoint My head with oil, but she has anointed My feet with perfume. So, I tell you, her sins, many as they are, are forgiven, for she has greatly loved! But the person who is forgiven little, loves little."

There was a slight stir among the guests, but no one spoke.

Jesus looked at the kneeling woman and said, "Your sins are forgiven."

She raised bright wet eyes to look directly into His face for the first time. She *could* look at Him now!

Jesus smiled warmly at the woman and repeated, for her heart's complete rest, "Your sins are forgiven."

Around the table now there was open shock. The disciples sat observing the Pharisees, who began to mutter and complain among themselves as though Jesus and His men were not present.

"What did we hear with our own ears? This man claims to forgive sins?"

"Who is this imposter, even to forgive sins?"

Another Pharisee threw down his silver fork in anger, and rose from the table. "We have witnessed blasphemy against the Lord God this night!"

In the midst of their outrage, Jesus once more reassured the grateful woman. "Your faith has saved you! Go in peace!"

The rising temper of the other guests did not escape Him, but He concerned Himself with the woman's peace of mind, because her heart was open to Him, in faith.

Chapter 38

"He Is Deranged"

Back in Capernaum from His second swing around Galilee, the crowds grew so large around Peter's house, where Jesus stayed, that it was impossible for anyone in the house to eat a meal in privacy! The people had gone wild with enthusiasm over Him.

Some of Jesus' relatives and friends attempted to take Him out of the public eye by force, saying, "He is deranged!" His relatives were small-town, backward folk, who instead of understanding His mission were embarrassed by all the talk about Him. Even His mother, Mary, was worried. Perhaps not so much by what Jesus did, but because her other sons were putting increasing pressure on her to try to stop Jesus.

"But Jesus is healing so many suffering people," she reasoned with her son James the day he came to her small house to complain about Jesus' public ministry.

"Even so, Mother, I am a businessman in Capernaum, and I have my family to consider! You can't imagine how many rumors go around about Jesus. We haven't lived in Capernaum long enough for me to be firmly established. When the people come to my place of business talking about Him, I find myself hoping against hope they won't find out He's my brother! He's in Peter's house right now, and heaven only knows what new madness He's up to! They're saying He's possessed of a devil! Let's go and stop him, Mother!"

At that moment, before an enormous crowd of people, including the usual jealous Pharisees and their scribes, Jesus was healing a blind and dumb demoniac.

The man was well known in Capernaum. For years he had been led about the streets by his brother, not only because he was blind, but because he was never in his right mind. He mouthed hideous sounds instead of words. When Jesus touched him, he was changed instantly from a helpless creature with a demented mind, into a whole man—sane, able to speak and to see!

All the people who watched the miracle were amazed and began to exclaim: "May not this be the Son of David?"

The mood of the crowd was swinging so strongly toward Jesus, the Pharisees who stood (as always) in the front row where they could question Him, declared: "Don't be fooled by what you have seen! This fellow does not expel demons except through Beelzebub, the prince of demons!"

Jesus turned this sharpest criticism to date into an opportunity. He taught the crowd from it!

"Consider what you have just heard from My accusers, then think for yourselves. Any kingdom divided against itself will go to ruin, and any city or home that is divided against itself cannot stand. If Satan expels Satan, he is divided against himself! How then shall his kingdom stand? Besides, if I cast out demons through Beelzebub, through whom do your sons cast them out? On this score they will be your judges. But if you see that I expel demons through the Spirit of God, then the kingdom of God has unexpectedly overtaken you!"

A wave of new excitement plunged over the crowd. Some saw His point. Could it be that the very *seeing* meant the kingdom of God had unexpectedly overtaken them?

Jesus looked straight at His accusers and continued, "Whoever is not with Me is against Me and whoever is not gathering with Me, scatters! You either declare both tree and fruit to be sound or you hold both tree and fruit to be bad, for the tree is known by its fruit. You brood of vipers, how can you speak honorably, evil as you are? For from the overflow of the heart the mouth speaks. A good man brings out good things from good accumulations, and a wicked man brings out bad things from bad accumulations. By your words you will be acquitted, and by your words you shall be condemned!"

Bristling with sarcasm, the scribes and Pharisees demanded: "Teacher, we should like to see your token of proof!"

Jesus answered them with a reference He knew they would recognize.

"A wicked and disloyal generation craves evidence and no evidence shall be given it except the sign of the prophet Jonah! For as Jonah was for three days and three nights in the sea monster's gullet, so shall the Son of Man be three days and three nights in the earth's heart. Men from Nineveh shall arise at the judgment along with this generation and shall condemn it, for they repented at Jonah's preaching; and indeed, One greater than Jonah is here!"

His young, strong voice held the crowd motionless and silent, wondering what He would say next.

"The southern queen (Sheba) shall rise at the judgment with this generation and condemn it, for she came from the ends of the earth to listen to Solomon's wisdom—and indeed One greater than Solomon is here!

"When the unclean spirit goes out of a person it roams through dry places looking for rest and does not find it. Then he says, 'I will go back to the house I left,' and comes and finds it vacant, cleaned and orderly. He then goes out to bring along with him seven other spirits worse than himself and they enter and live there. And the final condition of that person is worse than the first. So it will be with this wicked generation!"

There was a stir down the center of the crowd gathered around Him, as a young man pushed his way toward Jesus excitedly.

"Master, Your mother and Your brothers are outside. They want to speak to You right away!"

Jesus showed no annoyance at the interruption. His voice dropped some of its hard edge, but none of its energy.

"Who is My mother and who are My brothers?"

Sitting at Jesus' feet near Him, were His disciples—the Twelve and the few women who traveled with them to care for His needs.

He stretched out His hand toward this faithful group, and said, "Here are My mother and My brothers. For whoever does the will of My heavenly Father is My brother and sister and mother."

For those who had ears to hear, He was not belittling human ties, but deftly and surely He was lifting up the ties He knew possible in the kingdom He came to establish.

Parables by the Sea of Galilee

That same day, in the afternoon, the crowds around Peter's house grew so great Jesus once more had to move to the lake shore and teach them from Peter's small boat. The people, as eager now over His teaching as they had been about His healings, stood hundreds deep on the sandy beach. Some, for a better view, climbed up the precipices that formed the sheltered cove where Jesus taught.

His voice carried clearly to them where they sat and stood as He spoke to them now in parables, using ordinary images with which they were at home.

"A sower went out to sow, and in his sowing, some seeds fell on the footpath and the birds came and ate them. Some fell on rocky soil where they had little earth and sprang up quickly because the soil was shallow; but with the rising sun it was scorched and, having no root, it withered. Some fell among the thorns and the thorns grew up and choked them. But the rest fell on the good earth and bore a crop—some a hundred, some sixty and some thirty-fold. Whoever has ears let him listen!"

Next, He began to give them a series of short parables—all concerning the kingdom of heaven.

"The kingdom of heaven is like a man who sowed good seed in his field, but while his men were asleep, his enemy came and sowed darnel (weeds) among the wheat and got away. When the blade shot up and the wheat headed, the darnel appeared, too. The owner's servants went to him and said, 'Was not that good seed, Sir, that you sowed in your field? Where, then, did the weeds come from?' He said to them, 'An enemy has done this.' They asked him, 'Would you like for us to go and weed them out?' But the owner said, 'No, in gathering up the darnel, you might uproot the wheat along with them! Let them grow side by side until harvest time, and at harvest time I shall direct the reapers to collect the weeds first, to bundle them up and to burn them, but to bring the grain into my barn.'

"The kingdom of heaven is like a mustard seed which a man took and sowed in his field. It is the smallest of all seeds, as you well know, but when it grows up, it is bigger than any plant! Actually, it becomes a tree, so that the birds of the air come and roost in its branches.

"The kingdom of heaven is also like yeast which a woman took and buried in three portions of flour until it was all raised."

That evening, when Jesus had gone back to Peter's house, His disciples made a special trip from their own homes to ask Him a question.

"Why do You speak in parables, Master?"

"Simply because it is granted to you to know the secrets of the heavenly kingdom, but it is not granted to them."

He did not refer to all the people who heard Him, only His enemies. Nor did He mean that God had arbitrarily discriminated against those who opposed Jesus. They opposed Him because they refused to open their ears and hearts to His message!

"I speak to them in parables because they look and see nothing; they listen and neither hear nor understand. But blessed are your eyes, for they see—and your ears, for they hear. Now, listen to My explanation of the parable of the sower."

The men listened eagerly. They had hoped He would give them some private teaching so that they would better understand.

"When anyone hears the message of the kingdom and does not understand it, the evil one comes and snatches away what is sown in his heart. This represents the sowing on the footpath. But what was sown on rocky soil means the one who hears the message and at once accepts it gladly; but it takes no root in him; it does not last. Trouble or persecution arises on account of the message and at once he feels scandalized. And what was sown among thorns, means one who listens to the message, but worldly worries, and the enjoyment of wealth, choke the word and it becomes unproductive. But, what was sown in good ground means one who listens and understands the message. He bears fruit and yields, one a hundred, one sixty and one thirty-fold! He who has ears to hear, let him hear."

Before the men left Him that night, He told them they would be leaving again soon. Jesus wanted to try once more to reach the hearts of the people of Nazareth, with whom He had grown up.

He knew there would not be another chance to go back.

Chapter 39

"Where Did He Get All This?"

There was no violence this time in Nazareth when Jesus walked once more into the small synagogue where he had sat with His mother and Joseph, every Sabbath, as a Child.

As He sat down to teach them, His sisters thought He looked older. His deep, brown eyes were still full of love and caring for the people of His home town, but there was a new sorrow. Many of the same men and women who had attempted to kill Him on His last visit were there, but He spoke fearlessly of the kingdom He had come to announce.

The people eyed Him suspiciously, and seemed only to be tolerating Him, this time, for the sake of His family. They even whispered as He spoke, discussing His lowly background, naming His brothers and sisters.

"After all, is not this the carpenter's son?"

"Are not His sisters all still living in Nazareth?"

"Who does He think He is?"

"Where did He get all this?"

It was clear to Jesus that they neither knew nor cared where He got His message. He longed to reach them with the love of His Father, with all the energy of His strong, young heart! But they simply didn't care, and because of their unbelief, He worked very few miracles in Nazareth.

Outside the synagogue, the home-town friends nodded coldly at Jesus and His disciples. They ate dinner with one of His sisters, and then Jesus went out alone. He walked the same path to the same spot on the hillside where He used to sit and think, His eyes roaming the surrounding countryside, peopling it with David and Saul and Jonathan, and all those who made Hebrew history there. So much did He still care about the people of Nazareth that He marveled at their unbelief.

Peter and the other disciples who accompanied Him on this last visit home were far from philosophic about the treatment their Master received in Nazareth. They couldn't help defending Him! In fact, they looked for chances to do it.

James and John were especially angry at the people of Nazareth. Both brothers merited their nickname Jesus had given them. That Sabbath they felt like "Sons of Thunder," and they set out to let some of that thunder roll around the quiet little hilltown.

The first person they met was the old man who had owned the leather shop near where Joseph's carpentry shop still stood.

"Don't you remember the Master when He was a Boy?" John asked.

"Certainly I remember him," the old man seemed almost cross that John had asked the question. "Remember his whole family. Joseph was a hard-working man. Good carpenter, too."

"You must remember only good things about the Master, then." James was all set for an argument. "How is it that you people treat Him like He was a bad penny now?"

"He's too peculiar. Says too many funny things. We're good people here in Nazareth. We don't need no young upstart giving us a tongue-lashing!"

"Excuse me, Sir, I know you're an old man, but my brother James and I are His disciples. We're among the twelve He chose to be with Him all the time. We know Him! He doesn't give tongue-lashings."

"Not unless they're deserved," James cut in.

"Even then, He only speaks with the authority of His Father. The Master has come to fulfill the prophecies, and if you thick-headed Nazarenes would only realize it, He fulfilled another prophecy right in your synagogue this morning!"

The old man spit. "Didn't hear no prophecy fulfilled!"

"Matthew reminded us at dinner today," John went on. "The prophet Isaiah said, 'Behold my servant whom I have chosen, My Beloved in whom my soul delights; I will invest Him with my Spirit and He will announce justice to the Gentiles. He will not quarrel or shout, nor shall anyone hear His voice in the streets. He will not break a bruised reed; He will not extinguish a smouldering wick until He carries justice to victory. And the nations shall hope in His name!' "

"Can't see what that has to do with Joseph's boy, Jesus!"

"We see! We have eyes to see and we see. We are with Him all the time, old man. We saw Him heal and convince even the Samaritans!" John's enthusiasm ran high now.

The old man spit again. "Samaritans!"

"Certainly, we thought that way, too, until He taught us better.

And the Master had every right to yell and shout and get angry with all of you in the synagogue this morning, after the way you treated Him the last time He came to visit you. But did He do it? No, He did not. 'He will not quarrel or shout . . . He will not break a bruised reed!' The Master is firm sometimes, but He is always gentle."

"We've known Him to raise the dead, too!"

Joseph's old neighbor cocked an unbelieving, shaggy white eyebrow. "Jesus raise the dead?"

"A widow's son in Nain and a little girl about twelve years old. Her father, a man named Jairus, a ruler in the synagogue at Capernaum, begged the Master to come and heal his daughter."

"Well," the old man cut in, "if he's such a powerful healer, how come the girl died so he had to raise her from the dead? That is, if he really did raise her from the dead!"

"Oh, He did all right. But she died before He could get to her, through the huge crowds that followed Him that day."

John and James were interrupting each other telling the story.

"And one of the reasons He couldn't get there was because a woman touched His cloak in the crowd and was healed from a hemorrhage just by touching Him!"

The old man was needling them carefully now.

"Well, young fellows, it seems to me if he is so powerful this woman got healed just by touching the cloak he wore, it shouldn't have slowed him down much. How come he let this little girl die?"

John's temper was almost out of control now. "I wish you weren't an old man, Sir," he said, clenching his teeth and his fists.

"The Master took time to talk to the woman about her faith. He wanted her to know that her faith in Him was what healed her." John's voice was rising like his temper, and the old man clearly was pleased.

James felt the old thunder rolling in his head, too. He was shouting. "Sir, if the Master hadn't taught us to love our enemies, we'd not be so kind to you now!"

"The Master raised the girl from the dead, and we are the witnesses! He only took three of His disciples, one other fellow named Peter, and the two of us. My brother James, and me. We saw it with our own eyes."

"More miracles would have taken place here in Nazareth, too, if you people would only believe! Like when He cast the devils out of a poor man in the country of the Gadarenes. He healed that man and the demons went into a whole herd of swine!"

The old man laughed so hard the tears ran down his face. James and John grew suddenly and surprisingly quiet.

When he had softened his laughter a bit, John said, "Don't you care about the suffering of people, Sir?"

"What? Don't I care? Certainly I care. Look here, we're not bad men here in Nazareth. We're just ordinary good people."

"I've noticed it's the 'good' people who find it hardest to listen to the Master." James was not goading him now. The young disciple was wholly serious, and the old leather-worker seemed suddenly to take them seriously.

"Look here, you two really believe in this boy of Joseph's, don't you?"

"We know Him, Sir. We live with Him. We were on the fishing boat the other night in a storm so violent it terrified even those of us who have been fishermen all our lives! We all panicked and the Master slept through it."

"What does that prove?" The old fellow's question was not barbed this time.

"We saw Him calm the storm, Sir." John spoke softly now, but with more persuasiveness than when he was shouting.

"You saw Him do—what?"

"We panicked and shook Him awake. He was so tired from teaching all those people. Oh, Sir, they wear Him out because He gives Himself so freely to them. But we had to rouse Him! We thought we would be killed, the storm was so wild."

"Well, what did Joseph's boy do?"

"The Master stood up in the boat and spoke to the storm: 'Peace! Be still!' The wind went right down and there was a great calm."

The old man had John by the arm now. "You mean Joseph's boy talked to the—storm?"

John looked down at the little old craftsman and replied, "Yes, Sir. He spoke to the storm and the wind like He owned them!"

"Just the way He spoke to the demons in that mad man in the

296

Gadarene country, Sir. No one could even keep him chained any longer. He kept breaking out of iron chains! He lived naked. He was a wild man. The Master is from God. He controls the elements and He controls the demons."

The old man looked at them for a long time and then walked away, shaking his head.

Jesus of Nazareth did control the wind, disease, demons and death. The most difficult thing for Him, it seems, was to be *permitted* to control the human heart.

Chapter 40

Herod Was Extremely Sorry!

John the Baptist sat chained in his dark, narrow cell, cut from the solid rock under Machaerus Fortress, on a February night in 29 A.D. He scarcely knew it was night. The Palestinian sun he loved never found the rough, damp stone around him. After a few months John's mind was old; his young, strong body had grown white and soft. Only his heart hoped—not for release from the airless cell, but for the coming of the kingdom of God.

His disciples had told him that Jesus of Nazareth was holding the people spellbound with His preaching concerning the kingdom. His solitary heart clutched its hope doggedly. Surely the kingdom would come soon!

The tomb-still night was shattered suddenly by the clank of an iron door, so loud it made his ears ache. The clank was familiar. It meant another miserable pot of half-spoiled food was on its way. But in the middle of the night? Only one surly guard brought his food. Now, not one man, but several, walked heavily down the stone corridor toward his cell.

John got to his feet, shielding his eyes from the light that suddenly flooded his black, stony night. Five armed soldiers stood in the open door of his cell.

"What do you want?" John asked.

Two of the men grabbed him and held his weak arms pinned against their rough, brass-studded jackets.

"Has the kingdom come?" John cried. "Have you come to tell me the kingdom is here?"

One of the soldiers shouted an order nervously—too loudly for the close quarters. Another guard jerked John's head upright —and a heavy sword slashed!

The voice that cried in the wilderness was still.

Back in the ornate banquet hall of Herod Antipas, the laughing, carousing guests waited impatiently for the fulfillment of a whim of the king's new wife, Herodias. Her graceful daughter, Salome, had pleased Herod greatly as she danced for him at his birthday feast that night.

"Salome, my dear, you danced so magnificently, I will give you whatever you ask me—up to half of my kingdom!"

The young girl slipped away from the drunken king to get her mother's advice.

The beautiful pagan woman apparently loved Herod. Not only had she left his half-brother to be his wife, but when he was banished to Gaul in 39 A.D., she went with him of her own accord. But her darkened heart contained as much hate as love. Herodias hated John the Baptist because he had dared to speak out against her marriage to Herod.

"Salome, I have lived for this hour! My husband has never agreed to please me by executing that dreadful preacher. Now he will please me! He won't want to do it—I honestly think Herod is afraid of the Baptist—but the king is an honorable man. He has made you a promise. He will keep it."

Salome's mother smiled triumphantly as she sent her daughter back into the banquet hall, carefully prompted to say to Herod:

"I want you to give me, this moment, on a plate—the head of John the Baptist!"

It is said that Herod was "extremely sorry," but because he had promised, the head of old Elizabeth's son, John, was brought to the banquet hall of Herod Antipas. The girl, Salome, presented it grandly to her Mother on a big silver plate.

When John's disciples heard of it, they came and took his body and sorrowfully laid it in a tomb.

"Sheep Among Wolves"

So great were the crowds that followed Jesus and His disciples everywhere they went announcing the gospel of the kingdom, that His heart ached over them seemingly as never before. In every village and town in Galilee He was besieged with crawling, limping, clambering humanity, diseased in body and mind.

His body grew weary, but His God-heart longed not only to be able to do more for their pain-wracked bodies, but to give light to more darkened hearts.

The job was now too big for Jesus alone. His twelve chosen disciples and the women who accompanied Him helped all they could. But the preaching and the healing fell to Him.

In His heart, He knew it was time to send the Twelve on a

journey without Him. He could also go alone, and the kingdom could be preached thirteen times over!

Every man among the Twelve was glad and apprehensive when He called them to Him for instructions before they left.

"I know I am sending you out as sheep among wolves; therefore, be as subtle as serpents and as guileless as doves. As you go about, preach that the kingdom of heaven is at hand!"

"We are all willing to go, Master," Peter said, "and we'll all do our best at preaching—but what about healing the sick and casting out demons?"

He gave them power over depraved spirits, power to heal every disease, and detailed instructions for their journeys. They were to take no money along, not even a bag of supplies. They were to take only one change of clothing, one pair of sandals and one staff.

"The workman deserves his support. Whatever town or village you enter, inquire who in it is deserving and stay there until you leave that community. As you enter the home, give your greetings, and if the home is deserving, let your peace come upon it."

Jesus smiled and the men relaxed, as always, at His subtle humor, "If the home is undeserving, your peace will return to you."

As they all parted to go their separate ways for the first time, Jesus said to them encouragingly, "Whoever receives you receives Me and whoever receives Me receives Him who sent Me."

It was February when the Master and His twelve men went their separate ways into many towns and villages. While he was away, each one learned of the execution of John the Baptist.

In April, when the Twelve gathered around Him again in Capernaum, their excitement was great, but so was their grief for John. The disciples had been able to preach and heal! He was proud of their courage and their faith. They had passed their first test well! Jesus clasped every man's hand, and even Judas Iscariot, who had known little sympathy for tears, was unashamed of his own that day.

Superstitious Herod Antipas heard of the wonders Jesus was performing and he was greatly confused by all he heard. Some told him John the Baptist had risen from the dead. Others, that Elijah had appeared on the scene of his coveted power. Herod knew either man was a trouble-maker for kings! If this man *was* anything like either John or Elijah, it could cost him his power over the people.

"I have had the Baptist beheaded. He is well dead. Find this other man about whom I hear so much! I will tolerate no interference in my kingdom. Go find this Jesus. I want to see him face to face, and to deal with him also!"

Chapter 41

Five Loaves, Two Fishes and Five Thousand People!

Capernaum was crowded with pilgrims on their way to Jerusalem for the Passover when Jesus and His men returned. Jesus' extensive travels continued to heighten His fame. It was impossible for Him to find a place in all Capernaum where He and His men could be alone to talk over all that had happened to them on their last journeys.

They needed to be alone for other reasons, too. They were all weary. Among them, they had visited over two hundred cities and villages. Jesus, particularly, was grieved over the news of John's tragic death. He longed for some hours alone with His Father.

Jesus had also heard that Herod Antipas had sent men to look for Him. He was sharply aware of the increasing danger every time He appeared before a crowd! The rulers in the Temple and the Pharisees throughout Palestine were no longer the only enemies he had.

Jesus and the Twelve made arrangements to meet at the waterfront at dawn the next day, to cross the northern tip of the Sea of Galilee to a lonely, picturesque region near the City of Bethsaida. They left early to avoid detection, but a few fishermen saw them shove off into the quiet, gray water just after dawn.

Peter's boat scudded to shore on the wet, packed sand of the other side of the lake, some five miles away, and the Twelve followed their Master up the side of a mountain, each man looking forward to the retreat alone with Him.

The little band of men had just seated themselves comfortably to talk when they heard excited voices below. People were coming toward them from every direction! The news of their departure had leaked out and the multitudes began to run on foot, one group calling to another, until five thousand people now stood looking up toward Jesus and His men!

"Can't they leave us alone just one day?"

"We wanted to tell You all about our preaching trip, Master!"

The disciples grumbled, but Jesus stood up, waving His hand to the crowd, and welcomed them. He longed for time alone with His men, too. He needed the solitude in His grief over John. But He had compassion on this troubled, surging throng of humanity that looked to Him like shepherdless sheep, some crippled in their bodies, all hungry in their souls.

By late morning, over five thousand people sat or stood in the natural arena, listening to Jesus speak to them about the kingdom of God. He stood through the heat of the afternoon, healing their diseases, opening the eyes of the blind and the ears of the deaf.

Toward evening, His disciples grew worried.

"Master, don't You think You'd better dismiss the crowd?" Philip asked.

"Yes, Rabbi, this is an isolated spot, and it's a long walk to the nearest food!" Judas Iscariot was always practical. "If You dismiss them now, they'll have time before dark to walk to the surrounding villages. The people who have come all the way from Capernaum will have to find lodging, too!"

Jesus understood their concern, but instead of dismissing the people, He said to His disciples, "You give them something to eat! Philip, where shall we buy food, so they may eat?" He was testing Philip.

"Master, there are so many people here, fifty dollars worth of bread wouldn't give each person one bite!"

Peter's brother, Andrew, had a suggestion which didn't seem a very good one to him, but he ventured to make it.

"There's a lad here with five barley cakes and two fishes. He's offered them to us, but what are these for so many people?"

"I think it's time we stopped this foolish talk!" Judas cut in. "The sun has already started to go down and these people have to eat and sleep tonight."

Jesus smiled at the little boy who had offered his two fishes and five barley cakes, but ignored the disciples' arguments.

"Have the people sit down!" He said.

"Sit down?" Judas couldn't restrain himself.

Nor could Peter now. "Master, this mob will turn on You if you don't let them go to find food soon!"

"They don't seem anxious about it," John said thoughtfully.

Once more Jesus told them to have the people sit down. As usual, His men obeyed Him, even while they argued. There was plenty of room for the five thousand persons. The gentle hillside was soft with thick, spring grass and wild anemones. All the multitude sat down and waited, as they were told to do.

Then Jesus took the boy's loaves, gave thanks, and the disciples began serving. He did the same with the two small fish. Five thousand hungry people ate all they wanted!

"Now," Jesus said, "gather up the leftovers scattered on the ground, so that nothing may be wasted."

Ashamed and amazed, the Twelve scurried over the area where the people sat, and filled twelve baskets with leftover bread and fish!

When the crowd discovered what had happened, bedlam shook the evening countryside!

"This surely is the prophet who is to come into the world!" they cried.

The five thousand surged toward Him, shouting, "This man must be our king! We will make this man our king!"

Judas Iscariot was wild with excitement. Simon, the Zealot, shouted with the people. "The time has come! God has acted in our behalf!"

Peter and the others ran among the people assuring them Jesus was the One whom God had sent to be their king!

In the noise and jostle and confusion, Jesus slipped away from them all to a quiet place farther up on the mountain, alone to pray.

They looked everywhere for Him, but no one found Him this time. He had not come to be proclaimed king by a shallow-thinking mob who had just had their stomachs filled! He was already King in a kingdom even His disciples still did not understand.

Gradually, most of the five thousand people disappeared toward the villages and hamlets nearby. The Twelve stood at the lakeside with the twelve baskets of food.

"I wonder where He is." John was heartbroken, sensing they had disappointed Jesus.

"This is more than I can understand!" Judas complained. "The chance of His lifetime and He disappears!"

Andrew looked toward the mountain. "Do you think we should hunt for the Master? He'll want to go back to Capernaum, won't He?"

"What do you think, Peter?" Nathanael asked.

Peter had been sitting on the sand with his curly head in his big hands. He seemed more ashamed than any of the others.

"I'd rather die than let Him down like this."

They waited until it was dark, but Jesus did not come.

After awhile they decided they'd better not take a chance on making matters worse, so they got into Peter's boat and started back across the Sea of Galilee toward Capernaum, all of them confused as to why they had displeased Him.

Peter's small fishing boat sailed along at a good clip, as the rising wind pushed the black waves higher and higher.

By four the next morning they had sailed about three of the five miles back to Capernaum, when someone shouted, "Look!"

The men stared unbelievingly across the black water. There, walking toward them *on* the climbing waves, was what appeared to be the fully clothed figure of a man!

The man, which the terrified disciples thought must be a ghost, walked steadily toward them.

No one could speak. They could only gape at the figure now within several yards of the tossing boat.

"It is I!" The dear, familiar voice reached their ears and their hearts. "It is I!" Jesus called. "Cheer up! Have no fear!"

Peter shouted, "Lord, if it is You, order me to come to You on the water!"

Jesus shouted, "Come, Peter!"

Throwing off his cloak, impetuous Peter climbed down the side of the boat and started to walk on the water toward Jesus! The big man's heart swelled with joy, and as long as he looked at Jesus' outstretched arms, he made progress over the heaving water.

Then, Peter looked down at the waves!

As in a nightmare, he felt himself begin to sink, and cried, "Lord, save me!"

Jesus reached out His hand instantly and caught hold of His beloved disciple, saying, "Peter, you faint believer!" For a moment He held Peter with firm and loving hands. The big fisherman was totally dependent on his Master.

"Peter," Jesus said in a voice Peter never forgot, "why did you doubt?"

When they had climbed aboard the boat, the wind quieted at

once, and the other disciples knelt before Jesus and said, "Truly, You are the Son of God!"

With the wild wind tamed, they sailed smoothly and quickly to the other side of the Sea of Galilee, and landed at a place called Gennesaret, halfway between Capernaum and Magdala.

As in every other place Jesus went, the people of Gennesaret rushed to hear Him teach, and with them they brought their blind, deaf, and crippled relatives and friends to be healed. Time after time, men grabbed His garments, and as many as touched even the fringes of His clothing were made perfectly whole!

"I Am the Bread of Life"

By the time Jesus and His men returned to Capernaum, the crowds were there searching for Him!

A few of those who had been fed from the five loaves and two fishes on the other side of the lake knew the disciples sailed alone that night without Jesus. More than ever they were driven to find Him again. The next day they stormed the city, arriving in small boats and on foot, and found Jesus—still without time to rest— teaching in the synagogue at Capernaum.

"When did You get here, Rabbi?" the people asked. The last time they had seen Him was on the other side of the Sea of Galilee, when they tried to force Him to become their king!

Jesus said to the crowd, "Truly, I assure you, you are not looking for Me because you saw true signs, but because you ate of the loaves and were filled up! Do not work for the food that must decompose, but for the food that lasts through life eternal, such as the Son of Man will furnish for you. You must see that the Father has certified Him!"

It was customary for the crowd to discuss issues with a rabbi in the synagogue, and Jesus welcomed their questions.

A gray-haired man called to Him: "What should we do to accomplish the works of God, Rabbi?"

"This is God's work," Jesus replied, "that you believe in Him whom He sent!"

A young man who had heard Him often, asked: "What sign then, will you work, so that we may see and believe you? What will you perform? Our ancestors ate manna in the desert as it is written, 'He gave them bread from heaven to eat.' What sign will you work?"

He had already multiplied the five loaves. The young man knew this. He wanted Jesus to call the miracle a sign of His coming from God.

It was not the sign, so Jesus explained patiently, "Moses did not give you the bread from heaven, but My Father gives you the real, heavenly food *now!* For what comes down from heaven and furnishes life to the world—that is the Bread of God."

Then the crowd cried, "Lord, give us this bread all the time!"

Judas Iscariot sprang to attention. Here was the crowd once more demanding of Jesus! Surely this time He would not sidestep the issue.

The disciples waited excitedly for Him to speak again.

The ever-present Pharisees and Sadducees waited, too, hoping to trap Him.

Jesus stretched out His arms toward the people—His enemies included—and said:

"I am the bread of life! He who comes to Me will never hunger and he who believes in Me shall not suffer thirst any more. But you have seen Me and have not believed! Every one whom the Father has given Me will come to Me, and I will certainly not cast out anyone who comes to Me. For I came down from heaven not to do My will but the will of My Sender. And this is the will of Him who sent Me, that of all He gave Me I shall lose nothing but shall raise them up at the last day. For this is My Father's will, that every one who sees the Son and believes in Him shall have eternal life!"

He paused to let His words enter any open hearts among them. Immediately the ruling Jews began to grumble among themselves, because He had dared to call Himself the Bread that came down from heaven!

"The Bread of life, indeed! Isn't this Jesus, the son of Joseph who was a carpenter in Nazareth?"

"Yes, didn't many of us know Joseph? And doesn't his mother still live right here in Capernaum?"

"How does he dare say he came down from heaven!"

"Stop your mutual mutterings!" Jesus' voice was firm. "No one is able to come to Me unless the Father who sent Me draws him, and him I *will* raise up at the last day. It is written in the Prophets, 'And they shall all be taught of God.' Every one who has listened to and has learned of My Father comes to Me! Which does not imply that anyone has seen the Father except He who is from alongside of God; He has seen the Father. Truly, I assure you, the believer has eternal life."

The crowd listened restlessly. Some who had tried to believe grew frightened. They were devout Jews who had been taught from childhood that eternal life came only if a man obeyed the law!

Once more, Jesus entreated them. "I am the Bread of Life! Your ancestors ate the manna in the desert and they died. This is the Bread that comes down from heaven, so that anyone who eats of it may not die. I am the Living Bread that came down from heaven!"

The people stirred, some were highly agitated.

Jesus went on with enormous energy.

"If anyone eats of this Bread, he will live forever! And the bread, which I will give for the life of the world, *is my flesh!*"

This was too much for the Jews.

"How can this person give us his flesh to eat?"

"What kind of insanity is this?"

Jesus did not attempt to show them their blindness. He went right on offering them truth. He was not trying to be practical, He was being *true*. He was not seeking to express what man could do, but what God asks!

"Truly, I assure you, unless you eat the flesh of the Son of Man and drink His blood, you have no inner life. He who eats My flesh and drinks My blood, has eternal life and I will raise him up on the last day. My flesh is genuine food and My blood is genuine drink! He who eats My flesh and drinks My blood remains in Me and I in him. Just as the life-giving Father sent Me, and I live through the Father, so he who nourishes on Me shall live through Me."

Among the crowd, many who had followed Him from place to place began to think in their hearts:

"This is a difficult message! Who can stand listening to such talk?"

"This man is making himself one with the Lord God!"

Aware of their failing hearts, Jesus said:

"This aggravates you? Suppose you should see the Son of Man ascending to where He was previously? Listen to Me, the Spirit is the life-giver. The flesh does not help at all. The messages I bring you are spirit and life."

His shoulders sagged a little.

"But I know there are some of you who fail to believe."

He was right. From that day on, many of His followers who had heard Him regularly returned to their homes and no longer walked with Him.

He stood watching as the large crowd melted away, grumbling and complaining. Some deeply saddened, but leaving Him just the same.

When they were alone, Jesus looked at the Twelve.

"You do not want to leave, too?"

Peter took a step toward Him.

"Lord, to whom shall we go? You have the words of eternal life, and we have believed and have grown sure that You are the holy One of God."

Judas Iscariot was the only one of the little band of men who did not look at Him. His disappointment was too great. Nothing had gone the way Judas had hoped. Jesus' eyes darkened with sorrow. He looked from one man to another, and then said in a weary voice—no more than a whisper:

"Have I not chosen all twelve of you?"

"Yes, Master," John answered tenderly.

"Yet one of you is a traitor."

Judas looked at Him now, briefly. But none of the men understood what He meant.

Chapter 42

Visitors from Jerusalem

Recognizing the danger signals among the Temple rulers in Jerusalem, Jesus did not attend the Passover in the spring of 29 A.D. No doubt His thoughts traveled to the Holy City during the days in which His people once more celebrated the anniversary of their ancient exodus from Egypt. The Temple at Jerusalem was His Father's house, and He revered it with all His heart.

In no way did Jesus deliberately set out to break the written Law. His regular trips to the Jewish festivals, His Sabbath attendance at the synagogue, His deep knowledge of the Law, proved His loyalty to the faith of His fathers. He Himself had declared that He came to fulfill the Law!

His opposition lay in His understanding of the Law, which was so far from the Jewish interpretation that the ruling Jews could see Him only as a law breaker. The original conflict stood: With them, the letter of the Law was supreme; with Jesus, human need was supreme.

While the learned doctors and scribes sat in the Temple analyzing the intricacies of the written and oral law during the closing days of the sacred Passover Feast, Jesus stood almost a hundred miles away on a deserted Galilean hillside feeding five thousand people with a small boy's lunch!

When, at the close of the Passover, the Pharisees held a conference at which they decided to go to Him to expose Him to further analytical questioning, Jesus was sitting in the midst of a crowd of people in Capernaum, declaring Himself to be the Bread that came down from heaven!

The learned doctors hoped to find sufficient charges against Him to justify a trial before the Sanhedrin. Jesus had only one friend, so far as He knew, in this highest court—and the Sanhedrin had the power to condemn a man to death! At best, Nicodemus was still a somewhat furtive friend.

Along the Roman highways north from Jerusalem to Capernaum rode the carefully selected scribes and Pharisees, atop their tall camels, and with their rigid determination to find a way to be rid of Jesus of Nazareth.

As they neared the outskirts of the thriving city by the sea, Jesus, whom they wanted to see dead, was again declaring Himself to be the Bread of Life!

The regal visitors to Capernaum, of course, did not stay with Jesus or His disciples in their homes. The disciples were as suspect as their Master. The Pharisees would be in constant danger of ritual defilement in the homes of the men who followed this (to them) unorthodox Jewish Rabbi!

A Jew committed a most unspiritual act—a sin, in their eyes if he ate or drank from cups or plates from which sinners ate. It was well known that Jesus and His men ate often in the homes of sinners. Of course, the Pharisees reasoned, the utensils in the disciples' homes could not be trusted.

They came to visit Jesus, but the visiting doctors and scribes arranged for hospitality in the splendid home of a fellow Pharisee in Capernaum, where they took no chance of defilement.

To eat at the same table with the Rabbi from Nazareth and His assortment of energetic disciples would be a painful ordeal, but their mission was serious enough for the sacrifice. This Man, Jesus, had to be pinned down and stopped!

On the night of the banquet, each visiting Pharisee and scribe carefully washed his hands up to the elbow before reclining at the table of the Capernaum host.

Jesus and His men arrived together and reclined at the table, grateful for the good meal coming up—but they did not bother to give their hands a ceremonial washing!

Jesus knew His disciples realized the seriousness of the occasion, but He referred to it not at all—even in His manner. He was pleasant, gracious and courteous, nothing more.

Throughout the meal, He waited for the inevitable questioning to begin.

When it did, He was ready.

"Rabbi," began one of the scribes, with unguarded antagonism, "why do your disciples transgress the tradition of the ancients?"

Jesus looked at the lawyer with the quiet directness which always angered His persecutors.

"To what do you refer?" He asked.

"They do not wash their hands before eating!"

311

Jesus looked at His own lean, brown hands, making Himself one with His men. Then he asked:

"Why do *you* transgress the command of God through your tradition?"

"Explain that accusation, Rabbi!" a Pharisee demanded.

"Very well. Here is an example. God has commanded, 'Honor your father and mother,' and, 'He who curses father or mother must suffer death.' Is this correct?"

Jesus waited for someone to answer Him.

"Yes, we agree with that wholeheartedly."

"But you say," Jesus went on, "it is agreeable for a man to say to his father or mother, 'What you might get from me I now make as an offering at the Temple!' Therefore he need not honor his father and mother. If a man has dedicated his wealth to God, he can still use it to his own profit, but need not give it to help his needy parents! So you have made God's command spineless through your tradition!"

The Pharisees drew back, insulted to the core of their analytical beings.

Jesus went on, cognizant of the danger.

"You hypocrites—Isaiah rightly prophesied about you when he wrote, 'This people honor Me with their lips, but the heart they keep far away from Me. Uselessly they worship Me with their teaching of human commands.' You neutralize God's word through your tradition that you have handed down!"

The angered visitors from Jerusalem denied the charge.

Jesus replied calmly, "Do not deny it, since you do many things of that kind."

The carefully planned quiz session ended flatly for them, but the visitors did not give up. The next day when Jesus faced another crowd, they were in the front row. His message was a development of their conversation begun at dinner the night before.

"Listen and understand," He told the people. "What enters the mouth does not pollute the person. Nothing entering a man from outside can defile him! It is what comes *out* of a man that renders a person unclean. If anyone has ears to hear, let him hear!"

That night, when He met with His disciples at Peter's house, they were anxious and full of questions.

"Master, are You aware that the Pharisees from Jerusalem were shocked at hearing You say what You said?"

Jesus smiled wearily. "Even you do not understand?"

"We are trying to understand, Master, but what You said about nothing that goes in a man's mouth polluting him seems to set aside the Mosiac rules on eating." Nathanael was deeply perplexed. Each man had the same question.

"Do not be disturbed by them. Every plant My heavenly Father has not planted shall be uprooted. Leave them alone. They are blind guides of the blind! But if one blind person leads another, they will both fall into a pit."

The men nodded. They were doing their best to follow His thinking.

Finally Peter blurted, "Please explain more to us, Master! I don't think any of us really understands."

"Do you not know that whatever enters the mouth passes into the stomach and is thrown out into the drain? But what comes out of the mouth, comes from the heart. That pollutes a man! For out of the *heart* come evil designs, murders, adulteries, sexual vices, thefts, lyings and slanders. These pollute a person—but to eat with unwashed hands does not pollute anyone!"

His voice was intense, but quiet. They sensed a new urgency in Him.

Before they parted for the night, He told them they would be leaving their beloved Galilee at once. Since His enemies had bothered to come from Jerusalem to find Him, there was no choice but to leave.

Jesus was not afraid of them, but there was still so much to be done.

313

Chapter 43

"You Are the Christ"

Jesus and His men headed north to the vicinity of Tyre and Sidon, in Phoenicia. Healing the sick and preaching the kingdom all the way, they went west, through the Decapolis, back across the Sea of Galilee to Magdala, and completed their big loop to the northeast, at Caesarea Philippi, a thriving gentile city at the southern tip of Mount Hermon.

After their long, strenuous journey, the lush, green beauty of the region around Caesarea Philippi cheered the hearts of the disciples. They needed cheering. Daily, since their sudden departure from Galilee, they had grown more and more apprehensive of what lay ahead.

Jesus was calm, but the disciples sensed the new urgency growing in Him, and He spent more and more time alone with His Father.

Caesarea Philippi was a magnificently built city. Philip, Herod's son, had built it, and named it for his emperor, Augustus Caesar. Its surrounding natural beauty dwarfed the city, which was almost hidden from view by the tall-treed woods, the tangle of heavy, wild vines, and gigantic sculptured cliffs, shedding numberless waterfalls.

Jesus and His disciples stood some distance outside the city, watching a river tumble into the sunlight from the black depths of an immense cavern at the base of an abrupt rock wall which formed the side of a steep mountain. The river was a part of the upper sources of the Jordan; the cavern from which it roared out toward the valley, an ancient sanctuary of the god Pan.

In this beauty, in the midst of a gentile area, within sight of the heathen god's temple, Jesus stopped on a midsummer afternoon to talk to His men about the most important subject in history!

They were away from the Temple in Jerusalem, away from their familiar Galilean haunts—even away from their equally familiar enemies, the scribes and Pharisees. Standing on a deserted mountain path in a strange land, Jesus turned to them and asked the question, the answer to which His Father's beloved world needed most to know.

"Who do people say the Son of Man is?"

No one said anything at first. They had believed His identity variously, through the months. Surely they wanted to believe that their Master *was* the Messiah. More than once, the more impetuous among them—Judas, Peter or John, had almost asked Him outright. He had never discussed it with them, but now, having lived under His influence for so many months, the men were growing daily more aware. More aware of Him, more aware of the need for knowing, because of the nameless danger walking with them wherever they went now.

Jesus waited for them.

Those who had sprawled on the thick grass of the mountain trail got slowly to their feet.

Once more He asked: "Who do people say the Son of Man is?"

"Some say another John the Baptist."

"Others call You the prophet Elijah, who is expected to return, Master."

"Still others say you're another Jeremiah."

"Or one of the other prophets from the past."

Jesus did not need to know what the people thought. He wanted the men to summarize the situation for themselves.

John was thinking quickly now. "This means no one has a very definite idea about You at all, doesn't it, Master?"

Now Jesus turned the question to them, personally.

"But you, who do you say I am? Who do *you* say I am?"

The deep moment hung over them, silencing even the summer birds and the long, thin waterfall nearby.

They were closed in with Him.

He looked from one man to another, waiting.

"You are the Christ, the Son of the living God!"

The disciple who spoke had a big voice. It was Peter.

He had said it once before, in Capernaum, when most of Jesus' followers turned away from Him. This time it broke into the hot summer afternoon like a new thunder that would not stop there on that mountain path, in sight of the cave sanctuary of Pan.

Jesus laid His hand on Peter's big forearm, and gripped it. "Blessed are you, Simon Bar-Jonah, because it was not flesh and blood that revealed this to you, but My heavenly Father."

The disciples wanted to kneel and worship Him. Even at this holy moment, however, His humanity kept them all natural.

Jesus had more to say to Peter.

"I also tell you that you are Peter, and on this rock I will build My church, and the gates of hell shall not hold out against her!"

Big Peter glowed with the singular joy of having been assured by his Master that he had heard from heaven. The Father Himself had verified the identity of the Son of Man, and revealed it to Peter! On this truth the whole movement would be built!

Judas was elated. Now they could move ahead rapidly with the work of establishing the new kingdom on earth. Now, surely, they would see some visible results!

Excitement ran high among the twelve dusty travelers who had needed something to firm their wavering spirits; but the excitement was short-lived.

Jesus silenced their energetic plans abruptly by forbidding them to tell anyone that He was the Messiah of God! His own disciples must not be responsible for spreading a false idea among the people. The kingdom He came to announce could not be seen!

"This Must Never Happen to You!"

From then on, gloom hung over the men.

They stayed in the vicinity of Caesarea Philippi, in the long, blue shadows of snow-peaked Mount Hermon, for six days. Knowing their still-clouded minds, their inability to loose themselves from the traditions by which they had been bound, Jesus began to tell them something of what lay ahead.

He longed to cheer them up, but He could not and remain true to what He knew. And so, He taught them—slowly, carefully, day after day, realizing their lack of understanding, realizing the tension building, particularly in Judas Iscariot, who agitated for action! The execution of John the Baptist, although Judas was never associated with him, was a tremendous letdown to him. His Master could have saved John. Why didn't He? Restlessness and dissatisfaction spread like the branches of a thorn bush in Judas' heart when Jesus refused to allow the people to crown Him king! He *was* the King, why not admit it?

Still in the natural beauty of the vicinity of Philip's gentile city, away from the nagging scribes—even with Peter's heavenly revelation that Jesus was the Christ of God—Jesus had a difficult time teaching His men. Naturally, Judas spread his own unrest among them; but they were all unable to grasp the central meaning of the kingdom as the Master taught it.

He did not pamper them. He laid heavy demands on their faith, and continued with undiminished energy to get across the message which motivated His earthly life.

Large and small personality explosions occurred among the men. And, as usual, Peter's personality was prominent. He sat listening with the others one hot afternoon.

The Master was reviewing some of His recent teaching. In Magdala, before they had reached Caesarea Philippi, there had been an unusually bitter encounter with some Pharisees who demanded that Jesus give them a sign from heaven to prove His claims!

The men looked uncomfortable when He repeated His answer to them now.

"A sign? At eventide you say, 'Fair weather, for the sky is red,' and in the morning, 'A stormy day, for the sky is red and cloudy.' You hypocrites, you can distinguish the looks of the sky, but not the signs of the times!"

Point-blank, He had refused, knowing that signs merely change men's minds, not their hearts.

The discomfort of the disciples when He again brought up the subject was a more personal one, however. They well remembered what He had said to them, when that night they realized they had forgotten to bring food for their trip back across the Sea of Galilee.

"Look out," He had warned, "and keep away from the leaven of the Pharisees and Sadducees."

They had argued among themselves over His words, missing His point completely.

"He must mean to rebuke us because we brought no food."

Knowing their confusion, Jesus had pinned them down.

"Why these discussions among yourselves, faint believers? Because you brought no food? Do you not understand even yet? Do you not remember the five loaves of the five thousand, or a little later on, the seven loaves and the four thousand who were fed—and how many baskets there were left over for you to pick up?"

They remembered both times vividly, but they did not make the connection.

317

"How is it that you do not see that I was *not* talking to you about food, but that you should be careful about the ferment of the Pharisees and Sadducees?"

On the mountainside outside Caesarea Philippi, where Jesus was reviewing this important lesson, James said: "We realized finally, Rabbi, that You did not tell us to beware of the *bread* fermentation, but of the teaching of the Pharisees and Sadducees."

Jesus looked at them with growing concern, but also with still growing love, and said, "He who has ears, let him hear."

Then He went on to tell them the most startling thing of all! The thing that brought Peter crashing down to earth from his heavenly contact of a few hours before!

For the first time, Jesus told them that He must leave for Jerusalem and suffer much from the elders, priests and scribes, and be killed!

"But I will rise again on the third day!"

Peter heard only the first part.

The big, rough fisherman grabbed the Master's arm, jerked Him off to one side of the group and fairly shouted:

"Mercy on You, Lord! What do you mean by saying a thing like that? Look who You are! This must never happen to You!"

Jesus' mind raced back to the brown, trackless wilderness where He had spent forty days alone at the beginning of His ministry. In the voice of His much loved disciple, Simon Peter (who just a short time before had heard from the Father concerning Him), He recognized the voice of His temptor!

Jesus whirled to face Peter, and commanded, "You get behind Me, Satan! You are a snare to Me."

Peter's mouth fell open.

"What did You say, Master?"

"You are not now minding things divine, but things human!"

The others joined Peter and Jesus.

"How can You become an acting king if you expose Yourself to suffering and refuse to defend what we are all working to establish?" Judas demanded.

Jesus walked away from them slowly. The men followed Him. When they had all sat down again on the warm grass, He looked at them steadily and said:

"If anyone wishes to walk behind Me, he must deny himself, take up his cross and follow Me."

"Take up his *cross!*" Judas snapped. "You speak as though we are to put ourselves at the mercy of those brutal Romans! It is they who recommend crosses! We must offer the people a better life, better living conditions—no crosses! No denial! They've had enough!"

Jesus waited for Judas to finish.

"If anyone wishes to walk behind Me, he must deny himself, take up his cross and follow Me. For whoever wants to save his life shall lose it. But whoever loses his life for Me shall find it!"

Their love for Him as a human being was so intense, each man longed to please Him, but their frowns were deep, and they spoke little that evening as they walked together back toward the edge of the city, to the caravansary where they were staying.

Young John walked with his hand on Jesus' arm, but his mind could not take in what His beloved Master had said.

"Perhaps I don't need to *understand,*" John told himself as they walked along. "Perhaps loving Him is enough."

Chapter 44

"Sanction on a Mountain"

From almost all parts of the land in which Jesus and His disciples lived and worked, the broad, snow-sloped majesty of Mount Hermon could be seen on clear days. Three lofty peaks rising from the same giant beginning on the earth crowd themselves silently into the clouds and dominate the sweep of the land He loved.

Caesarea Philippi, where they had been staying for six days of concentrated personal teaching, spread itself in the angle of the lower reaches of Hermon. The city was touched hourly by the changing magic of its shadows, as mountain and sun met and communed and parted, leaving the death-white snowy slopes to relieve the darkness alone.

In the evening of the seventh day of their stay there, while the Sabbath sun poured fire over the western slopes of the mountain, Jesus and His three close friends, Peter, James and John, began the climb up the only path leading from the city to the lower heights of Hermon.

In the ugly face of what lay ahead, Jesus had chosen these three to go with Him to the mountain to pray.

As they climbed, Hermon lifted itself, bulking and flushed with color, immediately ahead of them. When purple shadows began to spread, Peter broke the silence of their climb as he spotted the Sea of Galilee, some twenty-five miles away, gleaming in its mounting of dim hills.

"Look at it!" the big fisherman said affectionately. "Can you believe that's our lake down there? Way down there, shining like that? That's *home* down there by the lake, and look how it looks from up here!"

Everything was going to look different to them all after that mountain journey. Peter's boyish wonder at the sight of the transfigured lake—the daily and familiar turned glorious—was merely a beginning.

The four climbed briskly, their healthy bodies energized by the clear mountain air; past the surrounding vine-tangled hills, stocked with mulberry, fig and apricot trees, through rising fields of pear trees, and oak groves, up rocky ravines to where the soil was dotted with dwarf shrubs. Then as the path grew steeper, they crossed the first ridge of snow, blotched with gravelly banks and grassy slopes.

Jesus stopped climbing. Below them now, they could see nothing but dim, earth outlines. It was dark, and the moon threw long, steel shadows over the rough-ribbed mountain, selecting only the patches of snow to reflect.

He could not see what lay below through the darkness, but down there was Nazareth. His home town, where He had been a devoted member of a devoted family.

Nazareth had rejected Him.

Down there was the Jordan River, where His cousin John had baptized Him at the start of His life's work.

John was dead now.

Down there lay Capernaum, His adopted city. "Home," Peter had called it. His mother lived there, and His brothers, who still resisted Him.

Hundreds of disciples had walked away from Him in the lovely, white stone synagogue at Capernaum, to follow Him no more.

Outside Capernaum was the flowering, green hillside where He had called the Twelve to Him. The men who would have to continue His work for Him soon.

None of them understood fully. One seemed in near revolt against Him.

Far to the south lay Jerusalem, the Holy City, and tomorrow, when the sun was high, the gold dome of His Father's house would shine again, and the sacrifices would be offered according to the beloved Law of His people.

But they would be offered by the men who wanted, at all cost, to be rid of Him!

He thought of the crowds of milling, jostling, needy people who had thronged Him. They were sleeping down there now.

They had wanted to make Him their king. In the power of God, He had refused them. He *was* their king, but they did not know how to enter His kingdom! His influence over them had boomeranged violently. The very fact of their enthusiasm forced the priests and Pharisees to fear Him as they would fear a dread disease. His sway over the people could bring an uprising against Rome, which in turn would mean more oppression and the loss of what power the Jewish religious rulers retained.

He had no notion of urging the people toward insurrection.

"Render unto Caesar that which is Caesar's," He had said.

But no one understood what He meant. The people wavered in their loyalty to Him because they did not grasp the true meaning of the inner kingdom which He came to announce. The Jewish rulers in Jerusalem were plotting His death because they understood even less the reality of the inner-kingdom.

Not once had He considered exerting earthly power over the people. He had committed Himself to God's higher way once and for all, during His forty days of temptation in the wilderness.

But He was utterly human, and the most painful thing a human being can be asked to bear is total misunderstanding.

He stood on the side of the high, black mountain now, bearing this cruelest pain. James and John and Peter stood with Him, their hearts full of intense human love, but with their understanding conditioned by the ways of the world which lay below them, still in the ancient night of spiritual darkness.

"We will pray now, to My Father."

Jesus needed to pray. His soul must lie calm within Him to the end. It must remain perfect in the unruffled quiet of His total self-surrender to absolute obedience to His Father. In His heart lurked no question as to the direction He must continue to take, regardless of the seeming failure of His mission on earth, but He needed to pray.

And He needed His three beloved friends to pray with Him.

They were there, as close as their confused hearts would allow.

They prayed.

Out of the open need in each of their hearts, contact with heaven became an almost humanly unbearable reality. Their audible prayers changed to silent communion, as the heaven-invaded moments moved by.

The climb up the mountain had left their bodies physically relaxed and exhausted. The high emotional experience of the communion with heaven passed its peak for James and John and Peter, and their minds and spirits relaxed helplessly.

The three men fell asleep.

It was not a sound sleep. Each man longed to stay awake and share in this rare experience to which He had called them. They fought to stay conscious, but they didn't win consistently. They slept and then roused themselves, and then drifted off again.

Jesus continued to pray. During a brief moment of semi-consciousness, all three men saw Him. And what they saw startled them wide awake!

As they watched, their Master was transfigured before their eyes. His dear, familiar face shone like the sun, and His clothes became whiter than pure light!

In the darkness of the mountain night, they were forced to shield their sleepy eyes from the radiance which fell upon Him, as though heaven itself had opened to earth!

Were they dreaming? Did they really see two figures bathed in the same light enter into conversation with Jesus? Two men out of their own nation's history stood talking earnestly with their Master, openly discussing His coming departure from this earth! They heard the name of the Holy City of Jerusalem mentioned. And all three men recognized the two bright visitors.

One was Moses, whom every Jew revered!

The other was the big-boned, fiery-hearted prophet, Elijah!

Could three men experience the same dream at the same time? They were *not* dreaming. Their still darkened understanding could not grasp the meaning of the conversation they heard, but they were fully awake now! Each of the three remaining himself, acting typically of his own human personality.

John stared in love and wonder and excitement at His beloved Master.

James was struck silent, too, and as usual, his high-strung emotions choked him as he watched.

Peter acted like Peter. Unable to let the glory go, he began to talk rapidly and excitedly. Jumping ahead to make big plans and impractical, though well-intentioned, recommendations:

"Lord, Lord," he sputtered excitedly, "it's wonderful for us to be here with You! If You approve, I'll build three tabernacles right here—one for You, one for Moses and one for Elijah!"

Peter's talk was cut short by heaven itself!

As the big, impetuous fisherman went on to elaborate on his

idea, a bright cloud overshadowed all three disciples, and out of the cloud a voice covered Peter's babbling:

"This is My beloved Son, in whom I am delighted! Listen to Him. Listen to Him!"

The disciples fell on their faces against the rocky mountainside in great fear, and lay there trembling in their deepest souls, as slowly the light faded, and the mountain became the mountain again.

Still unable to raise their faces from the ground, all three men heard the familiar footsteps nearby; they stopped close to the frightened men.

One after another felt the firm, quieting hand on their shoulders. Gently, reassuringly, Jesus touched each man and said:

"Stand up, now—all of you, and have no fear."

When they raised their eyes, they saw no one except Jesus, standing there beside them, alone.

The set of His shoulders and His head, silhouetted against a scattering of snow behind Him, quieted their fears. He was all strength.

He had received His sanction from the Father. He could go on as He had planned.

Moving a "Mountain"

As the four men went back down the mountainside, in the early dawn of the next day, Jesus gave them definite orders.

"Do not mention the vision to anyone until the Son of Man is risen from the dead!"

That Jesus would have to die was still too much for their hearts to bear, but the strength now in Him pressed their minds to obedience.

They were totally unable to discuss His death, about which they had heard Him speak with Moses and Elijah. But their questions, as they went down the mountain, showed a new understanding in their hearts of the message of the Old Testament Scriptures from which they had been taught.

A Messiah who would be killed, with the knowledge and apparent approval of the Lord God, was beyond blind belief to a devout Jew! To have such a thing discussed with the Messiah by Moses and Elijah was utterly impossible!

Peter and James and John *had* to experience what they saw

on the mountain. It began to open their understanding.

"Elijah came, Master, we saw him! But he did not come to the people—he came to You. Why do the scribes teach that Elijah must first come to the people in order that all things must be restored?"

"Elijah comes indeed, and restores all things, as the scribes teach. But I tell you that Elijah had already come and they did not recognize him! Instead, they did to him as they pleased, and in a similar way, the Son of Man is about to suffer at their hands."

The light rising in their darkened minds matched the light rising on the new day. They realized He was referring to John the Baptist, with the heart of Elijah!

Once down the mountain, they had not walked far when they came upon a heartbreaking scene.

A crowd of people shouted and argued with the nine disciples who had remained behind.

A father had brought his epileptic son to them to be healed. Nothing happened. The boy, caught in a severe seizure, lay writhing on the ground.

When he saw Jesus, the parent fell on his knees before Him and cried, "Lord, take pity on my son! He's an epileptic and suffers badly. He often falls into the fire or into the water. I brought him to your disciples, but they had no power to cure him!"

Jesus looked away from the man toward His nine disgruntled, embarrassed men. He loved them as much as the three He took with Him to the mountain, but they could not have benefited from the wonder the three saw! They were not ready.

"Oh, unbelieving and rebellious generation! How long shall I remain with you? How long shall I put up with you?"

Then he turned to the father. "Bring the boy here to Me!"

Jesus healed the epileptic boy and the crowd melted away.

As the disciples straggled along behind Jesus, one of the nine who had failed so miserably asked:

"Rabbi, why did we not have the power to expel that demon?"

Jesus' answer was not only direct, He made use of the failure to continue teaching them.

"You did not cast it out because of the quality of your faith. I assure you, if you have real faith the size of a mustard seed, you will say to this mountain, 'Move from here to there,' and it will move! Nothing shall be impossible for you."

Chapter 45

"Who Is the Greatest?"

They took a secret way back through Galilee to Capernaum.
Jesus led them across untraveled territory to avoid the crowds,
because of the urgency of the hour. Desperately, the disciples—
even Peter, James and John, who had seen His transfiguration—
needed to be taught concerning His coming ordeal.

Somehow He must prepare them. Their courage must not fail!
They must not be taken off guard by whatever might happen.

Recognizing the blocks to their understanding, He repeated
once more what He had said in Caesarea Philippi:

"Let these words sink into your ears! The Son of Man is about
to be betrayed into the hands of men, and they will kill Him, and
on the third day, He shall be resurrected."

Despair seized the men. Surely He was speaking, as He so often
did, in symbolic language. He could not mean that He, Jesus,
their Master, would permit Himself to be killed! They now knew
Him to be the Messiah of God. The Messiah would protect Himself for the good of Israel! No one dared question Him further.

Gloom hung above their whole journey.

John stayed closer to the Master than ever before. He seemed
afraid to have Him out of his sight.

Judas sat and stared at Jesus during their rest periods. His
impatience made him irritable with the other men. His disillu-
sionment was almost complete now.

"You act as though you're the only one who hoped for more
than this!" Peter barked at Judas as they once more entered their
home city of Capernaum, after the long trip.

"I seem to be the only one who is thinking!" Judas spit back at
him.

They parted to refresh themselves, promising to meet again
that night at Peter's house for more teaching.

James and John arrived first for the session.

"What do you make of everything?" John asked Peter.

"I don't know what to make of it, John. The Master is the same
and yet He's not the same."

"Judas is causing real trouble among us. I wish you wouldn't argue with him, Peter!" James was irritable, too.

"Look who speaks of argument," Peter nudged John. "One of the two 'Sons of Thunder'! Named by the Master Himself."

"But we can't expect Judas to believe as we do. True, we don't understand exactly what's going on, but after all—we saw what we saw on the mountain!"

Jesus entered the room where the men talked and they tried to smile encouragingly at Him, but couldn't think of anything very encouraging to say.

When the other men came, He began to talk to them quietly, attempting to relate the kingdom to their personal lives.

"Master, speaking of the kingdom—who really excels in the kingdom of heaven? Who is really the greatest?"

One man posed the question, but this was dear to all their hearts. This they could understand! They all chimed in.

"Yes, tell us—who really is the greatest in the kingdom?"

The disappointment on Jesus' weary, drawn face escaped them entirely. He turned to Peter and asked him to call his little boy into the room.

In a moment, Peter returned leading his three-year-old son by the hand. Jesus greeted the lad cheerfully, and stood him in the very center of the group of men. The boy showed no shyness whatever. He liked Jesus and he had no reason to question why he was called. He stood, smiling broadly, just glad to be there.

The Master's strong, slender hands squared the child's chubby shoulders, as He turned him to face the disciples.

"Look at him," Jesus said, "I assure you, unless you be converted and become as little children, you will certainly not enter the kingdom of heaven! Whoever humbles himself like this little child excels in the kingdom, and whoever receives one such child in My name, receives Me!"

Peter's son looked up at Jesus now. The Master had pulled the boy to Him, hugging him encouragingly, as He said:

"But whoever is an occasion for stumbling to one of these little ones that believe in Me, it were better for him to have a millstone hung around his neck and to be sunk in the depth of the sea!"

The disciples shifted uncomfortably. Here was another revolutionary idea! A kingdom in which childlike, guileless people were the great ones?

Jesus gave the lad a playful spank that said "thank you," and sent him scampering back to his mother. Then He turned to the men and went on speaking with an energy and drive in His voice that stunned them as much as His words!

"Alas for the world because of the occasions of stumbling. The occasions have to come, but woe to the person on whose account the tripping up occurs.

"If your hand or your foot hinders you, cut it off and throw it from you!"

His oriental imagery was striking home with the men. All but Judas leaned eagerly toward Him.

"If your eye hinders you, pluck it out and throw it from you!

"See that you disdain none of these little ones who believe in Me with the simplicity of a child's faith, for I tell you that their angels in heaven are forever looking at the face of My heavenly Father!"

Jesus stopped talking a moment.

"Rabbi, if You did not come to set up the kingdom, why did You come?"

Judas' question was carefully calculated. Once and for all, he must know Jesus' intentions. He had watched Him multiply bread for the hungry, heal the sick—even raise the dead. A kingdom on earth under the rule of this Man would *be* a heavenly kingdom, with plenty for everyone. Still He refused it. Judas spoke quietly, but his galling disappointment rasped through the repeated question:

"Why did You come?"

There was so much tenderness in the look Jesus gave this restless, bitter disciple, Judas had to look away.

"The Son of Man has come to save the lost. How does this seem to you? If a man has a hundred sheep and one of them strays, does he not leave the ninety-nine on the mountains to go out in search of the stray one? Judas? Does he not leave the ninety-nine on the mountains to go out in search of the stray one?"

Judas nodded, not trusting his voice.

"And if he manages to find it, I assure you that he is happier over the one than over the ninety-nine that did not stray. So it is not your heavenly Father's will that one of these little ones should be lost. The Son of Man has come to seek and to save."

The silence was deep and strangely tender.

Peter and James and John looked at one another, remembering the voice that spoke from the bright cloud over them on Hermon.

"This is My beloved Son in whom I am delighted. Listen to Him!"

Jesus was talking to them now about human relationships in the kingdom.

"Once more I assure you that if two of you are agreed on earth about anything for which you pray, it will be done for you by My heavenly Father. For where two or three have gathered in My name, I am there with them."

Peter's big brow was creased with deep thought.

"Lord, how often shall my brother act amiss toward me and I forgive him? Up to seven times seven?"

"No, Peter, I do not say up to seven—but up to seventy times seven!"

Chapter 46

Pressure From His Family

For over a year, Jesus had not gone to Jerusalem for any Jewish feast. The very priests in the Temple of God were carefully plotting to do away with Him, with as little inconvenience to themselves as possible. He did not go, for His time had not yet come; and so, He had led His disciples up and down in Galilee and through the northern Greek cities of the Decapolis, preaching and healing. Mainly, He had concentrated on intensive personal discussions with His men.

Now, in October of 29 A.D., it was time for the great Jewish Feast of the Tabernacles in the Holy City. Jesus was in Capernaum, where His mother and brothers lived. By now, His brothers were openly antagonistic. They hated the publicity and the wrangling and the gossip about Him.

James had long since stopped trying to pursuade Mary to join them in attempting to stop Jesus in what he considered His willful, headlong plunge toward destruction. James knew that his Brother was a unique Man. He had witnessed the unearthly miracles He performed. None of Jesus' brothers believed in Him, but their family name was involved in all that He did and so James tried one last bit of strategy.

Jesus' brother, James, was an intense young man, highly opinionated and ambitious, ordinary in his interests. He found Jesus at Peter's home in Capernaum and asked to see Him alone.

"I have come to you with the full agreement of our brother," James began. "We feel we have a right to speak openly to you. When I was growing up as a lad back in Nazareth, I looked up to you, Jesus. There was always something different about you. I couldn't call you stubborn, but you were never open to changing your mind once it was made up. Oh, I know and remember how kind you always were—and I expect you to be today. Either way it's all right with me—your reaction I mean—*if* you'll just once give my opinion some notice."

Jesus smiled at James with big brotherly affection.

As usual, He did not argue with him. As usual, He made James feel both at ease and uncomfortable at the same time.

"Now, don't get me wrong, I'm not angry with you. But we sense that you've been hiding from trouble in Jerusalem, and we think it's time to stop hiding!"

Jesus listened attentively.

"We want to know if you're going to the Feast of the Tabernacles with our caravan this year."

He shook his head—no.

James exploded then. "How do you expect people to believe you when you hide? Get away from here and go off to Judea. Let those who call themselves your disciples and those who do not, actually see you perform your miracles! Let the priests see you! Walk right into them. No one who seeks to be in the limelight as you do, does things where they cannot be seen." James shrugged and added sarcastically, "Since you insist upon doing these things, show yourself to the world!"

His brothers wanted Him out of Galilee and out of their lives.

Jesus put both His hands on James' shoulders and said quietly, but so firmly that there was no rebuttal possible:

"James, My time has not yet arrived. Your time is always opportune. The world cannot hate you; but it hates Me, because I testify about it. I tell it that its works are wicked. You go to the feast. I do not yet go up to Jerusalem. You see, My term is not yet completed."

James and his brothers left for Jerusalem with the usual caravan of pilgrims from Capernaum. When they arrived, James found Jesus the main topic of discussion and argument!

More than that, he found the ruling Jews looking for Him openly. In every milling crowd of pilgrims, the Pharisees and scribes had placed spies to check the temper of the people. They found heated disputes going on about the Man from Galilee in every group! Some flatly called Him good. Others said He was misleading the people. But as soon as anyone noticed a scribe or a Pharisee present, he stopped talking, for fear of punishment.

"Why did the Rabbi from Nazareth not come to the Feast?" the people asked among themselves.

"He's afraid to come!"

"They're out to kill him and he knows it. He's a strange one.

331

He has a way of knowing even what a man thinks in his own head!"

Overhearing the talk about Him, even James was glad He had not come.

"Why Do You Try to Kill Me?"

If James had listened carefully, he would have heard Jesus say that He was not going to the Feast of the Tabernacles—*yet*.

By the time the Feast was half over, Jesus and His men had arrived in Jerusalem, and James found his Brother sitting calmly on Solomon's Porch in the Temple itself, teaching openly in full view of everyone!

His words were so provocative and unique the people were once more amazed at His knowledge and authority.

"How does this man know literature without an education?"

Jesus replied, "My teaching is not Mine, but His who sent Me. If anyone wills to do His will he shall understand the teaching, whether it is from God or whether I speak Myself. He who speaks from himself seeks his own honor. He who seeks his sender's honor is sincere, and in him there is no deceit."

A group of irate Temple rulers had pushed to the front of the crowd around Jesus, on Solomon's Porch, where He sat.

How had He dared to make Himself available like this? The angry men in their silk robes could only stand silent and listen, however, because always they had to consider the crowds around Him, and His influence upon them. If the people rose up in favor of Jesus, the iron hand of Rome would put down the insurrection with such blanket violence that the priests and Pharisees themselves would be included!

When Jesus saw the rulers before Him, He looked directly at them and asked:

"Did not Moses teach you the Law?"

One Jew nodded stiffly.

"Yet none of you practices the Law! If you do, why do you try to kill Me? The Law declares, 'Thou shalt not kill!' "

Now, He had exposed both Himself and them. The crowd was shocked. How did He dare stand talking like that in public?

Someone back in the crowd shouted: "You must have a demon! Who is trying to kill you?"

The nervous group of Temple officials craned their necks to see the crowd's reaction. Some obviously knew they were plotting His death, others did not.

Jesus went right on speaking loudly and firmly.

"I have done a single deed—I healed a man on the Sabbath, and you are all still marveling about it! Look, because Moses established circumcision among you—though it did not come from Moses but from previous ancestors—you circumcise a person even on the Sabbath! If a person receives circumcision on the Sabbath so as not to have Moses' Law broken, are you enraged at Me for making a man entirely well on the Sabbath? Do not judge superficially, but judge fairly!"

Some of the citizens of Jerusalem began jabbering among themselves.

"This is the man they are trying to kill! Yet, here he stands in public talking like that and nothing is said to him!"

"Surely the rulers have not discovered that he is the Christ!"

"Who says he is the Christ?"

"Yes, we know where this fellow is from. When the Messiah comes no one will know where He is from!"

Jesus called out in a strong voice to break up their wrangling.

"Do you know Me and do you know where I am from? I have not come self-appointed! But He who sent Me is true. You do not know Him! I know Him because I am from His presence and He personally sent Me!"

This was too much for the listening rulers! They pushed back through the crowd and huddled with the Sanhedrin in the Temple, eager to plan His immediate arrest.

With tempers flaring, the priests and Pharisees tried to find some plausible scheme.

"We cannot be too careful with this rascal!"

"My opinion is that we have been careful too long. Did you not hear what he said out there on Solomon's porch? Such blasphemy my ears have never heard! He comes from the presence of the Lord God, indeed!"

"Still, we must be careful how we move in on him. You know we, by Law, cannot kill a man! But, we can have a man arrested."

"And we must be always careful of the people! Why, out there just now, I heard many of them say, 'When the Christ comes, will He achieve more signs than this one does?' I tell you, we must be careful—not of him, but of the people and of Rome!"

333

"Right! Pilate will brook no trouble during a feast time. Rome wants to control us with an orderly hand. We must move carefully. Yet, we *can* have a man arrested!"

At once, they called officers and sent them to arrest Jesus as He taught in the Temple. The officers went immediately to the part of Solomon's porch where He still sat, pouring out His heart to the people.

For a few moments, they stood listening, too.

"I will be with you a little while longer and then I go to my Sender. You will look for Me without finding Me, and where I am then, you are not able to come."

The men sent to arrest Him discussed this strange statement among themselves:

"Where is he intending to go, so we cannot find him?"

"He surely does not plan to visit the Jews scattered among the Greeks, or to teach the Greeks!"

"This man speaks strangely, indeed. What does he mean by saying, 'You will seek me and will not find me,' and, 'where I am you cannot come?' "

"Here he is right now! We can find him easily."

"Then, why don't we arrest him?"

"I don't know!"

"Perhaps we should listen a few more minutes. Maybe the crowd will thin."

The Master taught all that day, unharmed. The officers sent to arrest Him listened to His every word. When night came, they watched Him walk away with His men, to sleep.

The next day, which was the final day of the Feast, Jesus was back at the Temple again in full view. He stood with the enormous crowds watching the morning procession, led by the elaborately robed priests, carrying filled water pitchers.

Taking every opportunity now for still more teaching for the people's sake, He suddenly lifted His voice and cried out above the noise:

"Whoever is thirsty, let him come to Me and drink!"

The officers sent yesterday by the irate priests, were there again to watch Him. They had done nothing so far but watch and listen.

Jesus called out again, with all the energy of His compassionate heart:

"Whoever is thirsty, let him come to Me and drink! He who

believes in Me, just as the Scripture says, streams of water shall flow from his innermost being."

The arresting officers listened to the crowd's reaction, as its attention turned abruptly from the pompous line of marching priests to Jesus.

"This is really the prophet!"

"No—this is the Christ!"

"But does not the Scripture say that the Christ comes from the offspring of David and from Bethlehem where David lived?"

"That's right! And this man comes from Nazareth."

Two of the attendants wanted to seize Him then. No one laid a hand on Him!

After the parade, the priests and Pharisees confronted the officers angrily.

"How is it that on the second day since we sent you, you return to us empty-handed, without this imposter?"

"For what reason did you fail to bring him?"

The officers were silent a moment. One of them caught a glimpse of an old Sanhedrinist who was actually smiling! His smile gave the men courage.

"We did not arrest him, because no man ever spoke as this man speaks!"

Nicodemus' smile broadened as the priests and Pharisees exploded in anger.

"Surely, you are not misled, too! Have any of the real authorities believed in him? Have any Pharisees believed in him?"

The men looked at Nicodemus. He nodded briefly. Only the officers saw him. The priests went on raving.

"Has anyone who is anyone believed in this man? Only the rabble follows after him! They know nothing of the Law and are only accursed!"

According to the rulers, no one could experience eternal life who had no knowledge of the Law.

"We have no choice but to condemn this imposter from Galilee, and now!" a young priest shouted.

Nicodemus had said nothing. Now, the respected old ruler stepped forward and said: "But our Law does not comdemn a person without giving him a hearing and ascertaining his behavior, does it?"

His long years as a revered member of the Sanhedrin meant

nothing to the angry young priest who shouted rudely at Nicodemus:

"What's this? Are you not perhaps from Galilee, too? Investigate for yourself, old man, and see that no prophet comes to the fore from Galilee. This man is a fraud!"

Nicodemus was not impressed with the young priest's sarcasm. "But we have no actual charge to bring against Him!"

"Then we'll find one! In fact," the younger man smiled, and jerked his black, pointed beard delightedly, "I think I have just thought of something that will work very nicely! Yes, I'm sure it will work very nicely indeed. And we can bring it off right in front of the stupid people—tomorrow!"

The Sanhedrinists went to their lavish homes for the night. The crowds went to their homes and caravansaries.

Jesus went alone to the Mount of Olives.

Chapter 47

"Where Are Your Accusers?"

After a night alone with His Father, on the barren limestone ridge known as the Mount of Olives, Jesus arose just after dawn, walked down the slope of the ridge, across the Brook Kidron, and back into Jerusalem, to the Temple.

At that early hour, the people were already waiting for Him.

He had been teaching them for some time when He heard a commotion to one side of the crowd. Several scribes and Pharisees were rudely escorting a sobbing woman toward Him.

Two officers held her bruised arms, twisting them, as they forced her through the crowd. Her moans and short, sharp screams showed their unnecessary torture of a woman whose inner pain was already too much to bear.

She was in her twenties; perhaps under other circumstances, she would have been pretty. As they jerked and dragged her along the dusty ground toward the spot outside the Temple enclosure where Jesus sat, her long, unkempt hair straggled over her swollen eyes. Her robe was ripped and wrinkled.

More humiliating than her disheveled appearance was her shame.

Prancing at the front of the small procession of priests and Pharisees was the young priest who had tried to put Nicodemus in his place at the hurried meeting of the Sanhedrin the day before.

He was now about to put into operation the scheme in which they would be able to place a legal charge against Jesus.

The Master's heart turned in pity toward the woman as her accusers shoved her to the very center of the gaping crowd, directly in front of Him.

Nicodemus was with them, but stood apart from them, watching Jesus' every reaction.

"Teacher," the scheming priest said in mock outrage, "we need your help! This woman was caught in the very act of adultery. Now, Moses ordered in the Law to stone such as she. What do you say, Teacher?"

Jesus looked briefly at the priest, then at the wretched woman, who hung her head low, her tangled hair falling forward, making a welcome covering for her face. Had she wanted to brush it back, she could not have done it. The burly officers still clutched her arms, twisting them now and then, so that she cried out.

She could not look at Jesus. But the curious crowd milled around her, attempting to see her agonized face.

"What do you say, Teacher?" the priest pressed his question.

Jesus said nothing. He rose to His feet, then immediately stooped down, almost casually, and began to write in the dust of the ground!

For a moment, there was silence. Nicodemus stood on tiptoe to keep his eye on the Master.

The priests and scribes looked blankly at one another. When the crowd began to titter and chuckle, the officiating priest attempted to save his dignity by filling the silence.

"Well? What do you say, Teacher? Moses ordered in the Law, which I believe you know well, that a woman like this is to be stoned! What do you say?"

Slowly, Jesus rose to His feet and looked at each member of the accusing party of officials. Then He said with great authority:

"Let the sinless one among you throw the first stone at her!"

Stooping down again, He went on writing in the dust with His finger.

The silence was back. What was there to say? This time, the party of accusers could not look at one another!

Although he plainly was not with them in spirit, dignified old Nicodemus, the oldest among them, was the first to obey his conscience and walk away.

Then, one by one, all the accusing party, from the old Sanhedrinist to the young priest whose idea it had been to trap Jesus before the crowds, turned and hurried out of sight!

The officers who had been gripping her arms loosened their grips, and ran.

The crowd moved, too, like a wave, out of the Temple grounds and away.

Jesus was left alone with the woman, who still stood before Him. Now, she rubbed her arms and sobbed softly.

In a moment, Jesus raised Himself to His feet, and asked her: "Woman, where are your accusers? Has no one condemned you?"

"No one, Lord!" she gasped.

He was gentle with her, but firm, as with an injured child whose own disobedience had caused his injury.

"Then I do not condemn you, either. Go, and from now on, do not sin anymore!"

"Stone Him! Stone Him!"

That evening, during the lamp-lighting ceremony at the Temple, Jesus once more took advantage of the moment by lifting His voice to declare:

"I am the Light of the world! My follower shall not walk around in darkness, but has the Light of life."

A Pharisee shouted: "You are witnessing to yourself! Your testimony does not hold."

The Pharisees and ruling Jews did not disagree with the main theme of His message about the conduct of human life. Jesus' message was always based on the Scriptures they believed. Their opposition flared from their stark inability to believe His claims about His identity.

They simply could not recognize Him as sent from God!

"My testimony is valid," Jesus contended, "because I know where I come from and where I am going. You neither know where I am from nor where I go. You judge by human standards. I judge no one, and in case I do judge, My judgment is true, for I am not alone, but it is My Sender and I! It is written in your Law that the evidence of two persons is valid. I am witness for Myself, and My Father who sent Me witnesses on My behalf!"

The enraged Pharisee shouted; "Where is your father?"

"You neither know Me nor My Father. If you knew Me, you would know My Father as well. You are from below and I am from above. You are from this world. I am not from this world, so I told you that you would die in your sins. Because if you do not believe that I am He, you will die in your sins!"

"Who are you?" they shouted. "Tell us who you are!"

"When you have lifted up the Son of Man, then you will realize that I am He, and that I do nothing of My own accord, but tell the things just as the Father has taught Me. My Sender is with me. He does not leave Me alone, for I do inevitably what pleases Him."

339

The crowd around Him was large. Many believed in Him. To them Jesus said: "If you adhere to My teaching, you will truly be My disciples. You will know the truth and the truth will set you free!"

The others were enraged and insulted. "How dare you say we are not free! We are Abraham's progeny, and we have never been slaves to anyone."

Jesus was steady and strong in His reply:

"Truly, I assure you, everyone who commits sin is a slave to sin; but the slave does not forever stay in the home. The son remains in the home forever! So, if the Son liberates you, you are unquestionably free. I know you are Abraham's offspring; but you look for means to kill Me, for you have no use for My teaching. I relate what I have observed at the Father's side and you behave as you have learned from your father."

The Jews shouted indignantly, "Abraham is our father!"

"If you were Abraham's children, you would do what he did; but here you are seeking to kill Me, a Man who has told you the truth which He learned from God. Abraham did not act that way! You are doing your own father's works."

"Don't tell us we are born illegitimately!"

"We are not idolaters! We worship one God."

"If God were your Father, you would love me," He answered them, "for I came out of and am here from God! I did not come from personal motives—He sent Me. Why do you not understand My language? Because you cannot bear to listen to what I really say! Who of you convicts Me of sin? If I tell the truth, why do you not believe Me? A person whose origin is God, listens to the words of God. Because you are not from God you do not listen!"

"We're right!" the Jews shouted. "You are a Samaritan and you have a demon!"

"I have no demon," His voice was now deeply compassionate. "I simply honor My Father, and you dishonor Me. With assurance, I tell you, anyone who observes My teaching shall not taste death—forever!"

"Ah-ha! Now, we know you have a demon! Both Abraham and the prophets died and you say, 'If anyone observes My teaching, he will not taste death forever'!"

"You are not superior to our father Abraham, who died, are

you? And the prophets died also. Whom do you make yourself out to be?"

"My Father, whom you call 'our God,' gives glory to Me. Your father, Abraham, was extremely happy in the prospect of seeing My day, and he did see it and felt glad."

"Ha! You, Rabbi, are not yet fifty years old! And have you seen Abraham?" a Pharisee jeered.

The crowd was a howling mob now. Real fury swept it.

"Tell us, Rabbi," they jeered, "have you seen our father, Abraham?"

Jesus spoke clearly and His shoulders squared. "I tell you, before Abraham's birth—*I am!*"

He had dared use the sacred name of the Lord God given to Moses at the burning bush! No devout Jew even uttered this name aloud. He had called Himself "I Am!"

The mob broke its bounds. Dozens of men picked up stones to hurl at Him. Stones as big as eggs and bigger, to split a man's skull!

"Stone him! Stone him!"

"Death for a blasphemer against the name of the Lord God!"

The stones struck some of the bystanders, others glanced off the Temple wall. The mob, seeking to kill Him, turned on itself, under the pressure of its angry confusion.

Jesus slipped past them and escaped.

Chapter 48

"Welcome to My Home"

Twice more the Jews in Jerusalem tried to stone Jesus. Both times He escaped them. His time had not yet come.

Daily, He continued to teach in the Temple—to teach and to heal, fearlessly and steadily, facing a new attack each day by those who were determined to kill Him. There was a caliber of ordinary citizen always available to be aroused against Him by the clever members of the opposition. The stoning attacks seemed spontaneous. They were no more spontaneous than the action of any mob gone out of control with artificially inflamed violence. Among the crowds were always those who had come to believe in Him; but outnumbering them were the others, adrift on their emotions.

After the third attempt on His life, a pleasant-looking young man named Lazarus approached Jesus.

"Master, my sister Martha owns a nice home at Bethany, an easy walk from Jerusalem. I live there with Martha and my other sister, Mary. We would be honored if you would take refuge with us—for as long as you need our home."

That night, the Master and His men went home with Lazarus to Bethany.

For weeks both Mary and Martha had heard their brother talk of almost nothing but Jesus of Nazareth. The older sister, Martha, met Him at the gate.

"Welcome to my home, Master!"

Jesus' heart was warmed and encouraged by the very tone of Martha's voice. These had been days which left Him spent and battered. The incessant hecklers in the crowds to which He spoke now, tired a man's soul. A lesser man's nervous system would have collapsed under it.

"My sister Mary will be here directly. We are honored that You have wanted to visit with us. Please stay as long as You can."

He smiled and thanked her for her kindness. He thanked His Father, too. Jesus had not again had a home since He had walked away from Nazareth and His mother's house, almost three years before. His heart plunged gratefully into the normalcy and love He sensed in the comfortable house at Bethany.

"Your disciples can find lodging in the neighborhood," Lazarus told Him, "and we do hope You'll stay with us a long time, Master."

Jesus loved Lazarus at once. He was a quiet, gentle, personable young man, with an open, receptive heart. He loved Martha, too, although she was obviously the anxious type. Not outwardly as gentle as her brother, Martha was heavy set and talkative; but she made Him feel welcome, and He hadn't felt welcome anywhere since He left Peter's home in Capernaum.

Lazarus saw to His every need for refreshing Himself, and Martha returned to her kitchen.

While they waited for dinner to be served, Jesus and His men sat outside with Lazarus, discussing an incident which had occurred in Jerusalem, when Jesus had healed another blind man on the Sabbath.

"You see, Lazarus," Peter explained (to the Master's great delight), "as long as a man claims he knows all the answers, God can't redeem him! It's only when we realize we are blind, and need light, that light comes."

Jesus lost some of His weary look at Peter's clear explanation.

"The Master is the Light of the world," John said simply.

The Lord's heart overflowed with thanksgiving.

In the doorway of the house, a lovely, slender, dark-haired young woman stood listening, watching Jesus' every move. Slowly, now, she walked toward Him and sat at once at His feet.

"This is my sister Mary," Lazarus said.

Jesus smiled at her, recognizing another open heart. He was enjoying the personality picture He saw among the three well-bred people who had welcomed Him to their home.

Martha was considerably older, and had been mother and father to Mary and Lazarus. He could hear Martha ordering the servants about in the kitchen. She was adept at giving orders, sure that she ruled her domestic realm. He smiled inwardly, knowing her domestic realm ruled her!

Mary's heart ruled her. Women just did not join men in conversation as Mary had joined them. And yet, there was only childlike openness in her manner. She sat at His feet, longing for Him to talk.

343

"Master, are You too weary to repeat some of what I heard You say today at the Temple in Jerusalem? I want Mary to hear it, too."

Lazarus and Mary were obviously close.

"What about your other sister, Martha?" James asked.

"Martha? Oh, she'll get it second-hand," Lazarus laughed. "She's married to her kitchen!"

"Please tell me," Mary spoke to Him for the first time.

Jesus was glad for their interest. His voice was husky from speaking over the heckling crowds, but it never occurred to Him to refuse open hearts like those He saw in these two young people.

"Truly, I assure you," He said, "he who enters through the door of the sheepfold is the sheep's shepherd. He calls his own sheep by name and leads them out. When he has put out all that belong to him, he walks ahead of them and the sheep follow him. They know his voice. I am the door of the sheep."

He looked at the brother and sister with great tenderness.

"I am the Door. Whoever comes in through Me shall be saved, and he will go in and out and find pasture. I have come so they may have life and have it abundantly! I am the Good Shepherd. The good shepherd, you know, lays down his life for the sheep. I am the Good Shepherd," He repeated, "and I recognize My own. My own, in turn, recognize Me; just as the Father knows Me, and I know the Father—and I lay down My life for My sheep."

Mary's dark blue eyes were brimming with tears.

"We must pray the Lord God that You will not have to lay down Your life, Master! We need you," Lazarus whispered.

Jesus loved them both deeply. He knew they belonged to Him.

"I recognize My own. My own, in turn, recognize Me."

The two young people nodded vigorously, too close to tears to trust their voices.

"Mary! Mary!"

Martha's shrill voice shattered the tender moment, as she came hurrying across the yard, wiping her hands on a linen towel. Her exasperation and anxiety over dinner pushed her to a liberty she might not have taken with a guest in her home for the first time.

"Lord," Martha complained, as though she had known Him a long time, "don't You care that my sister is letting me do all the

344

work alone? A dinner for fourteen hungry men to prepare—and here she sits under the trees in the shade! Tell her to take hold with me!"

Some of the men chuckled. Jesus smiled at Martha, enjoying the naturalness she felt with Him, and said, still smiling, "Martha, Martha, you are anxious and bustling about many matters, when there is need of but few—or even of only one thing. Your sister, Mary, has selected the good portion. And she is not to be deprived of it!"

The tension was broken. Even Martha laughed at herself—a little.

At any rate, she didn't fuss anymore, but went on back to the kitchen. Soon Martha was calling, "Dinner is ready!"

The fourteen hungry men did not have to be called twice. Even Judas talked a little as they all reclined around Martha's loaded table.

For awhile, at least, they had a home.

Chapter 49

"The One You Love Is Ill"

Jesus walked the two miles over the Mount of Olives from Bethany to Jerusalem every day, to continue His teaching in the Temple, as long as possible. He spent each night at the home He had found with Lazarus and his sisters in Bethany. The quiet home refreshed Him, and He loved His new friends deeply.

One night He didn't come. The violence in Jerusalem broke against Him with such force He and His men left directly for Perea, beyond the Jordan River. It was January of the year 30 A.D.

Mile after mile, looping northward through Jericho and Ephraim, He preached to the multitudes who continued to seek Him out for His message, and for His healing touch upon their diseased bodies. Jesus seemed tireless. He worked almost without rest, a Man against the relentless motion of time.

He healed blind eyes, deaf ears, crippled bodies, sick minds and on one occasion, ten lepers—only one of whom remembered to thank Him at all. His men worked with Him.

Even Judas did not slacken his duties. As treasurer of the group, he bought their supplies, haggling for the best price, portioning out their funds. He was sullen and uncommunicative, but he worked.

In February, a boy found them at the end of a long, tiring day, with a message for Jesus from Mary and Martha back in Bethany.

"Lord, Lazarus—the one You love—is ill! Please come back at once."

Jesus frowned. The pain on His face was intense. They all loved Lazarus.

"He's near death!" the boy panted.

A bird sang too loudly. They noticed it now. A few minutes ago its song had seemed a part of the day itself, and it had been a good day.

Lazarus dying? The disciples could scarcely believe it.

"This illness is not to end in death," Jesus said suddenly. "It is for the glory of God, so that through it the Son of God may be glorified."

For two days they made no move to return to Bethany. Jesus

spent much time alone in prayer, apart from His men. "I don't think He's going to change His mind and go back now," Peter said.

"Who can tell about Him?" Judas scowled.

"It's too dangerous to go back to Judea now!" Thomas was adamant. "I'm sure He won't try it again."

"I hope not," John's face was tense with anxiety. "Nothing must happen to Him."

Matthew rubbed his hands over his brown, wrinkled face. "Everything would be lost."

"What's been gained?" Judas spoke to no one in particular. The men had begun to ignore his remarks mostly.

"I'd be lost without Him," John said.

"Sh!" Judas whispered. "He's coming back."

Jesus was walking rapidly, with long, sure steps cutting the distance between the disciples and the hillside where He had been praying.

The men stood up.

"Let us go back to Judea," He said.

"Go back and let them stone You to death? Think, Master, think what can happen!"

"Rabbi, we plead with You to be sensible."

"We just shouldn't go back now!"

Jesus let them talk briefly, and then He asked: "Are there not twelve hours in the day? If one walks about during the day, he does not stumble, for he sees the world's light. But if he walks about during the night, he stumbles because in him there is no light."

He had a certain length of time in which to complete His work, and He knew it. His "twelve hours" in which He would not "stumble," or be stopped. Knowing they did not understand His meaning, He also explained to them:

"Our friend, Lazarus, is asleep, but I am setting out to wake him up."

"But, Lord, if he is asleep, that probably means he will recover. That he has passed the crisis."

"Lazarus is dead!" He declared. "And for your sakes I am glad I was not present, so that you may believe. However, I will go to him now."

347

Thomas turned to the other men and said courageously, but expecting the worst: "Let us go, too, so that we may die with Him!"

They gathered their few belongings and began the day's journey back to Bethany.

"I Am the Resurrection and the Life"

Jesus did not trudge innocently back into danger that spring afternoon, as He and His disciples came within sight of the flat-roofed stone houses of Bethany. He made no effort to hide His return. That would have been futile, since Lazarus and his sisters were prominently known even in Jerusalem.

While they were still outside Bethany, word of His arrival reached the sisters by way of those who had come from the Holy City and its surrounding area to comfort the mourners.

Martha ran heavily toward them, already talking rapidly and bitterly.

"Lord, Lord, if You had been here, I know my brother would not have died! Why didn't You come? Why?"

Jesus gave her time to compose herself a little.

"You could have healed him," her voice softened. "And yet, even as I complain to You, Lord, now that I am face to face with You once more, I know that even now, whatever You ask of God, He will grant You."

Jesus said to her, "Martha, your brother will rise again."

For a minute she looked hopeful, and then covered her swollen, red eyes with her hands, realizing how long it might be before the promised resurrection of all the dead! Without any real hope but like one who wants to say what she knew was expected of her, Martha whispered:

"Yes—Yes, I know that he will rise again at the resurrection on the last day, but——"

Jesus lifted her head and forced her to look squarely at Him.

"Martha, I am the Resurrection and the Life."

She stepped back and stared at Him. Even the disciples had never heard Him say a thing like that!

"I am the Resurrection and the Life; the believer in Me will live even when he dies, and everyone who lives and believes in Me shall never, never die! Do you believe this, Martha?"

"Yes, Lord, I have faith that You are the Christ, the Son of God, who was to come into the world."

The knot of people who followed Martha from her home stood staring at Jesus. Some had seen the attempts to stone Him in Jerusalem. Martha took advantage of their preoccupation with the Master to slip away to tell Mary He was there, asking for her.

Jesus waited for Mary to come to Him outside the village.

Women customarily returned again and again, alone, to the tombs to weep. When those who had come to comfort her saw Mary rush from the house, they followed her, thinking she was returning to Lazarus' tomb.

Mary ran to Jesus instead, and fell at His feet weeping.

"Lord, had You been here, my brother would not have died!"

She didn't need to say any more to Him. He knew these words were said at the peak of Mary's faith. The same words from Martha meant a labored beginning. But a beginning just the same.

When He saw her great weeping, and that of the mourners with her, His spirit was indignant at death! A great stirring within Him to do battle with all that caused death in His Father's beloved world energized His weary body.

"Mary, where have you laid him?"

The mourners called, "Come and see!"

A storm of grief tore through Him. His soul trembled with the holy hatred of God for anything that caused suffering among His creatures. Jesus' shoulders shook with His own weeping as He walked toward the grave of His friend.

"Look," murmured one of the mourners, "look how He did love Lazarus."

Now, they had reached the cave-like tomb, dug out of the slanting side of the rocky garden hillside. A huge stone sealed its opening.

Jesus was in front now. He walked deliberately down the four stone steps leading to the grave's entrance and stood on the flagstones recently placed there.

Tears still wet His cheeks and beard, but He said in a clear, firm voice:

"Remove the stone!"

Martha's voice pierced the stunned silence of the crowd.

"Lord, by now there is an odor. It is four days!"

349

"Martha, did I not tell you if you will believe you will see the glory of God?"

They removed the stone, and Jesus began to talk to His Father quietly and naturally.

"Father, I thank You for having heard Me. I know You always do hear Me; but on account of the people standing here, I speak, so that they may believe that You have sent Me."

The spring breeze mingled the death and spice smells from the open grave with the garden flowers which Lazarus had tended and loved.

Jesus took a step back from the open grave and shouted:

"Lazarus, come out!"

Mary sobbed once.

Martha held her hand hard over her mouth and stared with the others at the dark, silent opening of the grave where they had laid the body of their beloved brother.

There was a scuffling sound, and a loose stone fell somewhere inside the tomb. The people gasped when their straining eyes caught the first glimpse of white. The body of Lazarus moved, sat up, and then hobbled out into the spring sun, bound hand and foot in the winding sheet, with the burial napkin still tied around his face.

Both sisters moved slowly toward their brother, who was trying now to get free of his grave clothes.

Jesus smiled exultantly, and said, "Untie him, and give him a chance to move!"

Many of the Jews visiting Bethany believed in Jesus from that moment on. Others hurried to Jerusalem to inform the Pharisees what He had done openly, not two miles from their strong-hold in the Holy City!

Chapter 50

"A Priestly Emergency Session"

"He has defied us at the very gates of Jerusalem!"

"The gall of this imposter, to raise a well-known Jew like young Lazarus from his grave! Just two miles from us, too."

"This latest exhibition of his has the people in an uproar. The Passover is little more than a month away. Pontius Pilate will brook no outbrusts among the people during a feast time!"

The chief priests (Sadducees) and the Pharisees had summoned a quick meeting of the mighty Sanhedrin. Once more, Jesus had come to the very gates of Jerusalem to perform the mightiest miracle of all. He had raised others from the dead, but that was in far-off Galilee. Here, He dared do it under the nervous noses of the Temple officials themselves!

"What shall we do?" the priests asked of the Sanhedrin, sitting in a solemn row of silk and gold before them.

"What shall we do? This man continues to perform sign after sign. If we let him go on this way, everyone will believe in him! The Romans will not tolerate an uprising among our people for any reason. They will come upon us and take away our positions, our place in the Temple, and our people! Our nation will be utterly destroyed!"

Caiaphas, that year's high priest, spoke softly, but under his silken speech he carried an impact upon the minds of men. Particularly upon jittery, troubled, luxury-loving men who wanted to be out of their difficult spot as quickly and conveniently as possible.

"I know some of you gentlemen feel we should show this man more leniency. You, Nicodemus, are one, I am well aware. I must say, however, you who would let him keep on at this rate do not know a thing!"

The silk-robed court coughed and shifted its position uncomfortably.

"You do not reason out that it is preferable for you to have one person die on behalf of all the people, rather than have the whole nation ruined!"

Nicodemus did not vote at all. Nor did Joseph of Arimathea,

and one or two others among the rulers who had also come to believe in Him. They too remained silent when the vote was taken. But by an overwhelming majority, it was decided that from that day on, definite plans would be laid to kill Jesus of Nazareth at the first possible opportunity!

No longer did He go openly among the Jews. Nicodemus saw to that. The old Sanhedrinist sent word to Him at the home of Lazarus in Bethany, where Jesus and His men were resting. They left at once for the desert country near Ephraim, and again He preached and taught and healed the thousands who came to Him.

In Jerusalem, it was Passover time again. The Jews who came early to the Holy City to consecrate themselves before the Feast looked first for Jesus!

"What do you think?" they asked one another, meeting in groups here and there in the Temple.

"Is he not coming to the Feast this year?"

The gossip circled His Father's house, but few dared mention Him by name. The chief priests and the Pharisees had given orders that anyone knowing where He was must report to them at once!

"Choice Seats for My Sons"

For almost a week, Jesus and His men had been on their way steadily south, from Ephraim, through Jericho, heading straight for Jerusalem.

The men protested. Judas tried unskillful, frantic, futile persuasion. Jesus heard them out, but His time had come. He had set His face toward Jerusalem, and toward the Holy City they went, steadily closer with each passing day.

Great throngs of people followed Him out of Jericho, and although He continued His steady progress southward, as usual, He worked without strain. He wasted no hours, but He always found time for more healing and teaching.

A week before Passover the tired travelers were joined on the way to the Holy City by the happy, singing caravans of pilgrims coming down from their beloved Galilee for the Passover Feast.

They all met old friends, and Jesus was cheered to find His mother among the crowd from Capernaum! With her, also, was her sister, Salome, the mother of His dear disciples, James and John.

The meeting among these members of His family was a deeply poignant one. His mother looked older, but when Jesus caught her up in His arms to hug her, she laughed and wept with joy.

Salome could not understand the mood of her two sons, James and John.

"They've always been hot-tempered boys," she said to Mary the first night they were with their sons, "but never morose and glum as they are now! I wonder what's wrong. Perhaps I should talk to Jesus and find out about my sons. I want to be sure everything is going well for them. After all, you know, Mary, they did give up a great deal to follow Him!"

James and John were not the only disciples whose anxiety and gloom set them painfully apart in the midst of their light-hearted relatives and friends. All the men were afraid and apprehensive. After all, their beloved Master was going to Jerusalem!

Nothing could stop Him now.

And the day before they met their families along the way, He had taken them aside on the road and said to them:

"Take notice! We are going up to Jerusalem and the Son of Man shall be betrayed to the chief priests and scribes; they will sentence Him to death and hand Him over to the Gentiles to be mocked and scourged and crucified, and on the third day He shall be raised."

This was the third time He had told them this.

To each man, it was still too horrible to believe! He *must* be speaking again in something like a parable. Desperately, they clung to this slim hope, not daring to question Him about it.

In spite of their aching hearts, James and John agreed readily to go with their mother, Salome, to speak to Jesus.

"After all, He's my nephew," the woman said, "and it's a mother's duty to see that her sons are well cared for."

The three came to Jesus, kneeling before Him, obviously with a special request.

"What do you wish?" He asked His mother's sister.

"Jesus, say that these, my two sons, shall sit one at Your right and one at Your left, in Your kingdom!"

He was not hurt that she had asked; but He was wearied and disappointed that neither of these, His close friends, had learned any more than that about the kingdom!

There were deep lines in His face as He answered her. Just before He began to speak to her, Salome noticed almost irrelevantly that at thirty-three years of age, Jesus was already graying at His temples.

"Salome," He said, "you do not know what you are asking." Turning to James and John, He asked: "Can you both drink the cup I am about to drink?"

"Oh, yes, Master. We can!"

"More than you know now, you shall indeed drink my cup," He said sorrowfully. "But to sit at My right and My left is not Mine to grant! It is for those for whom it has been prepared by My Father."

When the ten others heard what James and John had done, they were furious with them. Jesus called them all together and said firmly:

"You know that the rulers of the Gentiles lord it over them, and their superiors oppress them. With you it is different: Whoever among you wants to be great, must be your minister, and whoever wants to be first, shall be your servant! Just as the Son of Man did not come to be served, but to serve, and to give His life a ransom for many."

Even Judas could not remember a single time when this greathearted Master of His had not been eager to serve the lowliest person. Now, so close to His hour of danger, once more He had shown them all their own fiery egos!

Once more, their hearts reminded them that He had given His life to them along every dusty mile of every weary journey they had made together. He now asked for nothing more than the right to continue to lay down His life for His Father's beloved world.

The men were still locked in their selfish natures, but with all the strength of their human hearts they loved Him.

Even Judas' love, which was slowly twisting to hate, warmed itself for a last sweet moment as he watched his Master walk wearily but resolutely ahead of him, toward Jerusalem.

Chapter 51

"Fragrance Filled the House"

Six days before the Passover, Jesus and His disciples stopped over in Bethany, just two miles from the Holy City, where official word was out for His arrest.

They were to have dinner this time in the home of Simon, a leper whom Jesus had healed. His dear friends, Mary and Martha and Lazarus, were guests also; but apparently Martha could not resist serving Jesus the only way she knew how.

It was not her house, but she insisted upon serving the tables that night.

All around Him sat living reminders of the healing in the touch of a human life with His. Lazarus He had raised from the dead. Simon, His host, he had restored to health and society, by healing him of the outcast's disease. Martha was no longer bustling just for the sake of bustling. She served from her heart now.

And Mary—that night as He reclined at the table—poured out her heart of love to Him in the only way she knew. Martha's younger sister had never been a woman of questionable morals. Still, her darkened heart had been so filled with light by Jesus that she innocently repeated another tender scene at another table in the home of another Simon.

Halfway through the meal, Mary anointed His head and His feet with a pound of the costliest perfume, and dried His feet with her lovely, dark hair.

The whole house was filled with fragrance.

This was too much for Judas! He jumped to his feet and shouted angrily: "Why wasn't this perfume sold for 300 dollars— a whole year's wages—and the money donated to the poor?"

Mary hid her face, trembling. Judas' angry, darkened face caused even some of the men to turn away.

"I thought we were supposed to be concerned for the downtrodden! How is it we sit here gorging ourselves on rich food and allow this stupid woman to waste 300 dollars worth of expensive ointment for nothing!"

Judas was venting the bitterness and disappointment and

hostility which had been mounting in him during all of the last weeks of his strange, dark silence.

"Judas, leave her alone! Why do you embarrass her? Mary has treated Me nobly. You will always have the poor with you, and whenever you wish, you can benefit them. But Me you will not always have. She has done what she could. She has prepared My body with perfume for the burial."

Mary looked at Him and cried: "No, Master! It is only that I love You so deeply!"

Jesus smiled at her, encouragingly.

"I assure you, wherever this Gospel shall be preached over the whole wide world, what she has done shall be told as a memorial to her."

Judas crashed out of the brightly lighted dining room and ran the two miles across the Mount of Olives, over the Brook Kidron, to the home of the High Priest, Caiaphas, in Jerusalem!

The anger in the heart of the bitter young man turned to greed when he was received with such courtesy by the High Priest himself.

Judas had never felt appreciated. Now that he had agreed to betray his Master into the hands of the priests, he was at last being treated as the important person he had always longed to be!

On top of that, they were going to pay him money for doing it. Thirty pieces of silver. Not much; in fact, not enough. Only the price of a lame slave on the market!

But Judas would now be an important man among other important men!

And he began to think of just the right way to betray Him. The right way, and the most convenient way.

Entry into Jerusalem

Early the next morning, which was Sunday, they had left the home of Mary and Martha and Lazarus, to go on to Jerusalem. Near Bethphage, another small village between Bethany and Jerusalem, Jesus sent two of His men on a strange mission:

"Go into the village, and then and there you will find a donkey hitched and a colt with her. Unhitch and bring them to Me. Should anyone question you, simply say, 'The Lord needs them,' and without delay he will let them go."

The two disciples brought the donkey and its colt as He directed them. An enormous crowd was gathering around the Master. It was still the talk of the whole countryside that Jesus of Nazareth had raised Lazarus from the dead! Many in the crowd had seen it with their own eyes. Still others poured out of Jerusalem, toward the Mount of Olives down which He would ride. Many among these were pilgrims from Galilee, in the Holy City for the Passover Feast, soon to begin.

John rushed to spread his coat over the donkey. Then Peter covered John's coat with his. Before Jesus could seat Himself astride the small animal, two or three other disciples had shed their coats. Everyone longed to do something to help Him.

A spirit of high homage seemed to be growing among the ever increasing multitudes pressing around Him now. The people spread their coats on the road itself, for Him to pass over. Others cut flower laden branches from the spring trees and spread them on the road bed. From all directions, people streamed toward Him, waving palm branches and shouting:

"Hosanna! Hosanna!"

"Blessed is He who comes in the name of the Lord, even the King of Israel!"

They greeted Him with praises from the Psalms, but only Jesus, in His heart, knew they did not know what they said.

His disciples went along with the crowd, waving palms and shouting, proud of their Master. No one had expected Him to do anything like this! Their hopes rose sharply. Each man had fully anticipated arrest the moment they entered Jerusalem.

All except Judas.

Now, their beloved Lord was actually making a spectacular, triumphal entry into the Holy City! With the crowds cheering Him like this, the priests would not dare lay a hand on Him. It was too near Passover. The city was too crowded with Galileans.

"Ha!" Peter laughed, "they don't dare lay a hand on Him while the Galileans are here! They're a rowdy bunch. Old Pilate would clamp down on the Pharisees for sure if they gave this crowd any trouble."

Of course, the disciples thought He was at last announcing His identity! After all, why would He allow the crowd to follow Him like this, shouting and waving palms and singing His praises?

Jesus rode in silence up to the limestone ridge which marked the highest point on the Mount of Olives. Just across the Kidron valley, the Temple and the Holy City were bathed in morning sunlight.

Jesus halted the jubilant procession. For a long moment, He looked out over the same scene He saw at the age of twelve when He attended His first Passover Feast with Mary and Joseph.

He was still a young man, but that was His full lifetime ago. Even more clearly did He understand His deep love for the city of His people, the beauty of His Father's House, the plume of black smoke rising into the morning sky from the altars where the sacrifices to God were being made.

Those near Him in the crowd saw the anguish on His face, and heard Him cry, with tears streaming down His cheeks: "Oh, Jerusalem, Jerusalem! If you only knew *personally*, even today, how you might enjoy peace—but that is hidden from your eyes. For the time is coming when your enemies shall throw up ramparts around you, and shall encircle you and besiege you from every direction, and shall level you and your children within you to the ground, and shall not leave you one stone on another—because you did not understand when you were divinely visited!"

The happy, shouting procession of His disciples—now in the thousands—moved on toward Jerusalem, the city that broke His heart because His love could not stop trying to break through its darkness!

The shouting reached a joyous bedlam before they reached the city gates, and a few helpless but irate Pharisees, who trotted along to keep the situation under surveillance, shouted at Him:

"Teacher! Rebuke your disciples!"

Jesus answered His critics by saying: "I tell you, if these believers kept silent, then the stones would have to shout!"

No one dared lay a hand on Him inside the city gates because of the high spirit of those who danced and ran and shouted for joy ahead and behind Him, as He rode into the ancient city on the lowly donkey.

He went straight to the Temple, sized up the situation in the money changers' stalls, found it the same disgrace as it had been three years ago, but surprised even His disciples by turning almost at once to go back to Bethany.

There He stayed the night, and on the next day He once more headed for Jerusalem—this time walking quietly across the Mount of Olives with His disciples, without the protection of the crowds!

Inside the city gates, He went directly to the Temple, and into the market place where the stalls of the men who hawked sacrificial animals filled one entire wall of the Temple sanctuary! The money changers were doing a brisk business.

Without a word, Jesus once more took charge of the unholy situation. Here, at the darkening close of His earthly ministry, He drove the animals out of the Temple, turned over the money changers' tables, one after another, and released the caged doves!

When finally He turned away toward Solomon's Porch, even His disciples had to realize that the crisis was near. Either the priests must accept His authority or they must destroy Him!

There could be no other end to what had been begun.

Chapter 52

"The Last Meal Together"

The address of the house where Jesus and His men were to eat the Passover Feast was kept a secret until they arrived. What Judas was about to do was no secret to the Lord, and so He sent two other disciples to arrange for their meal.

They were to eat it in the quiet, private, upper room in the home of a faithful woman and her young son, whose name was Mark. Both were believers. Mark was unusually drawn to the Master.

When Jesus and the twelve disciples filed into their home, under cover of early darkness on Thursday night of the same week, the young man, Mark, found it difficult to stay downstairs. With all his heart, he longed to watch them, and to hear what would go on around the table his mother had prepared.

He stayed downstairs, but kept a close watch.

The laughter and joking among the Twelve was at an end. They entered the house quietly, everyone solemn except Jesus, who was merely silent, and deeply thoughtful.

"You would think His life was as safe as a baby's in a cradle!" John whispered to his brother, James.

The men reclined on couches at the low table, Judas on Jesus' left and John on His right. The table was well stocked with little salted fish, herbs, roasted lamb, preserved vegetables, bread, sauce, fruit and wine.

"If everything wasn't so tragic, I'd have laughed at Thomas on the way over here," James whispered to Nathanael. "He jumped at every twig we stepped on! Poor Thomas expects us all to be grabbed around every dark corner."

"Don't you?" Nathanael asked.

"Look! What's the Master going to do?"

Jesus had gotten up from the table, and was removing His robe. He wrapped a towel around His waist, picked up a basin of water, and walked behind the men as they lay on the couches in a semicircle around the table, He knelt at Matthew's feet and began to wash them!

The men were so shocked no one said a word, until the Lord was on His knees at Peter's feet.

"Lord! *You* wash my feet?" Involuntarily, Peter jerked his big, wide feet out of Jesus' reach.

"Peter," He said patiently, "just now you do not understand what I do; but you will later on."

Shaking both open palms at Him in refusal, Peter protested:

"You shall never, never wash *my* feet!"

Jesus looked at His dear disciple patiently.

"If I do not wash you, you are not sharing with Me."

This was more than Peter could bear. He quickly sat up on the couch, stretched out his hands and his feet and cried:

"Lord, then not only my feet, but wash my hands and my head, too!"

Gently, firmly, Jesus splashed the water over Peter's rough, calloused feet, explaining as He worked:

"A bathed person, Peter, does not need to be washed further than the feet, but is completely cleansed."

As He wiped Peter's feet tenderly with the towel, tears streamed down the big fisherman's broad face.

Jesus moved along the length of the table in silence, giving each man personal care.

Now, He was on His knees before Judas Iscariot, tenderly splashing the water over his slim, taut feet. Try as he did, Judas could not relax the muscles in his legs. The Lord dried Judas' feet, understanding the tension that gripped his heart.

Before He moved on to wash John's feet, He looked up at Judas from His kneeling position. Judas forced a cough, and jerked his head abruptly to avoid those eyes.

The Lord loved this disciple turned enemy. Tears sprang quickly to His eyes as the sin in Judas crashed against His sinless heart!

No words passed between them.

Jesus moved on to bathe the feet of John, who loved Him. When He had finished with all the Twelve, He said:

"Now, you are cleansed—but not all twelve of you."

Judas flinched.

"Not all of you are cleansed."

"What does He mean?" Thomas whispered behind his hand to Andrew.

Andrew didn't know either.

After Jesus had removed the towel and had dressed again in His outer garment, He once more reclined at the low table between Judas and John.

"Now, let Me ask you—do you understand what I have done to you? You call me 'Teacher' and 'Lord,' and rightly so, because I am. Then, if I, your Lord and Teacher, wash your feet, you surely ought to wash one another's feet, for I have set you an example so that you might do just as I did to you. A servant is not superior to his master nor a messenger to his sender. If you grasp these things, blessed are you if you practice them."

Judas ate rapidly, covering his nervousness, trying not to listen at all.

"I am not speaking of you all. The Scripture is to be fulfilled, and the Scripture says, 'The one eating my bread has raised his heel against Me!"

Judas' hands trembled. He held the loaf as Jesus quoted the Scripture. The thick crust jerked free suddenly, and a glass of wine spilled on the linen tablecloth.

"I tell you this right now, so that when it occurs, the rest of you will surely know that I am He."

Jesus' face had remained calm and almost serene until that moment. Now it was drawn with the pure pain of knowing, not only what Judas would do, but of the torment of Judas' heart, now fully in the black captivity.

The Lord's sinless heart brimmed with pain and love. The agony on His sensitive face was the hard, clean agony of grief, uncushioned by the sin of self-pity.

When He spoke again, the hearts of the eleven melted within them. Judas' heart kicked and clawed.

Jesus took a deep breath. "I have to tell you that one of you shall betray Me!"

He had hinted at this once before, in the synagogue in Capernaum, when so many of the people turned away from Him. It struck again like thunder into the quiet of the upper room.

Judas' hard eyes stayed fixed on his plate. The others spoke in muffled confusion, looking from one to the other—completely perplexed!

"Is it I?"

"Or I?"

"Not I, is it, Lord?"

Jesus was now breaking off a piece of bread from the loaf. Peter, who sat across the table from John, at Jesus' right, whispered hoarsely:

"John, ask Him who it is!"

John, leaning back, so that his head rested on Jesus' chest, asked, "Lord, who is it?"

He held the piece of bread over the center bowl of sauce now. Slowly, deliberately, He dipped the bread into the bowl. His quiet voice did not accuse, it merely stated.

"It is the one to whom I give this bite of dipped bread."

Judas allowed Him to place the piece of bread in his mouth. He chewed rapidly, glaring at each man around the table with open hatred now. He was free of them! For a moment, it looked as though his sharp, embittered face would break into laughter, something Judas rarely did.

The Lord spoke to Judas for the last time, quietly, as though He were sending him on an errand.

"Do quickly what you are going to do!"

Judas' foot caught in the hem of his coat as he bolted from the table; he ran down the outside stair and into the darkness of the night.

When the heavy door banged behind him, Jesus said:

"Now the Son of Man is glorified, and in Him God is glorified."

The men whispered among themselves.

"What does He mean?"

"Where did Judas go?"

"Did He send him to buy more food?"

"Little children, I am going to be with you but a little longer." His voice was full of sorrow and love. "You will be looking for Me and, as I told the Jews, where I go, you cannot come."

John grabbed His sleeve, as though to hold Him.

"But listen," He went on, "I give you a new commandment—that you love one another. Love one another, just as I love you. That's the way you should love one another. By *this*, everyone will recognize that you are My disciples—if you love one another."

"Lord, where are You going?" Peter choked out the words.

"Where I am going you cannot follow me now, but later on you will follow."

Peter was not satisfied with this. "Lord, *why* can't I follow You now?" His big voice trembled with emotion. "I will lay down my life for You!"

Jesus smiled at him briefly, almost sadly. "Will you lay down your life for Me?"

"Yes, I will! I will, I will!"

"Peter, I have to tell you—to assure you doubly, that the rooster will not crow tomorrow morning until you have denied *three times* that you know Me!"

"It Was Still Night"

It was still night. Darkness held the sky over Jerusalem. But the city had never grown quiet in the darkness of this night.

The narrow, ancient streets, usually given up to prowling cats and beggars asleep in the doorways, clanked and throbbed, echoing up and down their crooked lengths with angry shouts, barked orders, and the marching feet of soldiers in thick-strapped Roman sandals.

The city was crowded with Passover visitors, and as the night wore on, their excited, aroused chatter collected them in increasing numbers here and there in the vicinity of Caiaphas' house, and the Temple. Throughout the night, from bed after bed across the darkened city, rose the people to scurry from one scene of excitement to another.

Eleven of the twelve men who had followed Jesus scattered into the panic and confusion of this clamorous night.

The twelfth man roamed the scenes of the shifting drama, drawn like a murderer to the scene of his crime — hanging to the shadows, alone.

Judas had kept his bargain with the High Priest, Caiaphas. He had spent the last four tense nights with his Master and the other disciples on the slopes of the Mount of Olives. There was a garden there called Gethsemane, which Jesus loved. A private place, where He prayed and taught them time after time, under the ancient, gnarled olive trees. They would go there again that night when they finished eating the Passover feast. Could he be sure? Yes, he was very sure—and the spot was so private the arrest could be made easily without any public attention whatever.

Still running, driven by the same force that had sent him bolting from the upper room and the presence of Jesus, Judas arrived at Caiaphas' house with the news that the time had come. Caiaphas wasn't as lavish in his gratitude as Judas expected, but everyone, including the High Priest, did as he ordered.

By the time the impressive contingent of more than a hundred armed Roman soldiers had assembled at the Fortress Antonia,

Judas knew Jesus and the disciples would be on their way, at least, to the privacy of their favorite spot. The sight of the armed men in their short, pleated tunics, their chests covered with tough leather cuirasses, fringed, and studded with brass, made Judas' blood tingle. The soldiers adjusted their helmets and strapped on their swords.

He was going to be in the midst of real action at last!

Even the odd grouping of hand-picked priests and Temple dignitaries in their silken, tassled robes filled the embittered ex-disciple with a sense of his own power.

Only a few people had ventured sleepily into the darkened streets to investigate by the time the strange procession passed through the city gates, down through the dark valley of Kidron, across the brook, and up the familiar slope of the Mount of Olives.

Their lanterns and smoking torchlights made ugly, jumping shadows on the gray leaves of the twisted old olive trees of Jesus' favorite garden spot.

Judas raised his thin, narrow hand and the impressive expedition halted. He had told Caiaphas that he would lead him straight to Jesus by kissing the Man who had been his Master. Judas blinked into the darkness of the part of the garden where Jesus prayed. For a moment, he almost panicked. There seemed to be no one there!

Then a tall, straight figure stepped quickly out of the shadows directly beside Judas, and asked:

"For whom are you looking?"

"We're looking for Jesus of Nazareth!" a high Temple official snapped.

"I am He."

Suddenly the entire contingent stepped back; some fell to the ground in their confusion. No one expected it to be this easy!

"Whom do you seek?" Jesus asked again.

"Jesus of Nazareth!"

"I have told you—I am He."

This was too simple for Judas. Even now, the Master was making a fool of him! Determined to play out his important role to the end, Judas took three long strides toward Jesus and kissed Him.

"Judas," He said sorrowfully, "do you betray Me with a kiss?"

Peter, who had been hiding in the shadows of the garden with the other eleven, stomped into the eerie circle of flickering torchlight, drew his sword, and whacked off the ear of Malchus, the high priest's servant!

The servant screamed, and the priests began to shout for help from the hundred armed soldiers.

Jesus held Peter's arm firmly. "Put your sword away! The cup which My Father has given Me, shall I not drink it?"

Malchus still whimpered, holding the bloody socket.

Jesus touched him and restored the ear.

Then He stood facing them all, quiet and majestic.

"I told you I am He. Do you suppose that I cannot ask My Father and He would assist me with twelve legions of angels?"

He seemed almost to smile.

"Oh, but how then could the Scriptures be fulfilled? You have come with swords and clubs to arrest Me as though I were a robber, when daily I have sat openly in the Temple teaching, and you never seized Me. All this is occurring as it was written in the Scriptures. Once more, I tell you, I am He—so if you are after Me, take Me—but let these with Me escape."

The armed might of Rome seized Him, bound new, stout ropes around the arms He held out to them and the eleven disciples with Him escaped into the darkness of the garden.

A soldier grabbed what he thought was the robe of a young fellow who had been hiding in the bushes. When he ran, the linen cloth—all he had thrown on himself in his haste to follow Jesus, remained behind in the soldier's hand! The boy fled naked. It was young Mark, in whose house they had eaten their Passover feast.

Judas, totally ignored by the priests who had no more need of him, followed them back as far as the gate of Jerusalem, and then he, too, ran away into the shadows.

Now, he crouched among some low bushes outside the houses of Caiaphas, the High Priest, and old Annas, his father-in-law. Judas twisted his thin hands together, unable to stop.

Why had he done it? Why hadn't he realized their brutality? Did he think they would treat the Master decently? What made him think they'd make him a man of importance in their ignoble regime? How had he reached the dark place of betraying the only Person who had ever really loved him? Could mere impatience do this to a man? Could ambition do this to a man? Had he really thought he could force Jesus to establish an earthly kingdom?

Judas twisted his nervous hands and bit the blood from his thin, cracked lips.

Why couldn't he run now? Why couldn't he bring himself to turn away from the sight of his Master standing almost regally before bad-tempered old Annas, being badgered and humiliated like a criminal?

Annas was enjoying the sport immensely. His clever son-in-law, Caiaphas, "repaid" the old man for helping him become High Priest that year by giving him a crack at the Nazarene first. Annas was making the most of it.

Jesus, His wrists bound brutally tight with hard ropes, was answering one of the old man's sharp questions.

"Why ask Me this? I spoke openly to the world. I taught always in the synagogue and the Temple. I have said nothing in secret. Ask those who heard me."

The old priest growled in rage. "Impudent wretch!"

A guard struck Jesus a cracking blow to His face. A trickle of blood ran down His cheek as the guards pushed Him next through the doorway into Caiaphas' house.

He stood facing the entire Sanhedrin, on the trumped up charge of blasphemy against the Lord God of Israel!

Two local ne'er-do-wells had been brought in to witness against Him, both carefully instructed.

"I heard this man say," the first witness declared, " 'I have the power to destroy God's temple and build it again in three days!' "

"And did you hear the prisoner say the same thing?" Caiaphas prodded the other man of the streets.

"Yes, I heard this fellow say the same thing—that he could tear down the temple of God and build it himself again in three days!"

Caiaphas stood up, a good ten inches shorter than his prisoner, and asked: "Have you nothing to reply? What about their evidence against you?"

Jesus was silent.

Caiaphas, infuriated, shrieked: "I charge you, by the living God, that you tell us whether or not you are the Christ, the Son of God."

His prisoner looked at the little High Priest, unimpressed.

"As you say," Jesus said. "Besides, I tell you that shortly you shall see the Son of Man seated at the right hand of the Almighty and coming upon the clouds of heaven."

What happened then came as no surprise to Jesus.

"Blasphemy!" Caiaphas screamed. "What further need do we have of witnesses? What is your view?"

"He deserves death!" the others shouted, so loudly Judas could hear them from his hiding place outside.

Bedlam broke loose in the high priestly court. All present but Nicodemus and one or two others tore their costly garments to signify that they had witnessed blasphemy. They beat their breasts and struck Him in the face with their heavily ringed fists, time after time, shouting:

"Prophesy to us, Christ! Who struck you then?"

The priests of the Temple of God vented their anger on Him, until they stopped from their own exhaustion.

Judas wiped the blood from his own chewed lips as he crouched in the safety of the bushes outside Caiaphas' house. When he caught his next glimpse of the Master, his heart broke. The kind, open face was bruised and swollen. Blood ran from His eyes and ears and mouth, matting His brown beard.

He had done this! Judas alone was responsible. He broke from his hiding place to run again, but darted back when he caught sight of two familiar figures in the courtyard of Caiaphas' palatial home.

John and Peter crouched before the fire built there to warm those in attendance against the chill spring night.

A servant girl was talking to Peter.

"I know you—you were with Jesus of Galilee! I've seen you with him."

Peter shook his big, shaggy head firmly.

"I don't know what you mean!"

He and John got up and started toward the vestibule of the house. John knew Caiaphas' servants, and had managed to get Peter inside the courtyard, too, so they could at least watch from a distance. As they walked rapidly toward the house, terrified and anxious over what they had just overheard through the window opened to the courtroom inside, another servant girl pointed to Peter excitedly and cried:

"This fellow was with Jesus of Nazareth!"

Peter cursed, "I don't even know the man!"

In the crowded courtyard, a young man began to talk about Peter also. "There he is! That's the one who cut off my cousin's ear! I'm Malchus' cousin—that's the big fellow who pulled his sword when they arrested the Galilean last night!"

Peter was frantic. Frantic and trapped. He began to curse violently and shouted: "I do *not* know the man!"

One beat of time passed between Peter's third denial of His Master, before the night air was shattered by the loud crowing of a rooster!

Peter's heart shattered, too, and he ran out of the courtyard weeping bitterly. John ran after him.

"Let me go, John! Leave me alone," the big man sobbed, flattening himself miserably against the wall around the High Priest's palace, his brawny arms beating against the rough stone.

"I say to you, you are Peter—Peter, the rock."

Huge, wrenching sobs tore from his big chest and throat. The rock, indeed! He hadn't even dared admit to a mere servant girl that he knew the Master! A rock, indeed! A giant, rotting timber that collapsed in the first wind.

"Oh, you of little faith," he heard Him say again.

He slid down the wall to crumple in a hulking mass of misery on the ground.

Only a few hours ago, looking across the table at the Master, he had declared himself ready to die with Him! Peter, the weakling. Big Peter, the well-intentioned failure! How had he dared deny the Master? Wasn't it enough what they were doing to Him?

John stood leaning against the wall, his dark head buried in his arms. He had no comfort to offer Peter. His own heart was broken, too. He had run with the others from the garden at the sight of those bristling troops!

Could he ever make it up to Jesus? Would he ever get a chance to stand by Him again? Would he ever be able to speak to Him again? John slumped to the ground beside his friend, and both men sobbed helplessly.

Peter's voice was flat and dull when he spoke again. "I'd like to go to sleep now," he said bitterly. "Do you think I can? No! I did sleep, though, along with you and James back there in the garden earlier tonight when He really needed us!"

"Stop it, Peter!" John cried.

Peter kept on talking, like a man in a dream. A cruel dream that clung to him, numbing his tongue, so he could not express himself clearly, but keeping his heart sharp to more pain than it could bear! Peter had to keep talking about what had happened during those last few minutes with Jesus. He had to keep torturing himself and John (God only knew where James was by now) with the fact that the three of them had fallen asleep—sound asleep, mind you, right when the Master needed them the way He'd never needed them before!

Once more, He had selected the same three to go with Him in His hour of need. Once more, they had all fallen asleep.

So Peter happened to be the one who answered the Master's big question at Caesarea Philippi! What of it? He had been pretty proud of himself that day. Now, hunched against the stone wall of the High Priest's house—with the Master a prisoner—the big disciple almost wished it had been someone else who had declared Him to be the Christ that day! It would have made more sense.

He was ready to die with the Master, too! He had boasted about this at supper that very night. Then after the wonderful things the Master had said to them all, the crumbling "rock" had let Him down in His hour of horrible need in the garden.

Peter had meant to throw himself forever into the cause of His Master's ministry. With all his big, impetuous heart, he loved Him! He *had* thrown himself into the work. Peter had become the leader of the Twelve. From a rough, coarse-mouthed, hot-tempered fisherman, Peter had really become more or less the leader. He and James and John were closer to the Master in His deep moments than any of the others. The wonder of it all had saturated the uncouth mind of Simon Peter. He hung on the Master's every word!

"Seek and you will find . . . knock and it shall open to you."

Peter had knocked and the love of God had opened in the Person of the Master he loved. The Master he loved and disappointed and denied! He hoped he'd never hear another rooster crow again as long as he lived.

Peter wanted to die. But the Master was going to die instead!

"No!" the big man cried into the dreadful night around them.

"I don't want us to have let Him down over there in the garden,

John! I don't want that to be true!" He banged his fists against the rough stones and sobbed again bitterly.

John's voice was flat now, too.

"We did, though. We all three went to sleep, while He was on His knees, pouring out His heart to the Father. Asking that the cup might pass from Him, if possible. He doesn't want to die, Peter. The Master doesn't want to die."

"But I do!" Peter shouted again.

John went on numbly, so softly Peter scarcely heard him, nor cared.

"Twice He tried to keep us awake. I never saw Him the way He was over there in the garden tonight. Never in all the time I've known Him. Did you see His forehead when He finally came back to us the third time? There were big drops of blood running with the sweat, down His face. Big drops of blood and tears and sweat. He loves us and He loved being with us and He loves all the people so much, He wanted to keep on trying to make them see, I guess. He *hated* the thought of dying, but He said, 'Not my will, but Your will be done.' I heard Him say that."

Peter was thinking with John now. It helped, he decided, to know that John was in the same misery. Peter went on talking about the same thing. They suffered through the same heart now.

"I can hear Him say it to us, right after we reached the garden of Gethsemane tonight. He said, 'Sit down here, boys, while I take Peter and James and John and go to pray.' Then he took us apart from the others and we all sat down on that big rock together. John, that was the first time I ever saw Him in such distress! In all the tight places we've seen Him. He dropped His head in both His hands and shook it from side to side, like a man suffering all the pain all the men in the world had ever known!"

"Then is when He turned to us with that pleading look on His face and begged us to watch with Him! The Master begging *us* to help Him—" John began to sob again brokenly.

"Oh, yes, I said, 'I'll watch with You, Master. I'm the one who is ready to die with You!' When He came back to wake us the first time, He spoke right to me: 'Peter, you were not able to watch with Me for a single hour, were you?'"

Peter's guilt choked him. He grabbed his big chest and tried to smother the guilt there, but he only began sobbing again. He would carry this pain forever. He hoped he would. He was a sinful man. Peter had never denied this. He deserved to feel this pain. The Master was sinless. He didn't deserve anything that He was getting. None of it! *They* deserved it. Not the Master!

Both men scrambled to their feet shakily, roused from their self-condemnation by the fearful sound of the marching guard of soldiers. They would be taking Him somewhere else now!

Still ducking along in the safety of the shadows, John and Peter followed the sound. Jesus was being led to the dungeon beneath the Temple.

Peter hid his face, not able to look!

John stood white and shaken, unable not to look once more at his beloved Master, walking quietly, wearily now, between heavily armed guards, His face a mass of blood and bruised flesh. He, who could not break a bruised reed, was almost unrecognizable, even to John, who knew that face so well.

Peter couldn't look, but John watched them lead Him away to the dungeon to wait for morning, when there would be a hurried meeting of the mighty Sanhedrin—a hasty, almost "legal" formality. Then it would be officially the next step to take Him before the Roman Governor, Pontius Pilate, for actual sentencing.

For the remaining hour or so left of that night, the Temple prison guards in the dungeon beneath the Hall of Hewn Stone, where the mighty would meet, could amuse themselves by tormenting the Master until it was morning.

Morning was not far away, as Peter well knew. The rooster had already crowed.

Chapter 54

"Pilate Before Christ"

Old Nicodemus stood near the front of the crowd of people fanned out below the balcony of the Roman praetorium. With him was Joseph of Arimathea, another member of the Sanhedrin— a wealthy man, with a fine reputation, who had also come to be a secret believer in Jesus of Nazareth.

Neither man had been able to make himself heard at the emergency session of the night before. Both had left the council room ashamed, for the first time in their lives, to be known as members of the Sanhedrin. They stood now, in the early light of this dread day, apart; not with the crowd of calloused people, craning their necks to see the prisoner, not—certainly not—with the group of ornately garbed priests, huddled around their bound victim.

Nicodemus and Joseph of Arimathea were not called to the second session of the Sanhedrin that morning. Only those who would vote with Caiaphas were there. A bare quorum. The whole meeting had been a disgrace! Flagrantly they had broken the Law by not allowing the prescribed day go by before fixing His guilt. Everything about the trial of Jesus had been illegal. Jewish Law, as given by God, protected a man until he was found to be guilty. Their witnesses were paid, worthless men, whose word meant nothing.

Nicodemus had not jumped at any hasty conclusions about Jesus. Carefully, he had weighed and reweighed what the Master had said to him the night he visited Him. The old Sanhedrinist was grateful for the Master's understanding of his mental blocks to believing.

"You must be born again from above," He had said, explaining that He meant a rebirth of the spirit, not the flesh; an inner freshening that exposed a man's ordinary selfish arrogance and made him a child again. A rebirth of the inner life which made a man strong, by showing him not merely his own weakness, but assuring him of the love of the Father *in* that weakness. Jesus had said it was hard to grasp a spiritual truth—that the whole thing was like a wind moving in the workings of God; that you couldn't see where it came from or where it was going, but you knew it was there. The Master had also said something about the fact that God loved the world so much, He had sent His Son—in man's likeness—to suffer the burden of men's sins, and thereby give eternal life to anyone who aligned himself with the Son.

There, in the center of the huddled group of fear driven priests, stood the Man Nicodemus had visited by night; His wrists were raw and bleeding from the ropes by which He had been jerked through the streets of the Holy City all night long, and His face was battered beyond recognition. How tired He must be! Yet how He stood out from among the hunching, nodding, nervous priests—like a king!

Flanked by attendants, the Roman Governor, Pontius Pilate, stepped out onto the balcony of the praetorium and surveyed the strange scene below him. Then the arrogant Governor lifted his toga and descended—conscious of his exalted position—to a landing just above the prisoner and His accusers.

Pilate sat down on the judgment seat placed there especially for this incident, and asked in a bored voice: "What accusation do you bring against this man?"

Pilate was intolerably annoyed with the priests. He had to appease them somewhat—just enough to keep down trouble. He could ill afford for Tiberius Caesar to find out that he had lost control of the Jews. But here were these insufferable silk-robed rulers of a religious sect, refusing to enter his palace for fear of defilement at the Passover! They had roused him too early in the morning and forced him outside for this piece of nonsense and he was in a bad mood.

Caiaphas stepped forward and said ingratiatingly, "If he were not a criminal we would not have committed him to you!"

This was no charge. Pilate got up to walk away, saying sarcastically, "You take him then, and sentence him according to your mighty Law!"

Caiaphas' shrill voice stopped him. "According to our law, we have no right to execute anyone!"

Pilate's back was still turned to them. So they wanted an execution, did they? This was more serious than he thought. Tiberias had already criticized him for being too ruthless. He would have to give this his full attention now, in order to keep both sides happy! Either way, Pilate could come under condemnation from Rome. Rome wanted bloodless domination of these strange Jews when at all possible, and yet, he must keep the eccentric priests placated.

He continued his climb back up to his quarters, but ordered the prisoner to be brought to him in his private council room.

As he waited, Pilate paced the floor. Other men in his position had been recalled to Rome and divested of their offices over senseless clashes with these troublesome Jews!

He heard the sound of marching outside the door, and on his command, two officers prodded the bound prisoner into the room where Pilate stood.

The two faced each other.

Pilate strolled nonchalantly toward Him, looking Him up and down distastefully. A bloody sight so early in the morning.

The prisoner was a tall, strong-featured Jew. His priestly captors had worked Him over rather thoroughly. There were ugly abrasions on His face and neck and chest. His forearms were caked with blood from the ropes which had cut and rubbed and re-cut the flesh. Evidently they had been at Him for most of the night. But He seemed harmless enough. Calm, in fact, and totally unprotesting.

Pilate stepped back, still surveying Him closely. The country was full of would-be Messiahs, this much Pilate knew well. Word had reached him that this fellow considered Himself a king.

"Are you the King of the Jews?" Pilate asked sardonically.

The Governor was totally unprepared for the reply he got! It almost seemed as if the Man was personally interested in Pilate's answer.

"Do you say this of your own accord, or have others told you about Me?" Jesus voice was weary, but steady.

Pilate flared, self-consciously, "I'm not a Jew, am I? Your own nation and the chief priests have handed you over to me. What have you done?"

"My kingdom is not of this world," He said quietly. "If My kingdom were of this world, My attendants would have struggled to prevent My being delivered to the Jews. But really, the source of My kingdom is not here."

What a strange fellow! Pilate felt He was trying to communicate something to him.

"You are a king, then?" Pilate asked carefully.

His reply came quickly, without hesitation. "You have it right. I am a King. For this purpose I was born and for this I entered the world, that I might testify to the truth."

Pilate had been haunted privately by his own quest for truth. He did not interrupt the prisoner, who was saying with a quiet, intense energy, "Everyone who lives on truth, listens to My voice."

Pilate walked away from Him, then back. "What is truth?"

The prisoner looked at him in silence for a moment. Suddenly Pilate wanted to be rid of the whole thing! Before Jesus said any more, the Governor strode out of the room, down the stairs again to his judgment seat outside before the people.

The crowd quieted.

"I find nothing criminal in this man at all!" Pilate announced.

A roar of protest lifted from the crowd. "He stirs up the people by teaching all over Judea, starting in Galilee and all the way here!"

An idea struck Pilate. If this man is a Galilean, He should be tried by Herod Antipas! Herod was in Jerusalem, too, for the Passover.

Jesus was immediately jerked through the ancient streets toward Herod's quarters, the crowd following.

Pilate ordered his breakfast, relieved and satisfied with himself. He even wished his wife, Claudia Procula, were not still asleep. Today, he might enjoy her company at breakfast.

"His Blood Be on Our Children!"

Somewhere in the crowds around Herod's headquarters, Nicodemus and Joseph of Arimathea lost each other. Old Nicodemus hobbled along alone, leaning heavily on his strong, ornate cane.

He heard the people discussing the prisoner's appearance before the Tetrarch of Galilee.

Herod had been most interested in seeing Jesus of Nazareth at last. In fact, he had enjoyed the prospect of the interview—that is, until it got underway. The Master had stood before the puppet king Herod, who had murdered His dear friend, John the Baptist, in total silence!

Herod could make no sense of Him at all. Not knowing what else to do, he had decided He was a mere buffoon, a fanatic. Herod's soldiers amused themselves with Him for an hour or so, dressing Him in royal purple, befitting a king, and then dragged and jerked Him once more back to the praetorium to Pilate.

The Governor swept outside and sat down again in the judgment seat on the landing above the crowd, swearing to himself.

"You brought me this man," he shouted angrily, "as one who incites the people to rebellion. Here I have examined him in your presence and have found the man not guilty of any of your accusations against him! Neither, in fact, has Herod, for he has just sent him back to us. Observe that he has done *nothing* deserving death! So, since I must release one prisoner to you during your Feast, after a whipping I will let this fellow go!"

The people shouted in wild protest. The priests smacked their foreheads and stomped furiously.

Pilate thought of another prisoner he could offer them, a murderous, rebellious scoundrel named Barabbas. Surely they would prefer that he release Jesus above this dangerous criminal. Once more, he felt gratified with himself, and shouted confidently:

"Whom shall I release to you? Barabbas, or Jesus who is called the Chist?"

Their answer dumbfounded him.

"Barabbas! Release Barabbas to us!"

Pilate slumped in his chair, debating uncertainly what his next step should be. An attendant handed him a note in his wife's handwriting! Pilate unfolded it, annoyed with Claudia for disturbing him at a moment like this. The note read: "Do nothing, I beg you, to that innocent man for I was deeply affected this morning while dreaming about him!"

Pilate threw the crumpled note to the floor. What did his wife know of matters like this? He stood up, fuming as much at his own helplessness as at Claudia and the priests. For want of something new to say, he shouted:

"What shall I do then with Jesus, who is called Christ?"

"Crucify him! Crucify him!"

Pilate's voice split with desperation: "Why? Why? What wrong has he done?"

The blast from the throats of the people terrified even Pilate now: "Crucify him! Let him be crucified!"

The Governor stormed back inside, determined to let them have their way. Then he wavered. He had to consider what could happen to him when Rome found out! Perhaps he'd better just have the man severely whipped. Maybe that would satisfy these religious madmen outside.

He ordered Jesus taken to an inner cell. "The flogging of his life!" Pilate screamed at the officer, venting his own driven soul.

Nicodemus banged the stone pavement with his cane helplessly. Tears streamed down his wrinkled face and wet his long, gray beard.

"Honor has gone out of the world!" he screamed at the people. No one heard him.

Inside, Jesus had been stripped and was now being chained to a thick post. A burly guard picked up a three-thonged scourge, tipped with bits of lead and bone. The regulation number of lashes, according to Jewish law, was thirty-nine. Rome imposed no limit whatever. The guard began to whip Him, with no one counting. The bone and metal tipped whip ends whirred and slashed against His body in a steady rhythm. Again! Again! Again! Again! Again! The heavily muscled arm gave out at last. Jesus sagged semiconscious, His back and shoulders a raw, torn mass of bleeding stripes.

A soldier doused Him with a bucket of water. Then, to amuse themselves, other soldiers brought a mock crown they had made by weaving two-inch thorns together, and jammed it roughly down over His head, embedding the tough thorns. Blood streamed down His face, into His eyes and mouth. To go with the "crown" they put the purple robe back on Him, stuck a stick in His hand for a scepter and doubled up with laughter!

"Hail, King of the Jews!" they guffawed, bowing. Some of them slapped Him. Others spit in His face. Finally, one man jerked the stick from His hand, and whacked Him on the head with it.

Pilate came down to see Him then, and once more felt satisfied with himself. Surely, when the mob saw the way He looked now, they would relent.

Out on the platform above them again, the harried Governor shouted: "Look now, I bring him out to you, so you may know I find him not guilty!"

The rowdy Roman soldiers jerked Him, stumbling and bloody,

before the crowd. He stood swaying, wearing His brutal crown and purple robe. The crowd mumbled and buzzed.

Pilate shouted; "*Ecce homo*! Behold the man!"

The sight of Him lashed the crowd to greater fury.

"Crucify him! Crucify him!"

"*You* take him and crucify him!" Pilate was beside himself now, the conflict overwhelming him. Even his voice was failing. "I find him not guilty!"

"We have a Law, and by our Law, he ought to die because he made himself God's Son!" a priest cried.

In desperation, Pilate hurried inside, ordering Jesus to be brought to him once more. When they shoved Him into the room and closed the door, Pilate, in a state of high agitation, demanded, "*Where are you from?*"

Jesus gave him no answer. His eyes were almost swollen shut. Still Pilate felt totally *seen*.

"You do not talk to me, eh?" Pilate said pacing up and down before Him. "Do you not know that I have power to liberate you and I have power to crucify you?"

Jesus' body sagged and swayed. His mouth was scarcely recognizable as a mouth. Finally, He spoke hoarsely, but firmly through grotesquely swollen lips: "You have no power whatever of your own, but only what is granted you from above." He added sorrowfully, remembering Judas, whom He loved, "For this reason, my betrayer has greater sin than you have."

From this moment, for reasons he could not fathom, Pilate was even more anxious that He be set free. His morale broken, the once arrogant Governor dragged himself again to the balcony, and made one more plea to the people.

A priest shouted scathingly: "If you liberate him, you are no friend of Caesar's! Whoever makes himself king rebels against Caesar!"

Pilate's spine tingled at the name of Caesar. He turned quickly and went back inside. Jesus stood as he had left Him. The shattered Governor reached a trembling hand toward Him. Then drew back at the sight of His mangled flesh. His eye fell on the ropes hanging from His bound and bleeding wrists. Then with a surge of courage, Pilate grabbed the stained ropes and led Him out onto the balcony himself!

The Roman procurator dropped into the judgment seat. Jesus stood swaying beside him, His beaten body erect.

"Behold! Your king!" Pilate screamed at the Jews.

"Away with him!" they roared. "Crucify him!"

Pilate stood up, still holding the ropes.

"Shall I crucify your King?" he croaked weakly.

"We have no king except Caesar!" The moment had driven the Jews themselves to blasphemy against the Lord God!

An enormous riot was brewing. Pilate knew it well. He would give them their way, but first he took a basin of water and washed his hands over the crowd saying: "I am innocent of this good man's blood. It is your concern!"

And all the people answered: "His blood be on us and on our children!"

Then Pilate handed Him over to them to be crucified.

Lurking at the edge of the crowd, Judas heard the verdict with his own ears. Not minding to be seen now, he plunged through the scattering, yammering people toward the Temple, his eyes glazed and staring, his heart empty of everything except black remorse.

He had gained nothing. He had lost everything.

Holding out the ugly bag containing the thirty pieces of silver, he gasped, "I have sinned by betraying innocent blood!"

The priests laughed at him and refused the money. It was blood money. They could not defile themselves!

Judas threw it on the floor of the Temple, ran all the way to a deserted spot outside Jerusalem, and hanged himself.

Chapter 55

"Father, Forgive Them!"

Nicodemus had hobbled along wearily, as close as he could manage, beside the tragic procession that wound slowly, painfully, through the narrow streets of Jerusalem, out the city gates, to the place called Golgotha.

A brisk Roman centurion was in charge of the affair, his crisp commands easily heard. The crowd that followed Jesus now did not shout. It muttered and exclaimed; almost everyone talked a lot in order to endure or relish the tension. But for the moment, even the priests and scribes and Pharisees were not shouting.

For once, there were as many women as men—maybe more. Throughout His ministry, Jesus' tenderness and concern for women had drawn them to Him to serve Him quietly, unobtrusively, with deep gratitude that He recognized them as important in the kingdom of God.

Almost as soon as the rough, eighty-pound crossbeam had been hoisted to Jesus' raw and bleeding back, Nicodemus found himself with a companion for this strange, nightmare journey. A woman in her thirties, her face drawn and stricken. Mary of Magdala walked beside the dignified old Sanhedrinist in silence for the first agonizing steps of the journey, never once taking her eyes off the Man who gasped and stumbled under the crushing weight of the huge timber He carried.

Women didn't speak to men in public. But Mary of Magdala was not remembering custom. She wrung her hands, stumbling over the rough pavement stones, not watching where she walked.

"If only I could do something to help Him!"

Her words tore through the old ruler's heart, too. He had stopped shouting it, but his own outraged soul kept crying: "Honor has gone out of the world!"

On they moved toward the city gate. More and more women joined the crowds following Him on His last walk out of the Holy

City He loved. They beat their breasts and wept helplessly.

Once the women got past the Roman guards to reach toward Him despairingly. Jesus was not unmindful of them, even now.

He turned His beaten, disfigured face toward them and said: "Daughters of Jerusalem, do not weep for Me. Instead, weep for yourselves and for your children!"

They had just passed through the gates, when He stumbled and fell to one knee. The giant timber thudded to the paving stones.

Mary of Magdala sobbed uncontrollably. Nicodemus laid his old hand on her arm to comfort her.

One of the guards grabbed Simon, a Jew from Cyrene in northern Africa, in Jerusalem for the Passover, and forced him to carry one end of the crossbeam. This Man must not be allowed to die of exhaustion!

The two other doomed prisoners in the ugly parade had not been beaten. They were in excellent physical condition and handled their beams without trouble.

The trouble came with them, as it always did, when the soldiers would have to fight to keep the prisoners' arms stretched out on these rough beams, while they set the nails and pounded them through their hands into the wood, with sharp strokes of their mallets.

Perhaps they wouldn't have that kind of trouble with Him, the centurion thought. Jesus of Nazareth was already weak and injured.

Not a breeze stirred on the slightly elevated piece of ground—called Golgotha because it resembled the top of a man's skull. The air was hot and oppressive, as though the elements waited for a storm; but there were no clouds in the sky. Only the blistering, relentless sun.

The crowd milled about the soldiers and the three prisoners, coming as close as they were allowed, hunting vantage points to watch the proceedings. The two thiefs to be crucified with Him screamed and writhed despite the sedative, as they lay on their backs beside Him, while the nails bit through into the heavy timbers of all three crossbeams.

He lay quietly, having refused sedation, His tortured face upturned to the blank, hot sky, experiencing the same stabs of pain they felt.

383

The perspiring soldiers grunted and cursed, as they bound the arms of the condemned men securely to the beams to support their weight while they were being hoisted—their bodies swinging free—to the big uprights, already planted in the ground. Three soldiers heaved at ropes which ran in grooves over the top of the uprights, to lift each crossbeam with its dangling body. Another soldier standing on a stump beside each cross guided the heavy beam into a notch, where it was lashed into place.

The victim's legs were set, knees slightly bent, and then fastened with nails driven through the instep and sole of each foot.

Then the arm ropes were removed, and the waiting time began.

Across the surrounding field a small disconsolate group made its way to the execution. Mary Magdalene left Nicodemus, crying, "There's His mother!" She ran toward the newcomers and embraced Mary, both women weeping violently. Salome, His aunt, the mother of James and John, was there, and another faithful woman follower named Mary, the wife of Cleopas.

Only one of the Twelve came. Wanting desperately to make up for deserting Him the night before, John had come to be with Him that day.

Jesus' mother leaned heavily on John, as the little group moved horror-struck across the field toward Him, where He hung agonizing through the first moments on His Cross.

None of the small group who loved Him could speak for a long time. His mother stared unblinkingly at the dear figure hanging there. Irrelevant thoughts raced through her mind. Trying to cope with the hard fact of the spikes through His hands and feet, she remembered cutting His nails when He was a little Boy. He had spoiled her. His brothers, who came later, yelled and fussed when she trimmed their nails. Jesus sat patiently, making it easy for her. He always made things easier for her. There was only one hard thing. He had never been only her Son. He was God's Son, and she had always had to remember this.

The fact that He was God's Son, born through her human body, brought her to this pain-wracked hour! They were murdering Jesus, her Boy, because He *was* God's Son.

But couldn't God have saved Him?

Why couldn't the priests in God's own Temple see that Jesus was God's Son? She and Joseph had felt that the events surround-

ing His miraculous birth had been well announced by the Lord
God! In the Temple the day they took Him to present Him to the
Lord, as a tiny Baby, hadn't the old man named Simeon held Him
in his arms, and thanked God that he could see the Lord's salvation before he died?

Mary buried her face in her hands suddenly. Another memory
from that strange day in the Temple stabbed her heart! What
had old Simeon said to her? Especially to her?

"See, woman, this child is appointed for the falling and rising
up of many in Israel, and for a sign that shall be contradicted—and
a sword shall pass through your own soul—so that the reasonings
of many hearts may be revealed."

Pilate himself had lettered the sign that was fastened to the
Cross over Jesus' head: "The king of the Jews." Caiaphas protested
violently that the sign should have read, "I am the king of the
Jews."

Here was the "sign that shall be contradicted!" Mary's Son was
the King of the Jews. He was hanging on His Cross now, not
merely for His claim, but for the truth of that claim. His sinless
presence had driven the very priests of God to crucify Him on a
"contradiction"!

Mary leaned heavily on John's shoulder, pain drenching her
whole being. The sword was passing through her heart, as old
Simeon had warned.

John could stand inactivity no longer. Leaving Jesus' mother
with his own mother, Salome, the tormented young disciple
walked back and forth before the Cross of His Master.

He had not arrived until the work was finished and the waiting
time begun. Had the Master said anything? Every word of His
had always been important to John. Now, any word from Him he
must grab more eagerly than ever before.

He questioned the people. Had He said anything at all since
they put Him there? Had He been able to speak? Yes! The two
men had never met, but drawn by their bond of common grief,
Nicodemus told John what he had heard the Master say.

"As soon as they swung that crossbeam into place, I heard Him
pray!"

"What did He say?" John shook the old man impatiently.

"He said: 'Father, forgive them, for they know not what they
do'!"

385

John's shoulders slumped. His eyes filled with tears. "How like Him. How like Him—to say that."

Old Nicodemus stood erect and declared: "The words of the prophets are being fulfilled before our eyes, son. The words of David were fulfilled in one deed alone. In fact, in all of this horror. My old mind can scarcely take it in!"

Then Nicodemus told John that the soldiers divided His few belongings among themselves, according to the ghoulish custom at a time like this. Jesus was led to Golgotha in His own familiar garments; when they picked up his seamless robe, they fulfilled the Scripture by casting lots for it!

John's mind clutched at the familiar Psalm of David. How had he and the others been so blind? King David had already described this horrible scene in a Psalm! Described it in all its grotesque reality.

"I am poured out like water, and all my bones are out of joint. My heart is like wax melted within me; My strength is dried up like potsherd, and my tongue cleaves to my jaws . . . they have pierced my hands and my feet; I can count all my bones! They look, they stare at me; they divide my garments among them, and for my clothing they do cast lots." Men were not being executed on crosses when David wrote that Psalm!

John's brain swam crazily. Truth broke into his heart and mind with sickening sharpness. He fought to restrain his longing to run to the foot of that Cross and embrace the dear feet! He wanted some of the pain for himself. John had seen a few crucifixions and had heard the cries of the crucified. He heard the shrieks of the two thieves now, hanging on each side of Jesus, fighting the agony every dragging moment of the way. Most victims of a cross died screaming maniacs. He looked from one to another as the three hung there.

Before and after every terrible scream, the thieves' bodies wrenched upwards, raising their weight on the nails in their feet. The shriek of agony—then slowly the cords in their legs locked and swelled, forcing them back down. The Master did this, too, periodically, but He uttered no cry.

The nails were nothing compared to the muscular agony, the bones wrenching from their sockets, the slow, vicious cramps slicing like knives through the body, the taut flesh blocking the circulation of blood.

"I am poured out like water, and all my bones are out of joint ... I count all my bones!"

Several priests and Pharisees were at the front of the crowd around Him, in their usual places.

"He saved others," one of the priests screamed. "Now, let him save himself! If he is the Christ of God, the chosen one—let him save himself!"

John's fist doubled on impulse, then loosened. *"Father, forgive them, for they know not what they do."*

"He saved others, but it's plain he cannot save himself!"

"If you are the Christ of God, come down from your cross!"

The priests and rulers thumped each other on the back.

John looked toward Mary, His mother, wishing with all his heart that she would leave! At least they were managing to keep her fairly far away. John ran back to her.

"He trusts so much in God, let God deliver him now!"

Raucous laughter followed John, as he returned to the little group of weeping women. There was nothing to say. He could only support Mary with his strong, young arm, and pray.

Time dragged. The crowds stood watching, jeering periodically to break the monotony and relieve the tension.

Still standing near the crosses, Nicodemus heard one crucified thief mocking Jesus.

He was a mean-looking fellow, with a thick shock of stiff, black hair.

"Hey, you! If you're the Christ, save yourself and us!"

Then the old Sanhedrinist heard a strange and beautiful conversation. Immediately, the other thief called to the first man, trying to make himself heard all the way to the third cross.

"Do you not fear God, when you are suffering the same punishment?" His words squeezed past the pain. "We are suffering justly—you and I. We are getting our just deserts. But He—He has done nothing amiss!"

The thief who had just spoken was a younger man, with a light brown beard and hair. The ravings of the first thief added to his own pain. Periodically, he had looked over at the bushy-haired victim, wanting to silence him by any possible means!

Every time he looked at his fellow thief, however, he had been forced to look at Jesus, who hung between them. Now, the younger man spoke to the Lord Himself on the adjoining cross.

"Jesus?"

The Master turned His head slowly toward him, giving the boy His full attention.

"Jesus," the young man gasped, "remember me when you come into your kingdom!"

"I assure you," He said encouragingly, "*today* you will be with me in paradise!"

Nicodemus bowed his gray head. "I, if I be lifted up . . . will draw everyone to Me." He had heard Jesus say this. Now, he was seeing it happen.

Honor had gone out of the world; but the old ruler was taking hold of the truth that redemption exceeds honor in the true estimate of things.

Only one hour had passed. Often it took a man two days to die on a cross! John tried to keep Mary at a distance, but she insisted now that he take her closer.

"I'm afraid He can't see me, if I stay way back there," she said, as John led her to the Cross of her Son.

"I want Him to know I'm here with Him."

The disciple Jesus loved and His mother stood together at the foot of His Cross, hoping He would know they were there.

He saw them, and tried to speak to His mother, but the pain was too intense. His lips moved silently.

"We must move closer, John!"

A guard pushed them back. The crowd began to jeer again.

"Please be quiet!" John shouted at the yammering people. "If you have no pity for Him, take pity on this woman. She is His mother! He is trying to say something to her!"

Straining toward Him, her hands cupped behind both ears, Mary waited.

"Woman—see your son!" Slowly, agonizingly, He managed to bend His head toward John. Then He was looking straight at His disciple. There was nothing between them! Only love. The same old love, and more. John's heart reached toward His. Jesus was going to say something to him, too!

"John, see—your mother!"

He had given them both to each other for consolation, for comfort, for love. The hours of His giving dragged on.

The cruel hours of His giving dragged on.

Then a strange darkness began to crawl over the terrible scene. It crawled over Golgotha, over the Holy City, over the sin-scarred face of the earth.

Another darkness was invading Jesus' heart! A darkness experienced by no one who watched Him there. A dense, pain-choked darkness He endured alone. The one sinless Man becoming sin for His Father's world!

He had not cried out once during the ordeal. His courage held firm. But the great darkness was filling His heart now. He felt cut off from all light. The pressed down, concentrated darkness of all sin for all time!

A sob wrenched from His tortured throat, He twisted His head violently and cried:

"Loi, Loi, lama sabachthani? My God, My God, why hast Thou forsaken Me?"

Everyone heard it. No one understood its meaning. Some thought He was calling for Elijah to help Him.

John froze with fear. He had never heard the Master say a thing like that! God had never forsaken Him. David's psalm which foretold this dark day began with those words. What did it mean? John's heart was torn with confusion.

"Let not your hearts be troubled; you believe in God, believe also in Me." He had said this to them as they ate their last meal together the night before. The night before? A lifetime ago. But the words found their mark in John's heart. He had them now and they held him.

"In My Father's house are many homes. If this were not so, I would have told you. I go away to prepare a place for you. And when I have gone and have prepared a place for you, I will come again and take you along with Me, so that where I am, you also will be."

John looked at His agony on this darkest day and heard Him say again, "And where I am going, you know the way."

Poor, worried Thomas had argued: "Lord, we do not know where You are going, and how do we know the way?"

"I am the Way and the Truth and the Life; no one comes to the Father except through Me. Had you recognized Me, you would have known My Father as well. From now on you do know Him. Yes, you have looked at Him."

Philip still had not been satisfied. "Lord, show us the Father."

"How long have I been with you without your recognizing Me, Philip! He who has looked on Me, has looked on the Father."

Those who looked on Him hanging there between earth and sky that dark afternoon, looked on the heart of His Father.

John was quieted. He would need to be quiet now, for Mary's sake. The Master was growing weaker, His breathing labored and heavy.

"I—I'm thirsty!" He gasped.

Mary tried to break away from John to run toward Him!

Some one stuck a sponge full of sour wine into His swollen, parched mouth. He tried to swallow, but couldn't.

His life's blood pooled in the little ruts in the hard ground, dug out by the soldiers' feet. The drops came more and more slowly now.

Weakly, but clearly, He said: "It is finished!"

Mary sobbed and clung to John. Jesus wasn't dead yet. He breathed deeply twice. The old energy surged perceptibly through His wounded body, and lifting His streaked face toward heaven, He cried in a loud, strong voice:

"Father, into Thy hands I entrust My spirit!"

His head fell forward and He died.

A soldier ran his sword deeply into Jesus' side. Blood and water poured out.

At once the very elevation on which the three crosses stood began to tremble. Lightning ripped the darkened sky and thunder lost itself in the deeper rumbling of the earth, which cracked and trembled beneath the scurrying feet of those who stood there gaping. The centurion who had commanded the execution fell to his knees mumbling:

"This man was surely the Son of God!"

And at the moment He died, the heavy brocaded veil surrounding the Holy of Holies in the Temple at Jerusalem was ripped from the top to the bottom!

Nicodemus and Joseph of Arimathea hurried to the praetorium requesting an emergency meeting with Pilate. They were both too influential to be refused.

Their request was a strange one—ridiculous to Pilate. But he granted it. What could be lost by giving these foolish rich men their way? Let them have the body of the Nazarene!

The two friends of Jesus returned to Golgotha themselves to see to His torn body. Nicodemus took a basin and a cloth and washed off the crusted blood and grime. Litter bearers started toward the tomb in Joseph's lovely garden. He would bury his Lord in his own newly excavated tomb, where no other body had lain. Tall cedars and palms guarded the spot, planted with well-kept flowers, all blooming now that it was spring.

As they reached the tomb, His mother, John, Mary Magdalene and Salome followed them sorrowfully. Mary had to see for herself how He was cared for.

At the entrance to the grave hewn out of the limestone cliff, Joseph of Arimathea and old Nicodemus rubbed Jesus' limp body with ointments and then wrapped it with strips of linen, spreading the layers of cloth with reddish-brown resins and other preservatives.

The women watched, and John. No one could speak.

Mary sobbed helplessly as the men lifted His body and carried it out of her sight into the dark interior of the tomb. Then they rolled the huge stone in place.

Nothing more could be done now. What had been done was in great haste, before the Sabbath. Even in their agony to minister to Him in these last things, the final preparation of His body would have to wait until the Sabbath was over, according to Law.

Somehow John did not feel bitter about the delay. He knew, even in sight of the closed tomb, and even though the beloved voice was silenced, that his Master would always be, to him, at least, the Lord of the Sabbath!

The next day, Caiaphas and a handful of other priests and Pharisees made a Sabbath trip to Pilate's headquarters.

"We felt we should tell you, Sir, that this imposter said, while still alive, 'After three days I will rise again.'"

Pilate was thoroughly annoyed with them now.

"Indeed? What is this to me?"

"Just this, Governor: you can avoid trouble by giving orders to have his tomb safeguarded until after the third day is past. After all, his disciples—a rowdy lot of illiterates, could easily steal his body and then incite the people by telling them he has risen from the dead! Surely you can see that the final fraud would be worse than the first."

Caiaphas felt pleased with his well-phrased argument.

Pilate nodded, wanting to be rid of them. "The guard is yours. Go on—see to it yourselves, and make it as secure as you can."

Once more the priests and Pharisees hustled importantly through the streets of the Holy City, flanked by a group of Roman soldiers. When they reached the garden plot belonging to Joseph of Arimathea, two women sat across from the tomb of Jesus, their faces covered by thick, black veils.

It was no unusual thing to find women returning to a grave. The temple officials and soldiers paid little attention to them as they went about their work of sealing the great stone in place.

The women sat clinging to each other, afraid that the men would steal His dear body. But they saw the grave sealed. His body remained safely inside.

All of the priests and soldiers left but two. These were ordered to keep a close watch at the entrance to the tomb until they were relieved by other soldiers in a few hours.

"How will we prepare His body now, Mary?" His mother whispered to the young woman from whom her Son had cast seven devils.

"I don't know. But surely they will allow that much. Surely they will roll the stone away for us tomorrow when it is lawful to care for Him."

At the close of the Sabbath day, the women went to buy aromatic spices. They could do that much now, and first thing in the morning they would return.

For all that Saturday night, there was nothing to do but wait.

Chapter 56

"Where Have You Laid Him?"

Before dawn on Sunday, the first day of the new week, three sorrowing women hurried through the still silent streets of Jerusalem. They carried boxes of aromatic spices and vials of oil and rose water. This would be the last thing they could do for Him, whom they loved so deeply.

Mary, His mother, walked between Magdalene and Salome, leaning on them for strength. As they trudged across the wide field outside the city, toward the garden tomb, His mother murmured over and over:

"Who will roll the stone from the mouth of the tomb for us?"

The two women with her could only press her arm and answer her nothing. They didn't know either. But go they must, all of them. They were driven by their hearts.

"Surely the guards will help us," Magdalene said finally, when Mary kept repeating her piteous question. There wasn't much more hope of help from the tough Roman soldiers, but they had to try.

His dear body must be cared for by loving hands.

Down the flower-bordered path to the tomb, they walked single file now, expecting to be halted any moment by the gruff voice of one of the soldiers stationed at the tomb.

A bird began to wake up in the trees above them.

Still no other sound in the quiet, fragrant garden. Magdalene walked in front, down the path. She saw it first!

The stone was rolled away.

His mother stumbled, then lifted her heavy mourning veil to see more clearly. Magdalene and Salome threw back their veils, too. Slowly the three women moved toward the open grave.

It smelled of the spices and ointments with which Nicodemus and Joseph had rubbed His body. Magdalene stooped to look inside. Then she ventured in all the way, the others following her.

Salome screamed!

There, to their right, sat a young man dressed in a snow white robe.

"Do not be terrified!" The young man's voice was quiet and re-

assuring. "You are looking for Jesus of Nazareth, who was crucified."

"Yes!"

"He is risen! He is not here—see the place where they laid
Him!" His young voice echoed exultantly in the empty tomb. "But
go now, tell His disciples—and Peter—that He precedes you into
Galilee."

"Galilee?" His mother whispered.

"Yes, there you will see Him, just as He told you."

Then the young man was gone. The women hurried outside,
their hearts pounding. The trees seemed filled with awakened
birds now.

"Go back to rest awhile," Magdalene urged Mary. "I will run
ahead to tell Peter and John!"

"What's the matter with you, woman?" Peter rubbed his eyes,
forcing himself awake. "What's there to make you beat on a man's
door like that?"

"They—they've taken the Lord out of the tomb!" Magdalene
blurted. "Or, He's risen as He said—His mother and Salome and I
were just there and He's gone!"

"What?" John demanded, joining them.

"It's true, and we do not know where they have laid Him!"

Both men ran all the way to the garden tomb. Younger and
lighter on his feet, John reached the grave first, and looked inside.
Peter pounded up behind him, panting.

"What do you see, John?" he cried.

"He's gone, Peter! But His grave linen is still there!"

Peter pushed past John and went inside the empty tomb. There
were the linens—and the handkerchief which had covered His
face and head, still wrapped as though it had never been disturbed!

"Where is He?" Mary demanded, when she, too, had reached
the tomb again.

The two disciples did not answer her, but walked away home,
not knowing what to think. Knowing only that now they did not
even have His body!

Magdalene stood alone in the spring sunlight which filtered
through the tall cedar trees and picked out the dew which still
clung to the rows of pale blue flowers along the path to the

tomb. When she and the other women had seen the white robed young man earlier, their hearts had almost lost the dread weight. Now, she didn't know what to think. After all, Peter and John were two of His closest disciples. If they just turned and went home, what was she to think?

The weight rolled back on her heart. Was she to be deprived of even this last chance to show Him her love, her gratitude for all He had done for her?

For several minutes she stood like a helpless child, weeping. Then her heart drew her down toward the entrance to the empty tomb once more. Had the grief become too much for her mind? She clutched her head with both hands.

There, one sitting at the head, and one at the foot of the place where they had laid Him, were two angels in white. Together, as one lovely voice, they said to her:

"Woman, why are you crying?"

"Because they have taken away my Lord and I do not know what they have done with Him!" she sobbed.

Suddenly the tomb seemed to stifle her. She turned and flung herself out into the clear, sweet air. She breathed deeply, filled with revulsion at the thought of the blood-and spice-encrusted tomb!

Outside there was light, and it drew her to itself. The sweet scent of lilacs and white myrtle gave her the earth again and with it, life.

But what was her life now, with the Master gone? How could she ever believe in anything good again? All He had ever done was good. All He had ever been was kind and unselfish and good. All He had ever done was to give new life to twisted, scarred creatures like herself. All He had ever done was to heal and bless and forgive. Now, she had seen with her own tormented eyes all they had done to Him!

Again her weeping filled the quiet garden.

Suddenly she knew someone else was there. She whirled around and heard the same question the two angels had asked her inside the tomb!

"Woman, why are you crying? Whom do you seek?"

It must be the gardener, she thought absently. But it was someone, and she did need help.

"Sir, if you've carried Him away, tell me where you've put Him, and I'll take Him!"

"Mary!" Jesus' voice spoke her name tenderly, reassuringly. She threw back her veil and looked full in His face. It was He! Everything stood still.

"Master! My Master!"

He *was* alive! Walking the earth, with His goodness and gentleness and love. Her Saviour was alive! She dropped to her knees, and reached for His hand to kiss it and bathe it with tears of joy.

"Do not cling to me, Mary," He said gently. "For I have not yet ascended to My Father."

She still had to learn that she had not received Him back, like another Lazarus, merely restored to natural life. She must let Him go first, in order that she could have Him back forever—everywhere she would go. In everything she would do. Magdalene still had this to learn, but she obeyed Him and did not try to touch Him further. He was there. She could see His dear face. She could hear His voice. For now, that was enough.

He was talking to her again. "Go now, Mary, to my brothers and tell them that I said, 'I ascend to My Father and your Father, to My God and your God.'"

Mary went, her feet flying, her heart on wings. He had come to *her* first, calling her name, because she could not bear to give Him up!

Chapter 57

"Locked in With a Memory"

Jesus had not only given new life to countless women who followed Him, He had given them new prestige and value in their own eyes. Until He came, women were necessary conveniences. His disciples had not argued too much with Him where women were concerned, but quite evidently they did not share His respect for them as sensible human beings.

None of the eleven remaining men believed one word of the story Magdalene had told them! Peter and John had investigated the tomb for themselves—they knew His body was gone. But they had no hope that He had actually risen from the dead.

On Sunday evening, the same day He arose, ten of the eleven sat like men half dead, locked in the roof-top room where Peter and John were staying in Jerusalem. Periodically they checked the big wooden bar bracing the door. Every man among them was afraid. With His body gone, the Jews and Romans would suspect the disciples first!

Magdalene and Salome were to keep them supplied with food, slipping it in to them by night. The women had just left, in fact. They had brought bread, fish, fruit and wine. None of it had been touched. Not one man in the ten had an appetite.

They all sat slumped around the room, their faces lined and tense. Now and then someone spoke, but mostly they sat buried in the blackest despair a man could know.

It was all over. The long, weary, high road had ended in a pit. The light had gone out. There was no more direction. Only defeat. They were empty shells. Nothing remained but terror for their lives at the hands of the priests and Romans—and despair.

Their Master was gone.

From their various hiding places in the city, ten of the eleven had crept now to commiserate with each other. Judas had hanged himself. No one cared. They were just there together because they had all loved Jesus, and now they all shared His defeat.

Only Thomas was absent. This surprised no one. Thomas was different. A real worrier by nature. A man who thought deep thoughts inside himself, but who struggled perpetually. His doubts were not from the lack of the desire for faith. Thomas loved Jesus as much as any other man among them. His temperament was just different. Invariably, Thomas looked on the dark side of things. He was a pessimist from the start. A loyal, plodding, thoughtful pessimist. Not a coward. At least no more so than the others. A man hard to convince that things could turn out well in a world as black as the one he saw around him. That Jesus had been able to bring any hope to Thomas was a miracle. The hope had come, though. And once Thomas got hold of a thing, he kept it. He was not with them tonight simply because he could not share what pained him so deeply. No one knew where he was. Everyone was sure he was alone, brooding on his grief.

"Angels, indeed!" Peter snorted.

"What?" Andrew asked his brother.

"I said, 'Angels!' Those silly women with their dreams and visions."

All the men nodded. Women always used their emotions instead of their heads.

Jesus was dead. John, at least, had been right there at the Cross. The thought that *he* had not been twisted Peter's heart.

"A man is a hopeless case when even the Master's prayers for him go unanswered!"

No one commented. They all knew the big fellow was going over it again.

" 'I have prayed for you, Peter,' He said, 'Satan has asked permission to sift you all like wheat! But I have prayed for you, Peter, that your faith may not fail—and when you are converted, strengthen your brothers!' "

Peter groaned.

John paced up and down the room.

Nathanael stared, and was silent, except for an occasional enormous sigh.

Andrew sat in a corner against a wall, his face stony and taut.

Matthew, the once hardened, hated tax collector, could only whimper now and then, like an injured child.

Philip ran his nervous hands through his hair over and over, shaking his head in disbelief.

James and Simon and the others sat sighing or staring or groaning.

"Every word He said that last night when we ate the Passover with Him pounds through my head!" John seemed almost to be complaining. His heart broke all over again every time he remembered the smashed authority of His Master.

"I saw His blood run out on the ground! I saw His broken body! I wish I hadn't, but I did."

"Shut up!" Peter shouted. "Be glad you did."

John stopped pacing. "I am glad. I didn't mean that."

Matthew sat up suddenly. "He gave us instructions that night at the table! Maybe we should obey Him now."

Instructions?

"He told us to do what we did with Him that night in memory of Him! You remember? He broke the bread and blessed it and said: 'Take, eat, this is My body.' Then He passed around the wine chalice after giving thanks, and said, 'All of you drink of it, for this is My covenanted blood, poured out for many for the forgiveness of sins.' Do you remember?"

"Of course we remember," Peter said. "Here—we have bread and wine."

The men stirred, almost relieved. Here was something they could do.

Then no one spoke. Who among them could feel worthy to take the Master's place—to break and bless the bread, to pass the cup?

The grieving men fell back to their old despair. Maybe they could do it later. But not yet. No one could swallow anyway.

More heavy time dragged by. Simon the Zealot got up to test the bolt and the wooden beam barring the door, and sat down.

Peter slammed one fist into the other palm and groaned.

"You are the Christ, the Son of the living God!"

How *could* the Christ be dead?

A rapid, quiet knock at the barred door brought the men to their feet! More trouble. This could be it. Peter strode to the door, sick of his cowardice. He slid the bar from its improvised slots, unbolted the lock and swung the door wide.

Two disciples of Jesus stood there babbling excitedly. Cleopas, whose wife had been at the Cross, and Luke, a Greek, who believed in Him.

"We've seen Him! We've seen the Master. He's risen from the dead." The two men talked at once, but as their strange story tumbled out, their hearts sank within them because the ten close disciples plainly did not believe what they said.

The two had been walking along the road winding west from Jerusalem toward Emmaus, when a stranger joined them. They told Him about the tragedy at Golgotha, and about the foolish old wives' tales of the women, that their Master had risen from the tomb.

The stranger startled them by saying: "O simpletons! With hearts so slow to believe everything the prophets have spoken. Did not Christ have to suffer all this, so as to enter into His glory?"

He assured them there could have been no other way. An act by God Himself, more powerful than the sin which choked His world, had to take place! There could have been no other way. Then He had explained all the Scriptures. The men had begged the stranger to stop at an inn with them. He did, and when He broke the bread, they recognized Him.

It was the risen Jesus!

More hallucinations, the ten decided. When the visitors had gone, they double-locked the door and sank once more into their despair. *Poor Cleopas and Luke,* Matthew thought. *They were really pitiful. So desperately did they want Jesus to live, their minds told them He did!*

They had better not open the door again for anyone. It was common knowledge now that the priests had bribed the soldiers at the tomb to say the disciples had stolen His body. An open scheme to wipe out the remaining key members of His movement. The Temple guards would be looking for them at that moment. A sorry lot they were to be hunted. Dangerous to no one.

Doomed to die in defeat, like their Master.

Peter had been drumming his thick fingers on the table. Suddenly he stopped. A deep silence closed around them. Every man sat or stood motionless, as though fixed by some outside force. The silence grew almost unendurable. The stuffy room became a grave, its walls bending toward them.

Then a light they could not see shot through their minds and bodies. As one man, they sprang to their feet. There had been no other sound. The door was still locked and bolted. The shadowy light of their one olive oil lamp remained the same.

But there in the center of the room stood Jesus!

"Peace to you!" He said in that dear, familiar voice.

No one moved a muscle or an eyelid.

"Why are you disturbed and why are such doubts arising in your hearts? It is I!"

He looked around the room at each man individually, His eyes tender with affection and understanding.

"Look at My hands and My feet. See for yourselves that it is I, Myself."

Still the men stared numbly.

"Put your hands on Me and see." He smiled. "A ghost does not have flesh and bones as you see Me have."

He held out His hands and they saw the scars from the big nails. He lifted His robe and they saw the same scars on His feet.

All the men were filled with joy now, but they still could not express it. Understanding their locked emotions, He did an extremely natural thing. Something that would make it possible for them to feel at home with Him again. He asked casually: "Do you have any food on hand?"

Still unable to speak, John handed Him a piece of the fish the women had brought. He ate it in their presence.

The men began gradually to relax. Once more they sat around Him, and He taught them in the old familiar way.

"These are My teachings which I spoke to you about when I was still with you, that everything written in the Law of Moses and in the prophets and Psalms about Me must come true."

He then opened their minds to understand the Scriptures. When He finished, He said:

"So it is written, that Christ should suffer and rise from the dead on the third day, and that repentance, leading to forgiveness of sin, must be preached in His name to all nations."

The stony faces had come to life! His men wept with open joy.

"Peace to you!" He said again, and spread His hands toward them. As He did, a warm, gentle movement of air covered them in the stuffy room. "Receive the Holy Spirit! When He comes, if you forgive the sins of any, they are forgiven. If you retain those of anyone, they are retained."

Then He was gone.

Another motionless moment passed, and the men dropped to their knees like children, blurting their happiness, their new joy.

The pit was gone! The high road had no end, after all.

"Unless I See I Will Not Believe!"

While they were still rejoicing and clapping their hands and shouting praises to God, there was another knock at the bolted door. This time, it swung wide to another disciple. His grieving face only grew more tortured when he looked in on the scene of holy hilarity among his friends.

It was Thomas.

The men all talked at once.

Finally, Thomas got them stopped long enough to cry out of the anguish of his own tortured heart:

"Unless *I* see in His hands the print of the nails and put my own finger in the mark of the nails, and thrust my own hand in His side, I will not—I cannot believe it!"

Thomas stayed with them in the locked room for a week. The new hope in the hearts of the ten left him cold. Hour after hour he sat alone in a corner, tormented by his doubts, but unable to quiet the longing in him to believe!

Suddenly, soundlessly, as before—with the door still bolted against the Temple guards, Jesus came again and stood with them in the middle of the room!

"Peace to you!" He said.

Then He went directly to Thomas, who sat huddled in a corner, staring at Him. For a moment, He only looked at His troubled disciple with love.

Thomas pulled himself slowly to his feet.

"Reach your finger here and see My hands, Thomas. Put your hand into My side and become a believer!"

Thomas touched the scarred hands and side. A new heart grew where the old one had been. The heart so slow to believe was gone. He fell on his knees at Jesus' feet, and cried:

"My Lord and my God!"

Chapter 58

"Breakfast on the Shore of Galilee"

They believed the women now, and even remembered that Jesus had told them Himself, just outside the garden of Gethsemane, that after His resurrection He would precede them to Galilee.

It all seemed so clear now that they believed!

The men had been back in their beloved Galilee now for several days, with nothing to do but wait and fish.

One night, Peter, Andrew, James and John, Nathanael and Thomas had fished all night and caught nothing. At dawn, they were hauling in their empty net disgustedly, when someone called to them from the shore about a hundred yards away.

"Fellows, have you nothing to eat but bread?"

"No! We had a bad night," they shouted back.

"Then cast the net to the right of the boat and you will make a good catch!"

Whoever it was on the shore sounded sure, so they decided to try once more. When they did, they drew the net from the water with so many fish they had to dump some or break the net!

Then it dawned on John. "It's the Lord!"

This was too much for Peter. He jumped overboard and swam to shore in his eagerness to be with Him again.

When the others brought in the fish, Jesus had already started a charcoal fire, and was waiting to cook their breakfast Himself!

"Come on, boys, and have your breakfast," He called cheerfully.

Peter hung close to the Master all through the happy meal, which He served to them with His own hands. The big fellow's heart still ached over his denial of the Master. He longed to feel reinstated somehow. To feel a part of things in the old way.

Jesus knew this, but it would be a different way now. A way they would have to travel alone in a new sense. He had promised to send the Holy Spirit to them, but no longer would Peter be able to depend upon the physical sight of Jesus to give him courage. That kind of courage hadn't worked anyway!

After breakfast, the Master and Peter took a walk together. The

Master called him by his old name, Simon. Peter, the rock, had not remained a rock.

"Simon, do you prize Me more dearly than these do?"

"Yes, Lord, You know I love You as a dear friend!"

"Then feed my lambs."

Peter waited for Him to speak again.

"Simon," He asked again, "do you prize me dearly?"

The big man frowned now, then laughed weakly. "Yes, Lord, You know I love You as a dear friend!"

"Then tend my sheep," Jesus said, not explaining further. In a moment He asked again: "Simon, do you really love Me as a dear friend?"

Peter was deeply disturbed now. "Lord, You know everything. You know my heart better than I know it. You know I love You as a dear friend!"

"Then you will feed My sheep." He looked at Peter for a long moment, and told the big disciple about the kind of death he, Peter, would die, in order to glorify God!

"When you were young, you girded yourself and went about where you wished, Peter. But when you grow old, you will stretch out your hands and another will gird you, and take you where you do not want to go!"

This time Peter felt no fear, except that he could not be worthy to stretch out his arms on a cross and die as His Master had died!

Jesus laid His hand on Peter's, and said: "You will follow Me."

"I Am With You Always"

The Risen Master promised to meet them back in Jerusalem. Their faith was so high now that the men obeyed without question and returned to the Holy City unconcerned about the danger there a month ago. Jesus had been meeting them here and there, as their Risen Lord, and their joy was full.

The men were maturing at last.

He had met with them on a mountain near their homes in Galilee and although some of the men still had doubts, He dispelled them:

"All authority in heaven and on earth has been given to Me. Go out therefore, and make disciples of all the nations, baptizing them in the name of the Father and of the Son and of the Holy Spirit. Teach them to observe everything that I have told you. And, remember, I will be with you—right alongside you, all the days, until the very end of the age."

His words rang in their hearts as they waited for Him to meet them back in Jerusalem. In Galilee, He showed himself to 500 people, and went especially to His brother James, who believed in Him from that time on!

When He came to the Eleven waiting for Him in Jerusalem, as they had promised to do, He gave more definite instructions:

"Do not leave Jerusalem, but wait for the Father's promise which you heard Me tell. John baptized with water, but after a few days you will be baptized with the Holy Spirit!"

Would it be like the moment He had flooded their beings with warmth and light in the airless room the first time He appeared to them as their Risen Lord? A hundred questions crowded their minds. They sensed that He was leaving them, and even though they did not dread it as before, still they were not yet filled with His Spirit and understood so little!

"Lord, are You going to restore the kingdom to Israel now?"

Knowing they would remain earthbound in their thinking until His Spirit came to them, He could only attempt once more to explain in words that their minds could grasp:

"It is not your affair to know times or seasons such as the Father has placed under His personal authority. But you will receive power, when the Holy Spirit comes upon you, and you will be My witnesses both in Jerusalem and in all Judea, and in Samaria, and to the remotest end of the earth!"

He led them then once more to the Mount of Olives, where they had spent so many good hours together.

The men stood around Him, worshiping Him. Feeling at home with Him, and yet knowing a new thing was beginning.

Jesus looked once more at the beloved view of the Holy City. He looked down the slope of the Mount of Olives toward Bethany, where Mary and Martha and Lazarus lived. Then He lifted up His hands and blessed His dear ones.

As He was blessing them, He was taken up in a bright cloud before their eyes. Up, up the cloud carried Him as the men watched intently, joy and sorrow flooding their still very human hearts.

When He had gone from their sight, two men in white stood

with them on the familiar limestone ridge of the Mount of Olives.

"Men of Galilee," they said, "why do you stand gazing into heaven? This Jesus, who was taken up from you into heaven, will come again in the same manner in which you have seen Him entering heaven now!"

A deep, bright hope seized the disciples when the two heavenly visitors had gone. The familiar walk back to Jerusalem had never seemed so short. Straight to the Temple they went to praise God and to thank Him that they were no longer defeated men.

None of them understood how it would be, but to a man they sensed they would never be defeated again.

From the Temple, they returned to the same room where they had hidden during the three days of despair. Here they held a meeting to decide about finding a larger room in a larger house, where not only the eleven, but all the others who had followed Jesus, including His mother and the women, could come together to wait in prayer and rejoicing for the arrival of the promised Power from on high!

Their exclusive days were over.

Chapter 59

With One Mind—Together!

The same upper room in young Mark's mother's house was selected as their meeting place; and for ten days, one hundred and twenty who believed Jesus of Nazareth to be God's Christ prayed constantly and with one mind—together.

Something new was about to happen. Jesus had told them it would. That He had said it was enough for them. They were all eyewitnesses to the fact of His resurrection, and no one doubted that He was the Messiah. He had left His tomb. They had known Him again as their Risen Lord. They still did not understand His purpose for them, but they loved Him, and they were now loyal to Him.

They loved each other as never before, but not only were they *not* ready for the work ahead, they had no concrete idea of its nature. They were simply there—waiting and praying together, because He told them to do it.

The Eleven were there as a part of the group. He had personally chosen them, but to a man they had deserted Him, and now their leveled hearts accepted the fellowship of even the women whose stories of His resurrection had made them scoff.

With them also were His mother, Mary, and His brothers, who now believed in Him. Mary's presence in the upstairs room was a source of strength to the others. She was going to have Something of her beloved Son back again! He said His Spirit would come to give them power to begin a totally new phase of His work; and then He had added, "I, Myself, will come." No one understood the promise, but Mary's mother-heart leaped with joy at the prospect. He had never let her down. However He came, it would be right and it would be Jesus, and that was enough. Her own inner strength was added to by the new faith of her other sons in their Brother. To Mary's simple, woman mind, a glorious family reunion was about to take place! Her faith held, and with it, the faith of the others.

Nine days had passed since Jesus disappeared from their sight to return to His Father. They had been days of breaking barriers and deepening love among the little band of people who waited for His Spirit to come to them. It was the day before the Jewish Feast of Pentecost at the end of May, forty-nine days after the Passover. Because sea travel was safer at this time of year, Jerusalem was always more crowded with pilgrims for Pentecost than for any other feast.

Those who waited in the upper room had selected another man to take Judas' place. Peter conducted the selection—sincere as always, in his belief that it must be a man who had also seen the resurrected Lord. They prayed, but then they used a human method for making the choice. They cast lots! A good and devout man named Matthias won the appointment, but nothing more is heard of him. The hundred and twenty were still operating on the strictly human level. Their every act was sincere, but in their ignorance of God's purpose, they had again chosen the lesser way.

Their faith reached out to act, but it lacked the power and the wisdom to carry out even the first duty together, according to God's highest plan. They were there, they were waiting, they were praying with one mind and together, but the promised power had not yet come. They were doing the best they could, but their best had never been enough. It could not be now. The ninth day after His departure dragged past them. They tried to encourage each other as they went to their separate homes that night.

Mutual faith in Him brought them together again early on the tenth day, the Feast of Pentecost. Once more they were there waiting and praying with one mind, together. The crowds in the streets were noisy and for some of the waiting group, concentration was difficult, even though their long day had only begun.

The throngs of people outside were in a holiday mood. The annual trip to Jerusalem highlighted the year, particularly for those who came from distant places. Through the ancient streets the world met itself, as men and women jostled and laughed and talked together. There were Parthians, Medes, Elamites, Mesopotamians, Judeans, travelers from Cappadocia, Pontus, Asia, Phrygia, Pamphylia, Egypt, Cyrene, Rome, Crete and Arabia. All of them spoke either Greek or Aramaic during their stay in Jerusalem, although almost every known language was represented that day, as residents from the same localities met and gossiped or discussed everything together.

A little before nine in the morning of Pentecost Day, the sunlit Holy City was struck suddenly by what appeared to be a great wind, so strong the people fled the streets, crowding into shops and inns—anywhere to escape the blowing dust and debris.

There was no rain and no darkness. Only the great roaring from heaven.

It filled the upper room where the disciples waited, and over the head of each of the hundred and twenty there, flames appeared, separated and danced for a moment, as one after another among them was filled with the promised Holy Spirit, and began to speak and praise God in foreign languages!

Out into the street went the joy-filled men and women from the upper room in Mark's house, clapping their hands and praising God in words they had never heard before. Words which poured from them that day under the direct guidance of the Spirit of Christ, who now was able to direct them from *within!*

After the drive of the mighty wind died down, the crowds of devout pilgrims from all nations poured again into the streets of Jerusalem.

Everywhere they turned, they seemed to meet one or more of these Spirit-filled Galileans, praising God in languages every visitor understood!

That the languages were spoken correctly, no one doubted. What it meant, no one knew, but some thought the hundred and twenty were drunk on new wine. The foreigners in Jerusalem forgot their shopping and gossip and merry-making, and clustered around the followers of Jesus.

What happened next smacked of the clear, steady, sane "new wine" of the kingdom! A tall, heavy-shouldered man with a mop of unruly hair stepped to the center of the group. An hour ago, he was praying and waiting in excited confusion—an ordinary, uneducated, lovable, sincere, but unstable ex-fisherman, among other ordinary provincial people, in the upper room of a Jerusalem home. Now, he stood poised, steady, certain, choosing his words carefully, with the very wisdom of God. His own inner turbulence was replaced by the same energy he had so often admired in his Master, but could never imitate. The Eleven stood around him, the same energy lighting their faces, and the same quiet certainty squaring their shoulders.

These were not ignorant Galileans full of new wine. They were simple, believing men and women, full of God!

Big Peter stood in silence until the crowd stopped chattering; then he raised his voice and spoke with an authority that kept the silence around him.

"Jewish men and residents of Jerusalem, take note of what I say. These men are not drunk as you suppose. It is only nine o'clock in the morning! What you have seen and heard is what was spoken through the prophet, Joel: 'It shall be in the last days, says God, that I will pour out My Spirit upon all flesh.' This is what you have witnessed, and men of Israel, listen to me: Jesus, the Nazarene, was a Man divinely accredited to you through mighty works and wonders and signs, which God wrought through Him in your midst. This, you personally know, and He, under the determined will and foreknowledge of God, was betrayed by lawless hands, and you killed Him by nailing Him to a cross! But, God raised Him up by unfastening the cords of death. He could not be held in death's grip!"

Peter went on speaking firmly, his thoughts following each other with the very clarity of his Master.

"Brother men, it is fitting that I speak plainly to you about the patriarch David, how he died and was buried, and his tomb is with us to this day. So, being a prophet and knowing that God had sworn to him with an oath to seat one of his descendants on his throne, David was looking ahead, and spoke of the resurrection of Christ, that He would not be abandoned to the realm of the dead; neither would His flesh see corruption. This Jesus, God has raised up! Of this we are all eyewitnesses! *He* has poured out what you both see and hear.

"Without a shadow of doubt, then, let the whole house of Israel acknowledge that God made Him both Lord and Christ— this very Jesus whom you crucified!"

Many of those who listened to Peter that day had helped howl Jesus to His cross before Pilate. Now, their hearts were torn within them at what they had done!

"What should we do now?" they cried.

"Repent and be baptized, each of you, in the name of Jesus Christ for the forgiveness of your sins, and you will receive the gift of the Holy Spirit. After all, the promise is to you and to your children and to all those far away—as many, in fact, as the Lord our God may call."

There were added that day about three thousand believers.

None among the hundred and twenty seemed at all surprised at Peter's boldness. They shared it, too. It was the holy boldness of Christ Himself! His *life* had invaded theirs. They were still simple folk from Galilee, but now they could do more than try to be like Him, they could let Him be Himself *in* them.

They were not surprised, they were filled with joy and wonder. They were utterly *natural,* going about their Father's business without delay.

The new believers sat regularly at the feet of the Twelve for teaching, and the young fellowship met daily for the breaking of bread and for prayer. Awe fell over the Holy City, as these energized followers of the Nazarene performed the same signs and wonders He had done.

The believers soon were desiring to own everything jointly. They were so full of love for each other and mankind that of their own free will they began to sell their property and belongings and distribute the proceeds to anyone in need! Daily, new believers were added, and even among those who did not believe, His followers were loved and respected.

He was with them again in power. Their minds were on the Lord Jesus alone, and He kept their hearts unruffled and their courage high.

Chapter 60

"Why Are You Surprised at This?"

The familiar form of Hebrew worship was not neglected by the followers of Christ. Most of them were devout Jews, longing to help their fellow Jews see that their Messiah had come.

One day, Peter and John, now inseparable friends, went to the Temple for the three o'clock hour of prayer. As they walked toward the Beautiful Gate, two men were just placing a familiar figure at his daily post by the Gate where he could beg from those who passed by. He was a middle-aged man, helplessly crippled from birth. As the two disciples approached him, the man begged for money.

Peter and John stopped, looked intently at the poor fellow, saying, "Look at us!"

The man watched them closely, hoping for a gift, but Peter said, "I have no gold or silver, but I will give you what I have. In the Name of Jesus Christ, the Nazarene, walk!"

Gripping the helpless fellow by the hand, Peter lifted him to his feet. Instantly the bones in his feet and ankles grew firm! He jumped to his feet, then walked about all over the temple courts, leaping and praising God.

To see this man healed amazed the people. A crowd gathered around him in no time, and since the happy man kept clinging to Peter and John, they were the center of attention. Word flashed about the city and the people literally ran, crowding onto Solomon's porch, to see for themselves.

This was all Peter needed. Without a moment's hesitation, he began to speak to the crowd about His beloved Master who had taught them so often in this very corner of Solomon's porch.

"Men of Israel," Peter shouted, "why are you surprised at this? And why are you staring at us as if we had made this fellow walk through our own power or goodness? The God of Abraham, Isaac and Jacob, the God of our fathers, has glorified His Servant, Jesus, whom you disowned before Pilate—even when he had decided to set Him free! You disclaimed the Holy and Righteous

One and requested a murderer for your reward. You killed the Prince of Life, whom God raised from the dead—of this we are witnesses. By faith in His name, this man, whom you see and recognize, was strengthened. Faith in the name of Jesus of Nazareth gave him this perfect health you all now see!

"Now I know, brothers, that you behaved ignorantly, just as your leaders did." Peter's voice softened with an understanding the big fisherman would have laughed at before. "I know you and your leaders meant to be serving God. But even through your ignorant act, God has fulfilled what He had made known through all the prophets—that His Christ was going to suffer! So, repent and turn, that your sins may be wiped away and that seasons of refreshing may come to you from the presence of the Lord, as He sends Christ Jesus, who is meant for you! Brother men of Israel, for you primarily, God raised up His Servant, whom He sent to bless you, as each of you turns from his evil ways."

While Peter was still speaking, the priests and the Sadducees brought armed guards from the Temple to seize him.

Opposition to the new fellowship had struck, and it struck as it had with Jesus, following the healing of a crippled man. As Peter and John were hurried to jail their hearts rejoiced, remembering the Master's report to them concerning what happened to Him at the pool of Bethesda when His opposition struck its first open attack because He also healed a man.

Their Lord was back, carrying on His work in full power through them! When Peter and John looked at the crippled man at the Beautiful Gate of the Temple, the love of Christ Himself flashed from their eyes.

No longer was His power limited to the human body of Jesus of Nazareth. God reached, through as many as would believe that Jesus was the Christ, toward His whole beloved world!

The next morning Peter and John and the man whom they had healed stood surrounded by the high priestly clan, headed by Caiaphas.

Little Caiaphas, the High Priest, strutted past them, forced to look up at both Peter and John.

"Now, tell us," he inquired sarcastically, "by what power or what name have you done this thing?"

Peter cleared his throat and preached another sermon. This time to the very men who had sentenced His Master to the Cross.

413

The very men from whom he and the others had hidden in the locked and barred room after the crucifixion.

"Rulers and elders of the people," he began, filled with the Holy Spirit of his Lord. "If today we are being called to account for a kind service to a crippled man, then you and all the people of Israel should know that this man stands before you in prime condition, because of the name of Jesus Christ of Nazareth, whom you crucified and whom God raised from the dead! He is 'the stone despised by you the builders, which became the head of the corner.' And there is salvation through no one else; for there is no other name under heaven given among men by which we can be saved!"

John spoke, too, and the priests and members of the Sanhedrin marveled that these men without schooling should speak so freely and intelligently. They recognized them as having been with Jesus of Nazareth, who had dumbfounded them for the same reason!

John and Peter with their witness were ordered outside the Sanhedrin hall.

"What shall we do with them?" the important men asked one another. "Everyone in Jerusalem knows they have performed this notable sign—we cannot deny it!"

Fearing the love the people had for the disciples of Jesus, all the mighty high court could do was bring their prisoners back and warn them not to speak to one more person concerning the Name of Jesus of Nazareth.

Peter looked around the circle of richly robed authorities and declared calmly:

"Whether it is right in the sight of God to listen to you rather than to God, is for you to judge. As for us, we simply cannot help talking about what we have seen and heard!"

After more sharp warnings, equally disregarded by Peter and John, they released them. Back they went to share this new act of the Spirit with the fellowship of believers.

Everyone rejoiced and praised God, and no one was in need of anything, because everyone loved and acted under the guidance of the One who had laid down His life for love of them all.

Happy to Be Whipped!

The act of rejoicing among the close followers of Jesus, the

Christ, did not depend upon what happened to them. They rejoiced because He had come back in a way in which everyone could have Him all the time. They rejoiced and were happy because of Christ Himself.

Many signs and wonders continued to be done among the people of Jerusalem, through Peter and John and the others, and they all met together daily on Solomon's porch at the Temple. None of the Temple attendants dared join them, but they loved having them there, and daily these longing outsiders saw throngs of new believers added to their number—in plain view on Solomon's porch, where Jesus loved to teach.

Peter, no longer trying to impress anyone with his devotion, did so in a most amazing way. The big man's personality was so saturated with the Spirit of his Lord that people went so far as to bring their sick relatives and friends into the streets where Peter might walk. They laid them on mats and rugs, so that at least his powerful shadow could fall on some! When it did, they were healed. From all the surrounding towns, the crowd came streaming toward these simple, Spirit-filled men, carrying their sick and mentally disturbed, and everyone was healed.

The Christ of God walked the streets of the Holy City again in the men who loved Him, presenting an even more complicated threat to the little High Priest and all his political friends.

Once more, they made an arrest. All twelve Apostles were thrown into the public jail. But on their first night there, an angel of the Lord opened the prison doors, led them all outside, and said, "Now, go as usual, and take your places in the Temple, and keep on telling the people about this new life!"

All twelve men were at the usual place on Solomon's porch, at daybreak, teaching. When Caiaphas and his party summoned the Sanhedrin for their trial, the prisoners could not be found.

"The men you put in jail last night are standing right out on Solomon's porch teaching the people!" Caiaphas was told.

He didn't dare seize them by force. By now, the people respected the disciples so much they would have stoned the priests!

Caiaphas and most of the party wanted to destroy all twelve men. But a Pharisee named Gamaliel—a famous and revered teacher of the Law—convinced them that they should take no such drastic action.

415

"I advise you, gentlemen, do not touch these men; rather, leave them alone. For should this plan or movement of theirs be merely human, it will go to pieces. But, if its source is of God, then you are unable to crush them anyway. You might even find yourselves to be God-resisters!"

Caiaphas agreed reluctantly, but he could not bring himself to let them go without some punishment.

The Twelve stood before the bantam High Priest, whose very soul shook like his angry voice, as he shrieked:

"Not once—not once more will you mention the despised name of Jesus!"

Before the Sanhedrin itself, all twelve Apostles were severely whipped—each receiving thirty-nine lashes allowed by Jewish law. Not as many lashes as their Master had received, since He was whipped under Roman law, which set no limit. But every bleeding Apostle went out from the presence of the Sanhedrin happy indeed for being thought worthy to suffer disgrace for his Master's Name.

And they did not stop for even a single day, teaching and preaching Christ Jesus in the Temple and in their homes.

Chapter 61

God Went, Too!

The number of new believers increased with such speed that complaints began to come to Peter and the others concerning the distribution of the daily charities. This was inevitable since the Apostles themselves were attempting to teach, preach and carry out this important sharing of material goods.

Seven men were chosen, all of them Greek-speaking Jews, except Nicolaus, who was a Gentile proselyte from Antioch. The seven—Stephen, Philip, Prochorus, Nicanor, Timon, Parmenas, and Nicolaus—met with the Apostles who laid their hands on them and prayed. These were the first deacons of the new fellowship, and although their main duties were to serve the tables and distribute the food and other supplies, God was in them, and their service soon went beyond the material.

Stephen, a young man full of grace and power, began to preach and to perform notable signs and wonders among the people. God's touch was upon Stephen, and through him the fellowship grew even more rapidly. The opposition continued to be led by the High Priest, Caiaphas, and the Sadduceean party, but in spite of this, a large number of priests who dared to think independently of the Temple hierarchy joined the dynamic young fellowship of believers in Christ.

The teachings of Jesus had a particular appeal for Jews whose thinking had been influenced by Greek customs. These Hellenists were much more liberal in thought than the other citizens of Jerusalem, and the Sadducees of the priesthood grew violently concerned when more and more Hellenist Jews joined Peter and the others to follow the still living Christ. So many came to believe in Jesus that the entire group of followers ultimately called itself by the Greek name, *Ecclesia*—meaning "called out ones."

The *Ecclesia*, however, had not yet made any attempt to break away from the Temple. They still taught and met on Solomon's porch, alongside the other teachers of Israel, and were generally accepted as another sect within the Jewish faith.

When Stephen, the new deacon in the young church, began to

attract unusually large crowds around him on Solomon's porch, the irate priestly leaders engaged young Stephen in a series of debates. One brilliant young Jew from Tarsus, named Saul (Paul), debated over and over with Stephen. Each time, the zeal to protect and defend the faith of his fathers against what he considered the heresies of the *Ecclesia*, burned at Saul's soul until his once controlled mind turned fanatic. He could not defeat the strong, authoritative wisdom of the strangely powerful Stephen! Each time Saul lost a debate to him, his hatred flamed against all the new *Ecclesia* stood for.

Great crowds heard the debates, and fury heaped itself upon humiliation for Saul, because inevitably, new believers were added to the new, fresh *Ecclesia*. He not only lost the debates, he believed he saw the faith of his fathers weakened by the growth of the new sect.

Night and day Saul agonized under what he sincerely believed to be blasphemy against the God of Abraham. He hated the Name of Jesus of Nazareth, and his hatred hardened his zealous young heart, and fired his determination to wipe out the last man who dared call upon that Name!

When the debates failed, Stephen was brought before the Sanhedrin, after a trial with paid witnesses as false and unreliable as those who appeared against Jesus. As Stephen stood before the Sanhedrin to make his own appeal, not a member of the powerful court missed the light on his face. He spoke like a man *possessed* by light and sanity and insight. Carefully and forcefully Stephen covered the whole of Israel's history, from Abraham to the death of Jesus Christ. His young voice rang with the terrible authority of God Himself as he shouted:

"You stiff-necked and uncircumcised of heart and ear, you have always resisted the Holy Spirit—the same as your fathers! Which of the prophets have not your fathers persecuted? They killed those who announced the coming of the Righteous One. And now you have murdered Him—you who received the Law through the mediation of angels, and yet have not obeyed it!"

His speech had been long, and by the time he made that charge in the courage of the Spirit of the Lord he followed, the entire Sanhedrin was enraged. They tore their silk garments and shouted their verdict upon the young man who stood before them, looking up toward heaven, crying joyfully:

"At this moment, I see the heavens opened and the Son of Man standing at God's right hand!"

Stephen's Lord was *standing*, His full attention on His beloved follower!

Bedlam broke over the entire court. Dignity vanished, and the exalted members of the Sanhedrin held their hands over their ears to stop Stephen's voice. Shouting like men gone mad—young Saul of Tarsus among them—they rushed at Stephen in a body, and dragged him outside the city and began to stone him!

By law, the witnesses who appeared against the prisoner threw the stones. Big stones, to crack a man's skull, small sharp stones to put out his eyes—stones of all shapes and sizes flew at Stephen's young body and head, as he stood defenseless and poised, still looking up into heaven. They had tried to stone his Lord, too, with arms made strong by the violence of hatred unleashed to kill.

Young Saul of Tarsus stood on the sidelines, watching the coats of the witnesses who now were battering his hated enemy, Stephen, to his knees. Saul's broad, stocky shoulders heaved with every stone that thudded against Stephen's body, then fell in the growing pool of blood on the ground. Saul of Tarsus threw no stones, but with the full tension of his fiery soul, he consented to them. Stephen had not been beaten down to defeat even by his chisel-sharp words. Saul smiled grimly. Now this raving heretic, this enemy of the Lord God, was being battered ignominiously down, down into the blood and dust of the ground!

The crowd shouted wildly. Stephen had fallen to one knee, but now he was back on both feet. Swaying unevenly, but still looking up into heaven with that light on his face. Saul hated the look on Stephen's bruised and bleeding face. A man suffering what he must be suffering could not look that way, and yet he did!

"Knock it off!" Saul shrieked. "Knock that light off his face!"

Now Stephen was shouting, too, in a loud, clear voice.

"Lord Jesus! Lord Jesus, receive my spirit!"

Saul laughed too loudly, his poise gone. "Listen to that! They say that's what the heretic, Jesus, shouted from his cross! Even now, he imitates him—even now!"

Saul's laugh seemed almost twisted to tears.

A large rough stone caught Stephen on the side of his head and he fell to his knees, calling so clearly that each word struck the hysterical Saul like a sharp stone:

"Lord Jesus, let not this sin stand against them. Let not this sin stand against any of these men!"

Stephen crumpled to the ground and died.

One witness, gone out of control with the ordeal, threw two more stones at his limp body. Then there was silence.

For a moment, Saul swayed on his short, sturdy legs. He rubbed one hand hard over his face, as though to wipe away one thought he dare not keep. Then he smiled coldly, and strode straight up to the lifeless, still bleeding body of Stephen.

"We're well rid of him!" He kicked Stephen in the side, rolling him over so that his bruised and blood-caked face once more looked up toward heaven.

Saul only needed to verify the fact that he was dead. Suddenly, he kicked him again. This time he rolled Stephen over so his face no longer looked toward heaven.

Saul of Tarsus walked away then, swaggering.

He strode directly to the High Priest, Caiaphas, and secured permission to begin a house to house persecution of every follower of the Nazarene in Jerusalem! Personally, he directed their arrests. Men and women were dragged from their beds and flogged and imprisoned. The others fled from the Holy City. Everyone left but the Twelve.

Into all the Judean and Samaritan communities around Jerusalem, believers took the happy tidings of the Good News that Jesus was Lord!

Saul felt secure to get them away from the holy Temple. He had no way of knowing that God was no longer imprisoned there. Wherever members of the young, Spirit-filled church fled, God went, too!

More Places Than One

Stephen was gone, but loss had a peculiar effect on the early church. The Spirit was not limited. Like a mighty switchboard, the new life could be flashed wherever believers went! God would now always be in more places than one.

Philip, one of the deacons appointed with Stephen, fled to hated Samaria. Like Stephen, Philip became more than a deacon.

In Samaria, after Saul's persecution of the believers, Philip proved himself to be a great preacher. Day after day, to enormous throngs of Samaritans, Philip preached Christ. The people saw the signs and wonders he performed, they heard his message, and thousands believed.

One day Philip heard the Spirit of the Lord speak to him. "About midday, Philip, go down the road that runs from Jerusalem to Gaza—a lonely road."

It must have seemed a strange thing for God to order a man in the midst of a big series of successful meetings to start traveling down an almost untraveled road!

Philip obeyed.

After he had walked some distance down the lonely road toward Gaza, he saw approaching him a splendid chariot. Seated in the chariot, intently reading, was a dark-skinned man, richly dressed, his pudgy fingers heavily jeweled.

The Spirit said to Philip, "Go up and contact that chariot."

Philip began to run. When he caught up with the chariot, he heard the man reading aloud to himself from a portion of Scripture from Isaiah, which Philip recognized had been given him in the Temple of Jerusalem, where he had obviously gone to worship.

"As a sheep he was led to slaughter and as a lamb, voiceless before his shearer, so he does not open his mouth. In his humiliation, he was deprived of his trial. Who can tell the story of his offspring?"

The man was so absorbed in his reading he did not notice Philip running alongside his chariot, until Philip asked, "Do you clearly understand what you are reading?"

The wealthy man sighed, slapped nervously at the Scripture portion with his jeweled hand, and said, "How can I, unless someone guides me? But I want to understand. Desperately, I long to understand it! Please come into my chariot with me and teach me."

Philip, riding along beside the gentleman, learned that he was an Ethiopian eunuch, a high official in the government of Candace, the queen of Ethiopia. He was in charge of all her finances, in fact, and so it was all the more amazing that a man of such influence had traveled to Jerusalem in search of the true God. He had been to the Temple, and had received the portion of Isaiah's prophecy, but only God Himself knew that his heart was still in darkness. But God did know, and now that His Spirit had come, He could send Philip.

" 'As a sheep, he was led to slaughter . . . In his humiliation, he was deprived of his trial. . . . ' Tell me, I beg of you, about whom does the prophet Isaiah say this? Of himself or of someone else?"

With great joy, Philip told him about Jesus. The chariot rolled along the lonely road as Philip talked. Suddenly, the man cried out: "Look, here is some water—I believe that Jesus Christ is the Son of God! What is to prevent my being baptized?"

After he baptized the Ethiopian, the Spirit sent Philip all the way to Caesarea, to preach the good tidings.

The Ethiopian official, filled with the same Spirit, took the same tidings back to his land.

More and more, as His followers obeyed, God was reaching toward His beloved world at the same instant, and in more places than one.

Chapter 62

"I Am Jesus"

Saul (Paul) of Tarsus worked like a man possessed, in his growing fever to destroy all those who followed The Way. Not content with scattering all the believers but the Twelve into the Judean and Samaritan countryside, the zealous young man, still breathing out threats and murder, got letters of introduction from Caiaphas to the synagogues in Damascus. If there were any men or women known there to follow Jesus Christ, he would arrest them, bring them back to Jerusalem in chains, to be killed or imprisoned.

If Saul's dreams were haunted by the light on the face of the dying Stephen, it only fired his hatred for the name of Jesus. He doubled his efforts to hunt down and punish anyone who believed that Jesus was the Messiah of God.

Young Saul was born of Jewish parents in the city of Tarsus, in Cilicia, and his life to date (37 A.D.) had been strangely stamped with both the opposing cultural forces of his day. He was born and educated by his parents as a rigid Pharisee, but as a child he had spent his play time in a Greek atmosphere. A Hebrew of the Hebrews, a Pharisee, but also a Hellenist, Saul of Tarsus in his very personality was marked by the tension of the conflicting ideologies. He was intense by nature—the kind of man whose inner potential could drive him to great evil or great good.

With all his passionate heart, he longed to live up to the strict Pharisee's concept of the Law. He was well versed in the Scriptures, having sat at the feet of Gamaliel, the great Teacher of the Law in Jerusalem. Young Saul was a rabbinical student who studied because he could not help studying, so great was his longing toward the Lord God. He shunned defilement at every turn. Had he been a student in Jerusalem at the time of the trial of the Nazarene Carpenter before Pilate, Saul would have been among those orthodox Jews who refused to enter Pilate's hall "lest they should be defiled." But just as surely, young Saul would have stood outside among the other Pharisees, clamoring for the death of Jesus, the heretic, who had dared affront the majesty of the hoary Law!

His family name was Saul. To his fellow citizens outside his home synagogue, he was Paul. In his extreme youth, he learned to speak Greek fluently and was a lover of Greek poetry and art. Saul-Paul was a nearly desperate combination of dreamer-doer. A man of intensely strong feelings and ideas who, when he came to Jerusalem to study under Gamaliel, could have turned poet-priest or persecutor.

Driven suddenly to persecution by his hate-possessed young heart, Saul of Tarsus was rapidly becoming a young man to watch and encourage by those older ruling Jews, who saw in him the easy way out where the eradication of the new and troublesome *Ecclesia* was concerned.

The clever High Priest, Caiaphas, entertained Saul in his lavish home, catered to the young man's growing ego, and sent him on his way with real ceremony, to drag the believers in Jesus from their homes in Damascus.

Saul-Paul believed in the Lord God. He possessed a real Hebrew's sense of the holiness of God—the power of God. He merely hated the "blasphemy" of those who followed the (to him) dead memory of a Man who dared claim to be God's Messiah!

Saul's heart was not hard; it was young, and heated with hatred, filled with what he considered righteous indignation against those who "slandered" the name of the Holy One of Israel. Saul had not degenerated into a political-religious tyrant like the High Priest, Caiaphas. Sincerity drove the young man from Tarsus like a strong wind at his back.

He could not help pressing some distance ahead of the small caravan Caiaphas had provided for his journey, as they pushed behind them the slow, hot miles toward Damascus. The travelers had crossed the Jordan River at the Bridge of Jacob's Daughters, where the narrow, rushing torrent of water flowed through a thicket of blooming bushes and balsam trees. His attendants wanted to stop to enjoy the beauty and the cool highland air. Saul kept walking, more rapidly than before. He had forced back the weariness of his body for so long he no longer felt it. His hatred and his zeal energized his very soul, forcing him mile by mile toward his goal.

It was almost noon, but he refused to stop walking. Let the men stop to eat and catch up with him later. Catch up with him or endure his fury!

424

The sun had been bright all day in a flat, cloudless sky. Was it growing brighter? Some of the servants cried out, but he paid no attention to them. Desperately he tried to ignore the sudden blaze of Light around him. He shaded his eyes and kept walking, faster, faster. The Light grew brighter, brighter, brighter, and the stunned man stumbled and staggered.

Blinded to everything but the unbearable brilliance of the Light that dimmed the high noon sun, Saul of Tarsus fell to the sandy roadbed and lay there trying to cover his eyes against the Light that penetrated everything!

"Saul! Saul! Why do you persecute Me?"

He raised his head from the roadbed, trying to look for the source of the great voice that spoke his name. He could see nothing. He was completely blinded by the Light. Saul was not blinded to the possibility of a heavenly vision, however. His was a religious heart. When he could speak, he stammered:

"Who art Thou, Lord?"

That it was God who spoke, Saul did not doubt. An angel of the Lord God to encourage him on his mission! But what had the voice said about persecution? He must not have heard clearly. Something stronger than fear squeezed his heart. This time he shouted wildly:

"Who art Thou, Lord?"

The voice came again, strong, clear, almost sorrowful:

"I am Jesus, whom you persecute."

The Light pierced Saul's heart now. The same Light he had seen on Stephen's face! Stephen—bones crushed, still standing, looking into heaven, blood streaming—the Light on his face.

Stephen—asking forgiveness for Saul!

Forgiveness for Saul, the murderer.

The voice came again, understandingly, almost tenderly.

"It is hard for you to kick against the goads of your conscience, Saul."

Raising himself slowly, his strong, young arms trembling beneath the weight of his body, Saul stared blindly into the Light.

"Lord," his voice was hoarse and unfamiliar, "what would You have me do?"

"Do nothing now, Saul, but rise and enter the city of Damascus, and it will be told to you what you ought to do."

Paul stumbled along the rest of the way to Damascus, blind,

supported on either side by two of his servants, his inquiring mind riddled with questions. The men had heard the voice, but had seen no one. Had Saul really seen Jesus? His heart told him he had. Suddenly his heart was important to him as never before. Something had invaded his heart. The hatred was gone. He was mostly numb, but Something had happened in his heart.

In Damascus, they led him to the place where Caiaphas had arranged hospitality for him! The home of a ruling Jew named Judas, on the street called Straight, which ran through the heart of the city.

Judas expected a vigorous, immediate attack on the followers of Jesus of Nazareth. He had a list prepared for the young zealot, Saul. When two servants led a weary, confused, blind man to his door, Judas chose the part of courtesy, in deference to Saul's position with Caiaphas. He took him to his room and did not ask questions.

For three days, the blind young man fasted and grew accustomed to the new heart within him.

He wanted to find the followers of Jesus now, more than ever. But for a very different reason.

There lived in Damascus a simple, devout disciple of Jesus Christ named Ananias—one of those Saul of Tarsus had set out to arrest and bring in chains back to Jerusalem.

As Saul sat blind, and still stunned from his experience on the Damascus road with the living Christ, the same Lord who spoke to him appeared to His humble servant, Ananias, and called him by name.

"Here I am, Lord!" The Risen Jesus was so real to Ananias he was not surprised at the call. He was merely ready to listen.

The Lord Jesus said to him, "Arise, Ananias, and go into the street called Straight, and inquire at the home of Judas, for a man named Saul of Tarsus. He is there now praying. And, he has already seen a man named Ananias entering and laying hands on him, so he may regain his sight."

Understandable fear gripped Ananias' heart. "But, Lord, this man is notorious! He has done much to hurt Thy saints in Jerusalem, and he is here in Damascus to put into chains everyone who calls upon Thy name."

"Nevertheless, I want you to go," the Lord Jesus answered.

"He is My choice. He will be My choice instrument to carry My name in the presence of nations, and of kings, and of the sons of Israel. I will show him how much he will have to suffer on behalf of My name."

Ananias went to the street called Straight, was admitted at Judas' house, and sent to Saul's room. When he entered the room, the man every believer feared because of his cruelty sat alone—his face buried in his hands.

"Brother Saul?" Ananias' voice was kind.

Saul raised his sightless face in the direction of the voice. Ananias couldn't help noticing how young he looked! Young and almost childlike. Not fierce, not terrifying. Saul was no longer Saul, the persecutor of those who believed in the Risen Jesus. He was Paul, the still confused, puzzled, but new creature in Christ. He needed help. Ananias' gentle voice was like balm to his wounded soul. Paul had been pierced by the love of the Holy One of God. He felt lost now without his burning zeal to defend the Law of God. Suddenly, his life had lost its direction. He needed help. Not explanation, help. Without understanding why, his inner self recognized its first real peace. So no explanation was necessary. But he was a man of action. And the new life within him cried out for expression. He tingled with the knowledge that now, somehow—in some new way, his enormous energies were going to be used up. But Paul needed help in the delicate transition from hate to love.

When Ananias entered the room, Paul was suffering the intense pain of wounded love. Whose love had been wounded? His own? Saul of Tarsus had known love for his family, for a few friends. He had known love and respect for his teacher, Gamaliel. He had thought he knew love for God. But now, his heart ached with a kind of love about which he knew nothing! Did he know this pain for himself? For those whom he had persecuted?

Was it for *Jesus Christ* that he suffered wounded love now—in the darkness of these lonely, perplexed, but glory-filled days spent in the home of a man who would have hated Paul had he known?

Ananias' voice calmed him. He had been waiting for him. He needed Ananias. The touch of the simple man's hands on Paul's head brought tears of relief rushing to his sightless eyes.

"Brother Saul, the Lord sent me to you. The same Jesus who

appeared to you on the road you traveled. He told me to come so that you may recover your sight and be filled *now* with the Holy Spirit—His Holy Spirit."

Paul's shoulders straightened. He could see again, and he looked gratefully into the cheerful, wrinkled face of a man who loved him as a brother. A man he had come to murder!

New energy surged through his body as he smiled back at his brother in Christ. He had never lacked energy, but this was a different kind. There was no strain in it. It lighted his entire being. He felt there was nothing he couldn't do, even in his weakened condition from fasting for three whole days. Yet, somehow, whatever he would do from now on, this energy could not be exhausted.

Even when he was weak he would be stronger than ever before!

Immediately Paul was baptized—by old Ananias, who was not even a deacon in the young church at Damascus. He was simply Paul's brother in Christ. And Christ had said, "He is My choice!"

The spirit of the Risen Lord did not trouble Himself with formalities when His choice was involved. He simply acted through His available friends. Ananias was the Lord's friend.

Now, Paul longed to be His friend, too.

Without delay, the man who had come to arrest the followers of Jesus Christ began witnessing to this same Jesus openly in the synagogues of Damascus. So sure were his words, so captured was his heart, that within a few weeks Paul found himself a leader in the young church at Damascus.

The Jews were enraged. With as much enthusiasm as they had supported the promising young Pharisee, they now pursued him to kill him. One night, his close friends helped him escape over the city wall in a basket!

His suffering and hardship for his new Lord had begun. But even though Paul's very nature thrived on excitement, Christ had his attention. He burned with a desire to work, work, work for this Jesus Christ, but in him also burned an unfulfilled desire. Was it to know Christ better? Was the unfulfilled desire within him an expression of his own need for more knowledge of the person of his Lord?

Chapter 63

Peter and the Gentiles

The Twelve who remained in Jerusalem, despite Paul's persecution, continued to preach Christ, and the young church there again grew in numbers. They knew nothing firsthand of the conversion of Saul of Tarsus, but they had heard stories. All of them reserved judgment until they could see for themselves, since his reputation among them was so black. For three years, while he was alone in Arabia, no one heard anymore of Paul.

Peter traveled extensively, and about a year after Paul left for Arabia, he was in the sea-coast city of Joppa, in Judea. His work here had prospered. Not only did the Lord add many new believers to the church at Joppa, but Peter raised a faithful woman named Dorcas from the dead. He stayed for some time there, as a guest in the home of Simon, a tanner.

In Caesarea, the Roman capital of that district, a short distance north on the Mediterranean, lived a well-loved Italian Centurion named Cornelius. He was not only a great military leader, but Cornelius and his whole family led a God-fearing life. He was a Gentile, but somehow he had learned of the one God of Israel, and believed so sincerely that he not only practiced liberal giving to the poor, he was known as a man who worshiped God constantly. So close was Cornelius' communion with the Lord God that an angel of God came to him saying:

"Cornelius, your prayers and your alms have ascended as worthy to be remembered before God. Now, then, send men to Joppa, and have them call for Simon, surnamed Peter. He is lodging with a man named Simon, a tanner, whose home is by the seaside."

When the angel of the Lord had gone, Cornelius was overcome with a still deeper desire to know God fully. Immediately he sent two servants and a devout soldier under his command to find Peter in Joppa.

The next day, as the three men entered the outskirts of Joppa, Peter was on the roof-top of Simon's house, praying, until time for lunch.

As he prayed, he saw heaven opened and a wide sheet came

down, held up by four corners. In it were all sorts of four-legged animals and reptiles and wild birds. A voice said to him, "Rise, Peter, kill and eat!"

"By no means would I do that, Lord!" Peter replied earnestly. "Because I never ate anything undedicated and unclean!"

Once more the voice said, "What God has purified, do not consider unclean!"

This happened three times, then the sheet filled with live animals and reptiles and birds was taken up into heaven.

Peter sat, scratching his head, trying to figure out what the Lord was saying to him! Only the Gentiles ate undedicated meat. No devout Jew could touch unpurified food without defiling himself. And yet, the Lord had said whatever He had purified should not be called unclean!

Peter had reached no conclusion when he heard the three men sent by Cornelius calling at the gate of Simon's house, to find out if Peter lived there. Even this did not break up Peter's puzzling thoughts. He was getting nowhere in his thinking, but he kept at it so steadily the Spirit finally had to interrupt:

"Peter, take notice! There are three men looking for you. Get up and go down and travel with them unhesitatingly, for I have sent them."

Peter hurried downstairs, shouting to the three men.

"Here, I'm the one you are looking for. Why have you come?"

"Captain Cornelius, a just and God-fearing man, of good reputation among all the Jewish people, was instructed by a holy angel to have you brought to his house, so that he might hear your suggestions about the Lord God."

Peter went back with them to Caesarea, taking along some of the brothers from Joppa. Cornelius had invited his relatives and all his close friends to his home, and they were all waiting eagerly for Peter's arrival. So eager was Cornelius that he fell at Peter's feet and worshiped him the minute Peter stepped inside the courtyard!

"Get up, brother! I am a mere human being like yourself."

Peter lifted Cornelius to his feet, and as they walked together inside the house where the others were waiting, Peter said, "You are aware how a Jew is not allowed to associate with or to visit one of another race." Cornelius nodded. "But," Peter went on beneficently, "God has shown me not to call any human being unhallowed or unclean. For this reason, I have come unhesitatingly when I was sent for. May I inquire for what reason you sent for me, Cornelius?"

The Gentile Captain told Peter about his visit from the angel of the Lord, and reassured that the whole thing was from God, Peter began to preach Jesus to the people Cornelius had assembled at his house.

Without baptism, without the laying on of hands, in fact, even before Peter had finished his sermon, the Holy Spirit fell on all who listened! The circumcised believers who had come with Peter—and Peter himself—were dumbfounded at what God had done. But there were the Gentiles—with nothing to recommend them to the Most High except their open hearts, speaking in tongues and declaring the greatness of God!

Peter turned to the brothers who came along from Joppa, and said, "Would anyone refuse the water for their baptism, since they have received the Holy Spirit as we did?"

They decided not. So, Peter directed them in the name of Jesus Christ to be baptized. In spite of the strange irregularity, Peter could not resist their warm pleas to stay with them a few days. This meant eating with Gentiles, from "unclean" dishes, food that had not been purified in the Temple!

Back in Jerusalem, Peter had a lot of explaining to do to the circumcised brothers in Christ, including the other Apostles. He told the whole story, however, and asked:

"Since God granted them a gift equal to ours who already believed in the Lord Jesus Christ, who was I to hinder God?"

The brothers quieted down then, and although none of them, even Peter, began really to associate socially with the Gentile believers, they agreed at least in principle, that it must be that God had granted to the Gentiles, too, the right to the repentance that leads to life!

Chapter 64

Known to the World as Christians

Time and distance, which limited the earthly ministry of Jesus of Nazareth, now disappeared, in the careful economy of His Spirit. He had promised them that they would be filled with a new power. Now, the same Spirit which motivated Jesus energized the ordinary human lives of His followers, and directed their work in His behalf.

As the Spirit fell on the entire household of the Gentile Cornelius, Peter came to see that "God was no respecter of persons." He was no respecter of Apostles either! Nor of seeming tragedy and waste. Stephen was stoned to death, but the Spirit had moved out and beyond Jerusalem, within the life of every believer forced to flee the persecution of Saul of Tarsus. As a result, the love of God in Christ reached, not only into the Judean and Galilean countryside, but into Samaria and to the Gentile cities as far away as Phoenicia, Cyprus and Antioch.

At first there were no "leaders" in this new outward movement. The people who began to talk about Christ in these remote cities were merely ordinary followers of The Way.

One of the Spirit-filled members of the *Ecclesia* who went to Antioch-Syria to live was a well-loved man named Barnabas. The work grew there, among both Jews and Gentiles, until it seemed a good idea to establish a permanent church.

The Spirit sent Barnabas to hunt for Paul, who had returned to his home city of Tarsus after his three years in the desert. As assistant to Barnabas, himself not one of the Apostles, the active career of Paul, the greatest Christian missionary, began.

As Paul and Barnabas worked among the people of Antioch, the followers of Christ first came to be called *Christians*. Paul could have inspired the name. Christ filled his entire horizon by then. Literally, he *lived* Jesus Christ.

Paul was overjoyed to be needed in the new movement, and he had no delusions concerning the danger into which he walked. Before he returned to Tarsus to take up his old profession of tent-making in order to provide his own funds for preaching Christ in his home city, he had spent two weeks with Peter in Jerusalem. Peter was forced to send him away quickly, in order to save Paul's life.

From the first, this energetic ex-Pharisee meant danger to the ruling Jews, so he was never safe working in a city where Jewry flourished. Paul did not seek safety. He sought only ways of winning men and women to a living faith in the Saviour who had arrested him and saved him from his own destructive drives.

With his Greek background, he was the logical choice to take the Gospel of Jesus Christ to the Gentiles. From Antioch, Christianity began to spread to the Gentiles everywhere, when Paul and Barnabas, with young Mark as their attendant, set sail for Cyprus, to begin the first of Paul's three long missionary journeys.

The Christians were moving out toward God's beloved world through the man who had breathed threats and murder against them!

From Cyprus, the three men went to the mainland of Asia Minor. At Perga, a seaport city in the district of Pamphylia, young Mark left them abruptly to return to Jerusalem as Peter's assistant. That God's great missionary, Paul, remained a human being, is evident, when, in spite of his friendship for Peter, he became annoyed with Mark for leaving. Mark was Barnabas' nephew, but Uncle Barnabas chose to stay with Paul.

Leaving Perga, Paul and Barnabas traveled northward through Pamphylia to Antioch-Pisidia, the largest city in the Galatian uplands. Here Paul preached Jesus Christ to mainly Hellenized Jews in the synagogues. Far away from Jerusalem, in this Greek city, he was free to speak the truth in comparative safety.

"Now, I can assure you—sons of Abraham, and all here who revere God—that because God raised Him from the dead, you may have forgiveness of your sins through faith in Christ Jesus. By Him all that believe are justified from all things—all things from which you could not be justified by the Law of Moses!"

Had Paul said that in Jerusalem, he would have been stoned. In the synagogue of the Galatian city, where few of his listeners could even read the Hebrew Law, Paul found many eager listeners among the Hellenized Jews. Once he left the synagogue, the Gentiles literally crowded around him and begged for a better understanding of the good news!

Many believed in Pisidian-Antioch, but a small, hard core of ultra-conservative Jews in the synagogues refused to hear and tried to accuse both Paul and Barnabas of blasphemy against the Lord God.

To these Jews Paul shouted: "God's message must be told to you Jews first; but since you push it from you and do not consider yourselves worthy of eternal life, please take note: We are turning to the Gentiles! For such are the Lord's orders to us in the prophet Isaiah, 'I have set you for a light of the Gentiles, for salvation to the ends of the earth.' "

The Gentiles were glad, and the number of believers among them grew swiftly, until the word of the Lord was carried all over the country. But the conservative Jews began severe persecutions against Barnabas and Paul, and drove them out of the city.

This began the strange pattern of victory and persecution which marked almost every visit of Paul along the sometimes violent routes of his three long journeys.

In Lystra, because Paul preached with such eloquence, but in particular because he healed a man crippled from his birth, the people and even the priests of the temples of Jupiter and Mercury fell down to worship Paul and Barnabas as gods! The crowds went wild with adoration, drowning Paul's protests that they, too, were mere men—but men who had found eternal life in the Son of God.

The riot was broken up only when the ever-present element of legalistic Jews convinced the adoring populus that Paul and Barnabas were heretics who worshiped a false god! Adoration turned to hatred, and the very people who had been trying to worship them dragged Paul to the edge of the city and stoned him so severely they left him for dead.

He rallied in the strength of the Spirit, however, and as soon as he was able to travel, he and Barnabas left for Derbe. All along their way, they left behind them a small nucleus of Gentile converts, who formed their own churches. After a time in Derbe, the two men revisited the cities where the new churches had sprung up and then went back to Antioch-Syria to report their work to the church from which they had been sent out.

The Christians in Antioch were greatly encouraged by the results of their trip, but almost at once Paul ran headlong into new trouble. Trouble so serious that it threatened to choke off his new mission to the Gentiles almost before it had begun.

James, the brother of Jesus, had become the head of the Jerusalem church. James was a true follower of the Christ in his heart, but he was still a victim of the inherited exclusiveness of the Jews. James was pleased when Gentiles believed in Jesus, but he could not see allowing them to become Christians without first undergoing the ancient Jewish rite of circumcision. James had not yet seen the wide-open heart of the God of his fathers. The half-brother of the Lord Christ, who had stretched out His arms toward the *whole world* on a Cross, still insisted upon confining God to the traditional Jewish matrix!

Paul argued vigorously with the brothers James sent to Antioch to express his views. Finally, in a desperate effort to keep the door open wide to the Gentiles, Paul and Barnabas went in person to Jerusalem to discuss the matter.

Paul made a forceful presentation of the working of the Spirit among the Gentiles all during their journey. In a much more inclusive way he, like Peter, had found God to be no respecter of persons. He pressed his beliefs tenderly, firmly, conclusively.

Still James and his conservative faction protested that no one should be admitted into the fellowship without circumcision and a strict embracing of the entire Mosaic Law.

The divided brotherhood looked to Peter for his thinking on the matter. The big Apostle rose to his feet to speak his mind. He would have been less than human not to have realized at that moment that Paul's meteoric rise to prominence in the church threatened his own position. Confusing, to a lesser man than Peter had become, would have been the fact that Paul had not even been one of the original Twelve! Except in a vision, Paul had not seen Jesus of Nazareth in the flesh.

But Peter did not hesitate. He had come far in the years since his life had been filled with the very Spirit of the Master he denied three times on that dread morning before the crucifixion.

In his earnest, booming voice, Peter reminded them of his experience the day the Spirit filled the lives of the Gentile family of Cornelius. "He granted them the Holy Spirit just as He did to us. As he cleansed their hearts by faith, He did not at all discriminate between us and them. Now then, why be a trial to God by placing a yoke on the neck of the disciples, which neither our fathers nor we have been able to carry? Instead, we believe that we are saved through the grace of the Lord Jesus in the same way as they are—and *only* by His grace!"

James agreed, with a few minor reservations, and with him the other conservative brothers. The few restrictions they imposed annoyed Paul, but at least he could now go on telling the good news to the Gentiles for whom God had filled his heart with love.

The entire Roman world stretched before him now. A world steeped in darkness and confusion and greed. A world in which there waited men and women with hungry hearts to believe in the Lord Christ—but there were also those who waited for Paul, His missioner, with stones and whips and rods.

Paul, strengthened in his inner self by the Spirit of his beloved Lord, welcomed it all!

Chapter 65

The Upside-Down World

On his second missionary journey, a new group of helpers went with Paul. Barnabas wanted to take young Mark again. Because he had deserted them once before, Paul refused. With the new freedom given him among the Gentiles by the Jerusalem decision, he felt he should take no chances with a seemingly unpredictable young man like John Mark. This time, Barnabas left Paul and went his own way.

A devout believer named Silas became Paul's traveling companion; and when they revisited the new churches in the Galatian highlands, Paul found a young convert at Lystra whom he loved at once. The boy's name was Timothy, and Paul was his ideal Christian. Young Timothy could scarcely contain his happiness when he was invited by Paul to go with him on this second important mission.

Timothy was the son of a Jewish mother and a Greek father. He was ideally suited to accompany Paul, not only in background but in spiritual capacity. To keep down criticism of their work together, although Paul firmly believed Mosaic Law had been superseded by the grace of Jesus Christ, he circumcised Timothy. That they would always be running into those sincere but law-bound Pharisees who failed to grasp the meaning of God's grace, Paul well knew.

At Troas, two things happened. Luke the physician, one of the two disciples who talked with the Risen Christ on the road to Emmaus, joined the mission. Paul's health was already showing the effects of his strenuous life. He pushed himself constantly. The enormous amount of travel alone, in those days of sailing ships and haphazard accommodations, would have weakened any man. Paul had need of the kindly, devoted physician, Luke.

At Troas, also, God widened Paul's vision of the possibilities in the Gentile world. In a dream, he saw a man who cried pleadingly, "Come over into Macedonia, and help us!"

With Silas, Luke and Timothy, the now middle-aged Paul

set sail at once from Troas, and landed at Samothrace, an island lying between Troas and Neapolis, the nearest port city on the Macedonian coast.

Macedonia (now Europe) was thickly populated and highly civilized, the kind of place where Paul loved to preach the good news of eternal life through faith in Jesus Christ. It was the gateway to Greece itself, and it was in the Greek-speaking provinces where Paul had found the most eager reception. The thinking people there grew restless in the multi-godded religion of mythology. More than that, the Christian doctrine of love and understanding was not too far-fetched to the Greeks. They had been taught a credo of love and kindness by their philosophers. Love held a natural appeal for them. Paul found them hungering for a way to live out in their daily lives the religion of love which lighted his own life. The capricious gods of mythology offered them nothing in the way of inner power.

From Neapolis, Paul and his companions journeyed to Philippi, the leading city of the area. It was a late summer evening in 50 A.D. when they arrived. Paul took Timothy and went in search of the inevitable small group of Gentiles he had come to expect to find in every Greek city—those who had turned to the worship of the one God of the Jews, out of restlessness with their own gods. The group in Philippi was too small to have its own place of worship, so they met regularly for prayer on the wooded banks of the picturesque little Gangites River.

The eager handful of people invited Paul to speak to them, and the advance work of the Spirit of Christ showed up immediately! Lydia, a well-to-do businesswoman, became the first European convert, and with her came her whole family to be baptized by Paul in the bright waters of the little river. The grateful woman insisted that the travelers accept her hospitality, and that night they moved from their public lodgings into her beautiful home. Lydia's connections in Philippi led them to other open hearts, and before many days passed a strong young church met regularly in her house.

Then the other side of the strange pattern appeared. The inevitable trouble came also through a woman. A young slave girl, who earned money for her owners by fortunetelling, persisted in following Paul and his friends about the streets shouting, "These men are servants of the Most High God—they are announcing to you the way of salvation!"

No one could tell the girl's real intentions. She may have been making fun or she may have been sincere. At any rate, soothsaying was an accepted evil of the times. Even the high state officials consulted oracles before making decisions. The girl kept up her strange shouting for several days. At last Paul became annoyed—not with her, but with the evil that possessed her. He turned to the girl and spoke in a firm, authoritative voice;

"I order you in the name of Jesus Christ to get out of her!"

Instantly, the girl stopped shouting and became her true self—smiling, shy and quiet. When her owners discovered her money-making power was gone, they dragged Paul and Silas before the authorities.

"These men are Jews and they are creating a vile disturbance in our city! They advocate ways of behavior, which we as Romans ought neither to welcome nor observe."

Immediately the crowd turned against them, too. The irate magistrate gave Paul no chance to speak in his own behalf. Shouting above the clamoring mob, he sentenced Paul and Silas to be stripped and flogged and thrown into prison.

Five strokes from the three-thonged, metal-tipped whip used for public floggings brought blood spurting from the victim's back. Twenty strokes left him a mass of bleeding flesh. Paul could have avoided the whipping since he was a Roman citizen. But Silas was not, and Paul took the torture with his friend.

That night, their legs locked tightly in the wooden prison stocks, Paul and Silas began worshiping God. They sang hymns and praised the Lord Jesus Christ, and the Philippian jailer and all the other prisoners were dumbfounded! The first night of torment after a beating as severe as the one they experienced was usually spent in cursing and moaning. Not so with these Christian friends. They sang and thanked God that they had been counted worthy to suffer for His sake!

About midnight, a violent earthquake shook the prison to its deep, stone foundations. Such a disturbance in the earth should have tumbled the walls of the prison. Instead, the shackles of all the prisoners fell off and the doors stood open! The poor jailer was beside himself with fright. He would be held accountable if the men escaped. Paul saw him draw his sword to kill himself rather than face the fury of his superiors, and shouted:

"Do not harm yourself, friend! We are all here."

What could have been the ruin of Paul's Philippian efforts was turned quickly back to victory by the Spirit of God!

The terrified jailer grabbed a light, hurried to Paul and Silas, and fell to his knees, crying: "Sirs, what must I do to be saved?"

The poor man may only have meant, "How will I get out of the trouble I'm in?" Whatever he meant, the answer he got from Paul turned the tide for everyone concerned!

"Believe on the Lord Jesus," Paul urged, "and you will be saved! Not only you—but your family, too."

Paul's jailer became a joyful prisoner of Jesus Christ!

In the middle of the night, their new brother washed their wounds and cared for them. Then he took them home with him, where he and all his family were baptized into the warm, growing Philippian fellowship of those who loved Jesus Christ. The jailer's wife prepared a meal, and they all rejoiced together in the new bonds of love that made them one. Before dawn, Paul insisted that the jailer take him and Silas back to their cells.

When they were officially released, Paul, Silas, Timothy and Luke visited Lydia's house once more, encouraging the new brothers and sisters of the fellowship, and thanking God that His Spirit worked wonders in the midst of trouble.

Luke and Timothy stayed behind to strengthen the new church in Philippi, and when trouble struck its inevitable blow in Thessalonica, Paul and Silas' next stop, no one was surprised that their enemies accused the Christians of turning the world upside down!

They loved, and when possible, converted their enemies. They sang and praised God in suffering. When they were weak, they discovered strength.

Within them lived the very Life of the sinless Man of Galilee, who prayed for the darkened souls of the men who nailed Him to His Cross.

The Christians saw life from the viewpoint of *heaven.*

From the viewpoint of the earth-bound, it was thoroughly upside down!

God—Respecter of Everyone!

Paul never stopped learning. By the time he reached the Greek city of Athens, in the fall of 51 A.D., his heart had become so sensitive to the minds of the intellectual pagans over whom Christ longed that Paul proved himself once more to be God's choice.

The sincere but still Law-restricted Apostles and leaders in Jerusalem would have been lost, had they stood as Paul stood, surrounded by the Epicurean and Stoic philosophers of Athens. The always curious Athenians brought Paul to the center of the ancient Areopagus, demanding that he expound his philosophy. These men thrived on ideas. Anything new and novel received a hearing. Nothing shocked them. Very little moved them. They were the most difficult men to convince.

As he walked the streets of their beautiful city, Paul had been struck by the enormous number of idols. One, in particular, grabbed his attention, and he made full creative use of it, as he began his speech to these men who loved ideas above anything else.

"Men of Athens, I notice on every hand how God-minded you are! As I have examined your sacred objects, I found one altar dedicated to 'the unknown god.' "

Immediately, Paul had their interest. And of course, he set about immediately to tell them the *name* of the God who, to them, was still unknown. When he came to the resurrection of Jesus Christ from the dead, many scoffed at him and laughed aloud. But—some also believed. The mind of Christ was being formed in His devoted disciple, Paul, and the more clearly it was formed, the more closely Paul could identify—as Jesus had been able to do—with every type of human being.

Silas and Timothy rejoined Paul in Corinth, his next important stop. They encouraged him greatly with their reports of the good progress among the Christians at Philippi.

In Corinth, Paul stayed in the home of two converts, Priscilla and her husband, Aquila. They, like Paul, were tent-makers by profession, and during the year and a half that he remained in Corinth, Paul worked at his trade to support himself as he preached.

When Paul sailed in 53 A.D. for Ephesus, he left a strong church at Corinth, but it demanded his time and love, even as he traveled to other cities. And the Spirit began to work in behalf of the churches everywhere as Paul felt the need, time and time again, to write letters to those he left behind. The church at Corinth was almost entirely made up of Gentiles; men and women who had not known the background of worshiping the One God. Paul's philosophy of love appealed to them, but they seemed unable to remember to practice it in their daily lives.

In a letter to the Corinthian church, he wrote his great passage on the true characteristics of the love of God. The kind of love by which they themselves could live, because the Spirit of God lived in them.

Paul was no longer young. For love of Jesus Christ, he had endured three beatings by rods, five whippings, had been stoned and imprisoned countless times. Nonessentials had dropped away for him. Bearing about still joyfully in his body the scars of the Lord Jesus, Paul saw clearly and could write to his dear Corinthians that "Even though I speak in every human and angelic language, and have no love, I am as noisy brass or a loud-clanging cymbal. Although I have prophetic gifts and see through every secret and through all that may be known, and have sufficient faith for the removal of mountains, but I have no love, I am useless."

Hearing of their bickerings and selfish behavior patterns, and admitting his own personality needs, he ended the passage on the triumphant potential of love operative in the human personality: "When I was a child, I talked as a child; I entertained child interests; I reasoned like a child. But on becoming a man I am through with childish ways. For now we see indistinctly in a blurred mirror, but then we will see face to face. Now we know partly, but then we shall understand as completely as we are understood. There remain then, faith, hope, love—these three—but the greatest of these is love."

Paul was bound with this kind of love to his friends, Priscilla and Aquila, who had proven to be so helpful to him. They went with him to Ephesus, and remained there, while he went alone to Syria, to revisit the churches at Caesarea and Antioch.

While he was gone, a dynamic young preacher named Apollos came to Ephesus and began to draw huge crowds of followers. Priscilla and Aquila went to hear him preach. The eloquence and knowledge of the educated young Alexandrian drew the people to Apollos in huge numbers, but at once Priscilla and Aquila saw that the Gospel he preached was limited. Apparently, even with the broadening spread of Christianity, to that date (54 A.D.)

Apollos had not heard of the resurrection of Jesus Christ! He was still preaching the same message John the Baptist preached.

With love and tact, Paul's friends, the tent-makers, Priscilla and Aquila, closed the big gaps in Apollos' message. The sincere young man was teachable, and God once more proved that His Spirit was a respecter of no person and yet a respecter of everyone!

Chapter 66

Paul Set His Face Toward Jerusalem

The friendships Paul made at Ephesus were of the eternal variety. Wherever the Spirit wooed men and women into a deep fellowship with Himself, they were close to one another, too. Paul and the Christians almost ruined the local business in Ephesus, and the way in which the Spirit of Christ controlled the riot against them perhaps gave these Ephesian brothers an unusual bond of love.

Artemis (Diana) was the local goddess. And since the harbor at Ephesus had filled with silt, so that trade with other ports diminished to an alarming degree, the silversmiths controlled the Ephesian economy by the sale of statues of Artemis. So many people became believers in Jesus Christ the frustrated local businessmen started a riot. Once more, Paul and his brothers were rescued by a pagan authority, who stopped the riot against them for the sake of peace and quiet.

After the tumult ended, Paul called the Christians together, told them farewell and left for Macedonia to revisit and strengthen the churches there. On this trip, he also went to Greece, and was headed for Syria when a plot by the Jews to kill him changed his plans. He returned to Macedonia where Luke rejoined him, and sailed with him to Troas. His younger co-workers, Timothy, Sopater, Aristarchus and Secundus, Gaius, Tychichus and Trophimus, left their posts and met Paul and Luke joyfully at Troas in time to share the Passover Feast together.

The younger men, especially Timothy, were full of enthusiasm over the results the Spirit had given them in their separate missions. They talked excitedly and all at once. Paul loved them all, but the moments he spent alone with Timothy cheered his heart especially. His eyes were growing weaker, and he declared the tears of joy he shed on sight of Timothy, his beloved son in the Lord, helped them enormously!

On the first day of the week, the young evangelists and members of the local church met in an upper room with Paul, to hear him speak to them.

"I intend to leave you tomorrow morning at dawn," he said to them, unashamed of the quick tears once more brimming in his eyes. "And since I intend to leave you so soon, I warn you, I may talk to you a long time!"

"Talk all night, sir!" Timothy called affectionately.

The others agreed noisily, and then fell silent, as they listened eagerly to every word from the old Apostle's lips. Indeed, Paul did talk a long time! So long, in fact, that one young man named Eutychus dropped off to sleep and fell from the third story window to the ground below. When the people rushed down to him, the boy was dead.

Paul knelt beside the lifeless body of the young disciple, embracing him in his arms, saying, "Have no fear, his soul is still in him."

Eutychus returned to life, and Paul preached until dawn!

Paul and his companions made a few more stops after sailing from Troas, intending to return to Ephesus for one more meeting with the beloved friends there. But so intense was Paul's conviction that the Spirit was hurrying him back to Jerusalem in time for Pentecost that he decided to send for the elders of the Ephesian church to meet him at Miletus.

They came gladly. Gathered around Paul on the shore, before he sailed away from them, the Christians from Ephesus listened with love to the man through whom the Spirit had made them aware of God's grace in Jesus Christ.

"You are well acquainted with my behavior among you from the day I first set foot in Asia and all the while since," the great Apostle began, with the childlike unselfconsciousness now familiar to them all. "You know that I have served the Lord with all humility—in tears and in trials that befell me, due in the main to the plottings of my own people, the Jews. You know I never failed to tell you what was to your benefit and to teach you in meetings and in homes. You know how I bore testimony to both Jews and Greeks that they should repent before God and have faith in our Lord Jesus Christ."

He looked briefly toward the open sea, wiped his eyes, then turned back to them, speaking slowly and steadily.

"And now, you see, I am bound to the Spirit to go to Jerusalem, and what is going to happen to me I do not know—except that the Holy Spirit in one city after another testifies to me that bonds and afflictions await me."

The smiles turned to deep concern on the faces of the brothers who listened.

"However, I am not concerned about anything! Neither is my life dear to me except to finish my course and the ministry which I accepted from the Lord Jesus to bear witness to the Gospel of the grace of God."

Paul wiped his eyes again. "I know that you all, among whom I have gone in and out as herald of the kingdom, shall see my face no more. Be on guard for yourselves and for the entire flock over which the Spirit has appointed you overseers. Shepherd the church of God, which He has bought with His own blood."

The men gathered around Paul on the shore were weeping openly now. No one spoke, because they all longed for him to continue, hating the moment he would stop talking to them and sail away.

"So, brothers, I commit you to God and to the word of His grace, who is able to build you up and to grant you the inheritance among all those made holy. I have set my mind on no one's silver or gold or clothing. You personally know that these hands supplied my needs and those of my companions. I have in every way pointed out to you how, by working hard that way, the needy must be assisted, and that we should remember the words of the Lord Jesus, how He said, 'It is more blessed to give than to receive.'"

With these words, Paul knelt on the sand and prayed with them. Everyone wept openly, throwing their arms around Paul and kissing him, as many as possible clinging to his hands until the last minute!

All along the way to Jerusalem, wherever Paul stopped to encourage the saints, he was warned and warned again that it was unwise and dangerous for him to return to the Holy City.

He was not unmindful of their love for him, but finally he could contain himself no longer:

"What do you achieve, my brothers, by weeping and discouraging me? I am prepared not only to be bound, but also to die at Jerusalem, on behalf of the Lord Jesus!"

Paul Before the Sanhedrin

Luke, Timothy and the Greek youth, Trophimus, arrived in Jerusalem with Paul, bearing the collection from the Gentile churches earmarked for those in need among the Jewish Christians there. They were received warmly by Jesus' brother, James, and the others.

"I miss my brothers, Peter and John," Paul said, when he rose to make his report to the now quiet and somewhat unproductive Jerusalem church. "But they, too, are enjoying the blessing of having no homes of their own, except in Christ. Here on this earth, we have no continuing city, and those of us who travel in the bonds of the Lord Jesus Christ are made mindful of the eternal city to come."

The elders of the sedate Jerusalem church squirmed, but urged Paul to give them the details of his work among the Gentiles. This he did, in glowing terms, delivered the generous offering from the Greek churches, and prepared to leave at once for Antioch and then, he fervently hoped, for Rome.

James, however, urged him to stay in Jerusalem and do something publicly that might alleviate the continuing criticism among the Jewish Christians who still lived by the Law of Moses.

"You see, brother Paul," James explained diplomatically, "there are many believers who are still zealous for the Law. They have been informed about you that you are teaching all the Jews living among the Gentiles to turn away from Moses, telling them not to circumcise their children, nor observe the ancestral customs."

"I am merely telling them the truth," Paul retorted, "and the truth is that they do not *have* to be circumcised or observe the ancestral customs in order to receive the gift of eternal life. This comes by faith in Jesus Christ alone!"

James insisted, however, and Paul agreed to his plan, for the sake of peace. He would join four men chosen by James in a ceremonial purification in the Temple. This, Paul could do with a clear conscience. He was a Pharisee by background and did not propagate discarding Mosiac Law or Jewish custom. He merely refused to allow it to block anyone's entrance into the kingdom of God!

When the seven days required for the ceremony were almost completed, Paul was seized in the Temple by a group of Jews who shouted: "This is the man who teaches everyone everywhere against our nation, the Law and this Temple—and besides this, he has brought Greeks into our Temple and so has defiled this Holy place!"

These conniving Jews had seen young Trophimus, a Gentile, on the streets of Jerusalem with Paul, and so decided Paul must have brought him into the sanctuary of the Temple where no Gentile was permitted to go!

Paul was dragged outside the Temple, and the doors slammed behind him. The crowd grew quickly in numbers and fury, and the Jews were in the very act of trying to murder Paul when the report reached Claudius Lysias, the military commander in Fort Antonia, that all Jerusalem was in an uproar. As always, the Romans were trying to keep peace during a Feast day. It was the Feast of Pentecost and the city was crowded with pilgrims.

A detachment of soldiers rushed to the scene, and Paul's life was saved once more by the pagan authorities. There was so much confusion and so many accusations, the Commander could make no sense of any of it, so he bound Paul in chains and took him to jail in Antonia.

"Am I permitted to have a word with you, Commander?" Paul asked as they reached the Fortress.

"Do you speak Greek?"

"I do, and I am a Jew from Tarsus of Cilicia, a citizen of no insignificant city! I beg of you, please let me speak to the people."

With Claudius' permission, Paul took his stand on the steps of the Fortress, and in Hebrew, not Greek, told his story to the very mob who had tried to murder him a few minutes before. In detail, he explained how Jesus of Nazareth had met him on the road to Damascus, of his blindness, of his healing at the hands of Ananias, of his baptism and call to witness to the Gentiles in the name of Jesus, the Christ!

The crowd listened to him up to that point, then they began to shout like madmen: "He's not fit to live! Do away with him! Kill him! He blasphemes!"

No one could hear anyone speak after that. In the pandemonium that followed, the furious Jews tore their clothing, yelled, threw dust in the air and stamped the ground like men gone out of their minds.

In desperation, the Commander, Claudius Lysias, took Paul inside, and ordered him examined by scourging. As God's Apostle was being stripped, his arms stretched between the posts for beating, Paul asked: "Is it legal to flog a Roman citizen without trial?"

It was not, so they had him bound and thrown into prison.

The next day, determined to find out once and for all just why the Jews tried to murder Paul, the Commander ordered a session of the chief priests Annas and Caiaphas and the entire Sanhedrin, and had Paul brought down to face them.

With a straight look at the mighty Council, Paul said:

"Brother men, I have behaved myself in the presence of God with an altogether clear conscience to this very day!"

"Strike the blasphemer in the mouth!" old Annas shrieked above the shocked gasps of the Sanhedrin.

A trickle of blood ran down one corner of his mouth as Paul shouted: "God is about to strike you, you whitewashed wall! You, sitting here to judge me according to the Law, and ordering me to be struck contrary to that same Law?"

"You insult the High Priest of God!" someone yelled at Paul.

Always in command of his intelligence, even when his emotions flared, Paul replied calmly, "I did not know, brothers, that this man was High Priest. I would not have addressed him so had I known, for I *do* know it is written, 'You must not defame a ruler of the people.'"

For a moment, no one could think of anything to reply, but Paul's mind was turning rapidly, and his next remark threw the entire assembly into an uproar. Aware that one party was Sadducee (believing in no life after death), and the other Pharisee (holding strongly to belief in the after-life), he shouted:

"Brother men, I am a Pharisee, a son of a Pharisee—it is concerning the hope of the resurrection of the dead that I am being accused!"

The outburst grew to deafening proportions as the Pharisee and Sadducee members of the Sanhedrin attacked each other! Some of the Pharisees even tried to defend Paul, which, of course, set the Sadducees against them with such bitterness that the Commander ordered soldiers to hurry Paul from their midst and bring him back to the safety of his cell.

That night, the Lord Himself stood by Paul and said: "Take heart, Paul! For as you have borne Me witness in Jerusalem, just so, it is necessary for you to testify at Rome."

Paul's heart leaped with joy! For years he had longed to visit the Christians in Rome. In fact, he had written his longest letter to them while he was in Corinth. A letter in which he not only shared his desire to come to them someday, but in which he had confessed some of the deep problems of his own life before his conversion to Jesus Christ—and after.

"In my inmost heart, I admire God's Law; but in my whole natural make-up, I notice another law battling against the principles which my reason dictates, and making me a prisoner to the law of sin that controls my bodily organs. Man of toils and troubles that I am, who will rescue me from this body doomed to death? Thanks be to God because of Jesus Christ our Lord! So then, with my heart I serve God's Law, but my human nature is under sin's control. But for this very reason there is now no condemnation to those who are in Christ Jesus; (and behave in no flesh governed way, but in a spiritual way), because the lifegiving principles of the Spirit have freed you in Christ Jesus from the control of the principles of sin and death . . . And, who shall separate us from Christ's love? Affliction? Or distress? Or persecution? Or danger? Or sword? No, in all this we are more than conquerors through Him who loves us."

Now, the Lord Himself had assured Paul that he would go to Rome.

At daybreak the next day, forty Jews took an oath that they would neither eat nor drink until they had killed Paul; but the Lord was in charge. His Spirit worked quickly, through Paul's nephew, who got wind of the plot against his uncle, reported it to the Roman Commander, and by nightfall, Paul was on his way out of Jerusalem, to the capitol, at Caesarea, under military escort!

Chapter 67

In the Presence of Kings

Felix, the procurator of Judea (58 A.D.), was annoyed at the new disturbance the day a company of seventy horsemen rode with a prisoner named Paul into the magnificent courtyard of his palace in Caesarea. The soldiers handed him a letter from the Roman Commander, Claudius Lysias, informing him that he had rescued the prisoner from a Jerusalem mob. Claudius himself had found nothing worthy of bonds or death in the man Paul, but a plot against the prisoner's life forced him to send him under guard for safety to the Governor at Caesarea.

Five days later, Felix sat in the judgment seat and heard the accusations against Paul, presented by the high priest, Annas, through a lawyer named Tertullus. For all the insistence of the Jerusalem delegation, Felix could find no case for judgment. The Jews were upset over some theological point, and although he was married to a Jewess, Drusilla, Felix could not have been less interested in the religion of the Jews. He postponed the trial on the pretext of waiting for the arrival of the Roman Commander, Claudius Lysias.

Paul had spoken at the first hearing in his own behalf, however, and Felix seemed strangely interested in what Paul had to say. A few days later, he arranged for Paul to explain the Christian faith to Drusilla and himself. God had called Paul to speak before the mighty. This was his first real chance.

Paul spoke at length, with great interest and energy, of righteousness, temperance, and the judgment to come. He knew about Felix' background. Tacitus, the Greek historian, said Felix "exercised the power of a king in the spirit of a slave!" He was a bitterly cruel man. Paul's sermon caused him to tremble. Unable not to search his own life, Felix grew more and more restless. He listened intently as Paul offered the certainty of forgiveness and righteousness through faith in Jesus Christ. At times, Felix seemed close to repentance. Paul's words not only struck his heart, they offered God's way out of his tormented life.

Felix took his own way. He put the whole thing off.

"You may go now. When I can spare the time later on, I will send for you."

Felix wanted to keep peace with the Jews. In the months that followed, he hardened his heart toward Jesus Christ and toward Paul. Claudius Lysias had no plans to visit Caesarea. Felix stalled for two years. Paul was held a prisoner with no formal charge against him.

What about God's promise that he would go to Rome? Paul was no longer young. It was 60 A.D. If he had not made use of every moment of his semi-confinement at Caesarea by telling the story of Jesus to any who would listen, and by writing almost continuously to the churches he had founded, he would have despaired in his restlessness.

But he had learned to be content, in bonds or free. Day by dragging day, he lived rejoicing in the Presence of the One by whom all things were created in heaven and on earth. Jesus Christ was with Paul forever—before all, and in Him all things were framed together, including delays.

He Himself had told Paul he would go to Rome. Paul, with all his restless energy, could wait.

Felix was followed by another procurator of Judea, Porcius Festus, who was immediately informed by the Jews at Jerusalem about a dangerous prisoner left by Felix, named Paul.

"You will do us a great favor, honored Festus, if you will sentence this man to death at once!"

Festus was a fair man, and refused their request, saying it was not the Roman way to send a man to his death without proper accusation and a chance to defend himself.

The trial that followed amazed Festus. He expected the Jews to bring accusations of violence and sedition. Instead they could only declare that Paul had violated their Temple and undermined Jewish Law!

Had Festus been completely just, he would have released Paul. Instead, disliking the idea of incurring the hatred of the ruling Jews so early in his term of office, he asked Paul if he would mind to go to Jerusalem to stand trial. Knowing the Jews would attempt to have him murdered en route to the Holy City, Paul decided to exercise his right as a Roman citizen and appeal his case to Caesar himself. Festus granted his wish gladly. It seemed a good way to be rid of the whole sticky mess.

This presented more problems to Festus, however. He could not send Paul before Caesar (Nero) without a definite charge Nero would understand!

The last of the hate-filled Herods, Herod Agrippa, king of Judea, was due for a royal visit to Festus in Caesarea. For want of a better way, he decided to allow Paul to speak before Agrippa. Perhaps the king could help him think of a definite charge to make against his prisoner.

Paul was delighted with the opportunity! He was not merely seeking freedom, he wanted to get to Rome. And always, he gloried in the chance to witness for Jesus Christ before those in power. Agrippa's father had killed John's brother James, the Apostle, with a sword. His great-grandfather was the Herod who ordered the murder of every male child under two years of age, in his desperate effort to do away with the Baby Jesus.

When Festus told Agrippa about Paul, the king remarked, "I should like to hear the man myself—when can it be arranged?"

Elaborate arrangements were made for the next day. At the allotted time, to the blare of trumpets, King Agrippa and his Queen, Bernice, entered the magnificent audience hall of the palace at Caesarea, at the head of an impressive procession of the military and prominent citizenry, and took their places beside Festus.

At the Governor's order, Paul was led in, chained, between two guards. Festus spoke first, repeating that he had found nothing deserving of the death penalty demanded by the religious Jews in Jerusalem. He confessed he needed help even in wording the charge on which Paul had appealed to be heard by Caesar. Then Agrippa asked Paul to speak.

The Lord's great Apostle raised his arm in a characteristic gesture, his hand extended over the audience as though to bless them, and began to tell them of his own personal faith in Jesus Christ. Once more, he confessed his hate-filled persecution of Jesus and His followers. Once more, his face glowed as he recounted the details of his encounter with the Living Christ on the road to Damascus.

"From then on, O King Agrippa, I was not disobedient to the heavenly vision, but first to those in Damascus and in Jerusalem, and then all over Judea and on among the Gentiles, I preached that they must repent and turn back to God and practice living their lives in a way consistent with their repentance. On account of these facts, the Jews grabbed me in the Temple and tried to kill me. So, as I have enjoyed the help of God to this day, I take my stand witnessing to both small and great, without saying anything, however, except what the prophets and Moses said would take place—that Christ must suffer, and that He, as the first to rise from the dead, shall proclaim a light to our people and to the Gentiles."

Suddenly, Festus was so affected by his words, he called out: "You are raving, Paul! You are a great theorizer, but you lack common sense!"

Paul had been speaking directly to Agrippa, king of his own people, the Jews. He turned courteously to Festus, however, and acknowledged his outburst. "Most illustrious Festus, I am not out of my mind. I am giving utterance to words of truth and sane thinking."

With that, he returned to Agrippa. "The king knows about these matters, so that I unreservedly address him. I do not believe any of these things are unknown to him, for they did not occur in a corner! King Agrippa, do you believe the prophets? I know you believe . . ."

Agrippa smiled wryly.

"You are, with a little effort, convincing enough to make me a Christian!"

Paul knew the king was thinking, but he also knew the remark was overlaid with sarcasm. The Apostle did not smile when he replied:

"I would pray to God that both by little and by much, not you alone, but all who are now listening to me today might be in my condition—not including these chains, of course."

Agrippa had heard enough. All he could bear to hear. He stood up. With him stood the Governor and Queen Bernice and all the other important guests. In a private conference, far enough from the prisoner so he could not hear, Agrippa concluded a little sadly—washing his hands of the whole thing: "This man has done nothing that deserves either death or prison. He could be set free if he had not already appealed to Caesar. Too bad."

It was not "too bad" to Paul. He had preached Christ before two governors and a king, and now he would be taken to Rome to tell of his Lord before Nero himself!

Chapter 68

The Long Voyage to Rome

Luke used the more than two years of Paul's imprisonment at Caesarea to collect material for the writing of his Gospel. He was along to attend his beloved friend, however, when Paul and the other prisoners bound for Rome were at last allowed to board a ship from Adramyttium, late in August of 60 A.D.

With Paul also, to care for his needs, was his loyal friend Aristarchus from the church in Thessalonica. Shipping was a dependable means of travel, but only during the summer months, and they had gotten a late start. The prevailing Mediterranean winds were, at that time of year, an important consideration.

Julius, the Captain of the Imperial Regiment, in charge of Paul and the other prisoners, was an admirer of the Apostle, and whenever possible he saw to it that he received every courtesy. On the second day out, in fact, when they docked at Sidon, Captain Julius allowed Paul to visit his friends, and there was great rejoicing among the Christians at this unexpected chance to see him again.

From Sidon they sailed along the south coast of Cyprus, obeying the contrary winds, then at Myra in Lycia Captain Julius found an Alexandrian ship bound for Italy. Sailing was so slow that it was nearly October before they reached Crete. Captain Julius respected Paul and listened carefully to the Apostle's warning that they should stop there for the winter. But the Captain had confidence in the ship's helmsmen, and since most of the crew voted to go on, hoping to reach Phoenix and spend the winter months there, he ignored Paul's warning.

Then, what was at first a helpful breeze which sent their ship speeding along through the blue waters, suddenly became a raging northeaster that threatened to drive them across the Mediterranean to the shoals off North Africa!

Unable to head against the violent wind, they gave up trying and let the ship drift. Running south of a small island called

Clauda, they struck sail and drifted. Next day, the danger was so great the crew threw the cargo overboard, and on the third day, the ship's tackle.

For many days the storm was so severe they saw neither sun nor stars, and the last hope of being saved was gone.

The crew was so frightened, most of the men had not eaten for days. Paul began to fear for their sanity. He was a prisoner on the ship, but the only strong personality in the face of their common crisis.

He stood among the nervous men and said: "Men, you should have listened to me and not drawn this hardship and damage on you by putting to sea from Crete. But even now, I advise you to cheer up! Not a life among you will be lost—only the ship will go down. For this night there stood by me an angel of God, whose I am and whom I serve. He said, 'Have no fear, Paul! You have to stand before Caesar (Nero), and so you can be assured that God has granted you all that are sailing with you.' So, be of good spirits, men! For I have faith in God that it shall happen just the way He has told me. But—we will have to be stranded on an island, first."

On the fourteenth night of the aimless drifting, at the mercy of the capricious wind, the sailors thought they were nearing some shore. They took soundings at intervals and found they were. Fearing the possibility of wrecking on the rocky reefs, they cast four anchors and longed for daylight.

Some of the more terrified sailors tried to abandon ship in the lifeboat, under the pretense of casting the anchors. Paul shouted at Captain Julius that unless all the men stayed with the ship they would not be saved! Obeying Paul, the prisoner, as though he were the ship's captain, the frightened men cut the small boat's ropes and let it fall into the sea—empty.

At dawn, Paul urged them all to eat. "For fourteen days now, you have been on the alert for danger, but have eaten no food. I beg you to eat something, men! It will keep you strong. Believe me, not a hair of your heads will be harmed!"

Paul himself gave thanks to God and ate. This gave the men courage and they began to eat, too. There were 276 men on board, and by now they all listened to everything Paul had to say.

In the full light of day, no one recognized the coast, but they spotted an inlet with a beach, into which they hoped to run the ship. After cutting the anchor ropes and loosening the rudder lines, they hoisted the foresail to the wind and made for the beach.

The men shouted for joy, but Paul, who knew they were going to lose the ship, stood waiting for what happened almost at once! Suddenly they struck a shoal, and the ship's big prow dug into the rocks, while the stern broke into splinters under the force of the wind-driven sea.

The crew panicked, wanting to kill the prisoners so they would be unable to swim away and escape. Captain Julius, to save Paul's life, stopped them, ordering all who could swim, prisoners and crew alike, to jump first and head for shore. The others he ordered to cling to fragments of the ship.

They all reached shore safely.

It was, they learned from the hospitable and cultured natives, an island called Malta. Around the fire, built for them in spite of the driving rain, they were welcomed by the Maltese people.

Paul, in an effort to help, gathered a bundle of branches along the beach and threw them on the fire. Suddenly a large viper, driven by the heat, crawled from the sticks and fastened its fangs onto Paul's wet hand!

The Maltese shouted: "This man must be a murderer! He was saved from the sea, but the goddess, Justice, will not allow him to live! We will see him die before our eyes—a victim of this poisonous snake."

Calmly, thanking God, Paul shook off the writhing viper into the fire and showed them his hand, with no wound in it!

Still they expected him to swell up and die from the venom. When, after an hour or so, nothing happened, they began to shout: "This man is a god, himself!"

Paul told them about Jesus and assured them that he was only a man under the protection of God.

They were well treated and entertained in the home of the chief of Malta, named Publius. Learning that Publius' father was seriously ill with dysentary and fever, Paul laid his hands on the old man and prayed. He was healed immediately, and when word of this spread around the island, Paul found himself conducting a large meeting! The islanders brought all their sick and demented friends and relatives to him, and he healed them all in the name of Jesus Christ.

After three months, toward the end of February, when the

weather permitted, they set sail again on another Alexandrian ship. and all their needs were more than supplied by the grateful Maltese islanders, who had come to love Paul dearly.

By the time they reached Rome at last, in March of 61 A.D., the human heart of Paul needed the kind of love and encouragement he received from the Roman Christians who came to meet him from as far away as the Forum of Appius and the Three Tabernacles.

"I am yearning to see you, so that we may be mutually strengthened by your faith and mine," Paul had written to those same Roman Christians over three years before.

Now he was there, with no fear of his coming ordeal before Nero. In his heart was only gratitude to God that He had gotten him to Rome at last.

Chapter 69

In Chains, Without Hindrance

Captain Julius delivered the other prisoners to the captain of Nero's guard, but Paul, although he wore chains and lived twenty-four hours a day with a Roman soldier to guard him, was allowed to rent his own apartment in Rome.

The first thing he did, after moving into his small quarters, was to contact the leading Jews of Rome. With typical courage, Paul walked right into what had always been his trouble area—the Pharisee and Sadducee leaders among his own people. He invited them to his apartment, and standing before them in chains, his Roman guard nearby, Paul began to speak to them earnestly.

"Brother men, although I have committed nothing whatever against our people, or against the ancestral customs, I was still delivered to the Romans as a prisoner from Jerusalem! When they examined me, they wanted to set me free, because I am innocent of any act that deserves death. But when the Jews objected, I was forced to appeal to Caesar—not that I harbored any complaint against my nation. But it is because of the continued accusations of the Jews that I wanted to talk to you."

Paul raised his arms, to show them his chains.

"In fact, I am in chains now because of the Hope of Israel!"

The roomful of Jews did not look antagonistic, merely wary. Speaking for the group, one man said:

"We have received no letters from Judea about you, nor has any of the brothers arrived here in Rome with a bad report or gossip about you personally. However, we feel it is fair that we hear from you, yourself, what you have in mind. After all, we do know that this heresy you preach is denounced everywhere!"

Paul arranged for a date for them to bring others and return to his apartment, to hear his message from his own lips. As he waited, he prayed much for the churches he had founded, and wrote a letter to the church at Ephesus, which was circulated widely among the other churches:

"I never fail in giving thanks for you as I mention you in my prayers, that the God of our Lord Jesus Christ, the Father of glory, might grant you a spirit of wisdom and of revelation for an understanding of Himself—granting you illumined eyes of the heart, so you may know the nature of the hope for which you are called. What a wealth of glory is the inheritance He grants among the saints, and how overwhelmingly great is His power for us believers! . . . And so I exhort you, prisoner as I am in the Lord, to conduct yourselves worthy of the calling you have received. Conduct yourselves with unalloyed humility and gentleness, in a loving way patiently to bear with one another, making every effort to preserve the unity of the Spirit by the binding power of peace. One body and one Spirit, just as you received your calling, too, with one hope—one Lord, one faith, one baptism; one God and Father of all, who governs all and pervades all and is in us all."

On the appointed day, the Jews arrived in numbers and Paul once more began his explanation of his faith in Jesus Christ. He explained the kingdom of God from his own personal testimony, attempting to persuade them about Jesus, both out of the Law of Moses and from the Prophets. He talked from morning until the sun went down!

Some believed, but others scoffed at him. There was no harmony among them, but for the first time, neither was there open opposition. The Roman imprisonment was indeed a strange one. Its very lack of action tried Paul's restless disposition. He waited for his enemies from Jerusalem to make accusation against him before Nero. The days inched by, and still nothing happened.

But Paul was not idle. The strange circumstances of his imprisonment allowed him almost complete freedom, and he preached the kingdom of God and explained the teachings of Jesus Christ to all who came to him.

One of his closest friends was a young man named Onesimus, a runaway slave from the city of Colossae, where Paul had founded a church. Onesimus became a believer in Jesus Christ through his friendship with Paul, and they soon discovered that his owner was a wealthy Colossian whom Paul had also led to Christ. Onesimus and Paul became such close friends the fugitive slave moved into the same house with Paul and served him from a grateful heart.

Close association with Paul, however, meant close association with Christ, and soon Onesimus knew he had to go back to his owner and give himself up. When he left for Colossae, he took a letter from Paul to Philemon, his wealthy owner and Paul's friend.

"Although in Christ I feel very free to give you directions as to your duty, I prefer to make my appeal on the basis of love. Here I am, then, as Paul the old man, yet now a prisoner of Christ Jesus, appealing to you on behalf of my son, Onesimus, to whom I became father while in my chains. Once he was useless to you, but now he is helpful both to you and to me. (I am assuming that you know, dear Philemon, that Onesimus means 'useful'!) I am sending him back to you and my heart with him. . . . For he was parted from you for awhile, perhaps, for this very reason, that you might have him forever—no longer as a servant, but better than a servant, a beloved brother in the Lord. So, if I am your partner, then welcome him as you would me. And if he cheated you at all, or is in debt to you, put it down against me. I, Paul, am writing with my own hand and I will refund it."

The great Apostle believed that salvation came through faith alone, but he understood fully the demands of the Christian faith on the personal life of all men who embrace it.

The next months of Paul's imprisonment were bearable after Onesimus' departure, not only because Luke returned to him, but his beloved Timothy came, too, to cheer his heart.

Writing letters to the churches occupied much of his time. In the same year he wrote his personal letter to Philemon (62 A.D.) Paul also wrote an important letter to the church which met in Philemon's house in Colossae. Word had reached him that the Colossians were being influenced by false teachings. Someone had been telling them that Paul's Gospel was incomplete; that they needed Christ, but also that they needed mediation by angelic creatures, if they were to travel the path from earthly darkness to heavenly light.

To them Paul wrote with force and poesy: "He has already rescued us from the control of the darkness, and has transferred us into the kingdom of the Son of His love, in whom we have redemption (through His blood), and the forgiveness of sins. He (Jesus Christ) is the likeness of the invisible God, the first-born before all creation! By Him all things were created in heaven and on earth, the visible and the invisible—whether thrones or lordships or rulers or authorities—they are all cre-

461

ated by Him and for Him, and He is Himself, before all, and in Him all things are framed together."

In 63 A.D., three years after he reached Rome, Paul was still waiting and still writing to his beloved churches. Nero, the murderous twenty-seven-year-old ruler of Rome's world empire, was turning from brilliant young man to fiend more rapidly with the passing of every day.

Nero was born about the time Paul became a Christian. At eighteen, he became Emperor of Rome. Under the totally evil influence of Poppaea Sabina, a beautiful woman who caused the assassination of Nero's mother, the young ruler began to change from a reasonably moderate and careful thinker into the cruel, nearly irrational monster who murdered his first wife in order to marry Poppaea, and then kicked her and their unborn child to death!

Paul waited to appear before this twisted, extravagant, hate-filled man. God had said he would stand before Caesar, and so he waited without fear, reasonably certain that he would be killed.

In his letter to his dear friends in Macedonia, at the church at Philippi, Paul wrote:

"I eagerly desire . . . as always, that the honor of Christ may be enhanced in my body (here in Rome before Nero), either through living or through dying. For on my part, to live *is* Christ, and to die would be gain! . . . I feel the pressure from both sides. I have a yearning to take my leave and to be with Christ, for that is by far the better part, but on your account it may be more necessary that I remain in the body."

The next year, two-thirds of the beautiful city of Rome burned to the ground! As it burned, the half-mad, murderous young Nero sat on the porch of his palace, playing his lyre and chanting odes about the burning of Troy.

He was suspected of ordering the destruction of the city himself, but Caesar was beyond punishment; and his whim was to turn the tragedy into a merciless persecution of the Roman Christians, who by that time were almost numberless!

To divert the wrath of the people from himself, Nero accused the Christians of having set the city on fire. They were herded into underground catacombs and fed to ferocious lions in the sports arenas of Rome. Many of them were lighted like torches and burned alive to give light at night in Nero's garden!

This was the Caesar to whom Paul had appealed his case.

With hundreds of his dear friends waiting death in the catacombs, and hundreds more meeting it daily to glut one man's cruelty, Paul was a desperately needed steadying influence to those remaining few believers who managed to slip in and out of his small apartment.

Paul was growing old and well aware that every tragedy-filled day that passed moved him nearer his death. Timothy had been gone for over three years. He was needed in the young Gentile churches in Asia, but Paul missed him painfully.

On a warm September night in 67 A.D., the aging Apostle sat alone, his dimming eyes straining to see the large letters, as he wrote with his own hand to his beloved son, Timothy:

"I would remind you to keep alive the flame of God's gracious gift which is in you, since the day I laid my hands on you. For God has not given us a spirit of cowardice, but of power and love and self-control. Feel no shame, therefore, about bearing witness to our Lord or about me, His prisoner, but share my suffering for the Gospel by virtue of the power of God, who saved us and called us with a call for dedication—not due to any doings of ours—but due to His own purpose and the grace that has been given us in Christ Jesus before time began. On this account, I suffer this way, but I am not ashamed. I *know* whom I have believed, and I am convinced that He is able to keep all I have committed to Him against that Day.

"I am already being poured out as a drink offering, and the time of my setting sail is near. I have fought the good fight. I have finished the race. I have kept the faith . . . Timothy, my son, make haste to visit me soon! Demas, our brother, has deserted me for love of the present world . . . Crescens has gone to Galatia, Titus to Dalmatia. Luke alone is with me. Get hold of Mark and bring him along, for he is helpful to me in service. And when you come, my son, bring along the heavy coat I left at Troas; also bring my books, and specially the parchments. My warm greetings to Priscilla and Aquila. And do hurry to arrive before winter! The Lord be with your spirit."

Before Timothy could reach Rome with Paul's books and warm winter coat, the Lord's great Apostle to the Gentiles was beheaded at the command of the thirty-two-year-old Nero.

Chapter 70

I Am the First and the Last

In the tragedy and turmoil of the Christian persecution during the last year of Paul's life on earth, the lonely Apostle missed learning that his old friend Peter was also a prisoner in the bonds of Jesus Christ, his beloved Master.

Before He ascended into heaven, Jesus had told Peter that he would die for His sake. And during his final days before the big, great-hearted fisherman was crucified, Peter, his shock of curly hair now turned gray, bent his head over a last letter of his own. Still fresh in the aging Apostle's memory were the high moments he had shared in his youth with Jesus, the Lord of his life.

"I think it is my duty, so long as I remain in this bodily tent, to keep you wide-awake by reminding you of these matters (of the kingdom life). For I know that shortly my body will be put off, as our Lord Jesus Christ made clear to me. Besides I will make every effort to enable each one of you to keep these things in mind after I am gone; for when we acquainted you with the power and coming of our Lord Jesus Christ, we were not accepting the authority of cleverly devised fables. On the contrary, we were eyewitnesses of His majesty, for as He was receiving honor and glory from God the Father, such a voice came to Him from the supreme glory, saying, 'This is My Son, My Beloved, in whom I am delighted.' And we (John and James and I) heard this voice from heaven, when we were with Him on the sacred mountain!

"Therefore, dear friends, forewarned as you are, be on your guard so that you may not be carried away by the stray wanderings of the lawless, and slip from your own moorings. But *grow* in the grace and knowledge of our Lord and Saviour, Jesus Christ, to whom be glory now and to the day of eternity."

During most of his life, Peter had not seen the Lord's open door to the Gentiles as clearly as Paul saw it. He and John spent themselves mainly as Apostles to their own people, the Jews. But at the close of their lives, both Peter and John were found ministering among the Gentiles, too.

This had to be, since no man could live as close to the Christ as they lived and fail to discover with Paul that the middle wall of partition had already been melted away by the Lord Jesus Himself, on His Cross.

The three great Apostles did not meet again on earth. John, the once hot-tempered son of Zebedee, outlived them all, and, three years after Paul was beheaded in Rome, John was writing letters to the Gentile churches in Asia, which Paul founded.

Like Peter and Paul, John as an old man was absorbed solely in the Person of His beloved Master, Jesus Christ. From Ephesus, in the year 70 A.D., John wrote:

"Little children, we announce to you about the Word of Life! He *was* from the beginning. We have heard Him. We have seen Him. We have looked at Him and our hands have touched Him. Yes, the Life has been revealed and we have seen and are witnessing and are announcing to you the Life Eternal, who existed with the Father, and who has been revealed to us. We *saw* Him, and we *heard* Him, and we are telling you, so you too may enjoy fellowship along with us. And this fellowship of ours is with the Father and with His Son, Jesus Christ.

"The message we heard from Him and announce to you is this: God is Light, and in Him there is no darkness at all!"

Sixteen years later, the Lord Jesus came once more to His beloved disciple, John, in a Revelation of Himself to the old man during his exile on the Isle of Patmos.

Paul was with Christ in life eternal. So were Peter and John's brother, James. So were all who had put their faith in Him as God's revelation of His own heart. But the Glorified Christ had messages for the churches Paul had founded. Only John was left on earth of the Twelve, to write what Christ had to say.

As he prayed, the old Apostle heard a voice like a mighty trumpet. "I turned to see whose voice was addressing me, and on turning I saw seven golden lampstands and in the center of the lampstands One like the Son of Man, dressed in a robe that reached to the feet and girded across the breast with a golden girdle. His head and hair as white as wool, as white as snow! His eyes like a flame of fire. His feet like precious ore as it glows in the furnace and His voice like the sound of many waters. . . . When I saw Him, I fell at His feet as dead. Then He laid His right hand on me and said, 'Do not fear! I am the First and the Last. I am the living One. I experienced death and now, behold, I am alive forever and ever! I hold the keys of death and of all its realm.'"

John's beloved Master wanted him to tell the church at Ephesus that He was aware of all their good works, but also that they had given up their first love for Him and for each other!

To the church at Smyrna, He told John to urge them not to dread what they would have to suffer.

The church at Pergamum had begun to throw stumbling-blocks in the way of new believers.

The church at Thyatira was to stop listening to a woman named Jezebel, who called herself a prophetess!

The church at Sardis was dead. John was to tell them to wake up!

To the church at Philadelphia, where love still ruled, He promised protection and care.

But the church at Laodicea received the bitter word—"I know your doings, that you are neither cold nor hot. I wish you were one or the other! But because you are lukewarm—neither hot nor cold—I am going to spew you out of My mouth!"

His hair was white as snow. His eyes like a flame of fire—but old John recognized the same authority, the same energy, the same faultless perception, the same love he had known in Jesus of Nazareth, as he and the Eleven had followed Him up and down the dusty roads of Palestine so many years ago.

This same Jesus, whom God had raised from the dead, had returned to His Father—alive forevermore!

Just as He had promised, Jesus had gone to prepare a place for John—for his brother, James, for Peter and Paul—for everyone who believes that He is the Christ, the Son of the Living God.

"Let not your hearts be troubled," He had said to them the night before He was crucified. "If you believe in God, believe also in Me. In My Father's house are many homes. If this were not so, I would have told you. I go away to prepare a place for you. And when I have gone and have prepared a place for you, I will come again and take you to Myself, so that where I am, you will be also."

His radiance was overpowering to John's old eyes. He had fallen to the ground as dead when he saw Him! But that dear, familiar hand touched his shoulder, and the voice like the sound of many waters spoke the dear, familiar words:

"Do not fear! It is I. I am the First and the Last."

It was the Master, who had been dead and who was now alive forevermore. He would come for John, and he would live forever, too, like the thief who turned to Jesus on the next cross—like Peter and Paul and James, in a place where they would all know each other as fully as they were known!

If it had not been so, He would have told them.

Bibliography

Atlas of the Bible (Nelson)

Barclay, William, *The Master's Men* (Abingdon)

Bowie, Wm. Russell, *The Story of the Bible* (Abingdon)

Bright, John, *The Kingdom of God* (Abingdon)

Cornell, George, *They Knew Jesus* (Morrow)

David, Richardson, Wallis, *20th Century Bible Commentary* (Harper)

Deissman, Adolf, *Paul, A Study in Social & Religious History* (Harper)

Edersheim, Alfred, *The Life and Times of Jesus the Messiah* (Eerdmans)

Kee and Young, *Understanding the New Testament* (Prentice Hall)

Keyes, Nelson Beecher, *Story of the Bible World* (Hammond)

Knox, John, *The Man Christ Jesus* (Willett, Clark)

LaSor, William Sanford, *Great Personalities of the Bible* (Revell)

Miller and Lane, *Harper's Bible Dictionary* (Harper)

Morgan, G. Campbell, *Acts of the Apostles* (Revell)

Neibuhr, Hulda, *The One Story* (Westminster)

Slaughter, Frank G., *The Land and the Promise* (World)

Stauffer, Ethelbert, *Jesus and His Story* (Knopf)

Wieand, Albert Cassel, *Gospel Records of the Message and Mission of Jesus Christ* (Eerdmans)

Wright & Filson, *Westminster Historical Atlas of the Bible* (Westminster)

Bible Reference Index Correlated with Chapter Divisions

471

473

(Compiled by Joyce Blackburn)